REGULATING RELIGION IN ASIA

In recent years, law and religion scholarship has increasingly emphasised the need to study the interaction of legal and religious ideas and institutions, norms and practices. The overall question that this scholarship explores may be stated as follows: how do legal and religious ideas and institutions, methods and mechanisms, beliefs and believers influence each other, for better and for worse, in the past, present and future?

This volume engages this area of scholarship by examining how law regulates religion, and how religion responds to such regulations. It examines underlying norms influencing state regulation of religion, and challenges emerging from such regulation. Importantly, this volume will go beyond the conventional enquiries that draw upon the Anglo-European approaches and experiences, and emphasise instead Asian perspectives in order to expand and build upon existing understandings about the complex relationship between law and religion.

Jaclyn L. Neo is Associate Professor of Law at the National University of Singapore (NUS). She specialises in constitutional law, human rights law and comparative constitutional law and religion. She is the sole editor of *Constitutional Interpretation in Singapore: Theory and Practice* (2017) and has been a guest editor for special issues of the *Singapore Academy of Law Journal, Journal of International and Comparative Law* and the *Journal of Law, Religion, and State*. Her articles have been published in the *International Journal of Constitutional Law* (I-CON), *Oxford Journal of Law and Religion, Human Rights Quarterly* and the *Singapore Journal of Legal Studies*.

Arif A. Jamal is Associate Professor at the Faculty of Law, National University of Singapore. He serves on the Executive Committee of NUS's Centre for Asian Legal Studies and as an editor of the *Asian Journal of Comparative Law*. His research and teaching interests include legal and political theory, law and religion and law in Muslim contexts. Arif's publications are forthcoming or have appeared in the *American Journal of Comparative Law*, the *Oxford Journal of Law and Religion* and the *Journal of Law, Religion and State*. His most recent book is *Islam, Law and the Modern State: (Re) imagining Liberal Theory in Muslim Contexts* (2018).

Daniel P. S. Goh is Associate Professor of Sociology at the National University of Singapore. He specialises in comparative-historical sociology and studies state formation, race and multiculturalism, Asian urbanisms, and religion, and has published more than forty articles on these subjects in journals and books. He has edited and co-edited several books, including *Race and Multiculturalism in Malaysia and Singapore* (2009), *Worlding Multiculturalisms: The Politics of Inter-Asian Dwelling* (2015), *Precarious Belongings: Affect and Nationalism in Asia* (2017) and *Urban Asias: Essays on Futurity: Past and Present* (2018).

Regulating Religion in Asia

NORMS, MODES, AND CHALLENGES

Edited by

JACLYN L. NEO

National University of Singapore

ARIF A. JAMAL

National University of Singapore

DANIEL P. S. GOH

National University of Singapore

CAMBRIDGE
UNIVERSITY PRESS

CAMBRIDGE
UNIVERSITY PRESS

University Printing House, Cambridge CB2 8BS, United Kingdom

One Liberty Plaza, 20th Floor, New York, NY 10006, USA

477 Williamstown Road, Port Melbourne, VIC 3207, Australia

314–321, 3rd Floor, Plot 3, Splendor Forum, Jasola District Centre, New Delhi – 110025, India

79 Anson Road, #06–04/06, Singapore 079906

Cambridge University Press is part of the University of Cambridge.

It furthers the University's mission by disseminating knowledge in the pursuit of education, learning, and research at the highest international levels of excellence.

www.cambridge.org
Information on this title: www.cambridge.org/9781108416177
DOI: 10.1017/9781108235983

First published 2019

Printed and bound in Great Britain by Clays Ltd, Elcograf S.p.A.

A catalogue record for this publication is available from the British Library.

ISBN 978-1-108-41617-7 Hardback

Contents

Notes on Contributors — *page* vii
Acknowledgements — xiii
List of Abbreviations — xiv

Introduction: Regulating Religion in Asia — 1

PART I THEORIZING REGULATION — 17

1 **Regulatory Markers** — 19
Arif A. Jamal

2 **Conceptualizing the Regulation of Religion: A Preliminary Framework for Inquiry** — 38
Jaclyn L. Neo

3 **The Role of Authority and Sanctity in State–Religion Conflicts** — 59
Shai Wozner and Gilad Abiri

4 **Jurisdictional versus Official Control: Regulating the Buddhist Saṅgha in South and Southeast Asia** — 79
Benjamin Schonthal

5 **Defining and Regulating Religion in Early Independent Indonesia** — 99
Kevin W. Fogg

PART II REGULATING RELIGION: STATE PRACTICE AND LEGAL NORMS — 117

6 **Principled Pluralism, Relational Constitutionalism and Regulating Religion within Singapore's Secular Democratic Model** — 119
Thio Li-ann

7 **Legal Regulation of Religion in Vietnam** 146
Bui Ngoc Son

8 **Regulating Buddhism in Myanmar: The Case of Deviant Buddhist Sects** 169
Nyi Nyi Kyaw

9 **The Bureaucratization of Religious Education in the Islamic Republic of Iran** 187
Mirjam Künkler

10 **Managing Religious Competition in China: Regulating Provisions of Charitable Activities by Religious Organizations** 207
Jianlin Chen and Loveday J. Liu

PART III CHALLENGES TO STATE REGULATION 231

11 **Regulating Religion through Administrative Law: Religious Conversion in Malaysia beyond Fundamental Rights** 233
Matthew Nelson and Dian A. H. Shah

12 **Legal Pluralism, Patronage Secularism, and the Challenge of Prophetic Christianity in Singapore** 256
Daniel P. S. Goh

13 **Equality in Secularism: Contemporary Debates on Social Stratification and the Indian Constitution** 276
M. Mohsin Alam Bhat

14 **Beyond the State and the Hawza: Legal Pluralism and the Ironies of Shi'i Law** 298
Haider Ala Hamoudi

Index 313

Notes on Contributors

Gilad Abiri is a JSD candidate at Yale Law School, where he also completed his LLM degree in 2016. Before coming to Yale, Gilad earned his LLM degree, summa cum laude, from Tel Aviv University; his master's thesis developed an account of deliberative democracy based on the moral theory of value pluralism. Gilad is a graduate of the Interdisciplinary Program for Outstanding Students at Tel Aviv University and has served as a research assistant and a teaching assistant in the fields of contract law, law and religion, and political theory. Gilad's academic interests lie in the intersection of political theory and law, and focus on constitutional law, law and religion, and democratic law. In his JSD dissertation, he develops a new theoretical account of the tense relationship between liberal states and religious groups.

M. Mohsin Alam Bhat is an assistant professor of law and Executive Director of the Centre for Public Interest Law at Jindal Global Law School (India). His research focuses on discrimination and exclusion, minority rights, and constitutional law and politics. He obtained his LLM and JSD from Yale Law School, where he worked on the law and social movement politics of Muslim affirmative action in India. He was Yale's Gruber Fellow in Global Justice and Women's Rights in 2015–16. He has previously clerked at the Supreme Court of India, and worked as a legal research assistant at the Permanent Mission of India at the United Nations.

Bui Ngoc Son is an assistant professor at the Chinese University of Hong Kong Faculty of Law. He was previously a Senior Research Fellow in the Centre for Asian Legal Studies of the Faculty of Law at the National University of Singapore. He holds a PhD in law from the University of Hong Kong. His research focuses on comparative constitutional law and theory, and comparative law from an interdisciplinary perspective. His monograph *Confucian Constitutionalism in East Asia* (2016) explores constitutional ideas and practices in the Confucian tradition and their contemporary relevance in East Asia. His second in progress monograph titled *Constitutional Change in the Contemporary Socialist World* examines changes to the constitutional systems in five current socialist countries (China, Cuba, Laos, North Korea, and Vietnam). His work also includes articles on Confucian law, socialist law, constitutional mobilization, popular constitutionalism, constitution-making, globalization of constitutional identity, and global diffusion of constitutional rights, published by *American Journal of Comparative Law*, *Law & Social Inquiry*, *University of Illinois Law Review*, *Fordham International Law Journal*, *Washington University Global Studies Law Review*, *Washington International Law Journal*, among others.

Jianlin Chen is an Associate Professor at the University of Melbourne Law School, joining in 2017 after starting his academic career at the University of Hong Kong in 2011. He obtained his LLB from National University of Singapore, and his LLM and JSD from the University of Chicago. He is qualified to practice in Singapore and New York. Bilingual in English and Chinese, Jianlin publishes widely, including a monograph titled *The Law and Religious Market Theory: China, Taiwan and Hong Kong* with Cambridge University Press, and nearly thirty journal articles with law journals such as *Columbia Journal of Asian Law*, *Law & Social Inquiry*, *Oxford Journal of Law and Religion*, among many others. His primary research interests include employing a combination of comparative perspectives and economic analysis to examine law and religion in Asia.

Kevin W. Fogg is a researcher on Southeast Asia based in the Faculty of History and Brasenose College, University of Oxford. His research looks at the place of Islam in Indonesia since independence, including his forthcoming monograph on the role of Islam in Indonesia's war of independence. Other articles and chapters have discussed subjects such as Indonesia's third Minister of Religion, script change and its impact on Muslim communities, Islamic socialism in Indonesia, and the convergence of Islamic and state education. His next major project focuses on mass Islamic organizations based outside of Java and what their evolution says about religious organizational life in Indonesia over the last century.

Daniel P. S. Goh is Associate Professor of Sociology at the National University of Singapore. He specializes in comparative-historical sociology and studies state formation, race and multiculturalism, Asian urbanisms, and religion, and has published more than forty articles on these subjects in journals and books. He has edited and coedited several books, including *Race and Multiculturalism in Malaysia and Singapore* (2009), *Worlding Multiculturalisms: The Politics of Inter-Asian Dwelling* (2015), *Precarious Belongings: Affect and Nationalism in Asia* (2017), and *Urban Asias: Essays on Futurity: Past and Present* (2018).

Haider Ala Hamoudi is Professor of Law and the Vice Dean at the University of Pittsburgh School of Law. He teaches contracts, commercial law, and Islamic law. Professor Hamoudi's scholarship focuses on Middle Eastern and Islamic law.

He has coauthored a casebook on Islamic law titled *Islamic Law in Modern Courts* and published numerous articles and book chapters in a wide variety of law school journals, university presses, and other scholarly venues, including a full length book on the Iraqi constitution entitled *Negotiating in Civil Conflict: Imperfect Bargaining and Constitutional Construction in Iraq*. He is also under contract to author a nutshell on Islamic law, focusing on Islamic law as it is relevant in modern legal systems. Professor Hamoudi is also the author of a blog on Islamic law titled Islamic Law in Our Times.

Arif A. Jamal is an Associate Professor of Law at the National University of Singapore (NUS). His research and teaching interests include legal and political theory, law and religion, and law in Muslim contexts. Arif's publications include *Islam, Law and the Modern State* (2018), and a range of book chapters and articles in journals including the *American Journal of Comparative Law*, the *Oxford Journal of Law and Religion*, and the *Journal of Law, Religion and State*. Arif serves on the Executive Committee of the Centre for Asian Legal Studies (CALS) at NUS and as an editor of the *Asian Journal of Comparative Law*.

Mirjam Künkler is a senior research fellow at the Swedish Collegium for Advanced Study (SCAS). Before joining SCAS, she taught Near Eastern Studies at Princeton University, where she also directed the Oxford–Princeton research cluster on "Traditional Authority and Transnational Religious Networks in Contemporary Shi'i Islam" and codirected the Luce Program on "Religion and International Affairs" for several years. Her books include *Democracy and Islam in Indonesia* (coedited with Alfred Stepan, 2013; published in Arabic as *Al-Dimokratia va al-Islam fi Indonisia*, 2016); *A Secular Age Beyond the West* (coedited with John Madeley and Shylashri Shankar), *2018; Female Religious Authority in Shi'i Islam* (with Devin Stewart, forthcoming 2019); as well as two volumes coedited with Tine Stein: *Selected Writings by Ernst-Wolfgang Böckenförde*, Vol. I (2017) and Vol. II (2019). Künkler has guest-edited special issues and symposia for the journals *Party Politics* (March 2013), the *American Behavioral Scientist* (July 2016), *Asian Studies Review* (December 2016), the *British Journal of Middle Eastern Studies* (January 2018), *Oxford Journal of Law and Religion* (February 2018), the *German Law Journal* (May 2018), *Constellations: An International Journal of Critical and Democratic Theory* (June 2018), and *Cambridge Journal of Law and Religion* (August 2018). She sits on the boards of various academic journals.

Nyi Nyi Kyaw is a postdoctoral research fellow at the Centre for Asian Legal Studies at the Faculty of Law, National University of Singapore. He specializes on Myanmar and is interested in religion, nationalism, human rights, law, social movements, and constitutionalism. His research has been published in the *Review of Faith & International Affairs*, *Journal of Immigrant & Refugee Studies*, and *Social Identities*.

He has also contributed to and plans to contribute to several edited volumes on Muslims, religion, Buddhist nationalism, and constitutionalism—all relating to Myanmar.

Thio Li-ann holds a BA (Hons., Jurisprudence) from the University of Oxford; a Masters of Law from Harvard Law School, and a PhD from the University of Cambridge. She is Provost Chair Professor at the National University of Singapore, where she teaches and researches public international law, human rights law in Asia, constitutional and administrative law, and comparative public law, with a focus on law and religion. She is a barrister (Gray's Inn, UK) and was a Nominated Member of the Singapore Parliament (2007–09). She is currently chief editor of the *Singapore Journal of Legal Studies* and formerly general editor of the *Asian Yearbook of International Law* and Chief Editor, *Singapore Journal of International & Comparative Law*. A prolific scholar, she has published more than 100 law review articles/book chapters and several books. She is the sole author of monographs including *Managing Babel: The International Legal Protection of Minorities in the Twentieth Century* (2005) and A *Treatise on Singapore Constitutional Law* (2012). She has also authored *Constitutionalism in Asia* (2014, with Kevin Y. L. Tan, Wen-Chen Chang, and Juinn-rong Yeh); *Constitutional Law in Malaysia and Singapore* (with Kevin Y. L. Tan, 2010); and *The Evolution of a Revolution: 40 Years of the Singapore Constitution* (Li-ann Thio and Kevin Y. L. Tan, eds., 2009).

Loveday J. Liu is a trainee solicitor at K&L Gates Hong Kong office. She graduated from the University of Hong Kong (PCLL, LLB) and LSE (MSc, Hons), and as an undergraduate spent one year at Tsinghua University School of Law for foundational studies. From 2016 to 2018, Loveday participated in the Supreme People's Court's project Compilation of Chinese Legal System Judicial Decisions, responsible for editing large volumes of judicial memoirs ("Shuotie") of late Tsing Dynasty. Loveday is developing an interdisciplinary research interest that looks to other social science subjects for understanding the working of law. Her publications include an article discussing the socio-legal impact of Uber entering Hong Kong that was published in 法律适用, and an co-authored piece on how Chinese Charity Law would shape the domestic charitable market in 财经法学.

Matthew Nelson (PhD, Columbia) is a Reader in Politics at SOAS (School of Oriental and African Studies), University of London. Before SOAS Dr Nelson taught at University of California at Santa Cruz, Bates College, and Yale University. At SOAS, Dr Nelson is a founding member of the Centre for Comparative Political Thought and the Centre for the International Politics of Conflict, Rights, and Justice. In 2009–10 he was the Wolfensohn Family Member in the School of Social Science at the Institute for Advanced Study in Princeton; in 2011 he was a Resident Fellow at the Woodrow Wilson International Center for Scholars in

Washington, DC; in 2014 and 2015, he was a Resident Fellow at the Zentrum für Interdisziplinäre Forschung (ZiF) in Germany. Dr Nelson has also served as an elected board member for the American Institute of Pakistan Studies (AIPS), the South Asia Council of the Association for Asian Studies (AAS), and the Religion and Politics Section of the American Political Science Association (APSA). His current research focuses on comparative constitutional politics and the politics of sectarian and doctrinal diversity in Islamic law and education.

Jaclyn L. Neo is Associate Professor of Law at the National University of Singapore (NUS). She specializes in constitutional law, human rights law, and comparative constitutional law and religion. She is the sole editor of *Constitutional Interpretation in Singapore: Theory and Practice* (2017) and has been a guest editor for special issues in the *Singapore Academy of Law Journal*, *Journal of International and Comparative Law*, and the *Journal of Law, Religion and State*. Her articles have been published in the *International Journal of Constitutional Law* (I-CON), *Oxford Journal of Law and Religion*, *Human Rights Quarterly*, and the *Singapore Journal of Legal Studies*.

Benjamin Schonthal is Associate Professor of Buddhism and Asian Religions and Associate Dean (International) for the Humanities Division at the University of Otago in New Zealand. Ben's research examines the intersections of religion, law, and politics in late colonial and contemporary Southern Asia, with a particular focus on Buddhism and law in Sri Lanka. His work has appeared in journals such as the *Journal of Asian Studies*, *Modern Asian Studies*, the *International Journal of Constitutional Law*, and others. Ben's first book, *Buddhism, Politics and the Limits of Law* (Cambridge University Press), appeared in 2016.

Dian A. H. Shah is an Assistant Professor at the National University of Singapore (NUS). She previously taught at the Faculty of Law, University of Malaya, where she remains a faculty appointee. Her research interests span the fields of constitutional history, comparative constitutional law, and human rights, focusing on issues arising from the interactions among constitutional law, religion, and politics in selected Asian jurisdictions. She is the author of *Constitutions, Religion and Politics in Asia: Indonesia, Malaysia and Sri Lanka* (Cambridge University Press, 2017) and coeditor of the book *Law and Society in Malaysia: Pluralism, Ethnicity and Religion* (2018). Dian currently serves as the deputy editor of the *Asian Journal of Comparative Law*.

Shai Wozner is a senior lecturer in Tel Aviv University Faculty of Law and the director of the Taubenschlag Institute of Criminal Law, Tel Aviv University. He received his BA in Talmud and Philosophy from Bar-Ilan University, and LLB, LLM, and LLD (cum laude) from the Hebrew University of Jerusalem. He was a fellow at the Shalom Hartman Institute in Jerusalem until 2007. In 2012–13 he was a Berkowitz Fellow at the Tikvah Center for Law and Jewish Civilization, New York

University School of Law. Shai Wozner is the coauthor (with H. Ben-Menahem and N. Hecht) of the three volumes *Controversy and Dialogue in the Halakhic Sources* (2002), and the author of *Legal Thinking in the Lithuanian Yeshivoth* (2016).

Acknowledgements

Most of the chapters in this volume were presented at a conference titled "Regulating Religion: Normativity and Change at the Intersection of Law and Religion", which was held at the Faculty of Law of the National University of Singapore (NUS Law) on 14 and 15 December 2015. The conference and this edited volume both benefitted from the generous support of a research grant provided by the Centre for Asian Legal Studies (CALS) at NUS Law.

We would like to thank the authors, both those who were present at the conference as well as those whose chapters were solicited thereafter, for their contributions to this volume. We also thank Cambridge University Press for its support in bringing this volume to fruition.

The research project and this edited volume would not have been possible without the help of several dedicated student assistants from NUS Law, and we thank the following for their work, especially for their assistance in preparing the essays contained in this volume for publication: Christopher Khew Wei Luen, Jacqueline Gwee Li Ling, Nguyen Vu Lan, Andrea Ong Hui Xian, KarLuis Quek, Sheiffa Safi Shirbeeni, Rachel Tan Xi'En, and Thaddaeus Tan Yong Zhong. Last but not least, we are grateful to Muhammad Nurshazny Bin Ramlan, research assistant at the Centre for Asian Legal Studies, for managing the editorial and publication process with great aplomb.

Abbreviations

ADJAR	Agama Djawa Asli Republik Indonesia
AMLA	Administration of Muslim Law
BN	Barisan Nasional
BSPP	Burma Socialist Programme Party
CHC	City Harvest Church
CPC	Country of Particular Concern *or* Communist Party of China
FCBC	Faith Community Baptist Church
ICCPR	International Covenant on Civil and Political Rights
IDF	Israel Defense Force
IRO	Inter-Religious Organization (Singapore)
JAKIM	Jabatan Kemajuan Islam Malaysia
JAWHAR	Jabatan Waqaf, Zakat dan Haji
LGBT	lesbian, gay bisexual, and transgender
MOM	Ministry of Manpower (Singapore)
MORA	Ministry of Religious Affairs (Indonesia)
MRHA	Maintenance of Religious Harmony Act (Singapore)
MUI	Majelis Ulama Indonesia (Indonesian Ulama Council)
MYR	Malaysian ringgit
NGO	non-governmental organisation
NLD	National League for Democracy
NRD	National Registration Department (Malaysia)
NU	Nahdatul Ulama
OCB	other backward classes
PAS	Parti Islam Se-Malaysia
PRC	People's Republic of China
RC	Revolutionary Council

SC	Scheduled Castes
SSMNC	State Sangha Maha Nayaka Committee
UDHR	Universal Declaration of Human Rights
UMNO	United Malay Nationalist Organization
USCIRF	United States Commission on International Religious Freedom

Introduction: Regulating Religion in Asia

I. RELIGION IN ASIA

Interesting trends are developing with respect to religion, and it is the proposition of this book that Asia stands at the forefront of these developments. While the study of law and religion has typically been dominated by the experience of Western jurisdictions in Europe and America and theoretical scholarship developed within these contexts has some relevance to understanding law and religion in Asia, this scholarship needs to be adapted to local situations. In particular, there is a need to take into account Asia's distinctive historical, demographic, and geopolitical contexts.

On the first, the historical contexts, most Asian states have had to grapple with encounters with colonialism, which brought the approach to arranging state and religion developed within the Western (Anglo-European) historical experience of Christian sectarian conflict that culminated in the Thirty Years' Religious Wars. Even the founding of America was rooted in Christian sectarian based pilgrimage. As such, when colonialism and decolonisation established new states, these were premised on a logic of the Westphalian nation-state that wrote itself, constitutionally, into existence as a political entity independent of the Roman Church or monarchies and their national churches. In the non-Western world, modern 'secular' state institutions were hoisted onto local societies in colonial situations, often involving the production of the very notions of religiosity and secularity that affected the nationalisms of both the coloniser and the colonised.[1] As such, while many Asian states adopted secular forms of government and appeared to embrace rational forms of authority that support such secular forms, religion has never retreated to the private sphere. There was no historical necessity; neither was there a forged political or philosophical consensus in which religion agreed to trade public influence for individual and group autonomy over religious affairs.

[1] Peter van der Veer, *Imperial Encounters: Religion and Modernity in India and Britain* (Princeton University Press, 2001).

Thus, the Western experience of religious pluralism as a basis for ordering state–religion relations is based primarily on the sectarian strife between divergent Christian creeds in the march to the modern nation-state. On the other hand, the non-Western experience of pluralism is defined by competing religious creeds and their participation in the public sphere, as well as sectarian innovations by religious entrepreneurs.

Second, in terms of demography, the Asia-Pacific region has the most religiously diverse profile in the world. This is according to the Pew Research Center's Religious Diversity Index, which also ranked Singapore, located within Southeast Asia, as the world's most religiously diverse country. The Index is based on the "percentage of each country's population that belongs to eight major religious groups, as of 2010", i.e. Buddhism, Christianity, Hinduism, Islam, Judaism, folk or traditional religions (including members of African traditional religions, Chinese folk religions, Native American religions, and Australian aboriginal religions), adherents of other religions (such as the Baha'i faith, Jainism, Shintoism, Sikhism, Taoism, Tenrikyo, Wicca, and Zoroastrianism), as well as the religiously unaffiliated (including atheists and agnostics). The closer a country comes to having equal shares of the eight groups, the higher its score on the Index.[2] The Asia-Pacific region has 24% Muslims, 25% Hindus, 12% Buddhists, 9% adherents of folk religions, 7% Christians, and 21% unaffiliated among its population. In comparison, Europe and North America have moderate levels of religious diversity, while the Latin America – Caribbean and Middle East – North Africa regions have low degrees of religious diversity.[3]

Such broad religious diversity in Asia is accompanied by a trend of rising numbers among its Hindu, Christian, and Muslim populations. In its report, Pew notes that the five widely recognised world religions – Buddhism, Christianity, Hinduism, Islam, and Judaism, which were the focus of its study, "collectively account for roughly three-quarters of the world's population".[4] A 2015 Pew Research Centre Report projects a 33.7% increase in the Hindu population within the Asia-Pacific region, compared to a 47.8% increase among the Muslim population and 32.8% increase among Christians in the region from 2010 to 2050.[5] Thus, even though the traditional notion of 'Asian religions' typically includes Buddhism, Sikhism, Hinduism, Shintoism, Daoism, and Confucianism,[6] Christianity, and, to a greater

[2] Pew Research Centre, 'Global Religious Diversity' (*Pew Forum*, 4 April 2014). www.pewforum.org/2014/04/04/global-religious-diversity/ (accessed 28 March 2018).

[3] Ibid. See also Zachary Keck, 'Asia Leads World in Religious Diversity' (*The Diplomat*, 9 April 2014). https://thediplomat.com/2014/04/asia-leads-world-in-religious-diversity/ (accessed 28 March 2018).

[4] Pew Research Centre, n. 2.

[5] Pew Research Centre, 'Asia-Pacific. The Future of World Religions: Population Growth Projections, 2010–2050' (*Pew Forum*, 2 April 2015). www.pewforum.org/2015/04/02/asia-pacific/ (accessed 28 March 2018).

[6] Bryan S. Turner and Oscar Salemink, 'Introduction: Constructing Religion and Religions in Asia', in Bryan S. Turner and Oscar Salemink (eds.), *Routledge Handbook of Religions in Asia* (Routledge,

extent, Islam have become major, though not majority, religions in the region. Indeed, whereas it has previously been observed that Christianity is "almost never defined as an 'Asian Religion'", Christian missionary activity established the religion early on in Asia,[7] and today it has oversized influence in many Asian countries. Besides Christianity, Islam, which spread through various means including by trade and the advance of Sufism, a mystical tradition of Islam, is today a significant religion in Asia.[8] Indonesia, located in Southeast Asia, is the country with the largest Muslim population in the world.

This depth in demographic range affects the regulation of religion in important ways. On the one hand, as different religious traditions with different practices, habits, and orientations are manifested, they raise different "accommodation demands." On the other hand, and even more fundamentally, they raise the question of what one is regulating when we regulate 'religion': what is, and is not, in the category of religion? What practices, values, and ideas are we regulating when we regulate religion? Thus, one set of emergent questions is how the terrain of regulating religion changes in different existing social contexts, especially between places where, in general, religiosity is robust, and places where it is not or may be declining, and how the fluid and altering social conditions in any of these environments will impinge on regulation. These 'on the ground' issues may be cast in light of a larger normative and theoretical challenge that also directly impacts the regulation of religion, namely how to deal with the challenge of regulating value diversity and plurality, especially when these are expressed religiously.

Third, in geopolitical terms, there is no single majority religion that dominates in the Asian region and different religions predominate in different countries and subregions. The constitutional arrangements in different countries within Asia therefore give priority to a range of different religions, depending on their majority status. This includes establishing particular religions as state religions. As an example, Buddhism is the state religion of Cambodia,[9] whereas Islam is the state religion in Malaysia,[10] Bangladesh,[11] Pakistan,[12] and Brunei.[13] In comparison, other regions of the world are dominated by a majority religion and their geopolitical approaches are dominated by this majority religion. Europe, North America, and Latin America–Caribbean are dominated by Christian majorities, i.e. 75%, 77%, and 90% of the population respectively. Countries within these regions also tend to

2014), 4. See also Michael D. Coogan and Vasudha Narayanan, *Eastern Religions* (Oxford University Press, 2005) and Donald S. Lopez, *Religions of Asia in Practice* (Princeton University Press, 2002).

7 Ibid.

8 See, for instance, Paul Wormser, 'The Spread of Islam in Asia through Trade and Sufism (Ninth-Nineteenth Centuries)', in Bryan S. Turner and Oscar Salemink (eds.), *Routledge Handbook of Religions in Asia* (Routledge, 2014), 109.

9 Constitution of the Kingdom of Cambodia 1993, Article 43.

10 Federal Constitution of Malaya 1957, Article 3(1).

11 Constitution of the People's Republic of Bangladesh 1972, Article 2A.

12 Constitution of the Islamic Republic of Pakistan 1973, Article 2.

13 Constitution of Brunei Darussalam 1959, Article 3(1).

give predominant status to Christianity within their constitutional orders. In the Middle East/North Africa region, 93% of the population are Muslims. Even in the second most religiously diverse region, sub-Saharan Africa, 63% of the population are Christians while 30% are Muslims.

II. ASIA AND SECULARISM

In light of these distinctive features of the Asian region, in terms of its historical encounter with religion and the modern state, the range and depth of its religious diversity, and finally its geopolitical complexities, there is a need to properly theorise the field of law, which mediates the relationship between state and religion. This theorising is particularly needed where secularism is applied to analysing law and religion practices in Asian states. Such analysis not only raises questions of fit, but should also give rise to questions of what secular and secularism means.[14] Theories that have been developed specifically within the 'Western' context may need to be rethought or even rejected in the non-Western contexts. For instance, using the secular frame developed within Western contexts runs the risk of interpreting the public role of religion in non-Western political formations in the current theoretical frame of state–church separation constructed to explain Western formations. To be more specific, let us examine three ways in which the Asian context may defy existing dominant theories about state, law, and religion.

First, the secularisation thesis never quite applied easily to Asia. This thesis dominated Western intellectual and political thinking in the 1960s and 70s. It posited that religion was in decline and on a trajectory to certain oblivion as societies developed economically and scientifically. These theories of secularisation, which occupied the field of sociology and other related scholarship, focuses upon the social consequences of the separation of the church from the state. José Casanova identifies three propositions encompassed within theories of secularisation: (1) the decline of belief, (2) the differentiation of public and private spheres (with religion being assigned to the latter), and (3) (related to the second) as marginalisation of religion.[15] The decline-of-religion sub-thesis postulates that "the process of secularisation would bring in its wake the progressive shrinkage and decline of religion until, some extreme versions added, it eventually disappeared".[16] In this sense, the idea of a secular state is extended to include the secular society, whereby "secularity consists in the falling off of religious belief and practice, in people turning away from God, and no longer going to Church".[17]

14 See, for instance, Neo's problematisation of secular constitutionalism in Singapore: Jaclyn L. Neo, 'Secular Constitutionalism in Singapore: Between Equality and Hierarchy', *Oxford Journal of Law and Religion* 5.3 (2016), 431.

15 Jose Casanova, *Public Religions in the Modern World*, 1st edn (University of Chicago Press, 1994), 7.

16 Ibid., 20.

17 Charles Taylor, A *Secular Age* (Belknap Press of Harvard University Press, 2007), 2.

On the other hand, the differentiation and marginalisation propositions may be collapsed into the 'privatisation' thesis, which postulates that "the process of secularization would bring in its wake the privatization and [logically] the marginalization of religion in the modern world".[18] Today, there is increasing contestation about the secular and secularism, which had for a long time presumed the viability of the secularisation thesis.

However, the challenge that Asia poses to the secularisation thesis is distinctive from the current contestation over secularism rooted within the Western experience. When scholars such as Peter Berger proclaimed the death of the secularisation thesis, they point to a "furiously religious" world,[19] where there has been the collapse of the "sacred canopy", which provided overarching normative regulation of society, replaced by rationalising modes of regulation marked by modern law and governance.[20] This presumes the existence of a sacred canopy as an existing normative framework for governance. Similarly, José Casanova's influential work on public religions theorises the phenomenon as *deprivatisation*, which assumes a prior privatisation. Indeed, for Casanova, the differentiation of social spheres and the declining influence of religion over the other spheres still hold true, but the new revival is seeing religion resist the shrinking and privatisation of its own sphere, pushing their way (*back*) into the public sphere to challenge dominant norms with their values.[21]

Within this context, Charles Taylor has called for a radical redefinition of secularism, thus to move the understanding of the term as pertaining to the relation of the state and religion to secularism as the proper response of democracy to diversity.[22] According to Taylor, there are four goals for a redefined secularism: to secure the freedom of religious affiliation for individuals, to guarantee the equality of all religions, to facilitate all religions to participate in the public sphere to determine society's identity and the governance of public goods, and to preserve religious harmony and comity.[23] We can see, explicitly in the third goal, the accommodation of the public role of religion. This accommodation is at the heart of attempts to rethink liberalism. As examples, Linda Woodhead[24] argues that strict secularism,

[18] Casanova (n. 15), 20.

[19] Peter Berger, 'The Desecularization of the World: A Global Overview', in Peter Berger (ed.), *The Desecularisation of the World: Resurgent Religions and World Politics* (Wm. B. Eerdmans Publishing, 1999), 1–18. See also Rodney Stark, 'Secularization, R.I.P. – Rest in Peace', *Sociology of Religion* 60.3 (1999), 249.

[20] Peter L. Berger, *The Sacred Canopy: Elements of a Sociological Theory of Religion* (Doubleday Anchor Books, 1967).

[21] Casanova (n. 15).

[22] Taylor (n. 17).

[23] Charles Taylor, 'Why We Need a Radical Redefinition of Secularism', in Eduardo Mendieta and Jonathan VanAntwerpen (eds.), *The Power of Religion in the Public Sphere* (Columbia University Press, 2011), 34–59.

[24] Linda Woodhead, 'Liberal Religion and Illiberal Secularism', in Gavin D'Costa and others (eds.), *Religion in a Liberal State* (Cambridge University Press, 2013), 93–116.

when it excludes public religious expression, is actually illiberal, while Derek McGhee[25] sees religion as integral to the founding and continued development of liberalism. However, Taylor's redefinition is much more radical than the accommodation of resurgent religion. Overall, the goals secure the place of secularism in overseeing and managing deprivatised *religions*, in the plural, as they tussle in the public sphere, not against secularism per se, but with each other. Thus, secularism derives its political legitimacy not in its liberal and rational departure from its religious opposite, but in its capacity to mediate religious differences and arbitrate religious conflict from a transcultural vantage point.

The focus of these contestations remains liberal democracies in the West, and the underlying philosophical concern has been with the viability of modern, or Western, civilisation, as we know it, and the role of Christianity. The contestation over secularism in the West has revolved around the extent of secularisation's reversal and thus the viability of secularism in contemporary times. Even Talal Asad speaks of a process of reversal – according to him, if religion was to become effectively deprivatised and cemented its role in the public sphere, then the differentiation of social spheres and declining influence of religion would surely be reversed.[26] Indeed, Casanova's position assumes the ineffectiveness of religion in reversing the inexorable march of secularisation, and therefore it sees the new revival as a rearguard reaction against modernity and the encroachment of secularism.

In comparison, much less is known of public religions in non-Western societies and the historical imbrications of non-Christian religions in the formation of secular postcolonial states. Thus, where other scholars noted similar experiences with political Islam, Hindutva, and other non-Christian religions in non-Western settings, it is questionable to what extent these non-Western experiences have been and can be compared to the Western Christian ones.[27] While modernisation has not brought about the decline and marginalisation of religion, scholars emphasise that, at the very least, there is secularisation in the sense of differentiation of public and private spheres, and correspondingly a decline in religion's dominance over 'public' spheres such as the political and the economic.[28] In a way, Taylor's more circumspect idea of secularity as the shift "from a society where belief in God is unchallenged and indeed, unproblematic, to one in which it is understood to be one option among others" is perhaps the most widely applicable.[29]

[25] Derek McGhee, 'Moderate Secularism in Liberal Societies?', in Gavin D'Costa and others (eds.), *Religion in a Liberal State* (Cambridge University Press, 2013), 117–34.

[26] Talal Asad, 'Religion, Nation-State, Secularism', in Peter van der Veer and Hartmut Lehmann (eds.), *Nation and Religion: Perspectives on Europe and Asia* (Princeton University Press, 1999), 178–96.

[27] Irfan Ahmad, *Islamism and Democracy in India: The Transformation of Jamaat-E-Islami* (Princeton University Press, 2009); Ian Harris (ed.), *Buddhism, Power and Political Order* (Routledge, 2007); Jyotirmaya Sharma, *Hindutva: Exploring the Idea of Hindu Nationalism* (Penguin Books, 2011).

[28] Casanova (n. 15).

[29] Taylor (n. 17), 3.

Second, there is increasing recognition that entanglement between state and religion remains the norm rather than the exception, even in highly modernised societies. For instance, Jonathan Fox's study of the extent of religion and state separation in 152 countries with populations of 1 million or more showed that the strict separation of religion and state is the exception whereas government involvement in religion is the norm.[30] Furthermore, the secularisation theories are not able to successfully explain why highly developed countries have differing state–religion relations, public influence of religions, and differing levels of individual religiosity. Ahmed T. Kuru's analysis of 176 countries in terms of their levels of development and official religion, using United Nations Development Programme's Human Development Index, in fact shows that more countries with high development (43%) have official religions compared with countries with medium (41%) and low development (5%).[31]

Asia not only represents an important crucible for investigating permutations of state–religion entanglement, but the degree and depth of state entanglement is also distinctive, and arguably greater. This is because, despite falling short of the separation of state and religion, Western Europe and North America continue to emphasise their 'secular' commitments and state neutrality as a way to manage religious plurality.[32] Furthermore, even in European states that constitutionally adopt a state religion or state church, such state–religion entanglements have been removed or become largely symbolic. Scandinavian countries such as Norway have amended their constitutions to remove the official status of the Norwegian State Church.[33]

Third, just as the secularisation thesis seems particularly incongruent when applied to Asia, post-secularism, which has emerged as a dominant line of scholarship in the Western context, seems similarly ill-fitting in its original terms but has to be reconceptualised to suit the Asian experience. This should not be entirely surprising. Habermas coined the term 'post-secular' specifically to describe the affluent societies of Europe, North America, and Oceania.[34] In the context of these, the idea of the post-secular may herald either an actual resurgence of religious faith, especially religious faith present in relatively new populations due to immigration patterns in some countries, or to a recognition of the persistence of religious faith, both of longstanding and more recent varieties. As discussed above, this is contrary to the received wisdom associated with the 'secularisation thesis' – namely the idea that

30 Jonathan Fox, 'World Separation of Religion and State into the Twenty-first Century', *Comparative Political Studies* 39.5 (2006), 537.

31 Ahmet T. Kuru, 'Secularism and State Politics Toward Religion: The United States, France and Turkey', *Journal for the Scientific Study of Religion* 48.4 (2009), 836.

32 See Silvio Ferrari, 'The Secular State in a Declining Europe: Beyond the End of the European Dream', *Journal of Religion and State* (2018, in press).

33 Elin Hofverberg, 'Norway: State and Church Separate after 500 years' (*Library of Congress*, 3 February 2017), www.loc.gov/law/foreign-news/article/norway-state-and-church-separate-after-500-years (accessed 28 March 2018).

34 Jurgen Habermas, 'Notes on Post-Secular Society', *New Perspectives Quarterly* 25.4 (2008), 17.

religiosity was in a slow but inexorable decline, particularly in the advanced countries of the West but extending after time to other countries as they developed. Critical to Habermas's use of the phrase post-secular is the idea that modernity no longer implies an inevitable march towards secularism or, as Talal Asad has put it, a straightforward narrative of progress from the religious to the secular is no longer acceptable.[35] What is important is that the notion of the post-secular marks a transition from a conception of modernity that was premised on a secular, or at least secularising, logic, to one in which the logic is neither necessarily secular nor religious. With respect to Asia, at the very least where current claims of post-secularism presume a resurgence of public religion, these seem ill-suited to understand a region where religion never quite relinquished its public power.

The applicability of ideas associated with the post-secular to Asia may be less incongruent if post-secular is thought of in terms more akin to Taylor's definition of secularity as a condition in which religious belief becomes simply one option among others.[36] Nonetheless, like all academic phrases, 'post-secular' has taken on a set of its own, diverse meanings. In 2012, the sociologist of religion James Beckford provided a useful accounting of the different senses of post-secular.[37] Among these differing understandings identified by Beckford is Inglof Dalferth's view:

> A society is post-secular if reference to religion or spirituality is no longer of basic, principal or indeed any importance at all for its self-understanding and self-definition ... Thus truly post-secular societies are neither religious nor secular ... They are neither for nor against religion(s) ... Rather, *they take no stand on this matter.* (emphasis in original)[38]

This understanding seems consistent with the view of the philosopher John Caputo, also cited by Beckford, who opines that 'the "post" in "post-secular" should not be understood to mean "over and done with" but rather *after having passed through* modernity ... '. Thus, a society is post-secular not because it necessarily rejects religion but because religion is optional or, in Taylorian terms, religious belief has no ontic necessity but is merely one option among many.[39]

Following from these points of incongruence, one may boldly suggest a differentiated study of law and religion in Western versus non-Western states. One should again not overstate the differences. This is because even within the 'West', the secularisation thesis has not entirely come to pass. While current data suggest that there are a growing number of people in the Western world who identify

35 Asad (n. 26).

36 On this, see Charles Taylor, *Modern Social Imaginaries* (Duke University Press, 2003).

37 James Beckford, 'SSSR Presidential Address – Public Religions and the Postsecular: Critical Reflections', *Journal for the Scientific Study of Religion* 51.1 (2012), 1.

38 Ingolf U. Dalferth, 'Post-secular Society: Christianity and the Dialectics of the Secular', *Journal of the American Academy of Religion* 78.2 (2010), 317, 324, as cited in Beckford, ibid., 11.

39 Taylor (n. 36).

as religiously unaffiliated,[40] such that religion may indeed be seen to be declining in one aspect, outside of the North American–Western Europe alignment however, religious affiliation continues to be vibrant and strong in most places (though with interesting exceptions). Therefore, while there appears to be a dichotomy between West and non-West, this is not a simple but a complex one. This dichotomy is, furthermore, itself becoming complicated by significant immigration flows from East to West that are changing and challenging the demographic realities and the religious landscape of the affected societies. Nonetheless, there are important points of distinction in Asia, being the most populous region in the world, with its own distinctive state, law, and religion encounters. We do not say that perspectives and analyses from outside of Asia cannot contribute to an understanding of the environment in Asia or to the development of principles relevant to the regulation of religion. However, we argue for a reflexive and dialogical approach to be taken in considering both theory and practices, between the analyses based largely on the experiences of the West and those of Asia. In this process, ideas and frameworks may need to be rethought and we should be alive to incongruences arising from the different demographic, historical, and geopolitical realities in Asia. In short, Asia deserves to be analyzed on its own terms.

III. REGULATING RELIGION IN ASIA: A LAW AND RELIGION APPROACH

This edited volume seeks precisely to analyse the regulation of religion in Asia on its own terms. It does not entirely reject existing theoretical accounts, as the chapters show engagement with current scholarship, but seeks to take seriously the experience and approaches of Asian states. While some chapters apply a normative framework that borrows from existing scholarship developed in the West, others seek to modify these frameworks based on the context of particular Asian states. This volume can be situated within an emerging major law and religion movement that is dedicated to studying the interaction of legal and religious ideas and institutions, norms, and practices. A large body of scholarship has gathered around the governance of institutions that, by their nature, have both spiritual and secular, and religious and political, dimensions. For instance, among the most perennial and prominent sites of such contests is the place of religion in schools. Charity and social welfare are becoming hotter areas of conflict, too, as religious communities play ever more prominent roles in providing charitable services. And in family law, headline battles today are over what *forms* of marriage should be recognised by the state – sometimes over the objection of religious groups, and sometimes at their insistence: straight versus gay marriage, contract versus covenant marriage, monogamous versus

[40] See Wim Hofstee and Arie van der Kooij, 'Introduction', in Wim Hofstee and Arie van der Kooij (eds.), *Religion beyond Its Private Role in Modern Society* (Brill, 2013), 1–11.

polygamous marriage, and more. An emerging battle concerns the fora in which marriage and family cases are adjudicated, specifically, the place of faith-based family laws and religious tribunals in governing the domestic lives of their voluntarily faithful.

This growing area of scholarship is commonly anchored in the crucial questions of the extent to which the export, transplant, or accommodation of discrete internal religious rules or procedures into secular legal systems vindicate religious group autonomy or protection, religious freedom, or constitutional rights. In comparison, 'regulation' is not normative but merely an analytical concept which emphasises state intentionality and the dialectical relationship between law and religion. Regulation is here understood, as Jaclyn Neo proposes in her chapter, as the *intentional intervention in the activities of religious individuals and communities, whether direct or indirect, through binding law or otherwise, and whether conducted by a public sector or private sector actors*. She suggests that using regulation as a conceptual tool to understand the state's relationship with religion is important as it pluralises the analysis of the state's relationship with religion, thus better reflecting the many points of legal and semi-legal encounters between the state and religion, beyond the usual parameters of constitutional and private law. This regulatory exercise arises as a result of the encounter of the state with religion as a matter of individual and group practices, as well as a matter of religious rules being incorporated into the state legal system. Therefore, for our purposes, the crucial question is not whether religion could be, is, and/or should be regulated, but what type of regulation and regulatory modes could be, are, and/or should be used to regulate this highly personal activity that could nonetheless pose some risks to the state such as providing an alternative source of socio-political mobilisation or as a source of intragroup conflict.

Regulation presumes a dialectical relationship between the state and religious groups/individuals, as well as between law and religion. It adopts a claim that many scholars now put forward about the dialectical relationship between law and religion. Thus, while law and religion can be conceptualised as distinct spheres of human life, they do not exist independently of one another. Instead, they are constantly crossing over and cross-fertilising each other. It is these points of crossover and cross-fertilisation that are the special province of the scholarly field of law and religion.

Furthermore, as discussed in Neo's chapter, interrogating the state's regulatory powers over religion should also serve to complicate claims about the relationship between regulation and religious freedom.[41] Wybraniec and Finke have argued, based on their study of religion cases from 1981 to 1996, that "even modest changes in the state's regulation of religion will have an immediate impact

[41] John Wybraniec and Roger Finke, 'Religious Regulation and the Courts: The Judiciary's Changing Role in Protecting Minority Religions from Majoritarian Rule', *Journal for the Scientific Study of Religion* 40 (2001), 427–44.

on the minority religions holding a tension with their surrounding culture."[42] They further conclude that "[r]eligious minorities are the first to benefit when religious regulations are lifted, and the first to be stifled when regulations are allowed."[43] This, they claim, shows an "inverse relationship between social power and the enforcement of state regulations."[44] This claim needs to be further investigated since some forms of regulations could arguably result in greater scope for religious freedom, particularly where such regulation is used to constrain excesses of religious majoritarianism. Majoritarian impulses may arise not only in terms of inter-religion relations but also from an intra-religion perspective.

IV. OVERVIEW OF THE CHAPTERS

This focus on regulation as international intervention frames this volume. As the various chapters show, the analysis is multidisciplinary and selectively representative. It does not seek to be comprehensive in methodology, disciplinary focus, and/or geographical coverage. Nonetheless, the chapters will show that regulation as a framework is used to go beyond the usual focus on courts and an over-emphasis on constitutional law. This is not to say that constitutional law is irrelevant but that it serves as only one area of state–religion encounter within the legal and semi-legal arena. As Jaclyn Neo's chapter emphasises, regulation can be direct or indirect, and can employ a range of regulatory tools, including co-regulation as an aspect of cooperation between the state and private agencies and self-regulation. Constitutional law and politics are also crucial insofar as they reflect the ideological orientation of state and society, whether liberal or non-liberal, individualist or communitarian.

It should here be noted that we do not in this volume seek to provide a comparative study of religion specifically, being cognizant of Clifford Geertz's lamentation that "[t]he comparative study of religion has always been plagued by this peculiar embarrassment: the elusiveness of its subject matter".[45] That said, we are also aware of the influence of what one might call the salient 'religious cultures' within Asia. Thus, we note three things. First, the landscape of religious cultures is markedly different in Asia than in other parts of the world. Hinduism, Buddhism, and Islam are present in many contexts of course, but they are particularly prominent in Asia. At the same time, while Christianity is present in Asia, looking at the region as a whole, it is not as major a religious culture as it is in other areas, especially

[42] Ibid., 441.
[43] Ibid.
[44] Ibid., 427.
[45] Clifford Geertz, *Islam Observed* (University of Chicago Press, 1968).

as compared to the West. Second, it will accordingly be important to recognise that the different religious cultures in Asia will shape the law and religion interaction in varied ways and hence give rise to different regulatory dynamics. For example, the different religious cultures may look to the law – or, indeed, not look to the law – in distinctive ways for accommodation, recognition, or even jurisdiction. However, because they are different, the religious cultures cannot be expected to approach these issues in similar ways. This draws on Geertz's insight about the challenge or elusiveness of comparison between what may be profoundly distinctive frameworks. Finally, it is important to keep in mind that Asia exhibits a high degree of 'mixedness'[46] in its religious cultures resulting both from high levels of religious diversity (as mentioned earlier), which includes the presence of significant religious minorities in certain countries (e.g., Muslims in Hindu-majority India, Buddhists in Muslim-majority Malaysia, or Hindus in Buddhist-majority Sri Lanka), as well as a diversity of interpretational outlooks within faith communities.

Accordingly, our volume opens with four chapters with different theoretical perspectives on the regulation of religion. The first is Arif Jamal's chapter, where he develops an account of regulatory markers as guidelines or principles for the regulation of religion. The five markers he proposes are fundamentally concerned with recognising and responding to the vast diversity of religion in Asia and embrace a capacious definition of religion, which moves beyond "essential practices", adopts dialectical regulation and regulatory dynamism and recognises epistemic plurality. His markers thus seek to respond to both inter- and intra-religious diversity as well as diversity from outside of religions. The markers emphasise both the need to be flexible because religion in Asia is not one thing, as well as to be serious "by acknowledging the presence of religion and allowing it to have a voice and play a role in normative debates".

In the next chapter, Jaclyn Neo builds upon the idea of regulation by developing, as alluded to earlier, an account of the concept of 'regulation' and highlights the range of regulatory modes that states have applied to negotiate their relationship with religion. She adopts existing regulatory terms such as public regulation, co-regulation, and self-regulation, thereby drawing from insights that have been developed within regulatory theory while not constricting her analysis to regulatory market assumptions.

Shai Wozner and Gilad Abiri's chapter furthers the volume's theoretical interrogations of regulation of religion. Their thoughtful exposition identifies

[46] For a discussion of 'mixing systems', see Esin Orucu, '"*Legal Families*" *and* "*Mixing Systems*"', in Esin Orucu and David Nelken (eds.), *Comparative Law: A Handbook* (Hart Publishing, 2007), 169–88.

contestation over ultimate authority as a foundational dynamic underlying the regulation of religion. Specifically, the chapter uses the case study of Israel's relationship with its ultra-Orthodox communities to posit that the conflicts between state and religious institutions are not merely about conflicts of ideology and value, but rather raise more fundamental and intractable issues in a dual, and mutually constitutive, dynamic of the competition for ultimate *authority* and the need to protect the sacred. Thus, their analysis pushes us to understand that there are deeper and more incommensurable logics operating in these interactions, which ordinary accounts of state and religion conflicts as grounded in clashes of ideology and values fail to capture, to their explanatory detriment.

This establishment of authority and power as connected to the construction of regulatory regimes underpins the next two chapters. Benjamin Schonthal's chapter focuses on the bureaucratic processes of regulating religion in Buddhist-majority states of South and Southeast Asia. He notes that before the state can purport to regulate religion, it must first define the status of religious groups. Accordingly, he argues that the legal regulation of religion is not just a bureaucratic process of subscribing religious freedoms, but rather, and more fundamentally, about delimiting the realms of civil and religious authority. While one might think that the character and attitude of the state vis-à-vis religion would deeply colour these processes, Schonthal uses his case studies to illustrate that "projects of managing religious and state authority in self-declaredly secular jurisdictions look surprisingly similar to projects of managing religious and state authority in legal regimes that neither claim to nor aspire to be rigorously impartial towards religion".

Kevin Fogg's chapter also examines the construction of regulation of religion through the political process of defining religion. His historical analysis is important as it shows how the power to define what constitutes religion formed an integral part of the regulatory regime and continues to be a basis for the exercise of regulatory power. His chapter is a lucid examination of the processes and actors involved in the consolidation of regulatory power, showing that a historical understanding is often times essential to interrogating foundational assumptions and goals of regulation of religion.

The next section comprises five chapters that highlight the various modes of regulating religion. In her chapter, Thio Li-ann identifies and evaluates five broad postures: controller, cooperative partner, consultative leader, constant calibrator, and culture war manager. Her study of Singapore highlights the informal forms of regulation, which is underpinned by legislation but takes place primarily at the informal and through what she has called the relational approach. Her chapter also shows the connection between regulation and constitutional arrangements. As she emphasises, '[c]onstitutions define the limits of public power in establishing the architecture of government and protecting rights, including religious freedom guarantees'. She argues that the Singapore government's approach is underpinned by a constitutional approach that can be characterised as 'principled pluralism'.

Bui Ngoc Son's chapter is important in highlighting the use of "formal laws to comprehensively and stringently regulate religion", which should be understood as an extension of the socialist ideology of the Vietnamese state. As he points out, the regulatory framework for religion in Vietnam should be seen as situated within broader institutional settings defined by four fundamental socialist attributes: the socialist regime, the ideology and strategy of "great unit", the principle of socialist legality, and statist human rights. His chapter is of special significance in uncovering the socialist attributes that shape regulatory approaches to religion, which could be relevant in examining other socialist regimes in Asia.

Nyi Nyi Kyaw's chapter examines a different face of regulation as applied to a majority religion. It discusses the regulation of Theravada Buddhism in Myanmar and the role of the State Sangha Maha Nayaka Committee, a supreme Sangha body established in 1980, in drawing the boundaries between legal/orthodox and unorthodox/illegal sects, ideologies, teachings, and practices. Kyaw argues that the work of the Committee represents a "political pact" between the state and the Sangha through which outlier unorthodox groups could be regulated, disciplined, and 'punished'. In that regard, the Committee performs functions that should be seen as crucially embedded within the state's regulatory regime directed at religion.

Mirjam Künkler's chapter addresses state regulation of religious education in the fascinating case of the Islamic Republic of Iran. It is particularly interesting as it presents an approach to regulation that is set within the context of a self-proclaimed Islamic state. Künkler uses previously untapped sources in Persian to demonstrate the gradual process of state regulation of the religious education sector. It also shows how private actors, particularly Muslim women, negotiate state regulation and use it to advance their own interests.

In line with this volume's multidisciplinary approach, Jianlin Chen and Loveday J. Liu's chapter employs market regulation theory to religion. Unlike Neo's chapter, which seeks to transform regulatory ideas when applied to religion, Chen and Liu's chapter assumes that religious activities can be regulated in the same way as economic activities. In other words, it introduces a religious-economic model that posits that the process in which individual religious choices are made are akin to decision-making processes in other realms of human activities, namely to maximise utility. Thus, in this chapter, the authors conceptualise law as performing the function of regulating religious competition.

The last section of the book comprises four chapters that expose the limits of regulation. There are three themes that thread through the chapters. The first is that the secular and the religious are produced by institutional politics conditioned by historical traditions and colonial legacies. The second is that the institutional politics are sparked by the social actions of individuals and communities responding to state regulation and vice versa. The third is that the institutional politics take place in the context of legal pluralism, in which the legal pluralism influences the politics and is at the same time impacted by the politics.

Matthew Nelson and Dian A. H. Shah's chapter discusses the landmark case of Lina Joy in Malaysia. Joy had converted to Christianity and sought to change the assignation of 'Islam' as her religion on her identity card. Her fundamental right to religious freedom was, however, mired in the procedural webs of the administrative state, in which legal regulation of religion was differentiated along state lines as well as along lines of religious authority, with Islam treated as a privileged preserve. Ultimately, in a majority two-to-one ruling rejecting Joy's appeal, the Federal Court determined that a person must renounce his or her religion only in accordance with the laws and practices of the religion. As Nelson and Shah argues, historical, constitutional, social and political contexts matter in the determination of administrative "reasonableness".

Likewise, Daniel Goh's chapter on the challenge of Pentecostal Christian megachurches to the authority of the administrative state in neighbouring Singapore shows that the legal pluralism that is applied to the regulation of different religions produces peculiar outcomes. Enjoying the greatest degree of autonomy from regulation, the megachurches nevertheless entered into legal face-offs with the state, as their prophetic calling led them to seek 'crossovers' to Christianise the secular realm. Goh examines two cases involving the policing of adultery among employees who broke employment laws and the deployment of church funds to meet cultural outreach objectives that broke corporate governance laws. Goh argues that the Pentecostals innovated hybrid interpretations of the law, combining constitutional rights, legal norms, and religious laws, to justify their standing as religious subjects operating in the secular sphere.

In the next chapter, Mohsin Alam Bhat continues with the focus on institutional and community actors. In the first place, Bhat shows how institutional actors reasoned, innovated, and produced Indian secularism and its slippages towards defining minority rights issues as "religious" and specifically "Muslim". Bhat discusses two cases, one in which the Muslim minority was denied affirmative action because of its supposed internal heterogeneity, and the other in which an influential opinion was made that Dalit Muslims should be excluded from affirmative action for Muslims because the former was not a religious but a caste identity. This elasticity of secularism and contradictions of regulating religion arise not from the conceit of institutional actors, but in their response to communities manoeuvring around markers of the secular and the religious to make demands on the state.

In the final chapter of the book, Haider Hamoudi turns to Shi'i Islamic jurisprudence and its relationship to the modern state. The high jurists of the decentralised Hawza pronounce doctrines over spheres of life that overlap with state jurisdiction. Current scholarly understandings see this as engendering conflict leading ultimately to the jurists seeking to seize control of the state apparatus. But the Islamic Revolution in Iran is more an exception than the norm. Hamoudi shows that the jurists of Najaf Hawza in Iraq seek instead to engage and negotiate with the state to carve out a 'religious' space where their pronouncements hold sway. The jurists thus contribute to the making of the legal pluralism and the tensed balance between the secular and the religious prevailing in many non-Western societies.

On the whole, therefore, one important common thread that ties the chapters together is that the diversity and complexity of state regulation in Asia matches the religious diversity and complexity present in Asian societies. Current approaches to the study of religion, law, and politics emphasise the tendency of state law, institutions, and actors to produce outcomes that discipline state subjects. They provide important perspectives on the operations of language, politics, and power in line with secular logics. Yet to the extent that they present an account of state power that is unitary, they overstate the degree to which states hold coherent views, manage the language and logic of state institutions and agents, and control the reception of their acts. In so doing, they may underplay the incoherence of secular logics and of state authority, when it may be precisely this incoherence that paves the way for new political and social possibilities.[47] By conceptualising the state's relationship with religion in regulatory terms, this emphasises the multiplicity of contact between them and the polycentric nature of the relationship. Consequently, regulation, rather than constitutional or private law approaches, provides a more complex picture of the state–religion relationship and the non-unitary or often non-monopolising nature of state authority.

[47] Iza Hussin, '"The New Global Politics of Religion": Religious Harmony, Public Order, and Securitisation in the Post-Colony', *Journal of Religious and Political Practice* 4.1 (2017), 93.

PART I

Theorizing Regulation

1

Regulatory Markers

Arif A. Jamal

I. INTRODUCTION

Asia's religious landscape is vast and diverse. This diversity also exhibits characteristics that make the Asian context notably distinctive from other environments and which, in turn, have implications for the regulation of religion in Asia.

This chapter presents a set of what I call 'regulatory markers' to address the regulation of religion, with a particular focus on Asia. The Asian focus is important because the markers posited in this chapter are presented especially to fit the diversity within Asia and, in this respect, draw on and help to explain the context of Asia.

I suggest regulatory markers also as guidelines or principles but without necessarily having a universal (or in this case regional) application, or having only one form of application. For an environment as large as Asia, a single form of application is neither necessary nor practical. At the same time, however, the markers suggest and point to shareable ideas. That is to say, the presentation of regulatory markers for Asia resists the position that we can say nothing across the space of Asia, even while acknowledging that we may not be able – at all times and in all places – to say the same things.

The first part of this chapter provides a contextual setting for the regulatory markers. I begin with a discussion of the demographic environment and then move on to outline three interconnected challenges towards the understanding of religion: the challenge of defining religion that arises from interfaith diversity, the complementary challenge of intrafaith diversity and, finally, the challenge of polarisation, which works both within religious communities and traditions, as well as between those with religious adherence and those without.

I then discuss a range of different roles that the state can undertake as a key regulatory actor, which vary from the rather obvious and explicit to more implicit and sometimes unseen. The elaboration of these different roles helps to outline the spectrum of regulatory responses available to the state.

These two sections then set up the presentation of regulatory markers that respond to the contextual settings and roles of the state. Ultimately, I argue that the diversity and presence of religion in Asia need to be responded to by a regulatory regime that is not only flexible to accommodate diversity but also takes the (potential) contributions of religious voices seriously.

II. REGULATORY CONTEXTS

A. *Demographics*

Religious demographics in Asia reflect a mixed and varied picture. I offer here a (non-scientific) random sample, relying on data from studies done by the Pew Research Center as part of their Global Religious Futures study, which has looked at the religious terrain in several countries around the world with projections up to 2050.[1]

The Pew research shows some countries in Asia with very high levels of religious affiliation both at present and expected in the future. For instance, Turkey is reported to have a 98% Muslim share of the population in 2010, and the same is predicted for 2050. Thailand is shown to have more than a 90% population share of Buddhists in 2010 and about the same is expected in 2050, though with a slight decline in the percentage of Buddhists and an increase in its Muslim population by 2050. Indonesia shows a more than 85% population share of Muslims in 2010 and the same expected in 2050, but with an increase in its Christian population by 2050 too. All three of these countries show an unaffiliated population of less than 1%. The results for India show that its population shares were 79.5% Hindus, 14.4% Muslims and 2.5% Christians with fewer than 1% unaffiliated in 2010, and by 2050 the population shares are expected to be 76.7% Hindus, 18.7% Muslims, 2.2% Christians and still fewer than 1% unaffiliated.[2] North East Asia, however, shows a significantly different religious landscape. Thus, in Japan, the Pew results predict that the unaffiliated percentage will rise from about 57% of the population in 2010 to about 67% in 2050, with a corresponding decline in the Buddhist population from about 35% (2010) to about 25% (2050).[3] In Hong Kong, the percentage of unaffiliated individuals is reported as 56.1% in 2010, *declining* to 49.1% in 2050, with an increase in the Christian population accounting for much of this change as it moves from 14.3% in 2010 to 18.9% in 2050.[4] In Taiwan, in 2010, folk religions represented 44.2%,

1 Pew-Templeton Global Religious Futures, 'Pew-Templeton: Global Religion Futures Project', www.globalreligiousfutures.org (accessed 1 March 2018).

2 Pew-Templeton Global Religious Futures, 'Religion in India' (2010), www.globalreligiousfutures.org/countries/india (accessed 1 March 2018).

3 Pew-Templeton Global Religious Futures, 'Religions in Japan' (2010), www.globalreligiousfutures.org/countries/japan (accessed 1 March 2018).

4 Pew-Templeton Global Religious Futures, 'Religions in Hong Kong' (2010), www.globalreligiousfutures.org/countries/hong-kong (accessed 1 March 2018).

Buddhists 21.3%, Christians 5.5% and unaffiliated 12.7%; the estimates for 2050 are folk religions 42.3%; Buddhists 20.5%, Christians 6.5% and unaffiliated 17.1%.[5] South Korea in 2010 showed Buddhists with a population share of 22.9%, Christians with 29.4% and unaffiliated with 46.4%, projected to change in 2050 to Buddhists 18.1%, Christians 33.5% and unaffiliated (almost unchanged) 46.3%.[6]

In addition to the foregoing, when one moves from numbers indicating religious affiliation to levels of religious diversity (which includes the religiously unaffiliated), Pew reports that of the global population, only 16.3% are religiously unaffiliated, with this percentage expected to *decrease* over time.[7] In terms of the geography of diversity, Pew notes, 'Half of the most religiously diverse countries are in Asia-Pacific region'.[8] Interestingly, it is in Asia and the Pacific, where more than three-quarters (76%) of the world's unaffiliated population resides, though 'only about one-in-five people (21%) in that region are unaffiliated',[9] and this number is quite skewed by one country China, which alone accounts for 62% of the world's total religiously unaffiliated. In comparison, the figures for Europe and North America are 18% and 17% religiously unaffiliated, respectively, and the unaffiliated make up smaller shares in the remaining regions. For instance, fewer than 1% of those who live in the Middle East–North Africa region are unaffiliated.

In another report, Pew notes that its 'study focused on five widely recognized world religions – Buddhism, Christianity, Hinduism, Islam and Judaism – *that collectively account for roughly three-quarters of the world's population*'[10] but in reading this we must also recall the situations in Asia such as Japan, South Korea and Hong Kong, which exhibit high levels of religiously unaffiliated populations now and expected in the future.

Thus, when looked at in the round and globally, the data suggest that what we are really seeing are conditions of heightening plurality – among religious traditions and among those with and without religious affiliation – which is captured in enhanced global religious diversity, with this diversity being especially prominent in the Asia-Pacific region. In addition, in looking at Asia we see that religions traditions such as Islam, Buddhism and Hinduism are quite prominent and may be majority traditions, whereas in the West these exist as minority traditions; similarly, Christianity is often a minority tradition in Asia though it is still the predominant tradition in the

5 Pew-Templeton Global Religious Futures, 'Religions in Taiwan' (2010), www.globalreligiousfutures.org/countries/taiwan (accessed 1 March 2018).

6 Pew-Templeton Global Religious Futures, 'Religions in South Korea' (2010), www.globalreligiousfutures.org/countries/south-korea (accessed 1 March 2018).

7 Pew Research Center, 'The Future of World Religions: Population Growth Projections, 2010–2050' (2 April 2015), www.pewforum.org/2015/04/02/religious-projections-2010–2050/ (accessed 1 March 2018).

8 Pew Research Center, 'Global Religious Diversity' (4 April 2014), www.pewforum.org/2014/04/04/global-religious-diversity/ (accessed 1 March 2018).

9 Pew Research Center, 'Religiously Unaffiliated' (18 December 2012), www.pewforum.org/2012/12/18/global-religious-landscape-unaffiliated/ (accessed 1 March 2018).

10 Pew Research Center, 'Global Religious Diversity' (n. 8).

West. This, therefore, provides some demographic context that we need to think about when considering the regulation of religion: a framework of different influences, and of diversity and plurality.

B. *Definitional Challenges*

Regulatory complexity does not arise just as a result of the diversity driven by religious demographics. There is also the important question of defining religion: that is, of deciding what constitutes 'religion' – as opposed to being categorised as a cultural, social, traditional, etc., phenomenon – and thus what falls within the purview of regulating 'religion'. In short, how do we define religion as a category for regulation?

Efforts to come up with a comprehensive definition have been tried by many thinkers from many disciplines but a comprehensive definition has eluded everyone. This chapter will be no exception. Indeed, even legal definitions have struggled to accommodate evolving realties, understandings and changing demographics so that what was 'not religion' in the past in some contexts has become religion later, and thus the anthropological question has entered legal discourses too.

For example, in *R (on the application of Hodkin) v Registrar General of Births, Deaths and Marriages*,[11] the UK Supreme Court had to address a claim by members of the Church of Scientology that they had a right to be married on the premises of a Church of Scientology in London. At issue was whether these premises were a 'place of meeting for religious worship' within the meaning of section 2 of the Places of Worship Registration Act 1855.[12] Depending on the definition, a valid ceremony of marriage could or could not be conducted on the premises of the Church of Scientology. In coming to its decision, the Supreme Court had to consider an earlier English decision in *R v Registrar General, Ex p Segerdal*,[13] in which the Court of Appeal held in a similar case that a different church within the Church of Scientology was not a place of meeting for religious worship. In *Segerdal*, Lord Denning said:

> We have had much discussion on the meaning of the word 'religion' and of the word 'worship', taken separately, but I think we should take the combined phrase, 'place of meeting for religious worship' as used in the statute of 1855. It connotes to my mind a place of which the principal use is as a place where people come together as a congregation or assembly to do reverence to God. It need not be the God which the Christians worship. It may be another God, or an unknown God, but it must be reverence to a deity. There may be exceptions. For instance, Buddhist temples are properly described as places of meeting for religious worship. But, apart from exceptional cases of that kind, it seems to me the governing idea behind the

11 [2013] UKSC 77, [2014] 1 AC 610 ('*Hodkin*').
12 (18 & 19 Vict c 81).
13 [1970] 2 QB 697 (CA) ('*Segerdal*').

words 'place of meeting for religious worship' is that it should be a place for the worship of God. I am sure that would be the meaning attached by those who framed this legislation of 1855.

He further stated,

> Turning to the creed of the Church of Scientology, I must say that it seems to me to be more a *philosophy* of the existence of man or of life, rather than a *religion*. Religious worship means reverence or veneration of God or of a Supreme Being. I do not find any such reverence or veneration in the creed of this church. . . . When I look through the ceremonies and the affidavits, I am left with the feeling that there is nothing in it of reverence for God or a deity, but simply instruction in a philosophy. There may be belief in a spirit of man, but there is no belief in a spirit of God.[14]

It was on the basis of the foregoing analysis that the Church of Scientology was held not to be a place of religious worship in *Segerdal*.

In *Hodkin*, Lord Toulson (with whom Lord Neuberger, Lord Clarke and Lord Reed agreed) held that 'In my view the meaning given to worship in *Segerdal* was unduly narrow, but even if it was not unduly narrow in 1970, it is unduly narrow now.'[15] In other words, Lord Toulson and the UK Supreme Court were able to move beyond the bias towards just conventional religions espoused by Lord Denning in the 1970s (when, note, Lord Denning thought that even Buddhist temples were 'exceptional' as places of religious worship) to adapt to minority or some might say fringe expressions as well.[16]

Segerdal and *Hodkin* were not cases from Asia, of course, but they do illustrate the challenges that arise in defining religion and how our understandings can change over time. Another legal example of this challenge that is again expressed legally has been the Supreme Court of India's 'essential practices test' for religions, which is discussed in the text that follows.[17]

In the context of Asia some have questioned whether the very category of 'religion' appropriately understands particular non-Abrahamic traditions. For instance, Prakash Shah has argued that

[14] Ibid., 707.

[15] *Hodkin* (n. 11) [61].

[16] I have discussed definitional issues and their impact in more detail in Arif A. Jamal, 'The Impact of Definitional Issues on the Right of Freedom of Religion and Belief', in Silvio Ferrari (ed.), *Routledge Handbook of Law and Religion* (Routledge, 2015), 91.

[17] See articulations of this doctrine in *Ram Prasad Seth v. State of UP* AIR [1957] All 411 (1957) IILLJ 172 Al, and especially *Mohd Hanif Quareshi v. State of Bihar* [1958] AIR 731 (1959) SCR 629. For a discussion, see Gautam Bhatia, '"Essential Religious Practices" and the Rajasthan High Court's Santhara Judgement: Tracking the History of a Phrase', *Indian Constitutional Law and Philosophy* (19 August 2015), indconlawphil.wordpress.com/2015/08/19/essential-religious-practices-and-the-rajasthan-high-courts-santhara-judgment-tracking-the-history-of-a-phrase/ (accessed 1 March 2018).

> When certain kinds of legal ideas, embedded as norms within the Western culture, which is constituted by a religion, Christianity, enter non-Western cultures that do not have religion, those ideas break down, become distorted, absurd or nonsensical, and induce conflict. The secular state engages in the process of suppressing what it implicitly regards as false religion or idolatrous practices.[18]

He further stated that 'A number of researchers have argued that the type of religion presupposed by studies of comparative religion and the human sciences more generally is Christianity.'[19]

Indeed, even when dealing with religions within the Abrahamic context, the question of how to understand the traditions and the impact of categories from the West formulated about Christianity may be raised. For instance, in discussing Islam, the Sunni tradition of the faith has often been called 'orthodox' Islam, while the Shia tradition of the faith has been called 'heterodox'. But there is an important question to be asked about whether these categories work when the tradition has not had the same structure of churches of as in Christianity to declare what is 'orthodox' and hence what falls outside of this as 'heterodox'.[20]

A framework premised either on the structure of the Abrahamic faiths, or indeed more specifically of Christianity, is obviously challenging for Asia, where non-Abrahamic traditions are significant in many jurisdictions. Even if we abandon efforts to come up with the perfect definition of religion, which we probably must, a more general understanding about the religious cultures in Asia must be considered. This understanding (let us not call it a definition) may in turn attract particular regulatory demands. The anthropological context of Asia thus displays a diversity with which we must grapple.

Interestingly, when the law has come to consider religion, explicit constitutional protections for freedom of religion per se (albeit often allied to freedom of belief or of conscience) are ubiquitous across different cultural and social contexts, including in Asia. As a consequence, as Jeremy Weber has argued:

> [O]ne cannot make sense of [these guarantees of] freedom or religion . . . unless one recognises that the freedom is founded upon the *affirmative valuing of religion*. Any coherent conception of the freedom depends upon the premise that *religious belief has special value and deserves special protection.*[21]

18 Prakash Shah, 'The Difference that Religion Makes: Transplanting Legal Ideas from the West to Japan and India', *ASJCL* 10.1 (2015), 81 (from abstract).

19 Ibid. Shah cites Markus Dressler and Arvind Mandair (eds.), *Secularism and Religion-Making* (Oxford University Press, 2011), 16–18, for this claim.

20 See on this the discussion in Robert Langer and Udo Simon, 'The Dynamics of Orthodoxy and Heterodoxy: Dealing with Divergence in Muslim Discourses and Islamic Studies', *World Islam* 48 (2008), 273.

21 Jeremy Weber, 'Understanding the Religion in Freedom of Religion', in Peter Cane, Carolyn Evans, and Zoë Robinson (eds.), *Law and Religion in Theoretical and Historical Context* (Cambridge University Press, 2008), 26–43 (emphases added).

Indeed, the fact that freedom of religion, as a nominated freedom, is so ubiquitous in constitutional and human rights documents attests to its historically grounded, as well as its currently recognised importance. Freedom of religion was, and is still, widely seen to be among the most important, foundational and critical of all freedoms – part of a sort of constitutional core.

In the context of this 'core value' of freedom of religion, closely aligned to the challenge of defining religion, is the issue of what different claims religions may make on the state and within society. Will different 'forms' of religion make different types of claims on the state and society precisely because of their different forms? For instance, works about both Muslim and Hindu law will discuss rules and principles relating to maintenance.[22] Adherents of these traditions would thus have the religio-legal resources available to seek recognition of these legal principles in state law but this would, of course, be different from other religious traditions that either did not have concerns about these issues or similar religio-legal resources because their traditions did not speak about these matters.[23] Thus, one of the regulatory challenges in Asia is the 'culture' of the different religions that are in the region. These religions' cultures may not only be different in theological terms from those of the West (or other regions) but, additionally, may be concerned with basically different issues on different terms.

C. *Intrafaith Challenges*

The discussion in the preceding sections has considered differences between faiths in terms of their structures, premises and orientations on an interfaith basis. To this discussion, however, must be added the context of intrafaith diversity. Intrafaith diversity may be distinguished from interfaith diversity in that it would be defined not on fundamentally different premises but rather on different interpretations or approaches. Be that as it may, interfaith diversity does not pose less of a challenge for the regulation of religion; indeed it may pose even greater regulatory challenges because it belies attempts to simplify diversity into religious groups, e.g., Christians, Hindus, Buddhists, etc., which could then be dealt with as single entities.[24]

22 By way of examples, see Wael Hallaq, *Sharia: Theory, Practice, Transformations* (Cambridge University Press, 2009), chapter 8 and Werner Menski, *Hindu Law* (Oxford University Press, 2003), chapter 12.

23 As an illustration, see Rebecca Redwood French and Mark A Nathan (eds.), *Buddhism and Law: An Introduction* (Cambridge University Press, 2014). The book contains a chapter by Timothy Brook on 'The Ownership and Theft of Monastic Land in Ming China' (chapter 12). The concern with monastic land may be (or may have been) significant for Buddhist law but it would not be so for Muslim law, for instance, as there is not a monastic tradition of the same type in Islam.

24 As an example of this phenomenon see discussions of the implications of different interpretations of Islam and Muslim law among Muslims in Singapore in Noor Aisha Abdul Rahman, 'Muslim Personal Law and Citizen's Rights: The Case of Singapore', *ASJCL* 7 (2012), 127, and among Indonesian Muslims in Nadirsyah Hosen, 'Halal and Hilal: How to Manage Islamic Pluralism in Indonesia?' *ASJCL* 7 (2012), 111.

Instead, the recognition of intrafaith differences accentuates the diversity present in religious communities, reminding us that shared identification with a particular religion does not mean that its adherents will share views about the expressions, claims or even values of the religion. The existence of these differences is particularly relevant to regulatory discussions because variances in expressions or values will likely result in distinctive types of claims being made on the state or on society – for instance, claims for 'accommodation' – and hence engender different regulatory responses. In other words, intrafaith diversity adds layers of nuance and complexity, emerging now not just between religions but also from within one religious tradition, to the regulation of religion.

D. *Polarisation*

Another important context impacting Asia is the emergence of heightened polarisation resulting from more assertive (or some might say 'fundamentalist') expressions of religious traditions. These expressions are manifesting themselves in different countries in Asia, and across a range of religious traditions. Examples of this phenomenon are well known and include the alignment between the Bharatiya Janata Party government and Hindu nationalism in India, which some see as advancing a pro-Hindu (and anti-non-Hindu and perhaps particularly anti-Islam) agenda or the reliance on parties of 'political Islam' in Malaysia or 'political Buddhism' in Myanmar and Sri Lanka.

The effects of these manifestations can result in polarisation in at least three ways. First, they may add to the polarisation between those who express adherence to a religion versus those who do not, when religious views are presented in assertive terms that may seem either aggressive or intolerant or to be making excessive demands in public life on those who do not hold religious views. Second, even for those who do hold religious views, and indeed, even for those of the same religious tradition, forms of religious expression that are especially assertive can be off-putting; in other words they can cause others within the same tradition to feel alienated from their co-religionists. Third, assertive religious expression is often linked to a sense of a 'purified' form of any one religious tradition, and thus more strongly demarcating the boundaries between one tradition and another. This can limit the syncretic space of religious plurality and hybridity and so more starkly polarise the distinctions between religions.

In sum, these forces may result in a multidimensional polarisation emerging in the socio-political environment, with external and internal dimensions: externally, between those of religion and those not, and internally within different understandings of a religious tradition. As 'assertive' religion is manifest in different parts of Asia today (e.g., India, Myanmar, Sri Lanka, Malaysia and others) these different facets of polarisation must be reckoned with.

Taking the foregoing into account, it is evident that in looking at Asia we must be alert to its identifiably different contexts. Concomitantly, we must also recognise that though there cannot be said to be one Asian pattern, we should understand the distinctive conditions that feed into the experiences (plural required) of present-day Asia and that will likely help to shape Asia's future.

III. THE ROLES OF THE STATE

The state is clearly a powerful regulator of religion, and thus when considering the range of regulatory responses available in light of the preceding discussion, we need also to be alert to the different ways in which the state can act. Indeed, one may conceive of a series of different roles the state can fulfil. In the following, I identify five.

The first role is that of the legislative state. This is perhaps the most easily seen variety of state action because it manifests in promulgated, written forms, either in legislation, or regulation made under legislation or in constitutional language. The state in this form may act in a variety of ways, including, for example, by providing general guarantees of freedom of religion (in constitutional language); by requiring, prohibiting or stipulating the terms of religious education offered in schools; by providing favourable tax status for religious establishments; by imposing registration or licencing requirements on religious organisation; or by legislating with respect to the giving of religious offence. Similarly, formal legal regulations may also be established to govern religious expression such as, for instance, for religious processions or broadcasting etc. The legislative state is explicit and has broad powers to reach into many areas of life and, of course, to make alterations to rules as it sees fit.

A second role is that of the judicial state. The state acts judicially in interpreting and defining the scope of its constitutional, legislative and regulatory provisions. Like its legislative role, this is a rather obvious state function but it is distinctive from the legislative role and significantly affects religious regulation. We can, for instance, consider the following judicial statements of courts in Singapore and Canada concerning the scope of freedom of religion to see the impact of the judicial state. The Singapore courts have said:

> I am of the view that religious beliefs ought to have proper protection, but actions undertaken or flowing from such beliefs must conform with the general law relating to public order and social protection. The right of freedom of religion must be reconciled with 'the right of the State to employ the sovereign power to ensure peace, security and orderly living without which constitutional guarantee of civil liberty would be a mockery'.[25] The sovereignty, integrity and unity of Singapore are undoubtedly the paramount mandate of the Constitution and anything, including religious beliefs and practices, which tend to run counter to these objectives must be restrained.[26]

[25] *Commissioner, HRE v. LT Swamiar* AIR [1954] SC 282.

[26] *Chan Hiang Leng Colin v. Public Prosecutor* [1994] SGHC 207, [1994] 3 SLR(R) 209.

And

> . . . although the pledge ceremony does not demand worship of the flag as a symbol, if a person held that understanding, that perception was a *philosophical choice*. It seemed clear to us that the appellant's interpretation of the pledge and anthem ceremony as a religious ceremony was a *distortion of secular fact into religious belief*. It is *not accepted as a religious belief* and is *not entitled to protection under the Constitution of Singapore*.[27]

This can be compared to the following statement of the Supreme Court of Canada:

> In essence, religion is about freely and deeply held personal convictions or beliefs connected with an individual's spiritual faith and integrally linked to one's self-definition and spiritual fulfilment, the practices of which allow individuals to foster a connection with the divine or with the subject or object of that spiritual faith . . . This understanding is consistent with a personal or subjective understanding of freedom of religion. As such, a claimant need not show some sort of objective religious obligation, requirement or precept to invoke freedom of religion. It is the religious or spiritual essence of an action, not any mandatory or perceived-as-mandatory nature of its observance, that attracts protection. The State is in no position to be, nor should it become, the arbiter of religious dogma. Although a court is not qualified to judicially interpret and determine the content of a subjective understanding of a religious requirement, it is qualified to inquire into the sincerity of a claimant's belief, where sincerity is in fact at issue. Sincerity of belief simply implies an honesty of belief and the court's role is to ensure that a presently asserted belief is in good faith, neither fictitious nor capricious, and that it is not an artifice.[28]

In looking at the preceding statements, we can see the judicial language expressing different senses of scope of guarantees of freedom of religion contained in the constitutional structure of both countries. The judicial state does this all the time, taking similar or analogous materials and articulating the meaning and limitations of the legislative provisions for the jurisdiction. The language of legislation is one thing; the meaning of that language when tested in specific circumstances is another and is ultimately determined by the judicial state.

Third, a slightly less visible – or at least less high profile – function is carried out by what we may call the administrative or bureaucratic state. By this, I mean to capture the state which applies norms or procedures to regulate in an ordinary, daily way, the way religion may express itself. The strictness of flexibility applied by the bureaucratic state is also part of the regulatory mix.

A colourful example of the operation of what I mean can be found, for instance, around some mosques in Singapore at the time of the communal Friday afternoon

[27] *Nappalli Peter Williams v. Institute of Technical Education* [1999] SGCA 41, [1999] 2 SLR(R) 529 (emphasis added).
[28] *Syndicat Northcrest v. Amselem* [2004] SCC 47, [2004] 2 SCR 551 ('*Syndicat Northcrest*').

prayers. One can observe the way in which parking enforcement is relaxed for a couple of hours in the vicinity of the mosques, allowing worshipers to park in places and in a manner that would not otherwise be permitted, except by the enforcement officials turning a blind eye, temporarily, to parking infractions. By operating in this way, the bureaucratic or administrative state in Singapore acts with a degree of flexibility that facilitates religious practice in an informal and implicit manner.

Fourth, the state can also act politically by making political statements that support or constrain the operation of religion by providing a broader or narrower political environment within which religion might operate. Examples of political statements include official greetings shared on the occasions of religious festivals, participation in religious celebrations by prominent public figures and more general statements affirming the religious (or multireligious) character of the nation. Consider, for example, ministers attending *iftar* dinners (to break the Ramadan fast) in the UK,[29] the issuing of greeting by the Canadian Prime Minister Trudeau for Diwali and Bandi Chhor Divas (for Hindu, Sikh, Jain and Buddhist communities)[30] and similarly by President Obama for Diwali[31], or the invocation and repetition of the value of the multiracial and multireligious character of the country by Singapore's Prime Minister Lee Hsien Loong.[32]

This is a soft form of regulation and indeed might not be seen by some as regulatory at all but I present it here because these political statements can indeed set an environment that might be either supportive (as the preceding examples are) or restrictive of the operation of religions. The political state can thus furnish an agreeable or disagreeable climate for its religious communities.

All of the foregoing can be captured in the 'expressive' function state. That is to say, the way in which the state in formal and informal ways, explicitly and implicitly, directly and by application, creates conditions for the scope and operation of religion and thereby in a holistic sense seeks to regulate religion. Unpacking these various roles of the state is an important precursor to delineating a set of regulatory markers

[29] Mark Hendrick and Stephen Williams, 'Ramadan: Written Question – 205630' (*UK Parliament*, 21 July 2014), www.parliament.uk/business/publications/written-questions-answers-statements/written-question/Commons/2014–07-14/205630 (accessed 1 March 2018).

[30] See video, '"I Have More Sikh Ministers Than Modi", Jokes Justin Trudeau' (*The Quint*, 12 March 2016), www.youtube.com/watch?v=gnZgDqO6Bd8 (accessed 1 March 2018).

[31] See video, 'US President Obama's Diwali Message 2016' (*ISKON Truth*, 27 October 2016), www.youtube.com/watch?v=Z_ysFpeTmWg (accessed 1 March 2018).

[32] Nur Asyiqin Mohamad Salleh, 'Singapore a Rare, Precious Example of Harmonious Multi-racial, Multi-religious Society: PM Lee', *The Straits Times* (Singapore, 20 July 2017), www.straitstimes.com/singapore/singapore-a-rare-and-precious-example-of-a-harmonious-multi-racial-multi-religious-society (accessed 1 March 2018). In fact, the topic 'multi-racial and multi-religious society' is a heading one can use to see speeches and statements by the prime minister and other senior political leaders in Singapore: see 'Multi-racial and Multi-religious Society' (*Prime Minister's Office Singapore*), www.pmo.gov.sg/topics/multi-racial-and-multi-religious-society (accessed 1 March 2018).

because these markers can relate and connect to the different ways in which the state can act to regulate religion.

IV. REGULATORY MARKERS

With the foregoing factors conditioning the landscape of Asia in mind, we can turn to the question of what guidelines and principles can best aid in regulating religion. We must locate these principles within the framework of heightened religious diversity and plurality (including of those who are religiously unaffiliated) in Asia as in other parts of the world, and the general persistence of high levels of religious affiliation in the region, with some notable exceptions. Indeed, in a world where levels of religious affiliation are predicted to increase, not decrease, over time, Asia may represent a significant portion of this increase. Some have referred to these conditions of diversity as heralding a 'post-secular' state of affairs. Using this concept, Zachary Calo has opined:

> The post-secular condition refers not only to a resurgence of religious faith and practice that might be measured on an empirical basis, it also refers to *a fragmentation in meaning* that undermines the universal aspirations of the secular.[33]

The fragmentation of meaning that Calo identifies implies that we are, almost everywhere, including in Asia, operating in conditions of heightened and perhaps more pronounced and polarising diversity. This diversity has many facets, as we have seen above and the markers presented in the text that follows are directed towards addressing these facets.

A. *Marker 1: Capacious Definition of the Category of 'Religion'*

The first regulatory marker relates to the challenge of defining religion. As noted earlier, one question that arises is how some of the prominent religious traditions may be defined as 'religion', particularly if they are not structured in 'Abrahamic terms' – i.e., asserting monotheism, and recognising prophets and revealed texts. Are understandings of religion too Abrahamic and can other types of religion fit within the category of 'religion'? This is a particular factor in Asia because certain major traditions in the region may not be defined in Abrahamic terms, or at least not entirely in these terms. In this context, it would thus be overly restrictive to confine definitions of religion within an Abrahamic framework. This is significant not just for Asia, of course, but the conditions in Asia may make it all the more pressing to be open to the varieties of religion.

33 Zachary R. Calo, 'Religion, Human Rights, and Post-Secular Legal Theory', *St John's Law Review* 85.2 (2011), 506 (emphasis added).

Thus, one regulatory marker must be to adopt an open-minded and capacious definition of religion in order to encompass the diversity in Asia. This would have to embrace theistic and non-theistic traditions, a range of practices and sources of religious normativity and, indeed, at least a consideration that traditions such as Confucianism, which might be seen to be primarily cultural or moral, might participate – in part at least – in being 'religious'.

To adopt a capacious definition means consciously to avoid certain all-too-simple pitfalls of understanding religion by way of core concepts that apply universally, across time and place. Rather, a capacious definition recognises that the contours of religion are coloured by the cultural context of locality. This approach therefore rejects a 'one size fits all' definition of any religious expression or of a regulatory paradigm. There are two aspects to be drawn out here: one is that a capacious definition must be open to religions that look different from the traditional or normal forms. For instance, a recent case in Canada involved the Ktunaxa Nation aboriginal community and their belief in the Grizzly Bear Spirit.[34] These beliefs may look very different from traditional forms of religion but need to be considered within a capacious understanding of religion. Second, even where there are traditional religions such as the Abrahamic religions that are at issue, one needs to be aware of their diverse local expressions, shaped by a range of contextual forces.

Of course, being alert to diversity does not make for easy definitions, or for definitions that are especially stable. But it respects the fact that simplified definitions of religion, or a particular religious tradition, can generate cack-handed regulatory outcomes because they are insensitive or inaccurate. In short, the context of Asia demands understandings of religion that are appropriate and responsive to the diversity of traditions and engagements that are present in the region, and this means that regulatory definitions will need to be broad and open to a variety of religious forms.

B. *Marker 2: Moving Beyond 'Essential Practices'*

The second, and related, regulatory marker is that certain types of legal tests that have already been developed, including in Asian courts, may not be fit for purpose taking into account the diversity present in the region. A key example is the 'essential practices test' mentioned earlier, developed in Indian jurisprudence, in particular for Hinduism. This test seeks to propose essential practices for religions, which can be protected, with other practices that are not essential, which would accordingly not be protected. As Ronjoy Sen says, the test has been used to determine which religious practices are eligible for constitutional protection, to adjudicate the

34 See *Ktunaxa Nation v. British Columbia (Forests, Lands and Natural Resource Operations)* [2017] SCC 54. For a discussion of the case and its implications see Dwight Newman, 'Implications of the *Ktunaxa Nation*/Jumbo Valley Case for Religious Freedom Jurisprudence' [2016] 75 SCLR (2d) 309; also published in Dwight Newman (ed.), *Religious Freedom and Communities* (LexisNexis, 2016).

legitimacy of legislation for managing religious institutions and to judge the extent of independence that can be enjoyed by religious denominations.[35] Such a test might seem at first blush a necessary aspect of regulation but it flounders when confronted by the diversity of forms of religion as discussed earlier. Indeed, as Sen further notes: 'The most striking aspect of the essential practices doctrine is the attempt by the Court to fashion religion in the way a modernist state would like it to be, rather than accept religion as represented by its practitioners.'[36]

Curiously, the Indian Supreme Court in *Tilkayat Shri Govindlalji Maharaj v State of Rajasthan*,[37] consistent with approaches taken in the UK and in Canada,[38] emphasised that the subjective (and therefore potentially eccentric) understanding of religion is something that the courts can both appreciate and protect. This case did not concern some minor or tangential religion's tradition in India but rather that greatly diverse set of practices that is 'Hinduism'. In confronting this variety, the court said:

> 60. In deciding the question as to whether a given religious practice is an integral part of the religion or not, the test always would be whether it is regarded as such by the community following the religion or not. This formula may in some cases present difficulties in its operation. Take the case of a practice in relation to food or dress. If in a given proceeding, one section of the community claims that while performing certain rites white dress is an integral part of the religion itself, whereas another section contends that yellow dress and not the white dress is the essential part of the religion, how is the Court going to decide the question? Similar disputes may arise in regard to food ...
>
> 62. It is true that the decision of the question as to whether a certain practice is a religious practice or not, as well as the question as to whether an affair in question is an affair in matters of religion or not, may present difficulties because sometimes practices, religious and secular, are inextricably mixed up. This is more particularly so in regard to Hindu religion ... Though the task of disengaging the secular from the religious may not be easy, it must nevertheless be attempted in dealing with the claims for protection under Arts. 25(1) and 26(b) [of the Indian Constitution] ...

As Sen suggests, and as the aforementioned decision of the Indian Supreme Court appears also to recognise, an approach to regulating religion that is premised on defining essential practices can have only limited purchase when confronted by the diversity within Asian contexts. Thus, another regulatory marker must be that legal tests for religious practices as constitutive of a religious tradition will have to be alive to diversity and accordingly should avoid definitions resting on essentials or essential practices of religions. This point is related to the foregoing definitional discussion. However, whereas that was focussed mainly on the range of candidates for religion,

[35] Ronojoy Sen, *Articles of Faith: Religion, Secularism, and the Indian Supreme Court* (Oxford University Press, 2010), 41.

[36] Ibid.

[37] AIR [1963] SC 1638, 1964 SCR (1) 56.

[38] See the British case of *Hodkin* (n. 11) and the Canadian case of *Syndicat Northcrest* (n. 28).

the point here is to understand the internal diversity, nuance and subtlety that can exist within any one accepted candidate and hence to avoid being reductionist.

C. *Marker 3: Embracing Regulatory Dynamism*

The diversity of religious understanding and practices will almost inevitably mean that religion will challenge existing regulatory arrangements – whether with respect to definitions, expressions or by pushing against other constraints – and the normative premises underpinning these arrangements. Moreover, such challenges are not likely to be static but dynamic, expressing themselves in myriad ways across times and jurisdictions. This is especially so given the range of cultural, linguistic, political and geographical contexts of Asia. Therefore, we must be prepared for religions to push the boundaries of our existing normative horizons, such that not only will existing categories of what is and is not religion need to be re-examined, but also the line between secular and its alternatives.[39] These observations give rise to a third regulatory conclusion, namely that all regulations will have to embrace its contingency and recognise that any regulatory framework will be subject to reconsideration and revision as new normative ideas are developed. At one level this may seem a banal point. After all, any regulatory framework must account for change either in the object it is seeking to regulate (say, financial products) or the environment of the regulation (say, financial products before and after the financial crisis of 2008–9). Why should the case of regulating religion be different? The case of religion may be thought initially to be different because it is not so much, on the one hand, that we will have 'new religions' (though there may be the emergence of some of these), nor on the other hand, that we might expect to have regularly any sudden paradigm-shifting changes in the environment of regulation religions like we had with the financial crisis of 2008–9 for financial products. Rather, we can expect that in responding to ongoing discussions and issues, religions in Asia will raise fundamental questions about the terms of debate within which issues are understood and expressed. One notable example of this is the current discussions about 'radicalisation' and 'jihadism' in Muslim discourse. In this discourse, both those who would purport to radicalise and those who oppose the narratives of radicalisation are drawing out new narratives from an existing religious tradition. So too, are different sides of the argument in debates about cow slaughter in India.[40] On this issue, it is

[39] One such horizon is the idea coming from American experience of the wall of separation between church and state. For a cardinal principle in US law, but one which may not have either the same influence or make the same sense in Asian (or other contexts) on influence, see David S. Law and Mila Versteeg, 'The Declining Influence of the United States Constitution', *NYULR* 87 (2012), 762, 805, that: 'Today, only about one-third of the world's constitutions provide expressly for a separation of church and state.'

[40] See Michael Safi, 'Cow Slaughter to be Punishable by Life Sentence in Gujarat' *The Guardian* (Delhi, 14 March 2017), www.theguardian.com/world/2017/mar/14/indian-state-government-life-sentence-cow-slaughter (accessed 1 March 2018), and Zeeshan Shaikh, 'Maharashtra Bans Beef, 5 Years

also the case that new narratives are being developed in light of current circumstances and political environments from longstanding traditions. The regulatory marker then is, simply put, that regulation must be alive to the shifting dynamics and articulations coming out of Asian discourses; regulation will only be *contingent* even when dealing with 'old' phenomena.

D. *Marker 4: Dialectical Regulation*

A fourth regulatory marker is that regulation must be seen as a *dialectical and discursive process*. Regulatory norms will be part of the discourse and not just the conclusion of the discourse. Legislative and judicially formed regulation, which might be viewed as the harder forms of regulation, should thus be conceptualised as what we may term 'decisional resting points', providing a (needed) decision for now but only as a resting point subject to being revisited in the future. Indeed, future reconsideration may take into account not just changed material conditions but also new value perspectives both in general as well as emanating from religious traditions. As Benjamin L Berger has said:

> By pluralizing the sense of what law and adjudication might offer to conflicts of deep normative diversity, one can find significant virtue in law's capacity to serve as a tool of adhesion, rather than ultimate decision, and a temporary relief from the hyper-realism of the politics of religious difference.[41]

In this respect, even the settled (for now) decisions are part of an ongoing journey rather than a final destination.

The dialectical anchor is designed to emphasise that given the fluid demographics as well as ongoing debates and interpretations – particularly in the vast and diverse space of Asia – regulating religion will remain an ongoing process. Regulation in this respect is not about 'solving for' the diversity of religion and the diversity that religion brings to society, rather it is about the more modest 'solving for now', by creating conditions in which this diversity is peacefully expressed and lived and can thereby nourish society.

E. *Marker 5: Enhancing Epistemic Plurality*

Finally, the fifth marker draws strongly from the fourth and extends the importance of a dialectical and discursive orientation beyond only the need to be responsive to

Jail, Rs. 10,000 Fine for Possession or Sale' *The Indian Express* (Mumbai, 27 January 2017), http://indianexpress.com/article/india/india-others/beef-banned-in-maharashtra-5-yrs-jail-rs10000-fine-for-possession-or-sale (accessed 1 March 2018). For an academic discussion see Shraddha Chigateri, 'Negotiating the "Sacred" Cow: Cow Slaughter and the Regulation of Difference in India', in Monica Mookherjee (ed.), *Democracy, Religious Pluralism and Liberal Dilemma of Accommodation* (Springer, 2010), chapter 8.

41 Benjamin L. Berger, 'The Virtues of Law in the Politics of Religious Freedom', *Journal of Law and Religion* 29.3 (2014), 378, 395.

changing interpretations as part of an effort to secure social tranquillity, within a consciousness of the limits of law. A dialectical approach is also important as a means to enhance epistemic plurality.

In this context, religious expressions can be seen as adding and expanding the epistemic range of our discourses.

For example, Tim Macklem has articulated the different bases of faith versus reason. Macklem writes:

> At its most basic level, the concept of faith describes the manner in which a particular belief or set of beliefs may be subscribed to by human beings. In that sense of the word, faith exists as a form of rival to reason. When we say that we believe in something as a matter of faith . . . we express a commitment to that which cannot be established by reason, or to that which can be established by reason but not for that reason.[42]

And later, 'Where the quest for reasons is impossible, but commitment is potentially valuable, faith can come into play.'[43] In saying this, Macklem too is asking us to understand the different epistemic grounding that may underlie religious faith. This is a basis in which the claims of reason are not the only metric and where faith commitments may exist 'beyond reason'. In a like manner, Rafael Domingo has discussed what he calls religion's 'suprarationality'. This he defines as more than religion being insulated from reason and evidence, as Brian Leiter posits,[44] but rather that '[suprarationality] refers to beliefs – and acts pursuant to them – that are neither defensible by reasoned argument alone *nor in conflict* with conclusions attainable by reason. In other words, suprarationality covers what is neither required nor ruled out by natural reason.'[45] For Domingo, an important implication of this assessment of religion is the legal 'right to religion', which 'establishes a constitutional limit on governments by protecting the suprarational capacity of the human person against political monopolization' and goes beyond freedom of conscience.[46]

So, the fifth marker is about adopting an approach that embraces the potential of religions to push the limits of our epistemic horizons and provide different metrics to consider. This is a diversity that goes beyond difference between religions or indeed different interpretations or understanding within a religion, and makes us confront the possibility of different epistemic bases that religion may present in our social discourses.

42 Timothy Macklem, *Independence of Mind* (Oxford University Press, 2006), 133.

43 Ibid., 138.

44 See Brian Leiter, 'Why Tolerate Religion?', *SSRN* (2008), https://ssrn.com/abstract=1012910 (accessed 1 March 2018), and his book, *Why Tolerate Religion* (Princeton University Press, 2014).

45 Rafael Domingo, 'Why Tolerate Religion? A Response to Brian Leiter', *SSRN* (2017), https://papers.ssrn.com/sol3/papers.cfm?abstract_id=2938693 (accessed 1 March 2018), 2 (emphasis in original).

46 Ibid., 3. I have discussed this matter in more detail in Arif A. Jamal, 'Considering Freedom of Religion in a Post-Secular Context: Hapless or Hopeful?' *OJLR* 6.3 (2017), 433.

V. Conclusion

In considering the regulation of religion in Asia, we must account for the context of the region. One of the major themes we have elaborated on is the diversity of religion in Asia. However, just noting diversity by itself is not saying much that is specific to Asia, since many contexts exhibit diversity. Rather, the terrains we have canvassed earlier reveal that the diversity in Asia has particular contours.

First, we have seen that Asia, and specifically the Asia-Pacific region, has some of the highest levels of religious diversity in the world. This gives Asian diversity a particular poignancy and edge because, while diversity is always a challenge, heightened diversity engenders even more complex and challenging conditions. Second, we have seen that religious diversity in Asia includes those who do not have religious convictions (the 'nones') and in some Asian jurisdictions large numbers who express no religious affiliation (e.g., South Korea and Japan); in other jurisdictions (e.g., Singapore) there are growing numbers who have no religious affiliation. Nonetheless, across much of Asia at present, there are high levels of religious affiliation and current projections suggest these affiliations will stay quite high in the years to come. Thus, in regulating religion in Asia, we will be regulating a social force that is currently robust and is likely to remain so for some decades. This presence of religion makes the environment of Asia different from other parts of the world – including the United States – where religious affiliation is, it appears, in some decline.

Third, Asian diversity spans in significant proportions both Abrahamic and non-Abrahamic religious traditions, including, among the latter, religious traditions that may not be conceived of in explicitly theistic terms. This landscape may raise questions about the definitions and categories of religion and add a layer of richness to the diversity of the religious landscape. The variegated environment is thus not just about a range of interpretations within one religious tradition (different Christian denominations, for example), nor even just about a religious 'family' (like the Abrahamic traditions, which might be said to share basic postulates), and this realisation means that Asia presents perhaps an even wider ambit to questions of what religion means compared to other environments.

Fourth, as we have seen, there are a range of ways in which the state can act in a regulatory capacity. These include the state acting explicitly via its legislative and judicial powers, as well as more implicitly in its expressive and administrative capacity. We must be cognizant of these different functional capacities in considering the regulation of religion.

Considering all of the foregoing, this chapter has proposed a set of regulatory markers to address the conditions of plurality of Asia. These markers basically emphasise flexibility and seriousness. Flexibility is important to respond to diversity. We need broad and flexible definitions of religion to accommodate the range of practices, values and forms of religion that may manifest themselves in Asia.

Concurrently, we will need flexible understandings and tests as to when religion is engaged. Flexibility here is tied to open-mindedness and the inclusion of diversity. Seriousness is also important and is distinguished by acknowledging the presence of religion and allowing it to have a voice and play a role in normative debates. The markers oppose a regulatory outlook that seeks to deal with plurality by curtailing variety in an effort to focus on what is shared versus what is particular. Such an approach has an impressive intellectual pedigree but runs the risk of leaving us with a public discourse of subtraction and a concomitant emptiness. It is thus that one of the regulatory markers that has been proposed is for legal regulation to operate in a dialectical and discursive fashion. In this paradigm, regulatory norms should be seen as providing decisional resting points – like a sort of regulatory precipitate – that exist to provide an answer for now but which are open to revision as the dynamics of religious diversity continue to churn. Regulating religion thus becomes embedded in an ongoing process in which the voices of religion are allowed, seriously, to raise normative challenges even to fundamental social issues within a narrative of continuing discourse.

As Bouma, Ling and Pratt have stated, the stakes are significant:

> These challenges [of how to deal with religious diversity] are not merely theoretical. People of what had been, for many, understood to be traditional or 'normal' religions now meet, live near, and work with people of different, indeed significantly other religious views and observances. The close proximity of different religions with their different theologies, values and cultures can be either socially enriching or communally destabilising. Emerging religious diversity has increased the possibility of religious-based conflicts in local situations, but that can also spread internationally. Therefore, management of religious diversity is critical to peace and sustainability both in local communities and among the nations of the world.[47]

Appropriate regulation, especially through law, may play an especially influential role in this management because of its capacity to serve as a tool of adhesion. This adhesion, even if it is only temporary, can respond to the challenge of the fragmentation of meaning mentioned earlier that emerges from the fact of the plurality of our value commitments and the diversity of our religious environment. To achieve this end, however, we would be best to operate from regulatory markers that forefront the vast and diverse religious landscape of Asia.

47 Gary D. Bouma, Rod Ling and Douglas Pratt, *Religious Diversity in Southeast Asia and the Pacific: National Case Studies* (Springer 2010), xvii–xviii.

2

Conceptualizing the Regulation of Religion

A Preliminary Framework for Inquiry

Jaclyn L. Neo[*]

I. INTRODUCTION

Modern states regulate religion. The degree and nature of regulation tend to depend on the state's precise constitutional commitments, its historical and contemporary relationship with religion, as well as other factors such as religious demographics and ideologies. For instance, in confessional states, religion is regulated as part of the governmental framework, whether through the imposition of conditions as a prerequisite to the allocation of funding, or through direct state provision of religious services such as the building of religious institutions and the administration of religious bureaucracies. Even in a strictly separationist state where there is an adamant insistence on the separation of state and religion, the state's regulatory powers are often exercised to control or to shape religious activity, including through its powers of registration and taxation. Indeed, the regulation of religion is not only a reality but often considered a necessity in many states. This is especially so because in most, if not all, societies, religion remains a critical aspect of social as well as political life. The state has to encounter religion and vice versa.

Thinking about the regulation of religion nonetheless requires an expanded concept of regulation. Indeed, the edited volume *Regulating Religion: Case Studies from Around the Globe* approaches the idea of regulating religion as "legal efforts to exert social control over such groups, especially through court cases, but also with selected major legislative attempts to regulate religious groups."[1] Another author defines regulating religion as "any treatment and practice from the state apparatus toward religious groups, or religious beliefs, or religious symbolism in

* An earlier version of this chapter was also presented at the Leiden Law School and I would like to thank Sofia Ranchordas, Hans-Martien ten Nappel, and other colleagues present at the seminar for their helpful comments. I would also like to thank Christian Hofmann, Daniel PS Goh, and Arif Jamal for their insightful comments on previous drafts. Andrea Ong Hui Xian provided valuable research assistance. All errors remain mine.

1 James T. Richardson, "Regulating Religion: A Sociological and Historical Introduction," in James T. Richardson (ed.), *Regulating Religion: Case Studies from Around the Globe* (Kluwer Academic/Plenum Publishers, 2004), 1.

a particular given nation-state based on the prescribed system of laws."[2] This use of the term regulation differs from the narrower conception of regulation that is commonly used in scholarship on the regulatory state. That scholarship tends to see regulation as the activities of an independent regulatory agency, set up by or facilitated by the government, to exercise regulatory functions outside of governmental functions, typically focusing on efficiency maximization. In contrast, there is now increasing recognition that regulation is a polycentric exercise that not only involves public actors and targets economic activities but also does more. Accordingly, in this chapter, I propose a modified version of what Koop and Lodge has proposed as an *essence-based* definition of the regulation of religion.[3] I define regulation of religion *as the intentional intervention in the activities of religious individuals and communities, whether direct or indirect, through binding law or otherwise, and whether conducted by a public sector or private sector actors.*

Adopting an expanded idea of regulation, this chapter sets out a preliminary framework for inquiry. It argues that such a focus on regulation pluralizes and complexifies the state's relationship with religion, extending the analysis beyond the traditional constitutional law and private (family) law approaches. It then identifies a range of regulatory approaches and provides illustrations of how these approaches are used to understand the regulation of religion. Lastly, it examines the regimes of regulation as differentiated by liberal versus nonliberal constraints. In doing all of these, it must be conceded that this chapter takes as its starting premise that the state does regulate religion, rather than whether the state can or should regulate religion.

II. RELIGION AS A SUBJECT OF REGULATION

A. *Why Regulation? Beyond Constitutional Law*

What is the value of using regulation to understand the state's relationship with religion? My argument is that regulation is a productive way of conceptualizing the state's relationship with religion, as it better reflects the many points of legal encounters between them, beyond the usual parameters of constitutional law and private law. In particular, a focus on constitutional law has tended to narrow the range of enquiries with respect to the relationship between state and religion to those implicating constitutional questions, dominated by religious freedom claims as well as the broader question of the proper boundaries between state and religion. A constitutional law focus would also tend to give disproportionate attention to judicial decisions. Indeed, Sezgin and Künkler characterize judicialization, defined

[2] Ismatu Ropi, *Religion and Regulations in Indonesia* (Palgrave Macmillan, 2017), 34 (emphasis in the original removed).

[3] Christel Koop and Martin Lodge, "What Is Regulation? An Interdisciplinary Concept Analysis," *Regulation & Governance* 11 (2017), 95, 104.

as the "ever-accelerating reliance on courts and judicial means for addressing core moral predicaments, public policy questions, and political controversies,"[4] as a form of regulation.[5] There is no doubt that judicial decisions influence religious behavior and even religious ideas, and are valuable resources for study. Courts often are "deeply involved in the social construction of religious freedom"[6] and judicialization serves to draw boundaries between protected and nonprotected religion, religious ideas, and religious practices. However, insofar as judicial decisions are not "intentional" interventions by judges, this chapter does not see them as falling within the definition of regulation of religion proposed here. This chapter thus departs from some existing conceptualizations of regulation of religion. Besides Sezgin and Künkler's, Richardson's definition also emphasizes court cases, though he also takes into account other legal efforts such as "selected major legislative attempts."[7]

Conceptualizing state–religion relations in regulatory terms thus goes beyond the current focus on constitutional law to analyze the relationship between the two. This is not to say that regulation of religion is not directly determined by a state's constitutionalized relationship with religion. For instance, constitutionally confessional states may have a wider scope to directly regulate religion as compared to liberal-separationist states that may be more constrained owing to their commitment to secular-liberal neutrality.[8] Furthermore, in constitutional settings where there is no culture of limited government dominating constitutional politics, there is likely to be greater space for the state/government to regulate religious activities.[9] Furthermore, regulation is likely to be more acceptable in societies with strong communitarian ethos. This coincides with Baldwin, Scott, and Hood's group and grid theory which suggests that hierarchist societies, characterized by strong group (the extent to which individuals are integrated into collectives) and strong grid (the extent to which transactions among individuals are governed by general rules, as opposed to being subject to ad hoc bargaining and case-by-case negotiations) are likely to favor "heavy reliance on generalized rules and organization" and this is founded on the shared assumption that individuals may need to be sacrificed for collective gain.[10] In contrast, individualist and egalitarian societies are likely to reject strong regulatory style favoring collective gains. Thinking about the relationship

4 See Ran Hirschl, "The New Constitutionalism and the Judicialization of Pure Politics Worldwide," *Fordham Law Review* 75.2 (2006), 721.

5 See, e.g., Yüksel Sezgin and Mirjam Künkler, "Regulation of 'Religion' and the 'Religious': The Politics of Judicialization and Bureaucratization in India and Indonesia," *Comparative Studies in Society and History* 56.2 (2014), 448.

6 Richardson (n. 1), 13.

7 Ibid.

8 See Jaclyn L. Neo, "Secularism without Liberalism: Religious Freedom and Secularism in a Non-Liberal State," *Michigan State Law Review* (2017), 333.

9 Pitman B. Potter, "Belief in Control: Regulation of Religion in China," *The China Quarterly* 174 (2003), 317; Richardson n. 1; Sezgin and Künkler (n. 5), 448.

10 Robert Baldwin, Colin Scott, and Christopher Hood, Introduction, in Robert Baldwin, Colin Scott, and Christopher Hood (eds.), *A Reader on Regulation* (Oxford University Press, 1998), 1, 23.

between political conditions and social conditions to regulatory range and styles is crucial to better understanding the relationship between religion and state, particularly in Asia, where there tends to be strong intentional intervention by the state into religious affairs.

Finally, interrogating the state's regulatory powers over religion should also serve to complexify a claim that any form of religious regulation restricts religious freedom and, in particular, disproportionately burdens minority religions.[11] Wybraniec and Finke's study of religion cases from 1981 to 1996 shows that "even modest changes in the state's regulation of religion will have an immediate impact on the minority religions holding a tension with their surrounding culture."[12] Furthermore, they conclude that "[r]eligious minorities are the first to benefit when religious regulations are lifted, and the first to be stifled when regulations are allowed."[13] This, they claim, shows an "inverse relationship between social power and the enforcement of state regulations."[14] This claim needs to be further investigated. For instance, some forms of regulations could arguably result in greater scope for religious freedom, such as where religious majorities are enjoined from preventing religious minorities from conducting their religious practices. Regulating religion to ensure peaceful coexistence, for instance, could result in greater scope for religious freedom than in a situation in which there is no state intervention but existing systemic discrimination against religious minorities. Regulating some forms of hateful religious speech may also, in some scenarios, enhance the capacity of religious minorities to practice their religion. Some may also argue that regulating religion in order to ensure the prioritization of individual freedoms could increase individual autonomy over religious practices. While this is not to say that regulation is always better for religious liberty than no regulation, a fuller picture concerning regulation and religious freedom requires a closer examination of the type of regulation, the modes employed, and the underlying motivation for the exercise of regulatory power.

B. *Expanded Idea of Regulation*

As mentioned earlier, this chapter proposes a definition of regulation of religion as *the intentional intervention in the activities of religious individuals and communities, whether direct or indirect, through binding law or otherwise, and whether conducted by a public sector or private sector actors*. This requires an expanded idea of regulation in three ways. First, it requires thinking about regulation as beyond an activity that

11 John Wybraniec and Roger Finke, "Religious Regulation and the Courts: The Judiciary's Changing Role in Protecting Minority Religions from Majoritarian Rule," in James T. Richardson (ed.), *Regulating Religion: Case Studies from Around the Globe* (Kluwer Academic/Plenum Publishers, 2004), 550.

12 Ibid.

13 Ibid.

14 Ibid.

addresses market failures and maximizes economic efficiency. While traditionally, regulation is directed at economic activity, e.g., the markets and actors in the market,[15] it is now seen as an activity that occurs in relation to a wider range of activities, such as family, education, reproduction, health, unemployment, government, etc. Social regulation is now part of regulatory activity within the state, which can govern any area of social or "natural" life,[16] including religion.

Second, regulation of religion involves not merely authoritative rules but a slew of nonbinding rules and modes of intervention. The emphasis on rules is seen, for example, in Hertog's definition of regulation as "the employment of legal instruments compelled by particular regime or government agencies or officials to comply with prescribed behavior and rules, and accompanied by a mechanism of monitoring and enforcement to achieve particular one or a set of goals."[17] Contrary to the previously dominant *command and control model* whereby one party would mandate rules and enforce compliance through sanctions,[18] modern-day regulation is now recognized to be far more complex, where the state adopts a wide range of regulatory modes and strategies to produce its desired outcome. When it comes to the regulation of religion, however, regulation has to be conceptualized as "encompassing all mechanisms of social control, by whomsoever exercised,"[19] as long as it involves intentional state activity (whether direct or indirect) targeting a specific subject or sphere of private activity. This would exclude from regulation "unintentional and *non-state* processes" even though these affect relevant behavior.[20] Intentional intervention indicates "governed, guided, controlled interference."[21]

Thirdly, regulation involves more than just public agencies and may involve semipublic or private organizations. This speaks to an existing debate as to whether regulation is carried out solely by state actors. Scholars have recognized that regulation is not merely a state activity and that semipublic and private actors also regulate. Black refers to polycentric regulatory regimes in which "the state is not the sole locus of authority" but where "state and non-state actors are both regulators and regulated."[22] Such a regime is "marked by fragmentation, complexity and interdependence between actors," and most tellingly, "their boundaries are marked by the issues or problems which they are concerned with, rather than necessarily by

15 Julia Black,"Decentring Regulation: Understanding the Role of Regulation and Self-Regulation in a Post-Regulatory World," *Current Legal Problems* 54 (2001), 104, 138.

16 Ibid.

17 Johan den Hertog, "General Theories of Regulation," in B. Bouckaert and G. De Geest (eds.), *Encyclopedia of Law and Economics* (Edward Elgar, 1999), 223–5 (emphasis added).

18 Baldwin et al. (n. 10), 9.

19 This is one of three main meanings of regulation that was identified by Baldwin, Scott, and Hood in a reader on regulation. The other two are "regulation as targeted rules" and "regulation as direct state intervention in the economy more generally": Baldwin et al. (n. 10), 1, 3.

20 Ibid., 4. Emphasis added.

21 Barry M. Mitnick, *The Political Economy of Regulation: Creating, Designing, and Removing Regulatory Forms* (Columbia University Press, 1980), 3.

22 Black (n. 15), 137.

a common solution."[23] Recognizing the regulatory role of nonstate actors means that one can expand regulation to include coregulation and self-regulation. Coregulation refers to collaboration between the state and private regulators to produce and/or enforce regulatory standards,[24] whereas self-regulation broadly refers to "some form of collective exercise on the part of non-governmental actors."[25]

Regulation of religion is furthermore closely connected to noneconomic goals and social policies. While some models of regulation see elected bodies as the only institution that can legitimately make value judgments that form the basis for social policies in a democratic state,[26] an expanded idea of regulation sees social objectives as legitimate regulatory goals. This is necessary especially because social regulatory bodies, including those that regulate religion, encounter a more complex mix of basic rationales and justifications for their work than economic regulators.[27] The focus on economic values is very much part of a dominant strain of regulatory theory focusing on *public choice*. However, there is recognition that economic values provide only a partial picture of the motivations underlying regulation and that noneconomic values, in the form of *public interest*, often exert strong influence over regulatory choices, even in the economic sphere. Indeed, as Mike Feintuck observes, "[i[f we unpack underlying regulatory concepts such as the precautionary principle or the public interest as applied to the media, we find a set of core values which are essentially political and contestable but which are embedded in legal discourse, and, perhaps more importantly, within the democratic settlement."[28] These values are embedded within the broader political and social context, or even the constitutional context. With respect to religion, constitutional principles serve as "an essential context" as well as a "justificatory basis for regulation."[29]

These points of distinction cumulatively support a wide-ranging definition of regulation of religion as *the intentional intervention in the activities of religious individuals and communities, whether direct or indirect, through binding law or otherwise, and whether conducted by a public sector or private sector actors*. In some countries, particularly those that commit to a strict separation of state from religion, such regulation would be quite limited to indirect regulation through binding laws. In other countries where there is no such strict commitment to the separation of state

23 Ibid.

24 See, e.g., the definition provided in Hans-Bredow Institute, "Final Report: Study on Co-regulation Measures in the Media" (2006).

25 Black (n. 15), 116.

26 Tony Prosser, "Models of Economic and Social Regulation," in Dawn Oliver, Tony Prosser, and Richard Rawlings (eds.), *The Regulatory State: Constitutional Implications* (Oxford University Press, 2010), 37.

27 Ibid., 41.

28 Mike Feintuck, "Regulatory Rationales Beyond the Economic: In Search of the Public Interest," in Robert Baldwin, Martin Cave, and Martin Lodge (eds.), *The Oxford Handbook of Regulation* (Oxford University Press, 2010), 39, 56.

29 Ibid., 53. Although there are difficulties with the capacity of constitutional principles to provide this public interest as they are usually less apparent and less clearly articulated.

from religion, regulation is likely to be more extensive and involve a more complex and polycentric regime involving an amalgam of public actors, semipublic actors, and private bodies, employing a range of regulatory modes.

III. MODES OF REGULATION

In this section, I will examine a range of modalities used to regulate religion. This includes legislative rules, regulation by public agencies, coregulation, and self-regulation.

A. *Legislative Rules with Regulatory Impact: General vs. Particular*

Many countries have a range of laws that intentionally intervene in religious activity. Such "intentionality" may not be immediately obvious, but some commonly found regulations that intervene in religion are registration requirements, zoning restrictions, tax-exemption conditions, etc. These laws may directly target religious activity or target them only indirectly. These have regulatory impact and fall within the definition of regulation of religion as they are intentional interventions in the activities of religious individuals and communities. In this regard, a distinction should be drawn between general laws that indirectly target religion as part of a bigger selected group or particular laws that directly target religion. As will be discussed in the text that follows, general laws are likely to be present in all states, whether liberal or nonliberal. In fact, they are likely to predominate in the regulatory relationship between state and religion in the liberal-secular state. In comparison, nonliberal states are not subject to liberal constraints and are more likely to use particular laws targeting religion.

One type of laws that is commonly found in most, if not all, states and which have regulatory impact on religion are registration laws. The regulatory impact of registration requirements depends on how onerous they are. Certain requirements may be imposed to require the lawful creation of a society or organization. These requirements can range from the administrative, e.g., having in place rules for proper management or control, to the more substantive, e.g., that registering the entity is not against public interest. Furthermore, the very requirement of registration brings about certain legal consequences for failure to comply; organized groups that do not register could be subject to penalties. I will discuss three forms of registration laws to illustrate the regulatory impact of laws on religion.

First, a general registration scheme may not directly target religious groups but could nonetheless have regulatory impact on them as an organized group falling within the general target audience of the scheme. As an example of a general registration framework, Singapore's Societies Act contains broad requirements relating to registration and regulation of societies, including religious societies. Since "society" is defined in the Singapore Act as including "any club, company, partnership or association of 10 or more persons," religious groups with more than 10 members must register. If they do not, they could be deemed an "unlawful society" and their activities will then become offenses under the Act. According to the Act, the Registrar is empowered to refuse to register any society representing, promoting, or discussing religion if he is satisfied that the society "is likely to be used for unlawful purposes or for purposes prejudicial to public peace, welfare or good order in Singapore." Even more expansive is the Registrar's power to also refuse registration if registration would be "contrary to the national interest."[30] Management, assistance, membership, attendance in meetings and activities, and publication of material, among others, are all punishable offenses if conducted under the auspices of an unregistered society.[31]

Second, a particular regime of registration may be enacted only for religion, with greater direct impact on religious activity. Such a specialist regime is likely to be more interventionist as it enacts laws that are specifically targeted at religion, and thus could impose greater restrictions that are most relevant for religion. In Vietnam, for instance, the 2004 Ordinance on Belief and Religion (2004) and the 2012 Decree detailing and providing measures for the implementation of the Ordinance on Belief and Religion impose various requirements on religious organizations to obtain legal status. A "religious organization" is defined as "a collection of the people who believe in a system of teachings, rules, and rituals and is organized into a certain structure which is recognized by the state." The Ordinance provides that the state will recognize only religious organizations that have followed the formal registration procedures. Furthermore, a religious organization must be registered at both local and state levels for at least 20 years in order to be officially recognized by the state and be protected by law.[32] A new Law on Beliefs and Religion took effect in 2018, and will continue to require faith groups to register with state authorities.[33] To illustrate the reach of such a regime, the regulations in Vietnam also require religious groups to register with the government for common events like annual religious festivals, conferences, and conventions.[34] In addition, the law requires any religious education to include "Vietnamese history and Vietnamese law" as core subjects.[35]

30 See section 4 of the Societies Act (Cap 311).

31 See sections 14 to 18 of the Societies Act (Cap 311).

32 See further: Chung Van Hoang, *New Religions and State's Response to Religious Diversification in Contemporary Vietnam: Tensions from Reinvention of the Sacred* (Springer International Publishing, 2017).

33 Ucanews.com, "Vietnam passes controversial law on religion," *Union of Catholic Asian News* (November 25, 2016), www.ucanews.com/news/vietnam-passes-controversial-law-on-religion/77714 (accessed October 8, 2017).

34 Luke Hunt, "Vietnam's Religious Law: Testing the Faithful," *The Diplomat* (January 12, 2017), http://thediplomat.com/2017/01/vietnams-religious-law-testing-the-faithful/. For more, see Chapter 7 by Bui Ngoc Son in this volume.

35 Ibid.

Third, registration requirements may be imposed only for a particular religion or religions. Such laws may be applied against the majority religion where the state regulates or administers the religion. For instance, in Malaysia, many constituent states within the federation require anyone teaching or professing to teach "any matter relating to the religion of Islam" to obtain a "tauliah" (i.e., a license to speak).[36] Failure to do so will render one guilty of an offence punishable by a fine and/or jail term.[37] Islam is the religion of the majority in Malaysia, and is constitutionally declared to be the religion of the Federation of Malaysia. Similarly, in Myanmar, a Committee (the *Ma-Ha-Na*) oversees the registration of Buddhist monks and nuns in Myanmar, and even issues orders and directives against Buddhist groups that it deems to have deviated from orthodox Buddhist teachings.[38] Thus, a majority religion may be subject to disproportionate control by a state's regulatory framework.

B. *Public Regulation: Religious State Agencies*

Greater research attention has been given to state religious agencies or bureaucracies in recent times.[39] Religious bureaucracies have not usually been conceptualized as regulatory agencies but considering the range of functions and the regulatory impact of these functions, it is here suggested that they can be analyzed as such. Bureaucratization affects religion in a myriad of ways, not least in delineating the boundaries of religion or the religious.[40] As Sezgin and Kunkler have argued, bureaucratizing religion "is often ridden with conflict and exclusion, as alternative sources of meaning and beliefs are systematically suppressed by agencies imposing statist notions of religion."[41]

Bureaucratization of religion, or more specifically Islam, is present in several Asian states. In Malaysia, for instance, religious bureaucracies have been established at the state as well as at the federal level, raising federal–state jurisdictional issues. The federal Islamic agency, known as JAKIM (Jabatan Kemajuan Islam Malaysia) or the Department for the Advancement of Islam in Malaysia, falls under the Prime Minister's Office and is given oversight in all matters related to the administration of

36 See, e.g., Syariah Criminal Offences Enactment (Federal Territories).

37 In the Federal Territories, Penang and Johor, the punishment is a fine up to RM5,000 and/or imprisonment of up to three years. In Selangor, the maximum punishment is a RM3,000 fine and/or two years' imprisonment. In Perlis, the fine is up to RM1,000 and/or a jail sentence of up to six months. Shahanaaz Habib, "Go beyond current mindsets," *The Star Malaysia*, March 26, 2017.

38 Myanmar, in *Keeping the Faith: A Study of Freedom of Thought, Conscience, and Religion* 321 (Human Rights Resource Center, 2014), 337. See further Tin Maung Maung Than, "The Sangha and Sasana in Socialist Burma," *Sojourn: Journal of Social Issues in Southeast Asia* 3.1 (1988), 26.

39 See, e.g., Sezgin and Kunkler (n. 5) 448; Walid Jumblatt Abdullah, "Religious Representation in Secular Singapore: A Case Study of MUIS and Pergas," *Asian Survey* 5.6 (2013), 1182.

40 Sezgin and Kunkler (n. 5), 451.

41 Ibid.

Islam outside the courts.[42] Furthermore, a Department of Waqaf, Zakat and Haj (JAWHAR, Jabatan Waqaf, Zakat dan Haji), also under the auspices of the Prime Minister's Office, administers Islamic alms (zakat) funds, waqaf (religious endowment), and haj (pilgrimage). JAWHAR's role is to standardize zakat administration across constituent states and make it more effective by "coordinating and strengthening legal procedures, regulations and management procedures,"[43] though the efficacy of such efforts has been questionable.[44] Zakat management is an interesting area of study on regulating religion not least because it entails an expanded idea of regulating but also because of the phenomenon of market interests being introduced into a religious activity. The marketization of zakat management under state-directed or state-sanctioned private institutions becomes questionable when they conflict, or indeed detract, from the traditional aim of zakat based on redistributive social justice and welfare.[45]

Another example of bureaucratic regulation of religion is Indonesia's Ministry of Religious Affairs ("MORA"), which is the lead agency at the national level for the administration of religious affairs.[46] It manages and channels state funds into private religious schools, subsidizes hospitals run by the country's large Islamic organizations,[47] organizes pilgrimages to Mecca for Muslims, and administers Islamic *zakat* and *wakaf*.[48] Besides these, the MORA also regulates religion and religious beliefs through a 1952 regulation that states that "for a community to be recognized as having a religion (agama), it had to profess an internationally recognized monotheistic creed with a holy scripture, embrace the idea of prophethood, and adhere to universal ethical teachings (i.e., teachings not exclusive to a particular race, tribe, or ethnicity)."[49] The MORA regulation clearly reflects a monotheistic Abrahamic understanding of religion, and in effect requires all religions to fit into that mould in order to gain state recognition.[50] Sezgin and Kuenkler have argued however, that the bureaucratization of religion has not escalated identity politics but MORA, in closely implementing the government's directives across the archipelago, managed to connect regulation of religion into the larger nation-building project.[51]

42 Johan Saravanamuttu, "Introduction," in Bernhard Platzdasch and Johan Saravanamuttu (eds.), *Religious Diversity in Muslim-Majority States in Southeast Asia: Areas of Toleration and Conflict* (ISEAS, 2014), 240.

43 Tim Lindsey and Kerstin Steiner, *Islam, Law and the State in Southeast Asia* (I. B. Tauris, 2012), 136.

44 Dominik M. Müller, "From Consultancy to Critique: The 'Success Story' of Globalized Zakat Management in Malaysia and Its Normative Ambiguities," *Globalizations* 14.1 (2016), 81.

45 See, e.g., Wzir Jahan Karim, "The Economic Crisis, Capitalism and Islam: The Making of a New Economic Order?" *Globalizations* 7.1–2 (2010), 105.

46 Tim Lindsey, "Monopolising Islam: The Indonesian Ulama Council and State Regulation of the Islamic Economy," *Bulletin of Indonesian Economic Studies* 48.2 (2012), 253, 255.

47 Sezgin and Kunkler (n. 5), 464.

48 Lindsey (n. 46), 255.

49 Sezgin and Kunkler (n. 5), 464.

50 Ibid., 465.

51 Ibid., 451.

C. Coregulation

Coregulation, in regulatory theory, commonly refers to collaboration between the state and private actors to produce and/or enforce regulatory standards. It stands in between public regulation and private self-regulation (which does not operate with direct state involvement).[52] Proponents of coregulation argue that it combines the flexibility commonly associated with self-regulation with the supervision and rigor of governmental rules.[53] The degree of collaboration between the government and the private organization sits along a spectrum. As such, self-regulatory bodies may sometimes become coregulatory bodies when they become more closely aligned with the state in standards-setting and monitoring. One such body that may have started out as self-regulatory but have become coregulatory with the state is the Majelis Ulama Indonesia/MUI (Indonesian Ulama Council) in Indonesia.

MUI was founded in 1975 and comprises almost all Muslim groups in Indonesia including the two largest groups – Nahdatul Ulama (NU) and Muhammadiyah. Although the then president, Soeharto, was closely involved in setting up MUI, it is not a statutory body or a government agency.[54] The charter establishing MUI was signed by ulamas at a meeting of the Council for Indonesian Mosques.[55] The President is listed as a patron of the council but there is no official decree or decision establishing it.[56] The establishment of MUI is crucial in regulating religion. Prior to the establishment of MUI, fatwas were issued by individual ulama or collectively by Islamic organizations. There was no centralized body for the issuance of fatwas, which could cover a whole range of matters including ritual, charity, pilgrimage, economics, politics, and other social problems. These fatwas have no legal effect and do not require the approval of government. Specifically, in the case of Indonesia where there is a plurality of Islamic organizations, with each organization also organized in separate branches across different provinces, fatwa making was a diffused enterprise. It is possible that fatwas from one organization may differ from those of other organizations; and/or that fatwas from different branches differ from others within an organization.[57]

The establishment of MUI is partially aimed at centralizing fatwa creation in Indonesia. MUI's main functions are to produce fatwas on legal questions, including dietary issues, as well as to advise the Muslim community, thus making it the leading institution in "the formation of policy on issues of Islamic legal tradition."[58] While

52 Hans-Bredow Institute (n. 24).

53 See, e.g., Neil Gunningham and Darren Sinclair, *Leaders and Laggards: Next-Generation Environmental Regulation* (Greenleaf Publishing, 2002), 104–5; Dennis D. Hirsch, "The Law and Policy of Online Privacy: Regulation, Self-Regulation, or Co-Regulation," *Seattle University Law Review* 34 (2011) 439, 441.

54 Lindsey (n. 46), 258.

55 Ibid.

56 Ibid.

57 Nadirsyah Hosen, "Fatwa and Politics in Indonesia," in Arskal Salim and Azyumardi Azra (eds.), *Shari'a and Politics in Modern Indonesia* (ISEAS, 2003), 169.

58 Lindsey (n. 46), 255.

the MUI is "nominally independent," it is endorsed and funded by the state. Lindsey thus terms it a "quango" or a "quasi-autonomous nongovernment organization."[59] Indeed, MUI's fatwas, like those of other Muslim organizations, do not have binding legal force, but the Indonesian state has at times put its weight behind these fatwas so as to give them legal sanction.[60] Specifically, a regulation now gives certain fatwas issued by MUI in relation to banking and halal certification binding force.[61] MUI's fatwas have also influenced state policy on Islamic legal traditions. The close relationship between MUI and the Indonesian government has been subject to some critique. Hooker, for instance, has argued that, at least from its inception to the 1990s, MUI's main function appeared to be to support and legitimize government policies.[62] Hosen nonetheless cautions that just because fatwas support government policies, this does not mean that they are not religiously based.[63] In the context of regulatory analysis, MUI's relationship with the state highlights the complexity of coregulation and the often evolving nature of this relationship. Indeed, it has been argued that while MUI often worked with and supported MORA under Suharto's authoritarian regime, it now more frequently asserts its independence from the state and has grown in influence, particularly in shaping state policy and public opinion through its fatwas.[64]

D. *Self-regulation*

Self-regulation refers to a system of regulation in which the regulatory target imposes commands and consequences upon itself.[65] It constitutes "some form of collective exercise on the part of non-governmental actors."[66] Self-regulation is a "principal controlling device" for a wide range of activities and this would include advertising, financial services, and many professional occupations,[67] and is often argued to be a better method for solving "market failures" than public regulation. Ogus argues that there are at least four reasons why. The first is that self-regulatory agencies normally have a greater degree of expertise and technical knowledge of practices and innovatory possibilities in the relevant area than independent agencies. Furthermore, information costs for the formulation and interpretation of standards are also expected to be lower for self-regulatory agencies. Second, monitoring and

59 Ibid.
60 Lindsey (n. 46), 258.
61 Lindsey (n. 46), 256–7.
62 M. B. Hooker, "Islam and Medical Science: Evidence from Malaysian and Indonesian Fatwas," *Studia Islamika* 4 (1997), 16.
63 Hosen (n. 57).
64 Lindsey (n. 46), 256–7.
65 Cary Coglianese and Evan Mendelson, "Meta-Regulation and Self-Regulation," in Robert Baldwin, Martin Cave, and Martin Lodge (eds.), *A Reader on Regulation* (Oxford University Press, 2010), 150.
66 Black (n. 15), 116.
67 A. Ogus, "Rethinking Self-Regulation," in Robert Baldwin, Colin Scott, and Christopher Hood (eds.), *A Reader on Regulation* (Oxford University Press, 1998), 374.

enforcement costs accordingly tend to be lower as interactions between regulators and the regulated are likely to be fostered by mutual trust. Third, self-regulatory standards are less formalized and are therefore easier and less costly to amend. Lastly, administrative costs of the self-regulatory regime are normally internalized in the trade or activity that is subject to regulation, and not borne by taxpayers as would be the case in public regulation.[68] Accordingly, while there are public interest justifications for self-regulation, self-regulation may also serve private interests particularly where such interests would otherwise be subject to regulation by public actors.

That said, it should be noted that self-regulation is multifaceted and is not entirely free from governmental influence. While self-regulation is often contrasted with public regulation, it has been observed that these should not be seen as dichotomous but as existing within "a spectrum containing different degrees of legislative constraints, outsider participation in relation to rule formulation or enforcement (or both), and external control and accountability."[69] Indeed, while self-regulation could be voluntarily initiated, many groups experience what Julia Black describes as "*mandated* self-regulation" where a "collective group is required or designated by the government to formulate and enforce norms within a broad framework set by government."[70] Self-regulatory rules may be private to the organization or association, but may have to be approved by a government minister or some other public authority.[71] Consequently, self-regulation may be a form of delegation of regulatory powers by the state. Furthermore, self-regulatory standards or rules may themselves comprise various forms with varying degrees of legal force. Some rules may be formally binding, presumptively authoritative, or purely voluntary or declaratory.[72]

With respect to religion, as will be further discussed in the text that follows, self-regulation may be seen as the most legitimate under a regime of liberal-secular constraints and most consonant with a commitment to the autonomy of religious individuals and groups. Furthermore, the liberal conception of religious freedom also tends to focus on the importance of religious autonomy and therefore self-regulation would be the most appropriate under such conditions. However, outside of this liberal-secular commitment, self-regulation may be subject to greater legislative constraints and take the form of mandated self-regulation. Religious organizations self-regulate when they conduct themselves according to internal rules. One interesting area of self-regulation, however, is in interreligious relations; indeed, interfaith rules of engagement are an important area of self-regulation among religious groups.

68 Ibid., 375.
69 Ibid., 376.
70 Black (n. 15), 118.
71 Ogus (n. 67), 376.
72 Ibid., 377.

In Singapore, for instance, the Inter-Religious Organization (IRO) comprises members representing ten significant religions in Singapore and regularly conducts interfaith dialogues. It works closely with the government and has been invited by the government to conduct prayers at public events such as the passing out parade of the Singapore Armed Forces and in memorial services involving national tragedies.[73] Furthermore, a Declaration of Religious Harmony adopted by key religious groups in the country sets out certain "ground rules" on inter-religious as well as state–religious interactions.[74] The declaration states that religious groups in Singapore shall always recognize the secular nature of the state, promote cohesion within society, respect each other's freedom of religion, grow our common space while respective diversity, foster interreligious communications, and ensure that religion will not be abused to create conflict and disharmony in Singapore.[75] These are nonbinding rules that clearly seek to temper some aspects of religious doctrine such as the call toward proselytization and the claim of salvational exclusivity. They are nonbinding in that there are no legal sanctions for noncompliance. The Declaration is portrayed as the product of a consensus among these national bodies, with the government's approval, as this presumably serves to legitimize the document.[76] Thus, while nonbinding, the Declaration is publicized and referenced by religious organizations as well as interfaith groups like the Inter-Religious Organization (IRO).[77] Consequently, the Declaration could be considered a form of self-regulation as it seeks to influence the behavior of religious groups even while it is endorsed by the government.[78]

IV. REGIMES OF REGULATION

Bearing in mind these different and broad-ranging modes of regulating religion, different regimes of regulation may employ different sets of regulatory modes depending on each regime's constitutional relationship with religion. In particular, though this is a general but not universal proposition, liberal-secular

73 Inter-Religious Organisation, Singapore (IRO), http://iro.sg/about/ (accessed Septemebr 28, 2018).

74 Ministry of Social and Family Development, Declaration on Religious Harmony, July 30, 2014.

75 Declaration of Religious Harmony, reproduced by the Inter-Religious Council of Singapore (IRO), http://iro.sg/about/declaration/ (accessed September 28, 2018). See also Explanation on the Declaration by the Religious Harmony Working Committee, International Council of Christian Churches website, www.iccc.org.sg/rhwcommittee.html (accessed September 28, 2018).

76 Ministry of Social and Family Development (n. 74).

77 Inter-Religious Organisation, Singapore (IRO) (n. 73).

78 Ministry of Social and Family Development (n. 74).

states tend not to regulate religion as strongly as compared to nonliberal states. This is because they are usually constrained by liberal commitments whereas nonliberal states, whether secular or more religious, are not similarly constrained but may instead see regulation as necessary to realize a common or public good.[79]

A. *Liberal-Secular Constraints against Regulation of Religion*

I have previously argued that a commitment to liberal secularism would constrain states from directly regulating religion in most ways.[80] This is because a liberal-secular state is constrained by two foundational doctrines: first, it must maintain religious neutrality, thereby not preferring or imposing any one vision of the common good over another[81] and second, it must prioritize individual autonomy, conceived of as equality and individual rights.[82] While I acknowledge that liberalism is an internally diverse and sometimes contested tradition,[83] these two constraints, I argue, sit at the core of most, if not all, liberal commitments. In fact, the idea that "government should be neutral on the question of the good life" has been called "the

79 Interestingly, Baldwin, Scott, and Hood's theory is consistent with this general observation. Using cultural theory, they use two fundamental variables in human organizations – group and grid. Group refers to the extent to which individuals are integrated into collectives whereas grid refers to the extent to which transactions among individuals are governed by general rule, as opposed to being subject to ad hoc bargaining and case-by-case negotiations. Dividing grid and group into strong and weak, one can identify four possible ways of life: hierarchism (strong group, strong grid), fatalism (weak group, strong grid), individualism (weak group, weak grid), and egalitarianism (strong group, weak grid). Thus, Baldwin, Scott, and Hood argue that hierarchist societies are likely to favor "heavy reliance on generalized rules and organization" and this is founded on the shared assumption that individuals may need to be sacrificed for collective gain. In comparison, individualist and egalitarian societies are likely to reject this regulatory style. Instead, individualists are more likely to prefer deregulation or light touch regulation. Egalitarian societies will stress highly participatory models of regulation. Finally, fatalist societies are likely to involve substantial state presence, though this does not necessarily take a regulatory form and often without social participation: Baldwin et al. (n. 10), 23.

80 Neo (n. 8).

81 See, e.g., Bruce A. Ackerman, *Social Justice in the Liberal State* (Yale University Press, 2010); Ronald M. Dworkin, "Liberalism," in S. Hampshire (ed.), *Public and Private Morality* (Cambridge University Press, 1978), 113–43; Paul Horwitz, *The Agnostic Age* (Oxford University Press, 2011); Peter Jones, "The Ideal of the Neutral State," in Robert E. Goodin and Andrew Reeve (eds.), *Liberal Neutrality* (Routledge, 1989).

82 The liberal assumption of constitutionalism is often assumed, such as where it is said that the protection of fundamental rights is a distinct feature of constitutionalism. Graham Walker, "The Idea of Nonliberal Constitutionalism," in Ian Shapiro and Will Kymlicka (eds.), *Ethnicity and Group Rights* (NYU Press, 1997), 154, 169. See, e.g., in Michel Rosenfeld, "Modern Constitutionalism as Interplay between Identity and Diversity: An Introduction," *Cardozo Law Review* 14 (1993), 497.

83 As Rawls notes, "there are many liberalisms," John Rawls, Political Liberalism 223 (1993), such that some have claimed that liberalism is an essentially contested concept; Larry Alexander, "Liberalism, Religion, and the Unity of Epistemology," *San Diego Law Review* 30 (1993), 763, 765; Ruth Abbey, "Is Liberalism Now an Essentially Contested Concept?" *New Political Science* 27.4 (2005), 461.

central idea" of liberalism.[84] Backer describes secular liberalism as privileging disestablishment.[85] Similarly, Horwitz points out that the modern liberal consensus is "at least ostensibly a position of genuine neutrality, in which the state is to take no position at all, whether on matters of religious truth or anything else."[86] He contrasts this with three other approaches to religious differences, which are (1) a jurisdictional settlement under which church and state retained coercive power within their own realms; (2) the imposition of religious orthodoxy according to the flag; or (3) toleration whereby there is an orthodoxy from which dissenters are free to depart.[87] Furthermore, proceeding from this liberal consensus, Horwitz argues, is a "protective view of individual religious freedom and a proscription against government establishment of religion."[88]

The regulation of religion is therefore particularly constrained within the liberal-secular state. It cannot directly intervene in religion where it would violate these two constraints, in particular the neutrality constraint. These constraints can be said to be reflected in a particular conception of religious freedom as prioritizing individual autonomy. However, it would be a mistake to think that the liberal-secular state does not regulate religion. There are at least three ways in which a liberal-secular state may regulate religion. The first arises through indirect regulation. According to the definition proposed earlier, regulation of religion includes intentional intervention that has an indirect effect on religious activity. Such indirect intervention may arise when facially neutral regulations cover a scope of activity that also includes religious activity. Thus, for instance, laws requiring all groups to register in order to have legal personality to hold property may not directly target religion but would include most organized religious groups. It is furthermore important to identify such indirect intervention through formally neutral laws especially because indirect intervention could also have a disproportionate impact on religious activity. For instance, facially neutral laws such as noise pollution restrictions could apply equally to all organizations and individuals but depending on the scope and content of such a law, it could have disproportionate impact on certain religious groups if it specifically applies during certain periods of time during the day when religious groups tend to broadcast their prayers. Thus, a law that limits noise pollution daily from sunrise to sundown may indirectly and disproportionately affect Muslim groups as they tend to broadcast their prayers, as compared other groups that do not broadcast their prayers. As such, it should be clear that a self-avowedly liberal state committed to the

84 Michael J. Sandel, "Freedom of Conscience or Freedom of Choice?", in James Davison Hunter and Os Guiness (eds.), *Articles of Faith, Articles of Peace* (Brookings Institution, 1990), 75.

85 Larry Catá Backer, "The Crisis of Secular Liberalism and the Constitutional State in Comparative Perspective: Religion, Rule of Law, and Democratic Organization of Religion Privileging States," *Cornell International Law Journal* 48 (2015), 51, 53.

86 Horwitz (n. 81), 10.

87 Ibid., 5–10.

88 Ibid., 10.

constraints of neutrality and individual autonomy may still regulate religion through facially neutral laws. The focus is on the impact, rather than on intention alone.

Second, because regulation may also occur through private sector actors, religion may also be regulated within liberal-secular states through self-regulation. Self-regulation broadly refers to "some form of collective exercise on the part of non-governmental actors."[89] Self-regulation tends to be the norm in states that grant broad autonomy to churches and, by extension, religious organizations. Many such states are committed to liberal-secular neutrality. Self-regulation permits a high degree of autonomy to religious groups. However, it is not entirely free from governmental influence. Furthermore, while self-regulation could be voluntarily initiated, in some countries, religious groups experience *mandated* self-regulation[90] where the state impose "guided" frameworks for religious groups to self-regulate.[91]

Third, while liberal-secular states may be constrained from imposing a particular vision of the good, this is only if the neutrality constraint is given equal or greater weight to the autonomy principle. One can nonetheless imagine scenarios in which the state may want to regulate religion in order to vindicate the autonomy principle, thereby subordinating the neutrality constraint. Indeed, authors such as Cohen have argued that political secularism (which appears to be a liberal-secular conception) does not presuppose that "the state must refrain from regulating religion or that religion must be relegated to the private sphere."[92] Highlighting the dualistic formula of the United States Constitution's First Amendment, she argues that it "*did not accord [religion] autonomy from state regulation*,"[93] neither does the constitutional arrangement allow for "*untrammeled self-determination or jurisdiction to religious associations*."[94] Instead, she argues that the state should intervene in religion to correct nonegalitarian gender practices by religious minorities.[95] For Cohen, the question is not whether to regulate religion but how to regulate religion to best reconcile freedom of religious association with the public's interest in equal liberty, antidiscrimination, and democratic citizenship.[96] She proposes a three-

[89] Black (n. 15), 116.

[90] Ibid., 118.

[91] Beyond Asia, see, e.g., a recent initiative in Zambia to develop a guiding framework for self-regulation of churches: "Govt consulting on the Church's self-regulation," *Lusakatimes* (July 29, 2017), www.lusakatimes.com/2017/07/29/govt-consulting-churchs-self-regulation/ (accessed September 28, 2018). A peer-review council mechanism which will form a self-regulatory framework in line with the constitution and the law body for churches have also been mooted in South Africa: Sipho Hlongwane, "Is there really nothing that can be done about the 'Doomed Prophet'?" *Huffpost* (South Africa, November 23, 2016), www.huffingtonpost.co.za/2016/11/23/is-there-really-nothing-that-can-be-done-about-the-doomed-proph_a_21612832/ (accessed September 28, 2018).

[92] Jean L. Cohen, "Rethinking Political Secularism," in Jean L. Cohen and Cécile Laborde (eds.), *Religion, Secularism, & Constitutional Democracy* (Columbia University Press, 2015), 113, 115.

[93] Ibid.

[94] Ibid.

[95] Jean L. Cohen, "The Politics and Risks of the New Legal Pluralism in the Domain of Intimacy," *I-CON* 10.2 (2012), 380, 393.

[96] Ibid., 394.

pronged approach. First, there needs to be a strong exit option. Second, top-down direct regulation and outright prohibition must be imposed when practices involve harm to members or to outsiders or when they contravene important public purposes and basic rights. Third, delegation of service provision to private providers must be subject to indirect regulation to ensure that they comport with constitutional principles.[97] Cohen's proposal presumes that the priority of the liberal-secular state is individual autonomy and that the state should intervene to regulate religion to ensure equal protection. This represents a much more direct intervention in religion than the other two modalities discussed before it.

B. *Regulation outside Liberal Constraints: Nonliberal Regimes*

In contrast, nonliberal states, even secular ones, are not similarly constrained from regulating religion. The term nonliberal is a wide-ranging one and could encompass anything from preliberal, semiliberal, and illiberal or antiliberal.[98] These various constitutional types are united as a category only by their negation of the principal liberal affirmations prioritizing individual rights and endorsing state neutrality.[99] Consequently, nonliberal states can privilege a substantive vision of the public good.[100] What this vision entails very much depends on the nature of the nonliberal entity. There are at least three forms of public good that motivate regulation in the nonliberal secular state. The first is peaceful coexistence or religious harmony, which itself tends to be linked to public order. The underlying claim is that interreligious animosity, if left unchecked, would threaten public order. In Singapore, for example, the idea of "racial-religious harmony" is a commonly invoked justification for state intervention into religious matters. It has been used to justify prosecuting religious speech for creating ill-will and hostility among different groups[101] as well as to justify passing broad-ranging laws directly regulating religious speech from the pulpit. One such law is Singapore's Maintenance of Religious Harmony Act empowers the government to issue a restraining order to any religious leader or persons of influence in a religious organization to refrain from speaking on a particular topic in his or her official capacity. Violations of such a restraining order constitute a criminal offense. The need for religious harmony (which in Singapore is

97 Cohen, "The politics and risks of the new legal pluralism" (n. 96), 394–5. See also Cohen, *Rethinking Political Secularism* (n. 92), 143.

98 Thio uses the term illiberal but I prefer the word nonliberal, which I argue is a more neutral term. Li-ann Thio, "Constitutionalism in Illiberal Polities," in Michel Rosenfeld and András Sajó (eds.), *The Oxford Handbook of Comparative Constitution Law* (Oxford University Press, 2012).

99 Graham Walker, "The New Mixed Constitution: A Response to Liberal Debility & Constitutional Deadlock in Eastern Europe," *Polity* 26.3 (1994), 503, 506.

100 Ibid.

101 See Jaclyn Neo, "Seditious in Singapore – Free Speech and the Offence of Promoting Ill-Will and Hostility between Different Racial Groups," *Singapore Journal of Legal Studies* 2011.2 (2011), 351.

intertwined with racial harmony) has arguably been elevated to constitutional or at least quasi-constitutional status.

It should here be clarified that peaceful coexistence or religious harmony is a social objective that could be present in both liberal and nonliberal states, as well as secular and confessional or even theocratic states. However, while liberal states are most likely to adopt religious tolerance as a way to maintain interreligious harmony, consistent with the liberal-secular constraints, nonliberal states are not similarly limited in achieving their objective and could be more interventionist in regulating religion to achieve religious harmony. Thus, laws aimed at ensuring religious harmony could have restrictive impact on religious groups, particularly religious minorities. In Indonesia, for example, the need for religious harmony has been used to justify and uphold a law restricting speech misusing or insulting religion.[102] Furthermore, a draft Law on Inter-religious Harmony[103] seeks to regulate "issues of public debate and controversy such as the concept of religious freedom, the criminal offence of blasphemy, the right to religious education, the need for guidelines on proselytization, and the permit application process for places of worship."[104]

A second public good could itself be the need to ensure religious uniformity. This is more commonly associated with religious constitutions or constitutions that prioritize a particular religion, most often the majority religion. Nonetheless, it is not a new idea; as Durham points out, prior to what he calls the Lockean revolution in religious liberty, it was generally assumed that social and political stability presupposed religious and cultural homogeneity.[105] Such homogeneity is thought to be necessary as a social glue and ultimate motivation for loyalty and obedience to the prevailing regime. Furthermore, there was an assumption that "religious truth required state implementation of religious beliefs."[106] Indeed, "it was thought that if a particular set of religious beliefs are true, their truth provides a natural rationale for implementing them."[107] An assertive claim for religious uniformity as necessary for social order can provide a strong impetus for laws restricting speech, religious proselytization, and even religious choice. Blasphemy laws and even apostasy laws have been argued to be necessary to ensure social order.

102 See Decision of the Constitutional Court No. 140/PUU-VII/2009 concerning the Request for Judicial Review of the Blasphemy Law, dated 19 April 2010. For further analysis, see Melissa Crouch, "Law and Religion in Indonesia: The Constitutional Court and the Blasphemy Law," *Asian Journal of Comparative Law* 7 (2011), 1.

103 For an in-depth discussion of the content and history of the law, see Melissa Crouch, "Shifting Conceptions of State Regulation of Religion: The Indonesian Draft Law on Inter-religious Harmony," *Global Change, Peace & Security* 25.3 (2013), 265.

104 Ibid., 267.

105 W. Cole Durham, "Perspectives on Religious Liberty: A Comparative Framework," in Johan D. van der Vyver and John Witte, Jr. (eds.), *Religious Human Rights in Global Perspective* (Martinus Nijhoff, 1996), 7.

106 Ibid.

107 Ibid.

For instance, some states justify restrictions on converting out of Islam as necessary to ensure the security and stability of the nation, though this is by no means a widespread view among Islamic scholars.[108]

A third, and related, public good used in nonliberal states is the need for social control. This is commonly associated with constitutional systems that are statist in their orientation, such as socialist constitutions. The state regulates religion as an aspect of social life though it often regards it with some suspicion or hostility because of its ideological opposition to religion and/or because religion has the organizational capacity to mobilize against the state. Under such conditions, religion is more likely to be closely regulated. An example of a state that sees the regulation of religion as necessary to maintain social order is the Peoples' Republic of China. As its Constitution states, citizens enjoy "freedom of religious belief" and state "protects normal religious activities," but these are subject to the limitation that "[n]o one may make use of religion to engage in activities that disrupt public order, impair the health of citizens or interfere with the educational system of the state."[109] Furthermore, the revised Religious Affairs Regulations that came into effect in early 2018 increased state oversight over religious activities such as online discussion of religious matters. This increased regulatory reach is justified as necessary to prevent the spread of "extremist" ideology and to protect China's national security against threats from religious groups.[110]

Nonliberal states may thus regulate religion strongly or weakly. Strong, even aggressive, regulation of religion may result in the systematic violation of religious freedoms. In comparison, a less aggressive approach may seem less violative of religious freedoms although it may simply be because the state has successfully co-opted religious groups. Beyond the current division between liberal and nonliberal approaches to regulation of religion, one can probably surmise another proposition, which is that the crucial factor determining how strongly the state regulates religion in a nonliberal setting is the *degree of threat religion poses to the public good and the political status quo*. The more religion is a perceived and/or real threat to the state, the more likely will the nonliberal state strongly regulate religion.

V. CONCLUSION

In conclusion, regulation of religion as the *intentional intervention in the activities of religious individuals and communities, whether direct or indirect, through binding law or otherwise, and whether conducted by a public sector or private sector actors*

108 For the former view, see e.g., Sulieman Abdul Rahman Al Hageel, *Human Rights in Islam and the Refutation of the Misconceived Allegations Associated with These Rights*, 2nd edn (Supreme Council for Islamic Affairs, 1999), 157–8. Contrast with Mashood A. Baderin, International Human Rights and Islamic Law (Oxford University Press, 2003), 118–25.

109 Constitution of the People's Republic of China, Art. 36.

110 China tightens regulation of religion to "block extremism," Reuters (September 7, 2017), www.reuters.com/article/us-china-religion/china-tightens-regulation-of-religion-to-block-extremism-idUSKCN1BI1IH (accessed September 28, 2018).

encompasses a range of legal as well as quasi-legal forms such as coregulation and self-regulation. The combination of these modes with public regulation responds to different regimes of regulatory enterprises that could broadly be divided into liberal and nonliberal approaches. Identifying regulation on these different levels and modes is important to highlight the many ways the state interacts with religion beyond the usual focus on constitutional and private law. This of course should not obscure the fact that, as Hussin has emphasized, the state is "not a unitary actor."[111] Further, the range of regulatory modes employed may at times conflict with one another. The state may also not be "fully in control of governed religion."[112] Religion may reject state regulation or, as the discussion on coregulation shows, may transform regulatory relationships in their favor. More research needs to be done to provide more theoretical analysis and empirical studies into the regulation of religion, including regulating religion in Asia. This chapter seeks to systematize a preliminary framework for inquiry so as to provoke further examination in this direction.

111 Iza Hussin, "'The New Global Politics of Religion': Religious Harmony, Public Order, and Securitisation in the Post-colony," *Journal of Religious and Political Practice* 4.1 (2018), 93, 104.

112 Ibid.

3

The Role of Authority and Sanctity in State–Religion Conflicts

Shai Wozner and Gilad Abiri

... it cannot be forgotten that considering the religious feelings of a particular individual is liable to violate the rights and feelings of another person. Thus, whether religious sensibilities are offended is a factor that cannot be considered in isolation. Rather, this must invariably be weighed against other factors, related to both the individual and the public at large.[1]

I. INTRODUCTION

Conflicts between state institutions and religious institutions are among the most intractable challenges facing liberal states.[2] The standard account in both political theory and law and religion of these conflicts is that they are mainly about ideology, values, and rights: the negative freedom enshrined in liberal constitutions clashing against the thick, positive normativity of religion.[3]

[1] See HCJ 5016/96 – *Horev v. Minister of Transportation* [1997] IsrSC 51(4) 1. Translation can be found in: http://versa.cardozo.yu.edu/opinions/horev-v-minister-transportation (accessed 31 October 2017).

[2] For an example of the rise of religious-based nationalist violence, see Jonathan Fox, 'The Rise of Religious Nationalism and Conflict: Ethnic Conflict and Revolutionary Wars, 1945-2001', *Journal of Peace Research* 41 (2004), 715. For an account of why religion is significantly more likely to cause intergroup conflict than other forms of identity, see Jeffrey R. Seul, '"Ours Is the Way of God": Religion, Identity, and Intergroup Conflict', *Journal of Peace Research* 36(1999), 553. For an analysis of the vulnerability of secular states to religious revolutions, see Michael Walzer, *The Paradox of Liberation: Secular Revolutions and Religious Counterrevolutions* (Yale University Press, 2015).

[3] We see this account as being made out of three propositions: (1) It sees the source of the tension over church and state as disagreement over values. (2) At the center of disagreement are liberal values such as autonomy, liberty, and equality. (3) If these disagreements over values are regulated properly (personal conscience is protected, policies are justified in correct ways), then conflicts of law and religion will be averted to a sufficient degree. Good examples of this account can be found in John Rawls, *Political Liberalism* (Columbia University Press, 2005). He seems to hold that if one regulates (somehow) the norms of public discourse to adhere to the principles of public reason, this will solve the issue of state legitimacy in the face of religion. The giving of the correct type of reasons leads to the ability to maintain social order in societies with a plurality of comprehensive doctrines, or moral world views. Indeed, it is the problem of what he called 'the fact of reasonable pluralism' – the existence of irreconcilable moral, religious, or philosophical doctrines – that his vision of 'political liberalism' comes to resolve. A similar notion can be found in the United States' First Amendment

In this chapter we challenge this view – arguing that this standard account is incomplete and inaccurate, and that it does not explicate the most compelling attribute of these conflicts: the deep intransience of all involved. This inflexibility is found even in cases of extreme state accommodation such as Israel's treatment of its ultra-Orthodox minority: the state allows them to independently control curriculum in schools while still receiving state funding; the state subsidises many *yeshivot* (religious academies); and finally, the state exempts them from mandatory military service. In the face of such extreme accommodation, one would expect the conflict and tension to abate. This does not seem to be the case.[4]

We wish to rectify the common account by turning our attention to two important dynamics: the struggle for ultimate authority and the need to protect the sacred. We will examine these dynamics in the context of Israeli society.

We suggest that the locus of the conflict of religion and state is in the struggle for authority – both real and symbolic. The tensions between state and religion do not result merely from ideological differences, but mainly from a competition over ultimate authority, or more accurately from a struggle over settling what the source of that authority is. This skirmish is held between the sovereign authority of the state and legislator, and the religious authority that undermines it. It takes place not only between those who claim authority, but also between lower social institutions (including the citizens) who are wrestling over the question of which authority they should be subjected to. It is important to notice that while in a disagreement over rights (or other values) both sides may acknowledge the opposing right and reach a compromise, a feud over authority is, by its very nature, uncompromising, as all sides wish to conquer the top of the hill.

The second dynamic enforcing the intransigence of both sides is their respective need to protect the sacred. In our opinion, a sacred social institution is one that is imagined by a certain social group as being grounded in an ultimate reality. These institutions have a semblance of inevitability and inviolability – qualities analogous to those often ascribed to the Divine – and like it they engender great fear and wonder.[5]

jurisprudence, where the centrality of the idea of protecting the freedom of conscience of religious minorities exemplifies the standard account well. See Patrick Weil, 'Freedom of Conscience, But Which One? In Search of Coherence in the U.S. Supreme Court's Religion Jurisprudence', *University of Pennsylvania Journal of Constitutional Law* 20 (in press).

4 Efraim Ben-Zadok, *Local Communities and the Israeli Polity: Conflict of Values and Interests* (SUNY Press, 2012); Asher Cohen and Bernard Susser, *Israel and the Politics of Jewish Identity: The Secular-Religious Impasse* (JHU Press, 2000).

5 One can divide the scholarship on the subject of the sacred into two wide tribes: phenomenologists on the one hand and culturalists on the other. The first kind examines the 'sacred' as a basic structure of the human experience of the world. The latter understands the 'sacred' as an identifiable quality of social life. The sacred is socially/culturally constructed within a specific historical context. For an exploration of this distinction see Gordon Lynch, *The Sacred in the Modern World: A Cultural Sociological Approach* (Oxford University Press, 2012). William James, Rudolf Otto, and Mircea Eliade are good representations of phenomenologists. Otto, in his *The Idea of the Holy* (Oxford University Press, 1958), defines the sacred as the experience of *mysterium tremendum et fascinans* (overwhelming and fascinating mystery); for him the holy constitutes a category of interpretation and valuation peculiar to the sphere of religion. For

Paradoxically, the perception of the sacred thing is that it is vulnerable and requires protection, similar to a taboo.[6] This perception exists especially in religious thought; and we think that it aggravates conflicts of religion and state, where the religious establishment feels committed to protect from desecration things they perceive as sacred. In such a case, religious citizens are not struggling for their own personal interests, nor are they trying to paternalistically impose their norms on others. In their eyes, what they are trying to do is to protect sacred entities – desecration of which is considered catastrophic. They find it very hard to compromise regarding the sacred object, because its interests are external to them. As we will discuss at length later, the protection of the sacred dynamic is central in Israel, where the land, the city of Jerusalem, and even the state are charged with religious meaning for different groups.

Despite the religious nature of this conception of the 'sacred', we think that a similar pattern exists in the liberal political world. The process of reification of the institutions of the state, rule of law, and democracy makes them into vulnerable sacred entities which require protection.

These two dynamics: the struggle over ultimate authority and the need to protect the sacred, represent, in our opinion, the major modus operandi of the sides in conflicts of law and religion – and the main reasons for its intractability.

The rest of this chapter will try and demonstrate the nuances of these theoretical arguments through an analysis of the legal and cultural discourse surrounding issues of law and religion in Israel. The first section will succinctly lay out a few relevant facts about conflicts of liberal law and religion in Israel. The second will turn to a discussion of the question of authority. The third will deal with the question of sanctity.

II. A FEW FACTS ABOUT ISRAELI LAW AND RELIGION

Israel is defined in its declaration of independence and in its basic laws (which function as a type of constitution) as a 'Jewish Democratic State'. Although the term

Mircea Eliade in *The Sacred and the Profane* (Harcourt Brace Jovanovich, 1987), sacred time, space, and things represent a more intense 'reality' around which the rest of the human world is structured. On the side of the culturalists we can find Max Weber, Emile Durkheim, and Peter L. Berger. In his book *The Elementary Forms of the Religious Life* (Oxford University Press, 2008), Durkheim divides human life into two symbolic realms: sacred and profane. The latter is the realm of routine experience that we can know through our senses. We experience this natural world of everyday life as comprehensible, knowable, and taken for granted. The sacred, in contrast, is separated from everyday experience; it is an object of worship, inspiring feelings of awe among its believers. Durkheim believes that the sacred is a socially constructed symbolic representation of society itself. Berger represents the most sophisticated version of sacred culturalism, in his book *The Sacred Canopy: Elements of a Sociological Theory of Religion* (Open Road Media, 2011), he elaborates the idea, stating that religion is the human enterprise by which a sacred social world is established. Since the sacred exists beyond the everyday, but is still experienced through rituals and symbols, it is experienced as both being independent of humanity and yet being accessible. The sacred social world is constructed on the concreteness of sacred social institutions. Our approach to the sacred is culturalist, and is roughly based on Berger's idea.

6 Mary Douglas, *Purity and Danger: An Analysis of Concepts of Pollution and Taboo* (Routledge, 2003).

'Jewish' here is not understood to indicate the supremacy of Jewish law and religion in state affairs, it is still clearly charged with religious undertones. Indeed, the legal and civil discourse in Israel delves intensively into the questions of how to bridge these two components. The common assumption is that conservative-religious Judaism cannot easily cohabitate with liberal democracy.[7]

As of April 2015, Israel has 8.35 million citizens, 75% of whom are considered Jewish, 17% Muslim, and the rest are Christians, Druze, and other smaller groups.[8] In the context of this chapter we will not be considering the conflicts of the Muslim religion and Israeli state, though the combination of religious and political strife makes these questions very important and interesting. Instead, we will focus on the Jewish religious population and its relation to the liberal state, which is usually associated with secular Jews. Israel's Jewish population is classically divided into five groups. According to the Israeli Bureau of Statistics, in 2011 43% of adults were non-religious, 23% traditional, 15% traditional-religious, 10% Religious Zionist, and 9% ultra-Orthodox.[9] These groups can be defined by their position on two axes – the first axis is the level of association with the Jewish religion and observance (from the secular to the religious), and the second is their attitude towards the Israeli Zionist state specifically and to modernity generally (this is the distinction between the more modern Religious Zionists and the non-Zionist ultra-Orthodox).

In many instances, conflicts of liberal state and religion in Israel reach the Israeli Supreme Court. This is the arena in which the sides expect the issue to be resolved. The fact that it is through the liberal court system that these conflicts are settled is not neutral; in fact, it is deeply contested. This is due to another disagreed-upon question that must be added to the list iterated earlier: which law should the state of Israel follow?[10]

Jewish law is central to Judaism, and covers, effectively, all facets of human life. Not only does it include substantial laws of ritual, prayer, and morality, but also an extensive system of criminal and private law. The root of Jewish law can be found in the Hebrew Bible as it was understood by the main rabbinic legal texts: the *Mishna*, *Talmud*, and subsequent rabbinic legal scholars.[11] Jewish law is extremely prolific, well developed, and sophisticated. It was practiced in most Jewish communities (that quite often had legal autonomy) all the way up to modernity. With the establishment of the State of Israel, many religious citizens believed the state should

7 See Ruth Gavison, 'Jewish and Democratic? A Rejoinder to the "Ethnic Democracy" Debate', *Israel Studies* 4.1 (1999), 44; Sammy Smooha, 'The Model of Ethnic Democracy: Israel as a Jewish and Democratic State', *Nations and Nationalism* 8.4 (2002), 475.

8 Israel Central Bureau of Statistics, *Annual Report* (February 2014).

9 Israel Central Bureau of Statistics, *Social Survey 2009: Jewish Tradition Observance and Changes in Religiosity of the Jewish population in Israel* (2009) (in Hebrew).

10 Y. Z. Stern, *Israeli Law and Halakha (Jewish Law) in Israeli Society* (Israel Democracy Institute, 2002), 103–42 (in Hebrew).

11 For a good review of the history of Jewish law, see Elliot N. Dorff and Arthur Rossett, *A Living Tree: The Roots and Growth of Jewish Law* (SUNY Press, 2012).

adopt Jewish law as the law of the land. For many reasons – among which are the facts that the Zionist movement was dominated by secularists and that the preexisting mandatory legal system was British – Israeli state law was generally based on traditional British common law;[12] and the legal elite, trained in colonial legal institutions, became agents of the spreading of liberal legal and political thought.[13] The tension born from the gap between Jewish law and the existing liberal common law has been present in all polemics on state and religion conflicts in Israel. This is due to the fact that the religious population usually mistrusts the courts, and does not lend full legitimacy to the Israeli legal system and courts.

Conflicts of the Israeli state with its religious population can be divided into two general types: imperialist and reclusive. These correspond respectively to the division between Religious Zionists and ultra-Orthodox. With the former group, accepting the Zionist project and its implementation in the modern state of Israel, and investing in its existence and success much religious ardor, the conflicts usually arise from political issues such as territorial compromise. This is an imperialist conflict because their religious prescriptions concern the general path the state should take. With the ultra-Orthodox, who reject the theological importance of the state of Israel (since it was founded by secular Jews and does not follow Jewish law), the issues usually revolve around their lack of equal participation in state institutions (mainly serving in the army) and other issues rising from their existence as a reclusive religious minority, such as: the content of education, state funding for religious institutions, etc. Clearly, questions and conflicts of religion and state in Israel are not merely a matter of theoretical and constitutional difficulties, but an integral part of a cultural-social polemic between religious citizens: ultra-Orthodox and Religious Zionist – comprising approximately 20% of the population, and the secular group.[14]

The ultra-Orthodox group in Israel has many nuances and subdivisions, the most radical among which completely reject the values and narratives of the secular Zionist state. In general, this population does not wish to be part of Israeli society and be exposed to the Western tradition. For this reason, they tend to promote cultural and geographic introversion (living in separate neighbourhoods and cities, having separate education systems) in a way that disconnects them from daily contact with surrounding cultures and allows them to adhere strictly to their form of religious life.[15] Some groups refuse to participate in Israeli elections, and accept no budgetary support from the state. They object to all religious leniencies, and insist on highly modest clothing and gender separation in most walks of life: from kindergartens, schools, and higher education, to the general public sphere (separate

[12] See Menachem Mautner, *Law and the Culture of Israel* (Oxford University Press, 2011), 35–41.

[13] Ibid.

[14] Mautner (n. 12), 99–158.

[15] See Nahshon Perez, 'The Limits of Liberal Toleration: The Case of the Ultra-Orthodox in Israel', *Journal of Church and State* 56.2 (2014), 223; Gila Stopler, 'The Ultra-Orthodox Community in Israel and the Right to an Exclusively Religious Education', in Susanna Mancini and Michel Rosenfeld (eds.), *Constitutional Secularism in an Age of Religious Revival* (Oxford University Press, 2014).

seating in buses, different hours for men and women in shops). On the basis of a religious law originating in the Hebrew Bible, they believe that homosexual relations are strictly forbidden, and they object to all legitimising gestures towards homosexuality. The supreme values in the ultra-Orthodox narrative are religious values. The ideal they educate towards is not to be rich, or achieve success in academia or in the public sector; rather it is to achieve high levels in religious experience, observance of Jewish law, and study of the *Torah* (the Jewish canon). Indeed, ultra-Orthodox society encourages all men to spend their time studying the *Torah* (a practice that usually takes place in *Torah* learning academies or '*Yeshivot*'), a fact that leads to extremely low employment among Israel's ultra-Orthodox society.[16]

One of the focal tension points between the state and ultra-Orthodox society is the refusal of the latter to allow its members to join the Israeli army. The rationale for not allowing women to be drafted is that it will harm their sense of modesty. Following intense struggles in the 1950s, it was legislated that women can receive a religious exemption from army service. For men the rationale is more convoluted. The official one, recognised by the state, but repeatedly challenged in the Israeli Supreme Court, relies on the inherent value of the study of *Torah*; and also argues that those engaged in *Torah* study represent an important intellectual and religious elite that should be exempt from army service.[17] This being said, there are clearly deeper reasons: the army is a mirror image of general society, and the cultures represented in it are exactly what ultra-Orthodox society is trying to seclude itself from. Also, army service depends on some acknowledgement of the Zionist narrative, which the ultra-Orthodox reject.

In recent years the ultra-Orthodox society has been going through changes. Some parts of this society are fortifying the walls and becoming more radical in their reclusion, but a large proportion wishes to take part in general Israeli society. More and more ultra-Orthodox join the army (though this is still far from the mainstream phenomenon), study in academic institutions, and join the work force.[18] One explanation of this shift is financial pressure, as most of the ultra-Orthodox population live well below the poverty line.

Unlike the reclusive ultra-Orthodox, the Religious Zionist population is deeply engaged both theologically and politically with the state of Israel.[19] Indeed, in the blessing for the state of Israel, recited each week in every Religious Zionist synagogue, the state is called 'the beginning of our salvation'. Religious Zionists serve in the

[16] Menachem Friedman, *The Haredi Ultra-Orthodox Society: Sources, Trends and Processes* (The Jerusalem Institute for Israel Studies, 1991) (in Hebrew).

[17] Menachem Mautner, 'A Dialogue between a Liberal and an Ultra-Orthodox on the Exclusion of Women from Torah Study', in Shai Lavi and Rene Provost (eds.), *Religious Revival in a Post-Multicultural Age* (Oxford University Press, 2013).

[18] Asaf Malhi, '"From Skullcap to Mortarboard": Academic Studies in Ultra-Orthodox Society', *Adult Education in Israel* 14(2015), 104.

[19] Dov Schwartz, *Religious-Zionism: History and Ideology* (Academic Studies Press, 2009).

army (in recent decades they have represented a significant portion of combat soldiers and officers in the Israel Defense Force [IDF]) and have a much more ambivalent relationship with Western culture and liberal-secular Israelis. As we have implied earlier, Religious Zionists start having problems with the state when it fails to meet their expectations, or when it does something that contradicts their theology and has implications in Jewish law or *Halakha*. The main point of conflict in recent decades has been around the mainly Religious Zionist settlement movement in the West Bank and Gaza. The process – which started with the Oslo peace process and continued with the Israeli evacuation of the Gaza Strip – both chafed against Religious Zionists' belief that the Land of Israel was given to the Jewish People by God.

In contrast to these two religious groups, Israel also has a large secular population with its own distinct ideology – dismissive of the existence of God and of the importance of Jewish tradition; instead, interested in promoting universal, liberal, values. These citizens see themselves as Israelis more than Jews (though these categories do interact). Since the early days of the state, its main mechanisms, namely the legislature, courts, army and academia, have been under strong 'hegemonic' control of the secular group.[20] This status quo has shifted somewhat in the last twenty years. This is especially apparent in the *Knesset*, where religious and traditional groups have significant, growing influence.[21]

III. THE STRUGGLE FOR AUTHORITY

A. *Values or Authority?*

The common understanding is that friction between law and religion is a matter of ideology and values, its roots lie in different conceptions of the good and divergent visions for the political. Liberal tradition and religious tradition are seen as reflecting binary, opposing values, which represent fertile soil for conflict.[22] The ideal of religion is characterised by total faith in and subservience to God and His representatives; while liberals and seculars conceive skepticism, autonomy, and individual liberty as their primary values. Religion is inclined to be particularistic while secularism advocates universal values. Religion supports prudery as opposed to the permissive licentiousness of secularisms. The history of religion is replete with

[20] Mautner (n. 12), 99–158.

[21] Ibid.

[22] For a general definition of this standard account of law and religion see footnote 3. This account is prevalent on Israel's op-ed pages; for recent examples, see Tomer Persico, 'Why Religious Zionism Is Growing Darker' *Haaretz* (16 May 2017), www.haaretz.com/opinion/.premium-1.789226 (accessed 16 May 2017); Irit Rosenblum, 'Declaring War on Israel's Secular Public', *Haaretz* (13 December 2016), www.haaretz.com/opinion/.premium-1.758627 (accessed 16 May 2017). The standard account is also dominant in Israeli academia; for an interesting example see Mautner (n. 17).

struggle and suspicion against novel (and perhaps heretic) scientific and philosophical development, while secular doctrines are rooted in philosophy and science.

This supposed clash of values can be easily seen in some of the examples already mentioned above: ultra-Orthodox Jews oppose homosexuality and public transport on *Shabbat*, and liberals see the limiting of these behaviours to be anathema to their basic values, such as autonomy, and to human rights, such as freedom of movement and expression. Similarly, on the issue of army service: the ultra-Orthodox view the imposition of a duty to serve in the army as harming their religious freedoms (to study *Torah*, to protect the modesty of women), while the liberals believe that equality and national security warrant an equal duty of service. These disagreements, and their proposed solutions, are about whose values should determine political and social life.

Legal scholarship is not exempt from this dichotomous conception of social reality. It often interprets conflicts between state institutions and religious groups through the lens of constitutional law. This prism, with its tendency to conceptualise in abstract categories of rights and equality, almost necessitates the understanding of conflict as a matter of disagreement over content. What follows then is an imposition of the conceptual legal structure of these core constitutional commitments onto conflicts of religion and state. The way this imposition usually appears in Israeli constitutional jurisprudence is through the narrative of 'balancing' the infringement of a constitutional right with harming the feelings of religious citizens. For example, balancing the right of the ultra-Orthodox population in Jerusalem to avoid their feelings being hurt by the LGBT pride parade on the one hand, and protection of the freedom of movement, expression, and the value of equality on the other.

In our opinion, this analysis is not exhaustive. We think that in many instances, the conflict between religious institutions and state institutions is, in fact, a struggle over the source of authority, hiding beneath the veil of ideals and values.

It is worth noting, in order to make our position clear, that we do think that these conflicts also concern the substance and content of ideals and values; but that without the prism of the struggle over authority it is impossible to grasp the whole picture. This lens especially allows us to better understand the radicalisation of the sides. If the struggle concerns only content, then compromises are easier to reach, a 'balancing' is always possible; but, if the conflict is over the source of ultimate authority, no side will budge as any compromise will threaten to undermine the very goal of the struggle. The Israeli Supreme Court often operates through the standard account of law and religion. An example is the case of *Horev v. Minister of Transportation*,[23] in which the court was examining an administrative edict that closed Bar-Ilan Street vehicle for certain times on *Shabbat*. The court held that 'the partial closure of the street during prayer times on the Sabbath, as per the Minister's decision, strikes an appropriate balance between freedom of movement and the

[23] *Horev* (n. 1).

ultra-Orthodox local residents' religious sensibilities and observant lifestyle'.[24] However, this compromise was not accepted by many in the ultra-Orthodox community, with demonstrations continuing.[25] This is a good example of a compromise over actual policy being met with continued struggle. In addition to the difficulty to reach a compromise, we also hold that often, the actual harm done to rights or values is negligible and thus cannot explain the magnitude of conflict, a fact that a discourse based on rights misses completely.

This use of liberal political theory, as embedded in constitutional law, is confusing a normative stance with social reality.[26] Using the lens of sociological/cultural theory, we view both liberal law and religion not only as institutions or sets of ideas or beliefs, but also as social worlds or cultures; by this we mean that they are a prism through which a meaningful order is imposed on the chaotic worlds of individual experience.[27] Both of these systems are comprehensive, in that they give order and meaning to many important facets of human life. These worlds are by their very nature precarious; this is especially true in situations where two or more social worlds pull and push at the same group of people. This vulnerability leads to a need for constant world maintenance, which is achieved by a variety of tools, or legitimations.[28] Indeed, 'two societies confronting each other with conflicting universes will both develop conceptual machinery designed to maintain their respective universes'.[29] The experience of one's social world being undermined is exceedingly hard and frightening, which explains much of the behaviour of groups possessing different social worlds in times of conflict. An important feature of this sociologically informed theory, and the reason it is useful for our argument, is that it is not mainly concerned with the ideological content of social worlds, or even with their philosophical assumptions and arguments, but rather with challenges to social world stability. This supports our argument that in the struggles of liberal law and religion in Israel, the issue at stake is not the specific content – but rather the very maintenance of the authoritative nature of their discrete social worlds.

In our context, then, we view both secular liberalism and Orthodox Judaism as comprehensive cultural groups maintaining discrete social worlds. These worlds provide order and meaning to their inhabitants. The ability to achieve a stable social-world is reliant on assumptions on the authoritative nature of social institutions: for

24 Translation found at: 'Horev v. Minister of Transportation | Cardozo Israeli Supreme Court Project' (*Versa*), http://versa.cardozo.yu.edu/opinions/horev-v-minister-transportation (accessed 17 May 2017).

25 'Bar Ilan Street Protests Resume after Court Rules against Closure', *Jewish Telegraphic Agency* (Jerusalem, 5 June 1997), www.jta.org/1997/06/05/news-opinion/bar-ilan-street-protests-resume-after-court-rules-against-closure (accessed 17 May 2017).

26 For an elaborate critique of liberalism on these grounds, see Paul W. Kahn, *Putting Liberalism in Its Place* (Princeton University Press, 2005).

27 Berger (n. 5), 22–3. For an account of law as a culture, see Benjamin L. Berger, 'Law's Religion: Rendering Culture', *Osgoode Hall Law Journal* 45 (2007), 277.

28 Ibid., 92–104.

29 Peter L. Berger and Thomas Luckmann, *The Social Construction of Reality: A treatise in the Sociology of Knowledge*, 6th edn (Doubleday, 1967), 108.

the liberal – the law and the state; for the Orthodox Jew – God and the rabbis. Because of this, often the preservation and maintenance of perceived authority is a central goal during conflicts between these two cultural groups; the urgency of the struggle over epistemic, cultural, authority has no relation to the importance (subjective or objective) of the actual subject of the struggle.

B. Religious Authority

As we have mentioned earlier, one of the main legal arguments put forth when "balancing" rights is that the feelings of religious minorities may get hurt. The LGBT pride parade hurts feelings, and so does public transport during *Shabbat*; these must be balanced with the right to free movement and speech. The argument of 'hurting feelings' is normatively weak; John Stewart Mill objected categorising this as 'harm' which justifies limiting the freedom of another person.[30] Daniel Statman argued against the prominence of the 'hurt feelings' argument in law and religion, stating that it focuses on mere pain and ignores the justifications for causing that pain. For him, 'such a shift in the locus of the argument would do more justice to its logical structure; would show more respect to the victims by saving them from the humiliating position of basing claims on mere pain; and would release us from the need to compare the intensity of the painful feelings of the sides involved'.[31] What is interesting is that when one looks closely at the arguments presented – both internally and externally – by religious parties during polemics, one sees that they almost never raise the 'feelings' argument themselves. If it comes up, it is only due to the fact that they understand that it is the only constitutional argument available to them. Furthermore, in the Israeli context, the 'feelings' argument is even less persuasive. This is due to the fact that the ultra-Orthodox understand to be an elite, a vanguard for the Jewish people. This sense of self-importance, combined with a dismissal of secular Judaism, means that they are absolutely not 'hurt' by seculars who belittle Jewish law or act in contradiction to its edicts.[32]

What, then, is the real reason that the ultra-Orthodox strongly oppose the LGBT pride parade and public transport on *Shabbat*?

The Jewish conception of the authority of God and his earthly representatives is clearly not uniform, and has shifted significantly over the ages. Our interest is in the contemporary cultural concept, an understanding of which will enable us to analyse current processes more effectively. Still, it is worthwhile to mention that in the *Talmudic* school of thought we find the conception of a significant limit to Godly authority. Especially well known is the *Talmudic* story of the 'Oven of *Akhnai*', in which sages are described as disputing the legal ruling of God and arguing that legal

30 John Stuart Mill, *On Liberty* (Longmans, Green, Reader, and Dyer, 1869), chapter 1; Daniel Statman, 'Hurting Religious Feelings', תרבות דמוקרטית (2000), 199.

31 Statman, ibid., 213.

32 See Mautner (n. 12).

authority is possessed by humanity, and not by God.[33] In a similar vein, revelation and prophecy have never been given legal powers in Jewish law (besides the original revelation to Moses in Sinai). The sages also present their activity in the development of Jewish law, which included the interpretation of God's words as well as the construction of new legal structures, as a wholly human endeavour. This anti-authoritarian theme in rabbinic thought also extends to human authority. In contrast with the Catholic conception of the infallibility of the Church, the sages are seen as obviously fallible. Indeed, there is a whole tractate of the *Mishna* (Tractate *Horayot*) which deals with the issue of what to do in the face of a rabbinic mistake. It is true that the common conclusion is that one must listen to *Halachik* authorities even if they are wrong, but the reasoning is utilitarian: keeping social order.

With this as a background, it is interesting to examine one of the main narratives and doctrines held by the ultra-Orthodox camp. This concept, developed in the early twentieth century, greatly increased the religious authority of the rabbis considered 'Gdolei Hador', that is, the greatest rabbis of their generation. This doctrine, called in Hebrew 'Da'as Torah',[34] expressed an ideal of complete subservience to Gdolei Hador, halachic, and religious authorities, and a duty of absolute obedience to their rulings and positions. An important ultra-Orthodox figure defined Da'as Torah as:

> That which Poskim [legal scholars] cannot prove from an explicit source, is decided upon by a thought-process which has been tuned and refined by tens of thousands of hours of Torah study (and with elderly Talmidei Chachamim [wise students] even hundreds of thousands of hours) which enables them to perceive where the pure truth lies. This process is called Da'as Torah – an opinion born out of Torah thought. Their thought-process has not been affected by secular and non-Jewish ways of thinking.[35]

In a way, this idea of Da'as Torah became the banner for the ultra-Orthodox community and the defining feature of its self-identity. An ultra-Orthodox person is one who subjects himself to gdolei hador and does not doubt their words. This subservience to the authority of certain men is seen as the essence of Jewish religiosity. The will of God is for us to obey these great men who represent His word on this earth. Although the ultra-Orthodox public is divided into different camps, which sometime disagree on who exactly are gdolei hador, in most times a leadership accepted by all comes into being. Either way, it is a matter of common

33 For a discussion of the story, see Izhak Englard, 'Majority Decision vs. Individual Truth: The Interpretations of the "Oven of Achnai" Aggadah', *Tradition* 15(1975), 137.

34 Jacob Katz, 'Da'at Torah. The Unqualified Authority Claimed for Halachists', *Jewish History* 11 (1997), 41; Lawrence Kaplan, 'Daas Torah: A Modern Conception of Rabbinic Authority', in Moshe Z. Sokol (ed.), *Rabbinic Authority and Personal Autonomy* (Jason Aronson, 1992).

35 Pesach Eliyahu Falk, *Sefer 'Oz Ve-hadar Levushah: Modesty, an Adornment for Life: Halachos and Attitudes Concerning Tznius of Dress & Conduct* (Feldheim Publishers, 1998).

agreement that this doctrine is what defines ultra-Orthodoxy. He who does not abide by the words of gdolei hador, even in trivial matters, is censured and becomes an outcast. It is also important to notice that in the definition offered earlier, Da'as Torah is also defined as an authority completely independent of western, secular, influences. Here, we get a glimpse of how central and explicit the issue of epistemic authority is for ultra-Orthodox society. They give the highest trust only to those who are completely independent of other cultural authorities. By blindly following leaders who have little to do with general Israeli Society – who are completely unaffected by it – the ultra-Orthodox have built a mighty cultural wall.

The authority of gdolei hador is based implicitly on the idea that the Divine inspiration they receive makes them infallible. This is the meaning of the expression 'Da'as Torah'; this idea penetrated ultra-Orthodox politics, and the two ultra-Orthodox parties in the Knesset declare that on all crucial decisions they abide completely to the words of the religious leaders.[36] This is important because it produces a type of agency problem. The rabbis order their representatives on how to act, and on what issues they should insist (e.g., the exemption of yeshiva students from army service); but the actual political battles are fought by politicians, whose main message to their secular counterparts is that they have no leeway to negotiate because they are merely following orders. This, combined with the fact that the actual decision-makers are completely disengaged from deliberations, creates an uncompromising political climate.

This situation explains why ultra-Orthodox individuals engaged in political polemics regarding law and religion often feel that they are fighting not only for a particular cause, but mainly in order to express their loyalty to religious authority. This dynamic applies regardless of whether the value fought over is important (even in internal terms of ultra-Orthodoxy), as what matters is the protection of religious authority.

Thus, when supporters of ultra-Orthodox service in the Israeli army raise powerful moral arguments (based on equality) or ones based in Jewish law (which is not clearly in support of the ultra-Orthodox position) it fails to resonate with the other side of the table. In the perspective of the ultra-Orthodox, the position held by glodei hador easily overcomes all arguments. In a certain way, the wobblier and untenable their position is in terms of morality and Jewish law, the better it expresses the absolute, blind, loyalty of the ultra-Orthodox to their rabbis.

If we examine Da'as Torah in terms of a tool of social world maintenance, we can see that its main function is one of separation. If, owing to the absolute inability to communicate Da'as Torah, the ultra-Orthodox are unable to explain their position to people who do not share their social world, this just concretises the difference between internal ultra-Orthodox discourse and external discourses. This is important to avoid the danger of being culturally influenced through political

[36] Cohen and Susser (n. 4).

engagement. By allowing rabbis who are uninvolved to make the final decisions, the ultra-Orthodox population can both be engaged in political efforts to secure its own interests, and still be a completely reclusive society: its social world left intact.

To conclude, the main issue in ultra-Orthodox discourse is the question of the nature of authority: Who holds it? Why do they hold it? Content becomes unimportant. If tomorrow the rabbis decide to permit serving in the army – there would be no practical problems in accomplishing this goal.

C. *State Authority*

We believe that non-religious discourse and actions in relation to law and religion are often also focussed on authority qua authority and cannot be explained by content alone. For example, both popular and academic discourses on the question of ultra-Orthodox army service utilise moral arguments of distributive justice and equality. Through the prism of these values it is difficult to justify the fact that a young secular person must serve in the army and risk his life, while his ultra-Orthodox counterpart can be exempt in order to study in a yeshiva (an exemption which is irrelevant for the secular soldier, as he is not interested in studying in a yeshiva).[37] This argument is based on the right to equality, which is also the main legal concept the Israeli Supreme Court uses in addressing the issue. This seems to us to be a rather weak argument. Even between those who do enlist to the army there is no substantive equality. It is true that all men spend three years in army service, but here equality ends. The service of an intelligence officer working in his Tel-Aviv office is quite different than that of the infantry man. Indeed, in the last few decades we have seen the tendency of Israeli secular elites to send their children to serve in elite intelligence units, where they receive training in IT and data manipulation, which helps them tremendously on leaving the army.[38] It is also true that de facto any soldier who does not want to serve in a combat unit can easily avoid doing so. Indeed, even equality in terms of contribution to the army is irrelevant. The Israeli army has an excess of personnel in many jobs (not in combat units or intelligence) – and many go through their army service merely shuffling papers. Thus, the frame of comparison is crucial. If we compare the contribution of essential personnel in contrast with that of the yeshiva student, we are justified in seeing it as vastly unequal. If we compare his contribution to that of a paper-pusher, we may find ourselves puzzling over who exactly contributes more. This is certainly true if we take into consideration the self-understanding of the yeshiva student: one of

37 Nurit Stadler and Eyal Ben-Ari, 'Other-Worldly Soldiers? Ultra-Orthodox Views of Military Service in Contemporary Israel', *Israel Affairs* 9 (2003), 17; Middle East Policy Council, 'Israel's Ultra-Orthodox Problem', www.mepc.org/commentary/israels-ultra-orthodox-problem (accessed 17 May 2017).

38 See Geoffrey Ingersoll, 'The Best Tech School on Earth Is Israeli Army Unit 8200', *Businessinsider* (13 August 2013), www.businessinsider.com/best-tech-school-is-israels-unit-8200-2013-8 (accessed 13 August 2013) and Inbal Orpaz, 'Welcome to the Employment Office of 8200', *TheMarker* (14 April 2014), www.themarker.com/career/1.2296657 (accessed 14 April 2014) (in Hebrew).

immense contribution to society. Looking at the situation this way undermines the view that there is strong inequality between yeshiva students and soldiers.

In our opinion, the actual ground upon which popular discourse and political groups (such as the centrist party Yesh Atid) demanding equal service in the army rely on is also the protection of authority. The struggle is between rabbinic authority (finding that the learning of Torah is of crucial importance), and secular authority located in the state and in the courts (seeing the same endeavor as worthless). What possibly enrages many from left-leaning liberals to right-wing nationalists here is the fact that the ultra-Orthodox clearly declare that they will not adhere to the authority of the law, the courts, or the army, but rather to that of the rabbis.

This argument arises explicitly in different contexts in Israeli civil discourse in sayings such as, 'It can't be that the rabbis set the agenda', 'Citizens loyalty should belong first and foremost to the state'. Through these and other similar expressions, we see that to a large extent what bothers people is not the actual drafting of ultra-Orthodox, but rather the rhetoric and justifications that the ultra-Orthodox provide for their actions. These undermine the authority of the state, which is a crucial part of the Israeli mainstream social world. We must also mention that in many other sectors of Israeli society, service evasion is quite common, not to mention the exemption of Palestinian-Arab citizens of Israel – all of which are usually not discussed in the same dramatic tones.

In recent years, following decades of political and judicial struggles, secular legislators tried passing a law which included criminal sanctions for ultra-Orthodox men who avoid army service.[39] The overwhelming ultra-Orthodox response was that they would be willing to go to jail and not be forcibly drafted.[40] Even if we are skeptical of the ultra-Orthodox declarations, there were also claims that the law would actually reduce the number of ultra-Orthodox enlisting (which was increasing) because of the antagonism produced among all parts of ultra-Orthodox society.[41] These arguments did not seem to faze the leaders pushing for equal service in the army. A possible reason for this is that the actuality of whether the ultra-Orthodox serve in the army or not does not actually matter for the world-maintenance goal of the struggle. It is true that if the ultra-Orthodox go, en masse, to prison, they may not serve in the army; yet, the authority of the law (which is a crucial part of the liberal social cosmos) will still be strongly asserted by the state. That the law would apply equally is more important than the question of who actually serves in the army.

39 Jonathan Lis, 'Knesset Passes New Draft Law, Which Includes Haredi Conscription', *Haaretz* (12 March 2014), www.haaretz.com/israel-news/.premium-1.579362 (accessed 17 May 2017).

40 Yair Ettinger, 'Israeli Ultra-Orthodox Confident Yeshiva Students Won't Be Drafted to IDF', *Haaretz* (23 February 2012), www.haaretz.com/israeli-ultra-orthodox-confident-yeshiva-students-won-t-be-drafted-to-idf-1.414219 (accessed 17 May 2017).

41 Yair Ettinger, 'The Fraud of the Draft Law: More Harm than Good for the Enlistment of the Ultra-Orthodox', *Haaretz* (14 March 2015), www.haaretz.co.il/news/elections/.premium-1.2589340 (accessed 14 March 2015) (in Hebrew).

Another example of the state acting in the authority-preserving mode is the uproar over women singing in the army. A few years ago there was great turmoil in Israel over an apparently very small incident. In a military ceremony during the Israeli army officer training course, a band which included female soldiers performed. A few Religious Zionist officer candidates asked to leave the hall during the performance, since their rabbis decreed that Jewish law prohibits listening to the singing of women. Their commanding officer refused to allow them to leave (or not attend the ceremony); a few of them disobeyed, arguing that the order infringes on their freedom of religion. They were tried, punished, and expelled from the course. The main arguments of the commanding officer were that leaving the hall was offensive to the female singers and exclusionary toward women, and also that soldiers should obey army commands and not to rabbinic edicts.[42]

In this case the soldiers were Religious Zionist and not ultra-Orthodox, but it seems that their main motivation for disobeying an order was to show their loyalty to rabbinic authority. Clearly, there are many voices in Jewish law which would have allowed the soldiers to stay in the ceremony. More than this, it is almost a consensus that the soldiers did not have to leave if the circumstances did not allow it, or if exiting the room came with a price.

This was not a disagreement over the law, nor was there an attempt to solve the situation without it devolving into a disobedience of an order. The soldiers felt committed to their rabbis, and more than this, they wanted to create a gesture of protest over the exercise of military authority by the commanding officer. The struggle was declaratory – the issue was who has the ultimate authority. This is also true for the army commander. Who would even notice if five soldiers left to go to the bathroom? Or called in sick? No one. What bothered the commanding officer was that his authority was being undermined.[43]

Another example has to do with the struggle against the implementation of the disengagement plan from Gaza (known by people who objected to it as 'the expulsion from Gaza'). Here also the apparent basis for disagreement was values (the land of Israel as a religious value vs. security or peace narratives), but it became clear that much of it was a struggle over authority. Some important Israeli rabbis (not necessarily ultra-Orthodox) decried that it was prohibited by Jewish law to cede control over land defined as 'Eretz Yisrael' to the Palestinian National Authority. This prohibition applies whether or not the Israeli government or legislators decided to cede

42 Amos Harel, 'IDF: Soldiers Cannot Skip Ceremonies with Women Singing', *Haaretz* (14 September 2011), www.haaretz.com/idf-soldiers-cannot-skip-ceremonies-with-women-singing-1.384288 (accessed 14 September 2011); Yair Ettinger, 'Top Settler Rabbi: Soldiers Will Sooner Choose Death Than Suffer Women's Singing', *Haaretz* (17 November 2011), www.haaretz.com/israel-news/top-settler-rabbi-soldiers-will-sooner-choose-death-than-suffer-women-s-singing-1.396180 (accessed 17 November 2011).

43 See Jonathan Lis, 'Chief of Staff: Religious Will Not Be Released from Official Events', *Haaretz* (27 December 2011), www.haaretz.co.il/news/politics/1.1602132 (accessed 27 December 2011) (in Hebrew).

territory. This is a good example of a clash between halachik authority and state authority. These rabbis, among whom was Rabbi Avraham Shapiro, who had been the chief rabbi of Israel a few years earlier, instructed soldiers who were commanded to participate in the disengagement plan to disobey the order, even if this meant going to jail. This created great agitation, and the army released statements declaring that soldiers must adhere to the command chain, and not to rabbis. Different rabbis released decrees objecting the call to disobey an order, arguing, instead, that in order to safeguard the fragile integration of religious soldiers in the army, they must obey the order to evacuate the Gaza Strip from Jewish Settlers.

It is telling to compare this case, and others like it, with the far more common cases of 'moral disobedience' from the left side of Israeli politics.[44] These cases usually involve soldiers refusing to serve in what they see as the occupied territories of the West Bank and Gaza. Here also, the perpetrators are indicted and put on trial, but it seems like the army is less troubled by it. The representatives of the state look at this as an ideological disagreement within the same 'camp' and not as a direct challenge to the social world authority of the state and the army. 'Religious disobedience', in contrast, is supercharged by all the threatening tensions between secular-liberal authority and religious-rabbinic authority.

Both the liberal social world and the religious social world rely on claims for deep cultural authority. On the liberal side, the emphasis is on the authority of the state and the law. Here, the concept of the rule of law, and the judiciary responsible for protecting it, replace God and the priesthood. The law, though we are all aware is created by interest-driven human legislators, is seen as a supreme value. The citizens are, essentially, subjects of the law. Both the existence of the state and the social well-being of all citizens seem to depend on the supremacy of the law. This sense of supremacy is maintained by elaborate rituals: the dress code for judges, the structure of courtrooms, court procedures, and more. Defying the dignity and authority of courts and judges is seen as a severe, criminal, act: contempt of court. These structures reflect very closely the ones meant to maintain the authority of the rabbis and the rule of God.

It is important to distinguish between two possible forms of authority that inform our argument. At times the subject of the argument of authority is made by the holders of the authority themselves: the rabbis, legislators, judges, and army commanders – all arguing that they are the ones who should be obeyed. In this case, authority wishes to cement its position in relation to competing authorities. Other times, the argument of authority is made by those who see themselves as its subjects: members of the secular-liberal cultural group arguing for the authority of law and the value of the rule of law, while religious cultural groups argue that it is God and

44 Ruth Linn, 'Soldiers with Conscience Never Die – They Are Just Ignored by Their Society: Moral Disobedience in the Israel Defense Forces', *Journal of Military Ethics* 1(2002), 57; Barak Medina, 'Political Disobedience in the IDF: The Scope of the Legal Right of Soldiers to Be Excused from Taking Part in Military Activities in the Occupied Territories', *Israel Law Review* 36 (2002), 73.

His representatives who should be seen as supreme. Many wars and conflicts around religious topics were fought by believers arguing over the source of true authority.

IV. PROTECTING THE SACRED

In this section we would like to explore the concept of 'sacred' objects and entities which we think is essential to an understanding of the tension between religion and the liberal state. We will start by exploring the idea that protection of the sacred is a major motivating factor in social conflicts around religious issues, first by showing how this idea helps us understand the behavior of religious groups, and then by arguing in short that this analysis also applies to the state.

Let us begin with an example. More than a decade ago, the first pride parade took place in Jerusalem. The city has a large ultra-Orthodox population. In the early years of the pride parade, the ultra-Orthodox passionately opposed the event.[45] In a striking contrast, the ultra-Orthodox leaders and populace were completely silent on the far more provocative parade which took place in Tel Aviv. More than this, some voices have explicitly called (and implicitly accepted) for the march to take place in Tel-Aviv.[46]

The common explanation for these different views is that Jerusalem is the residence for many Orthodox Jews, which results in their feelings being hurt by the parade. This is also how the phenomenon is understood in the legal context: the right to free expression and movement is balanced with the harming of religious feelings.[47]

We would like to suggest that this liberal prism both belittles and misunderstands the underlying dynamics of the situation.

What is infringed upon is not the feelings and peace of mind of the ultra-Orthodox population, but rather the perceived sanctity of the city of Jerusalem. For the ultra-Orthodox, the distinction between the parades in Tel Aviv (ignored) and Jerusalem (opposed) is not the size of the ultra-Orthodox population in the city, but rather the fact that Jerusalem is the holy city, while Tel Aviv is a profane, mundane one.

The concept of 'sacredness' as it is used here requires further explication. By describing Jerusalem as sacred, we do not mean that it is an exalted city or that it is closer to the Divine. Rather, the notion of sacrality we refer to is associated with the idea of 'taboo'. In the descriptions of classic anthropology we find the distinction

45 See Tzvi Trigger, 'Between Jerusalem and Umm Al-Fahm: The Pride Parade in Jerusalem and the Extreme Right Parade in Umm Al-Fahm in the Israeli Supreme Court's Rulings', *Hamishpat Law Review* 27 (2009), 61 (in Hebrew). It must be said that in recent years there has been a certain calm surrounding the parade. It became more conservative, and the ultra-Orthodox toned down the protest. That being said, recently an ultra-Orthodox man stabbed six people during the parade, killing one, but it was uniformly rejected by virtually all of the ultra-Orthodox leadership.

46 Chaim Shane, 'Please Do Not March in the Holy City', *Ynet* (18 June 2008), www.ynet.co.il/articles/0,7340,L-3557318,00.html (accessed 18 June 2008) (in Hebrew).

47 Statman (n. 30).

between two types of taboos: sacred taboo and impure taboo. In both cases the taboo can be an object, place, or person; and in both cases one must avoid going near a taboo (touching, entering a place, eating taboo food, having relations with a taboo person, etc.). Proximity to a taboo is seen as highly dangerous. The great similarity between the two taboos, the sacred and the impure, led James Frazer to wonder if there is any conceptual difference between them.[48] But as Mary Douglas showed in her classic work *Purity and Danger*, the major difference lies in the interest that the rule comes to protect. The impure taboo is not important in itself, and the distancing rule comes to protect the addressee of the rule. In contrast, keeping distance from a sacred taboo is meant, first and foremost, to protect it. This is the essential attribute of the sacred taboo – that it is vulnerable. Profaning a sacred object is seen as significantly harming it, which might result in great danger to the order of the world. A similar model exists in Jewish law and in other religions. Desecrating the sacred is not perceived as merely hurting the feelings of the believers, but as injuring the holy entity.

The construction of sacrality – that is, ascribing a dimension of sacredness to objects, places, people, and time – has a strong influence on directing behavior. The fact is that the world posited by religion both transcends and includes man. The sacred is confronted by man as a powerful reality other than himself. Yet this reality is addressed to him and helps him find himself in an ultimately meaningful order. Thus, the religious person finds herself with both the deep understanding of what is sacred, and the inability to compromise on the sacred.

The rules governing the sacred are not meant to protect the addressees of the law, but rather the interests of the sacred. It matters not who actually does the deed which harms the sacred. For the believer, standing idle while the sacred is profaned is impossible. Religion revolves around the sacred; it finds and sustains it in certain times, places, and people. The desecration of a sacred place, object, or person is understood as potentially world-destroying, a catastrophe.

So the protected interest of the ultra-Orthodox in their fight against the parade is not their feelings. They are also not especially interested in imposing their morals on the participants.[49] Rather, they care deeply about the perceived desecration of the holy city by what they call 'the abomination parade'.

The most radical group within the ultra-Orthodox population of Jerusalem are the 'Neturei Karta', that is – the guardians of the city. In their rhetoric, you will almost never find mention of having their emotions hurt; they will always refer to the 'Torah' or the sanctity of Jerusalem. The logic of sacrality produces an objectified

[48] James George Frazer, *The Golden Bough: A Study in Magic and Religion* (abridged edition, S. G. Phillips, 1959).

[49] Indeed, the major historian of Jewish Orthodoxy saw its defining trait as the disengagement with the rest of the Jewish population. See Jacob Katz, *A House Divided: Orthodoxy and Schism in Nineteenth-Century Central European Jewry* (Brandeis, 1998).

external interest for the religious group; it is not something that can be compromised.

The commitment to protect the sacred entity from desecration also helps understand what is dramatically called 'the Shabbat wars'. Ultra-Orthodox protest against the desecration of Shabbat in the public sphere, such as by driving and opening businesses during Shabbat. Here also, the common account assumes that the motivating factor behind the struggle is a paternalistic attempt to impose religious values, or preventing the hurt feelings of the religious man when he sees that others belittle what he sees as their duty. We believe that the main motive is the belief that the Shabbat itself is actually desecrated. From the viewpoint of the ultra-Orthodox, they must defend the sanctity of Shabbat. Tolerance and compromise are impossible, as he cannot relinquish what is not his in the first place. It is interesting to notice that the biblical commandment of keeping the Shabbat, such as in Exodus 31:16 – 'Wherefore the children of Israel shall keep the Shabbat' – is translated from the Hebrew verb 'shamor' which can also be understood as 'protect'. Thus, the commandment can be understood as protecting the Shabbat from harm by observing the rules.

At first, it appears that the mode of protecting the sacred is unique to a religious discourse; but, it is interesting to see that secular-liberal discourse has also developed a logic of sacrality and sacred entities that must be protected. In secular discourse these entities can be the law, democracy, the state, the nation, etc. All of these entities must be kept safe. The idea that secular state social institutions fulfil the same function as religious institutions can be traced back to (at least) Émile Durkheim. In his work Durkheim argued that something must replace the integration effect of religion in a secular society. He thought that the myths and symbols of nationalism as well as the passions it evokes are able to fill the void.[50] Ironically, as Mark Jurgensmeyer puts it, 'At the same time that religion in the West was becoming less political, its secular nationalism was becoming more religious.'[51] A famous variation of this point was made by Robert Bellah in his famous article, 'Civil Religion in America'. For him, civil religion was 'a collection of beliefs, symbols, and rituals with respect to sacred things'.[52] More recently, Anthony Smith suggested that the nation is a 'new religion of the people', one that is as 'binding, ritually repetitive and collectively enthusing'[53] as any other. Nationalism is a religion phenomenon which involves a 'system of beliefs and practices that distinguishes the sacred from the profane and unites its adherents in a single moral community of that faithful'.[54] In many countries, these religions of nationalism are deeply associated with democratic values, constitutionalism, and the rule of law. Seen this way, the

50 Émile Durkheim, *The Elementary Forms of the Religious Life* (Macmillan, 1912).

51 Mark Juergensmeyer, 'The Global Rise of Religious Nationalism', *Australian Journal of International Affairs* 64 (2010), 262, 263.

52 Robert N. Bellah, 'Civil Religion in America' *Daedalus* (1967), 1, 3.

53 D. Smith Anthony, *Chosen Peoples: Sacred Sources of National Identity* (Oxford University Press, 2003), 4–5.

54 Ibid., 15.

expression 'to keep the law' adopts a different meaning: to protect that institution of law from harm. We believe this rhetoric, often loudest in polemics with religious groups, come as a counter-weight to the sacrality-based arguments of religious groups. When the head of the open house – the organisation which runs the LGBT pride parade in Jerusalem – was asked why they would not be willing to move the parade to Jerusalem, she answered that they would be willing to compromise, but that doing so would harm democracy and the rule of law. The interest represented in the rule of law is reified into a sacred, independent entity that requires protection.

V. CONCLUSION

In this chapter we challenged the standard account of conflicts of religion and state, which sees them as being centered on questions of content; we suggested this account fails to explain the intractability of these conflicts, and that in order to gain better understanding, we should be aware of the dual dynamics of the struggle over ultimate authority and the protection of the sacred. In relation to the struggle over authority, we argued that the content of the disagreements between religious groups and the state often seems unable to plausibly explain the sheer intensity of this struggle and the public uproar it creates. We believe that this is due to the nature of competition over supreme authority, which naturally leads to a lack of ability to compromise. Complementing the struggle over authority is the need (especially, but not only, for the religious side) of protecting the sacred. The sacred is experienced as being supremely important, external to man, and vulnerable to desecration. It is hard to compromise over something held to be sacred because its interests are not your own; they are grounded in the eternal.

In a way, the two dynamics discussed in this chapter are mutually constitutive. The sacred, that which is inviolable, is experienced as being grounded in the foundations of reality. Being beyond human ken allows it to legitimate authority in a more effective way. The competition over authority between the modern nation state (in our case, Israel) and religion (in our case, Judaism) happens at this foundational level. At the same time, the idea that the sacred (and the legitimacy that is dependent on it) is vulnerable and requires protection is crucial in order to understand the competition over authority. Indeed, both the religious and the statist communities require and struggle for authority in order to be able to protect the sacred.

Our arguments were grounded in cultural interpretation; the primary importance of such an analysis is interpretative and descriptive. They gain a critical edge when contrasted with the standard account of law and religion. In this sense our essay should be understood as a critique of the shortcomings of the standard account. Although the types of arguments we engaged in do not lend themselves easily to the development of clear-cut prescriptive recommendations, we believe that in order to better handle these pressing issues, the struggle for ultimate authority and the commitment to protect sacred entities and values must be taken into account.

4

Jurisdictional versus Official Control: Regulating the Buddhist Saṅgha in South and Southeast Asia*

Benjamin Schonthal

I. INTRODUCTION

When scholars write about the legal regulation of religion, they often write about laws that limit the ways in which citizens express and practice religion. Common examples of regulating religion, therefore, include things such as ordinances restricting proselytising, ritual slaughter or amplifying religious prayers. These are common examples for a reason. According to most domestic constitutions and all major instruments of international law, proselytising, ritualising and praying are all legitimate objects of state regulation. This is because they are all understood to be 'manifestations' of religion, practices that – according to the logic these laws – emerge from, and are secondary to, individuals' religious *beliefs*.[1] Whereas practitioners may believe whatever they like, their religious practices can be limited in the interests of, for example, public order, public morality or the rights of others. Religious belief (the *forum internum*) is therefore the realm of pure freedom, while religious practice (the *forum externum*) is the realm of acceptable regulation.

If one starts from this common scholarly and legal perspective, it is easy to think of the legal regulation of religion in rather narrow terms, as approximating state interference in the outward activities, or manifestations, of religious individuals and groups. This perspective, however, overlooks another important feature of state law's influence on religion: the ways in which legal instruments and actors define and delimit religious institutions and authority. Before the state can regulate the practices of religious groups, it must first establish the status of those groups. That is, it must draw boundaries, sometimes overlapping ones, between those institutions and persons who embody and mobilise the power of the state and those who are considered to embody and mobilise the power of 'religion'. The legal regulation of

* Parts of this chapter are reprinted from my article, 'Formations of Buddhist Constitutionalism in South and Southeast Asia', *International Journal of Constitutional Law* 15.3 (2017), 705733.

[1] Elizabeth Shakman Hurd, *Beyond Religious Freedom: The New Global Politics of Religion* (Princeton University Press, 2015).

religion has, therefore, a central institutional or bureaucratic dimension, which is concerned less with protecting or circumscribing the religious freedoms of devotees than with clarifying and managing the boundaries of civil and religious authority.

Distinguishing civil and religious authority is, of course, not a new idea in studies of religion and law. The urge to prise apart or define 'church' and 'state' has been central to political and scholarly understandings of liberal legalism for centuries, and has been entrenched in legal ideals such as 'disestablishment' (in the case of the United States) and *laïcité* (in the case of France). What is new, in recent years, is scholars' insistence that these acts of separation are not and cannot be neutral acts of dividing and categorising an already-binary reality. Winnifred Sullivan, Saba Mahmood, Beth Hurd and others have demonstrated how the act of distinguishing religious and state authority requires that lawmakers identify what is 'religious' in the first place; and this, in turn, requires acts of administrative discretion and power – that is, regulation.[2]

Viewed as an act of regulation (rather than categorisation), projects of managing religious and state authority in self-declaredly secular jurisdictions look surprisingly similar to projects of managing religious and state authority in legal regimes that neither claim nor aspire to be rigorously impartial towards religion. If the defining feature of 'secular' law (the mandate to distinguish civil and religious authority) is itself an act of regulation then it also must be true that the defining feature of 'non-secular' law (the mandate to secure or support a particular religion) is equally an act of regulation.[3] That is, in regulating religious practice, both secular and non-secular legal regimes define and manage – that is, regulate – religious authority.

In this chapter, I want to make this point using two case studies taken from a group of legal regimes that has, to date, received inadequate attention in the literature on law and religion, the Buddhist-majority states of states of South and Southeast Asia (herein: Southern Asia). In their own ways, the legal regimes of Sri Lanka, Myanmar, Bhutan, Thailand, Cambodia and Laos all give special legal status and/or protections to Buddhism. Moreover, in each of these countries, lawmakers have engaged in projects of *Buddhist constitutionalism*, attempts to use written constitutions *and* other basic laws to organise power in ways that protect and preserve Buddhist teachings and institutions. While these legal projects have taken different forms, they have all involved attempts to manage the relationship between civil and Buddhist institutions, especially the institution of Buddhist monasticism, the *saṅgha*, which is traditionally understood to embody Buddhist religious authority.[4]

2 Ibid.; Saba Mahmood, 'Secularism, Hermeneutics, and Empire: The Politics of Islamic Reformation', *Public Culture* 18 (2006), 323; Winnifred Fallers Sullivan, *The Impossibility of Religious Freedom* (Princeton University Press, 2005).

3 Benjamin Schonthal, 'The Impossibility of a Buddhist State', *Asian Journal of Law and Society* 3 (2016), 29.

4 In focusing on the role of constitutions and basic laws in 'organising power' rather than limiting power, I follow the work of Nathan Brown. Nathan J. Brown, *Constitutions in a Nonconstitutional World: Arab Basic Laws and the Prospects for Accountable Government* (SUNY Press, 2012), 12.

Lawmakers in Southern Asia tend to talk about this process as one of supporting and protecting the monkhood, by assuring that both state and *saṅgha* perform their roles properly. However, as the following discussion will make clear, defining and managing the *saṅgha*–state relationship has involved clear strategies of regulation.

The two case studies examined in this chapter are those of Thailand and Sri Lanka, both Theravada-majority countries in Southern Asia. Using a comparative historical examination, I seek to explain how and why each country has come to adopt a distinctive mode of regulating the Buddhist monkhood: Thailand has developed a model of regulation which places Buddhist monks under governmental and royal control, while Sri Lanka has developed a model of regulation which manages the *saṅgha* by specifying for it separate areas of autonomy, or jurisdictions. I refer to these models of regulation as *official control* and *jurisdictional control* respectively.[5] Looking at the nineteenth- and twentieth-century histories of these countries, one can see how both modes of regulation emerge not simply as the product of elite decision-making, but develop in response to specific historical factors. These factors include the character of premodern and modern political regimes; the structure of Buddhist monastic hierarchies; and the presence or absence of monarchy, colonial regimes and military governments. Moreover, each model of regulation has produced its own distinctive types of regulatory crises involving state agents and Buddhist monks – crises that are ongoing today.

II. THAILAND: OFFICIAL CONTROL

Compared with its South and Southeast Asian neighbors, Thailand has the most complete and comprehensive legal and bureaucratic structures for regulating monks. Thailand's government recognises and oversees a formal monastic hierarchy that stretches, in theory, to all parts of the country. These structures of authority are bolstered and administered by special state institutions as well as a specific statute, the Saṅgha Act of 1962 (amended in 1991 and 2017), which is the third in a series of similar Saṅgha Acts enacted by Thai kings and governments since 1902.

As laid out in the 1962 Act, Thai monks come under the authority of a single monastic ruler, the Supreme Patriarch (Thai: *sanghkarat*; Pali: *saṅgha-rāja*), who is appointed by the king from a list of qualified candidates.[6] In reigning over the pyramidal structure of Buddhist monks in Thailand, the Supreme Patriarch acts on the advice of a council of senior Buddhist monks called the Council of Elders

[5] I have referred to these in 'Formations of Buddhist Constitutionalism in South and Southeast Asia', *International Journal of Constitutional Law* 15.3 (2017), 705–33.

[6] Until recently, the king followed a norm of appointing the most senior member of the Council of Elders. However, on 6 January 2017, General Prayuth and the Prime Minister issued an amendment to the Saṅgha Act specifying that the king has full discretion to appoint the *saṅgha rāja* (more on this later). Saṅgha Act (Amendment) No. 3 of 2017 as contained in *Royal Thai Government Gazette*, Vol. 134, Part II. (I thank Mark Charoenwong for pointing this out and Akbordin Rattana for translating the relevant section.)

(*mahatherasamakhom*), whom he partially appoints.[7] A lay bureaucrat, the Director-General of the Office of National Buddhism,[8] also sits on the Council as ex officio Secretary-General; and the Director-General's office serves officially as the meeting place for the Council (Article 13). Thus, in its administrative structure and physical location, the influence of the king and state officials over the Council is clear. State influence is further assured by the requirement that the Council gain the signature of the relevant minister before issuing an order to dismiss or appoint monks. When it comes to the powers of the Supreme Patriarch, the Saṅgha Act specifies that he may 'govern' the country's monks provided his *dicta* do not contravene the Theravāda code of monastic discipline (*Vinaya*), existing laws passed by the Council, or any of the orders and laws enacted by the state (Article 8).

Under the terms of the Saṅgha Act, the Supreme Patriarch and the Council of Elders – along with the state officers who participate in and help administer the Council – have formal, legal authority over monks in Thailand. The Council exercises this power through a carefully designed hierarchy that parallels that of Thailand's civil administration. The Council of Elders stands at the apex of a pyramid of 'ecclesiastical governors' (*chaokhana*) and subcouncils at the regional, provincial, district and sub-district levels. In principle, these authorities reign over the abbots of individual temples throughout the country.[9] The Act seeks to ensure the top-down power of this system by empowering higher-ranking officials to appoint lower-ranking ones (Article 22). In this way, the Council's orders and regulations are imagined to flow 'down' to individual temples. The Act also gives the Council final say in all matters of monastic discipline. By law, the Council has the power to disrobe monks who do not conform to its standards (Articles 24–30). This hierarchical network also gives the Council significant powers over movable and immovable temple property. The Saṅgha Act vests monastic property in trust with the individual temples (which are classified as juristic persons), while also giving the *saṅgha* hierarchy and Department of National Buddhism ultimate oversight over that property. Similarly, any new temple construction or renovation must receive approval from the Council (Article 32).[10]

7 The Council consists of monks who have reached the highest monastic rank (*somdet*, currently ten monks) along with several other monks from the second-highest ecclesiastical rank (*ratchakhana*). *Ratchakhana*-rank Council members are selected by the Patriarch, himself, and they serve for renewable two-year terms (Saṅgha Act, Arts. 12, 14). There are sixty-two levels of monastic rank in the modern Thai system and progression through the hierarchy is based on performance in state-administered ecclesiastical exams as well as one's service and reputation.

8 Before 2002, this was the Director-General of the Department of Religious Affairs. The change was made in response to popular demands that the official *saṅgha* should not be overseen by a bureau responsible for *religious* affairs, but special bureau for Buddhist matters only. Putsasi Theerasuvat, *Buddhism as a Factor in Thai Politics: 1963–1992*, PhD dissertation, JNU, Jawaharlal Nehru University, 118.

9 S. J. Tambiah, *World Conqueror and World Renouncer: A Study of Buddhism and Polity in Thailand against a Historical Background* (Cambridge University Press, 1977), 366.

10 Interview with Dr. Amnaj Buasiri, Deputy Director for the Department of Religious Affairs (Bangkok, Thailand, 21 December 2011).

In its conception and application, then, the 1962 Saṅgha Act is specifically designed to bring hierarchical order to the *saṅgha*, such that it can be regulated and, in certain cases, put to use by the state.[11] This fact is borne out in the history of drafting the 1962 version of the Act. Field Marshall Sarit introduced the 1962 law after his coup as a way to shore up the military government's power over the *saṅgha* and to repeal the effects of a 1941 law, which in Sarit's view had inappropriately introduced democratic and decentralised procedures into the national *saṅgha* hierarchy. As with Thai society generally, Sarit believed that too much democracy in the *saṅgha* would produce strife and dissension.[12] Starting in the 1960s, Sarit used the newly centralised system as a way to help put Thai monks in service of broader government goals. These goals involved deploying monks to combat communism in the North and East and helping inculcate among rural villagers a standardised 'national' (central Thai) culture, language, worldview and way of practicing Buddhism.[13]

A. *Nineteenth-Century Developments*

This modern system of centralised *saṅgha* administration grows out of a longer history of attempts to centralise, standardise and control monastic groups. While there is a very old history of royal control over the *saṅgha* in the lands that are today controlled by modern-day Thailand,[14] the origins of Thailand's contemporary Saṅgha Act can be traced more directly to the late 1700s. From 1782, following the establishment of the Chakri dynasty in Bangkok (the dynasty that still reigns today), Thai kings introduced a series of regulations and administrative decrees designed to standardise monastic life and bring it more closely under the control of the king. In 1782, King Rama I declared the first of ten '*saṅgha* laws' that aimed to regulate the activities of monks as well as the relationships between monks and laity.[15] These decrees proscribed certain behaviors, which were considered to be unbecoming for Buddhist clergy. They also empowered royal officers to audit monastic conduct and, if necessary, recommend that certain monks be disciplined.[16]

11 One of the first clauses of the 1962 Saṅgha Act clarifies that it is the Minister of Education, not the Supreme Patriarch, who shall have ultimate control over implementing the terms of the Act (Article 6).

12 Yoneo Ishii, *Saṅgha, State and Society: Thai Buddhism in History* (University of Hawaii Press, 1986), 113.

13 Thak Chaloemtiarana, *Thailand: The Politics of Despotic Paternalism* (Cornell University Press, 2007); Charles F. Keyes, 'Buddhism and National Integration in Thailand', *The Journal of Asian Studies* 30 (1971), 551.

14 Ishii (n. 13) 62; P. Jory, *Thailand's Theory of Monarchy: The Vessantara Jataka and the Idea of the Perfect Man* (SUNY Press, 2016).

15 C. J. Reynolds, *The Buddhist Monkhood in Nineteenth Century Thailand*, PhD dissertation, Cornell University, 1973, 36.

16 Ibid.

Over the course of the century, other Chakri kings expanded on the regulatory programs introduced by Rama I. In 1859, King Rama IV (King Mongkut) implemented a comprehensive registration system for all temples patronised by members of the royal family. This program required the abbots of those temples to submit registries of local monks to district officials, who would then convey them to Bangkok. By 1902, King Rama V (King Chulalongkorn) introduced the first Saṅgha Act, extending this system of registration to *all* Buddhist temples (royal and 'ordinary temples') within the newly established borders of the Thai state.[17]

The goal of these nineteenth-century reforms was the creation of a single, unified *saṅgha*, which – like Thailand's new, modern bureaucracy – would be uniformly disciplined, educated and loyal to the king. With these goals in mind, the Chakri kings attempted to integrate and reform the country's multiple monastic orders. Prior to these reforms, monastic groups (*khanas*) formed along multiple lines of affiliation, such as affiliations to a particular teacher, region or language. Thailand's monks were also divided into two major fraternities (*nikai*), which continue to operate to this day: the Thammayut, a small fraternity founded by then-Prince Mongkut in 1833 and associated with the royal family, and the Mahanikai, or 'great fraternity' consisting of all other monks.

In strengthening and centralising the monastic hierarchy, Chakri kings, and especially Rama V, sought to give the *saṅgha* more centripetal force. Although framed in the language of monastic purification and reform, this process of centralisation had the effects of elevating royal and state authority over that of monks. It was the king who appointed the Patriarch and other high-ranking monks, and those royally endorsed monks (disproportionately from the Thammayut Nikai) oversaw the promotions of monks underneath them. The system of ranks was reinforced by the hierarchical distribution privileges and honors. High-ranking clerics received honorary titles, cash stipends, preferred seating position in large ceremonies, monastic secretaries and assistants, explicit grants of authority over temples and temple lands and powers to adjudicate disputes among monks.[18]

From the middle of the century, bonds of blood further solidified the links between *saṅgha* and the king. Royal monks (princes in the Thai monarchy) increasingly came to serve as high-ranking members of the official *saṅgha*. In 1851, the Chakri dynasty achieved an unprecedented linking of royal and monastic power: a high-ranking prince in the royal family became the head of the kingdom's monks; and a high-ranking monk, who had been genealogically in line for the throne, cast off his robes to take the position of king.[19] These close familial links between monastic leaders and the royal family would endure for most of the nineteenth century, as would the disproportionate representation of Thammayut Nikai monks

[17] Ishii (n. 13), 72.
[18] Reynolds (n. 16).
[19] Ibid.

in the official monastic hierarchy.[20] This close collaboration of kings, royal officials and prince-monks would help to build a thoroughly state-controlled system for overseeing, disciplining, registering and credentialing monks.

B. Thai Regulatory Crises

The regulation of the *saṅgha* in Thailand is a project that has roots dating back more than two centuries. It is also a project driven by an attempt to use law and formal institutions to centralise and encompass the powers and authority of Buddhist monks. Although the formal *saṅgha* hierarchy does not influence all of Thai monastic life,[21] it does give rise to distinctive types of regulatory crises, involving struggles over the recognition and control of monastic groups that do not conform with the standards of practice endorsed by the Council of Elders. In fact, tense struggles of this type followed almost immediately after the introduction of the first Saṅgha Act in 1902 (a similar law to the 1962 Act) and have continued to crop up periodically in the intervening decades.

Between 1908 and 1935, a major struggle over monastic recognition and control took shape in the northern Thai region of Lanna, involving a charismatic monk from the northern Yuan tradition of Buddhism, named Kruba Siwichai.[22] By most accounts, Siwichai did not set out to rebel against centralised monastic authority. Rather, his transgressions resulted directly from the gradual extension of monastic regulations to Lanna, which, until the late 1800s, had existed as a separate tributary polity. On three separate occasions, *saṅgha* authorities charged Siwichai for violating rules of monastic discipline by engaging in what were, at that time, customary practices in Lanna. At the core of his trials was the accusation that Siwichai had performed illegal ordinations. What made them illegal was that Siwichai did not gain approval from the local state-appointed *saṅgha* official. They were also illegal because Siwichai, although a senior monk, had failed to register himself as an *upajjhaya*, a monk with the authority to ordain other monks. Refusing to renounce or reform his behaviors, Siwichai was detained on multiple occasions by representatives of the government. However, his popularity as a religious leader made it

20 Duncan McCargo, 'The Changing Politics of Thailand's Buddhist Order', *Critical Asian Studies* 44 (2012), 627, 637. McCargo calculates that, among the eight patriarchs of the Council of Elders between 1932 and 2012, five have been from the less populous Thammayut sect and only three from the more populous Mahanikai. More telling, though, is McCargo's estimation that Thammayut patriarchs held office for seventy of eighty years because the three Mahanikai monks had only short tenures in office.

21 Justin McDaniel, *The Lovelorn Ghost and the Magical Monk: Practicing Buddhism in Modern Thailand* (Columbia University Press, 2013).

22 Information in this paragraph comes from the MA work (in progress) of Thongtida Krawaengit as well as Katherine Bowie, 'The Saint with Indra's Sword: Khruubaa Srivichai and Buddhist Millenarianism in Northern Thailand', *Comparative Studies in Society and History* 56 (2014), 681; Katherine Bowie, 'Of Buddhism and Militarism in Northern Thailand: Solving the Puzzle of the Saint Khruubaa Srivichai', *The Journal of Asian Studies* 73 (2014), 711; Keyes (n. 14).

difficult for state agents to coerce him into cooperation. On several occasions over the course of his trials, Siwichai's supporters rallied to his defense, intimidating would-be state disciplinarians. In the end a tense détente was reached by Siwichai performing his obedience through signing a document pledging that he would abide by the terms of the 1902 Saṅgha Act, even though in practice his activities seem to have carried on.

The trials of Siwichai show early examples of how the project of centralising state authority over the monkhood generated conflicts over the activities and recognition of particular monks and monastic groups. By creating a hierarchical, centralised monastic institution, with a mandate to standardise and order monastic life throughout the country, the Thai state positioned itself and its official monastic body as the arbiters and enforcers of monastic orthopraxy. In so doing, it created the possibilities for implicating the state in conflicts over heteropraxy. In the case of Siwichai, conflicts over ordination (and other monastic activities) overlapped with conflicts over regional independence for Lanna: embedded in the contest between Siwichai and central authorities were other contests over Lanna's cultural, linguistic and political independence from Bangkok. Bangkok authorities viewed Siwichai not simply as a threat to their version of Buddhist orthodoxy, but also as a charismatic figure around whom political resistance might be organised.[23]

In recent decades, one can observe a similar pattern. As with Siwichai, contemporary Thai regulations have continued to generate conflicts over monastic membership and control, which often overlap with other salient political and social divides. Similarly, these conflicts have tended to involve Buddhist monastic groups that acquire popularity and wealth outside the official *saṅgha's* structures of power. In contemporary Thailand, the most important and influential Buddhist movement of this type is Wat Phra Dhammakaya, a temple and monastic organisation that started around 1970. In recent decades, the Dhammakaya movement has grown quickly. It is now the wealthiest Buddhist organisation in Thailand and one of the most popular. The group's teachings differ from the standardised Buddhism of the official *saṅgha* hierarchy. Dhammakaya recommends a special style of meditation, expounds a unique doctrine of enlightenment and advocates a style of religiosity that, for many critics, looks more like US-style mega-churches than traditional Thai temples. (Thammakaya's 800-acre temple complex outside of Bangkok attracts as many 100,000 worshippers on holidays.[24]) Teaching these practices and doctrines, and relying on a very sophisticated outreach and media apparatus, the Dhammakaya

[23] Kruba Siwichai is just one example. There are many other examples of Buddhist holymen who share similar characteristics. Taylor M. Easum, 'A Thorn in Bangkok's Side Khruba Sriwichai, Sacred Space and the Last Stand of the Pre-Modern Chiang Mai State', *South East Asia Research* 21(2013), 211; Amporn Jirattikorn, 'Buddhist Holy Man Khruba Bunchum: The Shift in a Millenarian Movement at the Thailand–Myanmar Border', *Sojourn: Journal of Social Issues in Southeast Asia* 31 (2016), 377.

[24] Rachelle Scott, *Nirvana for Sale? Buddhism, Wealth, and the Dhammakaya Temple in Contemporary Thailand* (SUNY Press, 2009), 52.

movement has garnered considerable support, particularly from upwardly mobile middle-class urbanites, including a number of powerful business and political leaders.[25] This popular support has also translated into financial support: through a variety of fund-raising efforts, coupled with the sale of merchandise and ritual donations, Dhammakaya has raised billions of baht. It has also attracted the scorn of critics who accuse the group of advocating an ethos of crass materialism.[26]

Under the centralised regime of monastic authority, the rise of a new Buddhist monastic group, with an alternative style of religious practice as well as a strong base of popular support, is threatening on two levels. On one level, *saṅgha* authorities in Thailand view Dhammakaya's version of Buddhism as a threat to orthodoxy, one that requires the reform or disrobing of heterodox monks. On multiple occasions, from the 1998 onwards, the Council of Elders, the Supreme Patriarch and government officers have filed charges against the chief abbot and monks of the Dhammakaya, including allegations of misappropriating temple property, misinterpreting Buddhist teachings, constructing improper Buddhist images, improperly marketing itself and falsely claiming to have performed miracles.[27] On another level, once labeled as heterodox, these groups, if powerful, can pose a second type of challenge to the official *saṅgha* and the Thai state. This challenge consists in the fact that monks who are accused of heterodoxy may refuse to accede to the *dicta* of the Council or Supreme Patriarch, even when those *dicta* are backed by the coercive powers of the state – thereby exposing the weakness of the official (monastic and state) system as well as confirming the de facto independence of monastic groups that can mobilise large numbers of people.

This is exactly what has happened from the 1990s to 2017 in the case of Dhammakaya. *Saṅgha* authorities have found it extremely difficult to control or 'downgrade the status' of a movement so popular and powerful.[28] For example, during the course of investigations from 1998 to 2000, the chief abbot of Dhammakaya refused to attend a number of disciplinary meetings. In addition, he publicly challenged the moral authority of both the official *saṅgha* authorities and of state officials. Although the chief abbot ultimately agreed to transfer certain property titles out of his own name and into a temple trust (a key demand made by officials), state authorities appeared to have no choice but to drop all other charges.[29] This

25 Rachelle Scott, 'A New Buddhist Sect? The Dhammakāya Temple and the Politics of Religious Difference', *Religion* 36(2006), 215; James L. Taylor, 'New Buddhist Movements in Thailand: An "Individualistic Revolution", Reform and Political Dissonance', *Journal of Southeast Asian Studies* 21(1990), 135; Edwin Zehner, 'Reform Symbolism of a Thai Middle-Class Sect: The Growth and Appeal of the Thammakai Movement', *Journal of Southeast Asian Studies* 21 (1990), 402.

26 Rory Mackenzie, *New Buddhist Movements in Thailand: Towards an Understanding of Wat Phra Dhammakaya and Santi Asoke* (Routledge, 2007), 90.

27 Scott (n. 25), 138.

28 One proposal was to downgrade Wat Phra Dhammakaya from a monastery to a meditation centre. Danna Marie Cook, *Wat Phra Dhammakāya: Competition and Authoritative Conflict with the Thai Monastic Elite*, MA dissertation, Arizona State University, 2009, 56.

29 Ibid.

retreat from prosecution reflected the influence of Dhammakaya supporters, which, like the supporters of Siwichai in the early 1900s, succeeded in using popular and political power to defend the group's independence.

Today, the situation has grown even more tense, with the Thai junta taking a much more aggressive posture towards investigating and charging the head monk of Dhammakaya. As before, the chief abbot has refused to cooperate with special investigators and has ignored summons. This time, however, the regime responded by ordering a massive, police siege of Dhammakaya's main temple, blocking people and essential supplies from entering, in an effort to force the abbot out of hiding. As before, 'disciplining' Dhammakaya has been challenging, requiring drastic and alarming power-plays on the part of the state. In pursuing Dhammakaya, the junta has taken a no-holds-barred approach and made use of emergency-style powers (listed under the controversial Article 44 of the interim 2016 Constitution) to reassert the state's position as the ultimate supervisor and arbiter of legitimate monastic authority in Thailand. In early 2017, the regime even took the dramatic step of amending the Saṅgha Act to give the king (and the regime) even greater say in appointing the Supreme Patriarch. General Prayuth pursued this amendment, most observers note, in order to avoid the appointment of a senior Mahanikai monk who – although he served as acting Patriarch after the death of the previous Patriarch in 2013 and was nominated for the position by the Council of Elders – had been resistant to the junta and friendly with Dhammakaya's head abbot.[30]

As seen in the case of Kruba Sivichai and Dhammakaya, particular types of crises accompany Thai-style *saṅgha* regulations. These regulations give the state formal powers to control monks though creating and overseeing an official monastic hierarchy. This official hierarchy has, however, been unable to exert total control over popular monastic groups and has led to significant conflicts at the margins. Where the state cannot formally co-opt and control popular monastic movements, it creates tense standoffs between semi-autonomous monastic groups and the state *saṅgha* authorities. This essentially leaves state and official *saṅgha* authorities with two options for dealing with would-be independent sects: controlling/coopting them or disrobing them – making monastic conflicts a high-stakes game that, as recent events indicate, a control-minded regime cannot afford to lose. On the other side, monks who value autonomy, or object to the state-monastic curriculum, or feel slighted by the system of ranks and promotions are left with few options too. They must either operate outside of the system, as in the case of Siwichai (or the reformist movement, Santi Asoke[31] or Thailand's Buddhist nuns[32]); or seek some kind of

[30] 'Senior Monk Backs Off as Saṅgha Act Amended' *The Nation* (Thailand, 30 December 2016), www.nationmultimedia.com/news/national/30303136 (accessed 18 March 2017).

[31] Mackenzie (n. 27).

[32] Martin Seeger, 'The Bhikkhunī Ordination Controversy in Thailand', *Journal of the International Association of Buddhist Studies* 29 (2009), 155.

awkward accommodation within the system, as in the case of Dhammakaya in the late 1990s; or, in extreme cases, directly resist state control and risk being the targets of coercion, as in the case of Dhammakaya since 2016.

III. SRI LANKA: JURISDICTIONAL CONTROL

If Thailand's mode of monastic regulation gives power to royal and government officials, the Sri Lankan mode gives significant power and autonomy to monks themselves. As in Thailand, there are sociological and historical reasons for this. Saṅgha regulation, in its Sri Lankan guise, emerges within a monastic milieu different from that of Thailand. Sri Lanka's monastic orders are far more decentralised and autonomous than those of Thailand. In fact, the desire to protect monastic autonomy was a key driver in writing the 'Buddhism Chapter' of Sri Lanka's current constitution, which gives to Buddhism the 'foremost place' and obligates the state to protect and foster its teaching and institutions. Sri Lanka's constitution drafters decided on the phrase 'foremost place' as an alternative to declaring Buddhism the 'state religion' because of pressure from the island's Buddhist monks. Those monks rejected the proposed phrase 'state religion (Sinhala: *rajyāgama*)' worrying that it might give state officials supervisory powers to regulate Buddhist monks.[33]

As the story about constitution drafting indicates, Sri Lankan monks have been very resistant to attempts on the part of the state to exert control over the monkhood. Sri Lanka has never developed an equivalent to the Thai Council of Elders. No single island-wide hierarchy, official or unofficial, structures the monkhood. Separate hierarchies exist within each of the island's three major independent fraternities, or *Nikāya-s*: the *Siyam Nikāya, Amarapura Nikāya* and *Rāmañña Nikāya*. (The fraternities are named for the areas to which they trace their ordination lineages: Siyam or Siam, and Amarapura and Rāmañña in present-day Myanmar.) The Siyam Nikāya is the largest and oldest fraternity; and it has its headquarters in Kandy, the site of the island's last Buddhist kingdom (until its conquest by the British in 1815). The Rāmañña and Amarapura Nikāya-s were established later and have their major centers in the southern and western parts of the island. Roughly half of the island's monks belong to the Siyam Nikāya, while the rest divide among Amarapura and Rāmañña Nikāya-s.[34]

Although Buddhists in Sri Lanka often refer to the island's monks as part of a single great community of monks (*mahā-saṅgha*), in practice deep principles of division separate the fraternities. These divisions relate to location, pupillary lineage

[33] Benjamin Schonthal, *Buddhism, Politics and the Limits of Law: The Pyrrhic Constitutionalism of Sri Lanka* (Cambridge University Press, 2016), chapter 4.

[34] Department of Buddhist Affairs of the Government of Sri Lanka, *Vihārasthāna hā Bhikṣūn Vahansē Saṅgaṇanaya ('Censurs of Bhikkhus and Temples')* (Government Press, 2012). Obtained from the Department of Buddhist Affairs in 2013. The official statistics here calculate the monastic population as follows: 53% Siyam Nikāya, 28% Amarapura Nikāya and 19% Rāmañña Nikāya.

and especially caste (*kula*).[35] Moreover, two of the three major fraternities are also internally segmented, containing dozens of autonomous subgroups: these are called chapters (*pārśava*) in the case of the Siyam Nikāya and, confusingly, called 'fraternities' (*niyāka* [I will use the lowercase 'n' to distinguish in transliteration]) in the case of the Amarapura Nikāya.[36] These subgroups go by different proper names, maintain distinctive organisational structures and perform their own separate higher ordination ceremonies.[37] They also differ slightly in how they dress, interpret disciplinary codes and practice rituals. In 2012, the Department of Buddhist Affairs, the government office charged with liaising with the island's monks, recorded eight separate subgroups within the Siyam Nikāya and twenty-one separate subgroups within the Amarapura Nikāya.[38] Other statistics from 1989, quoted by one scholar in 2002, put the total number of sub-fraternities at forty-three.[39] In both cases, one can assume that the actual number of independent subgroups is larger than reported figures, as those figures do not include non-registered subgroups.[40] In some cases, separations among these subgroups may be almost as great as those of the fraternities.

A. *Regulating Monastic Property*

Already one can see that, compared to the closely centralised and regulated hierarchy of the Thai system, the Sri Lankan government recognises *saṅgha* segmentation at many levels. The depth and persistence of this segmentation relate closely to the ways in which the monastic groups and the state regulate monastic property, which differ considerably from those in Thailand. In most Thai temples, the chief monk, or abbot, administers temple property in consultation with a group of lay trustees. Officially, this happens under the supervision of regional, district, provincial and country-wide superior monks. By contrast, in most Sri Lankan temples, the abbot – or *vihāradipati* (literally 'temple governor') – has considerable independence and relatively little oversight from the state. While there are some formal statutory restrictions on what abbots may and may not do with temple property (see later), they have considerable discretion in the use and transfer of property. Moreover, and in further contrast to the Thai system, civil courts rather than

35 Kitsiri Malalgoda, *Buddhism in Sinhalese Society, 1750–1900: A Study of Religious Revival and Change* (University of California Press, 1976).

36 The Rāmañña Nikāya alone is free from formal subsects. However, other principles of division apply. According to one author writing in the mid-970s, the Rāmañña Nikāya did indeed include splits into two 'sections' according to caste lines. Urmila Phadnis, *Religion and Politics in Sri Lanka* (South Asia Books, 1976), 55.

37 Steven Kemper, 'Reform and Segmentation in Monastic Fraternities in Low Country Sri Lanka', *The Journal of Asian Studies* 40(1980), 27.

38 Department of Buddhist Afffairs of the Government of Sri Lanka (n. 35).

39 Ananda Abeysekara, *Colors of the Robe: Religion, Identity, and Difference* (University of South Carolina Press, 2002), 178.

40 Ibid.

monastic tribunals have ultimate authority for adjudicating disputes over temple lands in Sri Lanka. In Sri Lanka, property disputes often appear first in monastic tribunals (*adhikaraṇa-s*) or assemblies (*sabhā-s*) within a given monastic chapter. However, if disputes cannot be resolved there, they can be (and in many cases are) appealed to civil courts, where civil court judges hear them. This means that Sri Lanka's civil courts see a considerable number of cases involving disputes among two or more monks over the control of temple property. One lawyer who appears regularly in these types of cases estimates that there are approximately forty cases per year.[41]

If the regulation of the *saṅgha* in Thailand is felt primarily around the regulation of membership, hierarchy and discipline, in Sri Lanka it orients primarily in the adjudication of disputes over temple property. In addition to the texts and procedures used by fraternities (and subchapters) to manage property disputes, two bodies of state law also address these disputes: an ordinance, introduced first in the late colonial period, called the Buddhist Temporalities Ordinance (temporalities being the term given to the matter of Buddhist properties by the British, who first drafted a law of this type [see later]); and a body of common law that dates back to the early 1800s, before the introduction of any statute or ordinance, referred to as Buddhist Ecclesiastical Law.

The Buddhist Temporalities Ordinance (most recently amended in 2013) lays out rules for how to manage the property of Buddhist temples. For all 'ordinary' Buddhist temples, which constitute the vast majority of temples on the island, the Ordinance specifies that property is controlled by a trustee who is appointed for a five-year term by the abbot of the temple. As the abbots may appoint themselves as trustees, today in Sri Lanka most abbots are also trustees for the temple. The Ordinance prohibits trustees from selling land or property or from using temple income for purposes other than maintaining the temple, supporting monks, paying temple workers, promoting Buddhist education, performing regular rituals, assisting the poor and covering administration costs and legal expenses related to the preservation of temple property.[42] The Ordinance also charges the Commissioner of the Department of Buddhist Affairs, usually a career civil servant rather than an expert in Buddhism, with monitoring the rules. However, Commissioners rarely intervene punitively in monastic affairs, which means that abbots/trustees have considerable flexibility in how they acquire, use and dispose of temple income.

Thus, in a context of decentralised authority, the temple abbot has significant control over monastic life: he manages temple property, governs local monastic affairs and has fairly independent authority over the monks who reside with him.[43]

[41] Interview with a lawyer and specialist in Buddhist ecclesiastical law who regularly appears in these cases (17 December 2014, Colombo).

[42] Buddhist Temporalities Ordinance No. 19 of 1931, amended most recently by Buddhist Temporalities (Amendment) Act No. 3 of 1992. Section 25.

[43] Steven Kemper, 'The Buddhist Monkhood, the Law, and the State in Colonial Sri Lanka', *Comparative Studies in Society and History* 26(1984), 401, 26.

As a result, the post of abbot remains highly sought-after and contested. A general rule-of-thumb applies to the appointment of an abbot. He should be the most senior, qualified successor to the previous abbot, in a system of 'student-after-student' succession.[44] (Senior, in this case, refers not to a monk's age but to the number of rainy seasons that the monk has passed in robes since he was ordained.[45]) Despite this overarching norm, however, numerous types of disagreements can occur, involving questions such as: Can an abbot hand-pick a successor who is not the eldest pupil? How should succession proceed in cases where incumbents or successors disrobe?[46]

Unlike the rules for using temple property, which are laid out in statutes, courts assess incumbency claims according to Buddhist Ecclesiastical Law (see later). The size and scope of the corpus are vast. One recent volume, representing the most comprehensive analysis to date, refers to more than 200 Supreme Court judgments.[47] The various guidelines for determining succession collected in this law derive from a mixture of sources, including rules of monastic comportment contained in Pali texts, testimony from senior monks and customary practices at temples as described by government officials, monastic residents and lay patrons.

B. The Nineteenth Century

Sri Lanka's mode of regulating the *saṅgha* gives significant power and autonomy to monks. From one perspective, this approach reflects *and* encourages the deep segmentation of Sri Lanka's monkhood: a decentralised *saṅgha* requires structures of regulation that permit decentralised control of temples and monks; and decentralised control of temples and monks makes possible further segmentation. From another perspective, however, historical factors seem determinative. Rather than the result of regulatory decisions made by successive Sri Lankan governments in response to a segmented monkhood, the legal regulation of the *saṅgha* can also be seen as growing out of policies introduced by the British during a period of direct colonisation – something that Thailand did not face.[48]

[44] An early explanation of this form of 'pupillage' is contained in G. W. Woodhouse, 'Sissiyanu Sissia Paramparava and Other Laws Relating to the Buddhist Priesthood', *The Ceylon Antiquary and Literary Register* 33 (1916).

[45] Hans-Dieter Evers, 'Kinship and Property Rights in a Buddhist Monastery in Central Ceylon', *American Anthropologist* (1967), 703.

[46] H. W. Tambiah, 'Buddhist Ecclesiastical Law', *Journal of the Ceylon Branch, Royal Asiatic Society*, NS 8(1962), 71.

[47] Wickrema S. Weerasooria, *Buddhist Ecclesiastical Law: A Treatise on Sri Lankan Statute Law and Judicial Decisions on Buddhist Temples and Temporalities* (Postgraduate Institute of Management, 2011).

[48] This is not to say that Thai history was not profoundly impacted by the history of colonialism. Many scholars point to an 'indirect' political and cultural colonialism in Siam and link the centralisation of the Siamese state in the late nineteenth century to pressures felt from the British and French powers in

Colonisation affected Sri Lankan Buddhism in many ways. However, when it comes to the relationship between government and monks, colonialism's most consequential legacies come from its dismantling of the institution of kingship. In 1815, the British deposed the last king of Sri Lanka, the ruler of the highland kingdom of Kandy. This change posed several dilemmas for the antagonistic symbiosis between monks and kings. Without a king, who would exercise traditional royal prerogatives to purify the *saṅgha* of heterodox monks, to donate land and money to the *saṅgha* and to act as final arbiter in monastic disputes?

British colonists initially took over these roles themselves. Yet, starting in the 1830s, colonial policies started to shift and British governors gradually moved to extricate themselves from responsibilities for local religions. As it related to the *saṅgha*, British officials transferred to colonial courts many of the powers formerly assumed by monastic bodies and kings. Using Buddhist texts (in translation), evidence from senior monks and the brokering of local court mediators and translators, British (and later Ceylonese) magistrates gradually took responsibility themselves for adjudicating disputes over monastic property, incumbency and succession according to British common law notions of property and trusts.[49] This process, over time, altered legal and popular understandings of monastic property. Monastic lands and assets came to be treated *neither* as something endowed to the temple by the king or the state, *nor* as something imaginatively held in trust for the entire monastic community (referred to in early Buddhist texts as 'the *saṅgha* of the four quarters'), but as something controlled by specific senior monks. That is, by the late colonial period, British civil courts had crafted a body of case law and a corpus of legal knowledge that legitimated and defended the fiduciary powers of a single individual: the temple abbot.[50]

As in the era of kings, intra-fraternity hierarchies and tribunals continued to exist. However, by the second half of the nineteenth century, the powers of these bodies had declined in the face of the growing powers of civil courts. According to the terms of Sri Lanka's colonial and post-colonial legal systems, the judgements of monastic tribunals were not enforceable by the state. Moreover, they were only of advisory value to courts; and judges regularly ignored and overturned the decisions made by monastic bodies.[51] In contrast to nineteenth-century Siam – where kings and their officers created new, official, centralised hierarchies of *saṅgha* authority – in

the region. Rachel V. Harrison, *The Ambiguous Allure of the West: Traces of the Colonial in Thailand* (Hong Kong University Press, 2010).

49 On this last category see Vijaya Samaraweera, 'An Act of Truth in a Sinhala Court of Law: On Truth, Lies and Judicial Proof among the Sinhala Buddhists', *Cardozo Journal of International & Comparative Law* 5 (1997), 133.

50 S. Kemper, 'The Buddhist Monkhood, the Law, and the State in Colonial Sri Lanka', *Comparative Studies in Society and History* 26 (1984), 401 (n. 44).

51 One lawyer who regularly appears in these cases estimates that civil court judges overturn to the decisions of monastic tribunals in approximately 30% to 40% of these cases. Interview (Colombo, 17 December 2014).

nineteenth-century Ceylon, colonial legal structures disempowered existing monastic hierarchies by empowering individual abbots. This, in turn, created new opportunities and incentives for the formation of novel subgroups. With control of temple property vested in the figure of the abbot (and not the broader chapter, fraternity or monkhood as a whole), schismatic monks had little to lose in the way of material resources by separating from the parent fraternity – and lots to gain.

C. Sri Lankan Regulatory Crises

Clearly, devolved control of temple property and the decentralised nature of Sri Lanka's monkhood have generated conflicts over monastic property. However, they have also generated specific types of regulatory crises over doctrine, discipline and religious authority. Consider, for example, a very recent and very public legal dispute involving the right of a Buddhist monk to drive a car.[52] Central to the case, which lasted ten years in the island's High Court and Supreme Court, was the question of whether the government would violate its duties to 'protect and foster' Buddhism by permitting a Buddhist monk to drive a car (something that monks do not normally do in Sri Lanka). Dozens of monks, lay donors and government officials participated in the case, which generated considerable acrimony and anxiety among Buddhists on the island. On the one side was Ven. Paragoda Wimalawansa Thero, the monk who requested the license, supported by approximately twenty other Buddhist monks, many of them abbots of small semi-urban temples. In submissions to the court, this group insisted that driving was essential to Buddhist monks because it allowed them to fulfill their many religious duties more efficiently. These duties included conducting rituals, teaching Sunday schools and ministering to lay persons. On the other side were some of the most well-known senior monks on the island, including the recognised head monks of the three overarching monastic fraternities (big 'n' *Nikāya*-s). They objected to Wimalawansa's petition, insisting that, by driving, Buddhist monks would be transgressing traditional standards of comportment. Therefore, they argued, the state's clear constitutional obligation to protect Buddhism also entailed an obligation to deny monks the legal right to drive.

In tracking the arguments made for and against Wimalawansa, both in the courtroom and in public media, one sees clearly how the decentralised nature of Buddhist authority and property in Sri Lanka has made disputes about monastic discipline – or Buddhist orthodoxy, in general – so contentious. Both Wimalawansa and his opponents offered compelling evidence, taken from Buddhist texts and customs, to attack or defend, respectively, the acceptability of monks' driving. Both cited Pali sources and pointed to important Buddhist principles. Yet, in the

[52] Ven. Dr Paragoda Wimalawansa Thero in SC 84/2007 (SC/Sp.LA/ 240/2007, CA Writ. App. 1978/ 2004), unpublished decision in possession of the author.

absence of an official or island-wide monastic hierarchy, there was no supreme ecclesiastical authority to evaluate the merits of the evidence. Each side claimed its own authority to speak for Buddhism. Wimalawansa repudiated the interpretations and authority of the senior monks who gave evidence against him, insisting that they had no authority to judge the behavior of individual abbots.[53] Conversely, Wimalawansa's opponents claimed that he and his supporters were rogue monks who had no authority to demand changes to customary standards of Buddhist monastic comportment, nor to justify those changes in terms of Buddhist doctrine.

When the Court of Appeal eventually passed judgement on the matter, rejecting Wimalawansa's petition, this too provoked a crisis of authority. In justifying its decision, the appellate court offered its own interpretations of monastic discipline. Yet, in doing this, the court, consisting of two Buddhist lay persons, could not help but dictate standards of discipline to Buddhist monks – a reversal of the normal ordering of Buddhist knowledge and power in Sri Lanka's decentralised monastic system. Therefore, in the end, the court's decision managed to upset both parties, including the 'winning' side![54]

The driving license case is not unique in Sri Lankan history. Over the last five decades, one can point to similar legal, political and social conflicts.[55] Legally, one finds a number of cases in which Buddhist monks face off in court over the acceptability of certain types of behavior, with both sides claiming to be authorised voices for Buddhism. Aside from driving, monks have clashed in court over the issue of Buddhist monks working as social workers and lawyers. Unlike in Thailand, civil courts find themselves in a double-bind of being called on to resolve the doctrinal and disciplinary disputes that inevitably arise in the context of a decentralised *saṅgha*, while at the same time not being able to claim the official and traditional religious authority to do so.

Similar conflicts have occurred in the political domain. Since the 1940s, Buddhist monks, interest groups, lay organisations and others have participated in fierce conflicts over the questions of whether monks should participate in politics and if the government should regulate monks. In both matters, monastic autonomy has won out. Today, Buddhist monks serve as very powerful political agents in Sri Lanka. Unlike Thailand, which has entirely disenfranchised monks and other religious leaders,[56] Sri Lankan monks not only vote; they also contest and hold public office, including seats in the national parliament. As of 2016, there were least two monk-led political parties: the fairly unsuccessful *Bodu Jana Peramuṇa* (the Buddhist People's

53 Interview with Ven. Paragoda Wimalawansa Thera. In Waskaduwa (Colombo, Sri Lanka, December 2015).

54 Benjamin Schonthal, *Buddhism, Politics and the Limits of Law: The Pyrrhic Constitutionalism of Sri Lanka* (Cambridge University Press, 2016), chapter 6.

55 Benjamin Schonthal, 'Securing the Sasana through Law: Buddhist Constitutionalism and Buddhist-interest Litigation in Sri Lanka', *Modern Asian Studies* 15(2016), 1956.

56 Tomas Larsson, 'Monkish Politics in Southeast Asia: Religious Disenfranchisement in Comparative and Theoretical Perspective', *Modern Asian Studies* 49(2015), 40.

Party) led by the aggressive monastic nationalist organisation, *Bodu Bala Sēnā* (army of Buddhist power); and the influential *Jātika Heḷa Urumaya* (the national [Sinhala] heritage front) or JHU, which first rose to prominence in 2004 and whose members continue to hold influence in parliament.

This is not to say that the Sri Lankan government has not tried to pass legislation similar to the Saṅgha Act in Thailand. Since the 1940s, Sri Lanka's successive governments have repeatedly attempted to create a national council of Buddhist monks and lay persons to oversee, among other things, the discipline and organisation of the *saṅgha*. More recently, in early 2016, the Sri Lankan government even introduced a bill called the 'Therawadi Bhikkhu Kathikawat Bill' designed to give the high-ranking monks of individual monastic chapters (*parśava* and *nikāya*) greater legal powers to discipline individual monks within their own fraternities (similar to powers given to the Thai Council of Elders). In all cases, these legal interventions failed owing, in large part, to opposition by the island's monks wary of any state encroachments (supported by many of the island's opposition politicians).[57]

In Sri Lanka, the regulation of the *saṅgha* has recognised and amplified existing lines of segmentation among monastic groups. This has led not just to disputes over temple property but to more general disputes over who has the authority to speak for Buddhism and/or regulate the behavior of the *saṅgha*. The regulatory dilemmas of monastic regulation in Sri Lanka do not provoke crises of official membership and control (as in Thailand) but crises of authority, characterised by an unsettling atmosphere of non-resolvability when it comes to questions about who officially is entitled to speak for Buddhism. If, in Thailand, regulatory crises call into question the legitimacy of the Council of Elders and their powers over the monks, in Sri Lanka the regulatory crises call into question the very possibility of Buddhism being a singular doctrinal, institutional or monastic whole. In all of the disputes described earlier – from the case of the driving monk, to the matter of monks in politics, to the disputes over creating island-wide bodies to supervise monastic affairs – one sees dramatically the deep diversity concerning the ways that monks govern themselves as well as understand and mobilise Buddhist norms.

IV. CONCLUSION

The legal regulation of religion in South and Southeast Asia involves state limitations on things like proselytising, ritualising and praying. However, equally importantly, regulating religion involves the organisation and oversight of religious

[57] Benjamin Schonthal and Asanga Welikala, 'Buddhism and the Regulation of Religion in the New Constitution: Past Debates, Present Challenges, and Future Options', CPA Working Papers on Constitutional Reform, No. 3 (13 July 2016), www.cpalanka.org/wp-content/uploads/2016/08/Buddhism-and-the-regulation-of-religion-in-the-new-constitution-Working-Paper-3.pdf (accessed 18 March 2017).

institutions and authority. In the contexts of Buddhist constitutionalism in Thailand and Sri Lanka, the management of the Buddhist monkhood constitutes a key focus for regulation. That is, defining and supervising Buddhist clerical institutions and power have been absolutely central tasks for government officials, lawmakers and judges.

Within the framework of Buddhist constitutionalism, Thailand and Sri Lanka have adopted virtually opposite modes of regulation, provoking different types of regulatory crises. In Thailand, kings, civilian governments and military regimes have created and consolidated a system of *official control* (including an official *saṅgha* hierarchy), through which they have attempted to bring monastic authority more firmly under the control of the state. When this strategy has failed, or has been challenged, it has contributed to regulatory crises in the form of contests over monastic control and membership, placing semi-autonomous monastic groups in direct conflict with the state and official *saṅgha* authorities. In Sri Lanka, colonial and independent governments have pursued a system of *jurisdictional control*. Rather than establishing an official monastic hierarchy, they have produced and maintained legal structures that devolve significant autonomy to the abbots of individual temples, while also claiming to block state intervention into monastic affairs. Where regulatory crises emerge in Sri Lanka they tend to be crises of authority, arising from the fact that no single monastic or governmental body claims total, official power to speak for Buddhism.

What is important to note is that both modes of *saṅgha* regulation involve high degrees of state involvement and, thus, reflect what J. P. Nettl once called high degrees of 'stateness'.[58] This stateness is obvious in the Thai case. One can see clearly in Thailand's system of official control the marks of state power: from the appointment of the *saṅgha-rāja*, to pyramidal structures of rank, to the administration of temple assets. Stateness is less obvious in the jurisdictional control of Sri Lanka's *saṅgha*; nevertheless, it is present. The creation of a strongly devolved *saṅgha* hierarchy, with the appearance of autonomy from state control, requires the delineation and management of jurisdictional boundaries; and that delineation and management requires, in turn, a strong network of state institutions, including courts, bureaucratic officers and parliament. Put another way, jurisdictional control – although it presents itself as the antithesis of state regulation – requires and involves a high degree of state involvement and indirect regulation.

It is, then, not coincidental that Thailand and Sri Lanka, the two states I chose as examples of opposite forms of monastic regulation, are the two Buddhist-majority states in South and Southeast Asia with the strongest legal and political institutions: the degree to which states are able to regulate monastic institutions varies directly with the infrastructural and institutional power of the states themselves, no matter which mode of regulation they adopt. Moreover, the mode of monastic regulation

58 John P. Nettl, 'The State as a Conceptual Variable', *World Politics* 20(1968), 559.

reflects political and religious history. In Thailand, the combination of strong monarchs, military governments and concerted projects of legal and political centralisation have directly contributed to creating and maintaining a centralised system of official control. By contrast, the British dismantling of monarchy in Sri Lanka and the subsequent empowering of temple abbots through the colonial law gave further impetus to processes of monastic segmentation that were already underway on the island. And this, in turn, virtually guaranteed that post-colonial politicians in Sri Lanka would have to maintain a system of jurisdictional control.

As these examples show, the legal regulation of religion, although a multiplex phenomenon, centrally involves the management of the relationship between state and religious authority – even in situations in which states themselves disavow that management. In fact, one might argue (as certain scholars have) that there is as much regulatory activity required in managing state and religious authority in the self-declared secular contexts of the United States or France as there is in jurisdictions that give special status or prerogatives to religions.[59] Scholarship on the legal regulation of religion would, therefore, do well to reconsider not just the diverse strategies of state control operating in ostensibly similar jurisdictions (as I've tried to do here for two Buddhist-majority countries in Southern Asia), but also to consider similarities in the state management of religion among jurisdictions that are normally seen as opposed.

[59] Winnifred Fallers Sullivan and Lori G. Beaman (eds.), *Varieties of Religious Establishment* (Ashgate Publishing, 2013).

5

Defining and Regulating Religion in Early Independent Indonesia

Kevin W. Fogg

I. INTRODUCTION

In a July 2016 interview, the Indonesian Minister of Religion, Lukman Hakim Saifuddin, told *Gatra* magazine: 'Defining what is a religion is not so easy. If you try to define it from a sociological point of view or a theological point of view, they can be very different.'[1] This task, though, is the crux of ongoing contestation in the Indonesian government, as the legislature works to pass a Bill on Protecting Religious Groups (*Rencana Undang-Undang Perlindungan Umat Beragama*). Defining religion, and in the Indonesian case creating a recognized list of defined religious communities, is the first step in regulating religious life in this diverse, non-sectarian state.[2]

Defining a religion in this modern age is a challenge not only for developing states such as Indonesia. In Europe and the United States, groups such as the Church of the Flying Spaghetti Monster (whose followers call themselves Pastafarians) or the Jedi Knights confuse categories of religion for the purposes of the census or identity documents.[3] One can also point to the Chinese state's practice of identifying unwanted groups (like the Falun Gong or the Church of the Almighty God) as 'unauthorized cults' so as to restrict their freedom, even while allowing since the 1980s the limited practice of some recognized world religions.[4]

1 'Mendefinisikan Agama Tidak Sederhana: Wawancara dengan Lukman Hakim Saifuddin' *Gatra* (Jakarta, 20 July 2016), 21.

2 Although the Indonesian state is not based on a single religion, the first pillar of the national ideology is 'Belief in the One Almighty God', making Indonesia non-sectarian, rather than secular. This also underpins the regulatory environment in which the government involves itself in religious life.

3 Samantha Grossman, 'Woman Wins Right to Wear Colander on Her Head in Driver's License Photo', *Time* (New York, 16 November 2015), http://time.com/4114369/pastafarian-colander-license-photo (accessed 1 March 2017); 'Austrian driver allowed "pastafarian" headgear photo', *BBC News* (London, 14 July 2011), www.bbc.co.uk/news/world-europe-14135523 (accessed 1 March 2017); 'Census returns of the Jedi', *BBC News* (London, 13 February 2003), http://news.bbc.co.uk/1/hi/uk/2757067.stm (accessed 1 March 2017).

4 Cheris Shun-ching Chan, 'The Falun Gong in China: A Sociological Perspective', *The China Quarterly* 179 (2009) 665; 'China cult murder trial: Two members sentenced to death', *BBC News* (London, 11 October 2014), www.bbc.co.uk/news/world-asia-china-29581195 (accessed 1 March 2017).

While well-established states tend to engage in the process of defining and regulating religion in the context of heavy institutional inertia and established interests, a newly emergent state could engage in such definitions without the same limitations. The latter is thus an ideal case study of how state definitions can determine the boundaries of religious belief and practice. This chapter uses the example of Indonesia in the first decades of its independence, when it was still setting up a regulatory regime for religious life, to highlight the importance of the definition of religion as the crux of religious regulation.

In the early years of Indonesia's independence, endless possibilities existed for determining the relationship of the state to religion. Although Indonesia had proclaimed its independence in 1945, the Netherlands – as the former colonial power – rejected this proclamation and reinvaded the country, initiating a war of independence. Only with the dawn of the new decade did the state apparatus have the opportunity to function in a non-conflict situation. One of the state units that was just finding its feet at this time was the Ministry of Religion. This cabinet-level ministry was created in 1946, approximately six months after the proclamation of independence, largely as a concession to traditionally educated Muslims who were not qualified to work in other parts of government but who wanted some patronage and some recognition of the role of religion in society.[5]

The recognition they sought was not in the law, per se. After some controversy (and causing continuing controversy later on),[6] Indonesia included *no* reference to Islam or to Allah or to Muslims in its constitution, making it for a long time one of a very few Muslim-majority countries in this situation.[7] Instead, the constitution enshrines 'Belief in the One Almighty God' (*Ke-Tuhanan Yang Maha Esa*), as the first principle of the Five Principles or *Pancasila*, Indonesia's national ethos, thus also making it the first pillar of the state. This allowed for the creation of the Ministry of Religion, but in the letter of the law, the nature of the One Almighty God and the ways in which citizens could practice their beliefs about God were unspoken at the dawn of the independent state.

The institutional instinct of the new Ministry of Religion to create regulations was complicated by the fact that Indonesians had many diverse ideas about religion. The classic anthropological study of Clifford Geertz, *Religion of Java*, provides the most well-known example.[8] Despite the fact that all of the groups he described were ostensibly Muslim, Geertz found it most effective to categorize Muslims according

[5] On the conditions surrounding the creation of the Indonesian Ministry of Religion, see Kevin William Fogg, *The Fate of Muslim Nationalism in Independent Indonesia*, PhD dissertation, Yale University, 2012, 110–14.

[6] The Jakarta Charter controversy is thoroughly discussed in Fogg (n. 5), 67–75, and in R. E. Elson, 'Another Look at the Jakarta Charter Controversy of 1945', *Indonesia* 88 (2009), 105.

[7] Masykuri Abdullah, 'Ways of Constitution Building in Muslim Countries: The Case of Indonesia', in Birgit Krawietz and Helmut Reifeld (eds.), *Islam and the Rule of Law: Between Sharia and Secularization* (Konrad-Adenauer-Stiftung, 2008), 56–8.

[8] Clifford Geertz, *The Religion of Java* (first published 1960; University of Chicago Press, 1976).

to the degree of syncretism and the type of admixture that was found in their practice. Even the title of the book pointedly declines to call this Islamic religion but rather talks about the 'Religion of Java' as though this stood apart from Islam. Geertz's categories of *santri*, *abangan*, and *priyayi* have been much contested in the intervening decades, but no one has seriously denied the high level of syncretism in Javanese Islam.[9]

If the question 'What constitutes religion?' continues to befuddle governments the world over, a key corollary question, 'What constitutes Islam?', as suggested by Geertz and later responses, poses particular challenges to governments like Indonesia where this religion is normative. Is it possible for a modern state to adopt an anthropological approach similar to Geertz's and accept local practices that are neither scriptural nor universal as the normative definition of Islam?[10] In the case of early independent Indonesia, the Ministry of Religion's functionaries had no desire to find out. At the societal level, Indonesian Muslim leaders had been working for generations, possibly centuries, to tamp down the admixture of local elements and promote text-based orthodoxy. This process has been broadly successful in inducing a long, slow march towards Arabo-orthodoxy; the work of Michael Laffan,[11] M. C. Ricklefs[12] and Nico J. G. Kaptein[13] unpacks some of the figures and processes that pushed that trend forward from the colonial to the independence era. The Ministry was thus staffed by workers inclined to promote definitions that were less tied to local practice and more tied to the scriptural practices they sought to promote.

The early independence period was a particularly exciting time because the new government had to decide how it would respond to these efforts to promote a certain understanding of religion. In other words, would the government prioritize protecting each person's right to believe and practise as they wished (and thus keep Islamization in check), or would it support the homogenization of religious practice within recognized categories? The context for these decisions was a country recovering from a decade of war with a large number of new, often syncretic, local religions and a government eager to exercise its newly achieved powers. The following

9 Major contributions to this debate have included Mark R. Woodward, *Islam in Java: Normative Piety and Mysticism in the Sultanate of Yogyakarta* (University of Arizona Press, 1989); Timothy Daniels, *Islamic Spectrum in Java* (Ashgate, 2009); Saiful Muzani, 'The Devaluation of Aliran Politics: Views from the Third Congress of the PPP', *Studia Islamika* 1.3 (1994), 177; and most recently M. C. Ricklefs, *Islamisation and Its Opponents in Java: A Political, Social, Cultural and Religious History, c. 1930 to the Present* (NUS Press, 2012). Ricklefs argues that syncretism has fallen sharply over the twentieth century.

10 The heated ongoing debate about the current Indonesian administration's program to promote 'Islam Nusantara' (Islam of the Archipelago) might be seen as a debate over textual normativity and normativity from local practice.

11 Michael Laffan, *The Makings of Indonesian Islam: Orientalism and the Narration of a Sufi Past* (Princeton University Press, 2011).

12 Ricklefs (n. 9).

13 Nico J. G. Kaptein, *Islam, Colonialism, and the Modern Age in the Netherlands East Indies: A Biography of Sayyid 'Uthman* (Brill, 2014).

discussion will focus on the Ministry of Religion,[14] its efforts to define and regulate religion, and the outcomes in Indonesian society. The process of definition undertaken by a government ministry is different from the process of definition undertaken by the courts: within a ministry, definitions can be made in the abstract (instead of amid a specific disagreement over rights and status) and the believers being defined need not be represented, so they may not be aware of the process or have any input on it. Thus, studying this aspect of the definition and regulation of religion is an important complement to legal studies based in case law.

The first step of the process of definition was coming up with the legal structures and reasons to define religion for this new state, which was followed by efforts to inventory the religious beliefs that existed in the population. When it came to the process of actual definition and regulation, though, it was clear that Indonesia took a very different approach to world religions, heterodox groups well outside Islam, and heterodox groups closely linked with Islam. The definitions and actions of the Indonesian state in this early period continue to impact religious life today, as can be seen in the debate over the pending Bill on the Protection of Religious Communities.

II. LEGAL STRUCTURES

In its Provisional Constitution of 1950, the Indonesian state was very clear about the right to freedom of religion. Article 18 guaranteed that 'Every person has the right to freedom of religion, conscience, and thought', explicitly echoing Article 18 of the Universal Declaration of Human Rights.[15] According to Indonesia's leading constitutional scholar at the time, the Indonesian constitutional clause was modeled after the Universal Declaration and should be understood to include all of its provisions (including a man's 'freedom to change his religion and belief, and freedom, either alone or in community with others and in public or private, to manifest his religion or belief in teaching, practice, worship and observance').[16] Furthermore, the Indonesian government explained in the open session of Parliament that adopted the Provisional Constitution its belief that 'in the future, our country will constitute

[14] Although the official translation of *Kementerian Agama* is the Ministry of Religious Affairs, the original Indonesian name is very straightforward and is correctly translated as the Ministry of Religion. Contrast this with its regional branch offices, *Kantor Urusan Agama*, which can be aptly translated as Religious Affairs Offices. The Ministry's name is telling because it suggests that there was a desire or aspiration right from the start to speak directly to the regulation of religion, and not merely to public practices or social consequences of religion.

[15] Universal Declaration of Human Rights (adopted 10 December 1948) UNGA Res 217 A(III); cf. Undang-Undang Dasar Sementara Republik Indonesia 1950, Pasal 18: 'Setiap orang berhak atas kebebasan agama, keinsjafan batin dan pikiran'.

[16] Soepomo (ed.), *Undang-Undang Dasar Sementara Republik Indonesia: Dengan Sekedar Tjatatan dan Keterangan dibawah Tiap-Tiap Pasal Menurut Pendjelasan dan Djawaban Pemerintah kepada Parlemen R.I.S.*, 3rd edn (Noordhoff-Kolff, 1950), 26–7.

an archipelago in which every kind of religion can live fruitfully and peacefully, as a good example to the world'.[17]

However, the broad guarantees of Article 18 of Indonesia's Provisional Constitution were tempered slightly by Article 43, which reads as follows:

1. The State is founded on Belief in the One Almighty God [*ke-Tuhanan jang Maha Esa*].
2. The state guarantees the freedom of each resident to embrace their own religion and to practice according to their religion and beliefs.
3. The government gives the same protections to all religious groups and associations that are recognized [*jang diakui*]. Giving support in any form by the government to religious officials and religious groups or associations is done on the basis of equal rights.
4. The government keeps watch so that all religious groups and associations are faithful to the laws, including legal regulations that are not in writing.[18]

The limitations introduced by this Article – such as 'recognized' religions and 'faithfulness to the laws' – were probed and tested in the 1950s. Still, the overall principle of freedom of religion was generally upheld in the Provisional Constitution, with one leading Islamic politician claiming in 1950 that the Indonesian constitution 'protected citizens who want to practice their religion, whatsoever religion regardless of its content and form'.[19]

III. WHY DEFINE RELIGIONS?

Given such a legal framework that specifically claims 'recognition' as a role of the state, one can ask why the state would want to have this power. Of course, the most nefarious reasons are often the quickest to jump to mind – such as the desire for social, or even theological, control of religious life. However, in the case of early independent Indonesia, the evidence does not generally lean in that direction, at least not for the 1950s when this Provisional Constitution was written and promulgated. Although greater control was to be a focus of government policy in later decades, the initial impetus for defining and regulating religion seemed to be driven by two goals, one generally positive and one a little less so, but neither of them about controlling belief.

The first goal was social harmony among religions.[20] In a nation with a broad spectrum of religious beliefs, this had been a concern from the earliest days of

[17] Ibid.

[18] Ibid., 46.

[19] Abu Hanifah, *Soal Agama dalam Negara Modern*, 2nd edn (Tintamas, 1950), 51.

[20] The idea presented here as 'social harmony' was framed in various ways in documents from the Ministry of Religion. Sometimes this was presented positively, as part of the Ministry's duty to 'protect diversity and tolerance between groups of every religion, belief, and stream [of thought]'. Other times

independence. One example from Aceh makes this very clear. A circular from the local nationalist committee, dated just two months into the national revolution in 1945, instructs residents of Aceh to be united: 'Respect each other's beliefs (Religions). Religious differences cannot become a stumbling block in the Struggle of the Indonesian People. Do not do anything that could offend each other's religious sentiments.'[21]

In the 1950s, this goal of promoting social harmony through the regulation of religions became more bureaucratically entrenched and required some initial efforts to define religion and religious beliefs. There were moves in some areas to set up ecumenical boards with representatives from different groups to smooth interreligious relations. This was not always successful because not every area had large enough religious communities to sustain such an effort (a sheepish official from Wajo in South Sulawesi wrote to his governor in 1952 explaining that with only three Christians in a basically Muslim regency, it would be difficult to run an interreligious board[22]). In other instances, the goal of social harmony became a bit more questionable, as when local Ministry of Religion officials wanted to stop the proliferation of a group called 'Partij Agama Ahlissunati-Waldjamaati Padjenekang' (Pajenekang [District] Religious Party of the Ahlussuna Waljamaah), which they believed 'was made intentionally to make a mess of religion' and which had elicited protests from mainstream groups that saw them as blasphemous.[23] In this case, the effort to define the group as something other than a religion (here, as a political group of rabble-rousers) was ostensibly for social harmony purposes but may have violated the highest principles of the Provisional Constitution.

The second goal of the Ministry of Religion in defining and regulating religions was slightly more suspect, and it came especially from the lowest-level functionaries. This second goal was to channel to specific types of religious leaders the potential patronage that could come through religious work, most notably in the area of marriage, where many low-level bureaucrats in the Ministry of Religion made a significant amount of their living from fees for officiating Muslim marriages. If non-orthodox groups were also able to officiate marriages, it would shut the valve on this lucrative source of side-income for Ministry of Religion bureaucrats.

(even in the same documents), this could be presented negatively, such as to 'decrease tensions and crisis situations' or to avoid 'bothering public safety and order'. See Arsip Nasional Republik Indonesia, Koleksi Kabinet Presiden RI, 1950–59, #91, Menteri Agama RI: surat tanggal 17 Januari 1955 tentang tugas pegawai Kementerian Agama mengurangi ketegangan sosial, dengan lampiran.

21 Arsip Propinsi Naggroe Aceh Darussalam, Koleksi Keresidenan Aceh, 1945–49 and 1951–55, #67, Maklumat Ketua Pusat Komite Nasional di Kutaraja no. 4 tanggal 15 Oktober 1945 tentang Kerukunan Ummat Beragama.

22 Arsip Sulawesi Selatan, Koleksi Kantor Wilayah Departemen Agama Propinsi Sulawesi Selatan, Periode Tahun 1947–90, #270.

23 Arsip Sulawesi Selatan, Koleksi Kantor Wilayah Departemen Agama Propinsi Sulawesi Selatan, Periode Tahun 1947–90, # 108, Kepala Kantor Urusan Agama Propinsi Sulawesi: Surat tanggal 28 Agustus 1952 tentang Laporan politik dan perkembangan aliran agama.

As such, restricting the definition of religions (thus restricting who could officiate marriages) was in the bureaucrats' interests.

This became a more acute issue across the archipelago in the 1950s. A 1954 Prime Ministerial Decision on sects specifically notes that sects were misleading the people on legitimate marriage.[24] The attorney general gave further details in a 'Top Secret' letter to the Ministry of Home Affairs, chronicling the story of the self-styled 'Agama Pantja Sila' (agama meaning 'religion', Pantja Sila referring to 'Pancasila', the Indonesian national philosophy of Five Principles) officiating 'wild' (i.e., unauthorized) marriages in several areas of Java.[25] The phenomenon of local sects, often heterodox offshoots of Islam, conducting their own marriage ceremonies was not restricted to Java. In the Makassar area of South Sulawesi, a sect called 'Patuntung' with some 3,000 followers would arrange its own marriage ceremonies involving special mantras that centred on a Divinity called 'KaraEng Kaminang Kamaya' (translating roughly to 'The More-Powerful God').[26]

The spectre of marriages officiated by unrecognized religions was not even the greatest threat perceived by religious officials. Even worse was the danger of marriages that were entirely secular, with no religious role at all. One such marriage was listed in Solo, Central Java, where the officiant was from the local Indonesian Communist Party branch.[27] Losing control over marriage meant mainstream ulama not only losing some authority in their local communities, but also losing the income they would receive from families for conducting marriage ceremonies; losing this influence and income to the Communists would be the bitterest possible outcome.

This concern about patronage was the second consideration, then, for the Indonesian Ministry of Religion as it undertook efforts to define and regulate religion in the early independent state.

IV. ASSESSING WHAT RELIGIONS EXISTED

Having set up the legal structures, the next task in defining religions was the effort to inventory Indonesia's religious groups, communities, and beliefs as they existed. During the Revolution, there was no time to engage in a census or in religious surveys, though the religious holidays provide some rough reflection of how the

24 Arsip Propinsi Naggroe Aceh Darussalam, Koleksi Keresidenan Aceh, 1945–49 and 1951–55, #68, Keputusan Perdana Menteri no. 167/P.M./1954.

25 Arsip Propinsi Naggroe Aceh Darussalam, Koleksi Keresidenan Aceh, 1945–49 and 1951–55, #68, Surat Kedjaksaan Agung to the Menteri Dalam Negeri no. Plk. C/ 1198/446, Sangat Rahasia, Jakarta (19 March 1954).

26 Arsip Sulawesi Selatan, Koleksi Kantor Wilayah Departemen Agama Propinsi Sulawesi Selatan, Periode Tahun 1947–90, #106, letter from Kantor Urusan Agama Kabupaten Makassar (31 December 1951).

27 Arsip Propinsi Naggroe Aceh Darussalam, Koleksi Keresidenan Aceh, 1945–49 and 1951–55, #68, Surat Kedjaksaan Agung to the Menteri Dalam Negeri no. Plk. C/ 1198/446, Sangat Rahasia, Jakarta (19 March 1954).

government understood religion. In 1948, the Ministry of Religion announced eight Islamic holidays (Maulid, Mi'radj, 1 Ramadhan, Nuzul Qur'an, Idul Fitri, Idul Adha, 1 Muharram, Ashura), four Christian holidays (Good Friday, Easter, Ascension Thursday, Christmas), and four 'Chinese' holidays (Chinese New Year, Confucius's Death Day, Tsingbing, Confucius's Birthday).[28] Clearly, Islam and Christianity were at the forefront of the government's mind, but it is interesting how Confucianism came third because subsequent governments refused to recognize Confucianism from the late 1950s until the presidency of Abdurrahman Wahid in 1999.[29]

Another example of the government's perception of the religious affiliations of its citizens can be found in estimates by ranking government officials. Abu Hanifah, a leading Islamic politician who served as Minister of Education in the first post-revolutionary government, wrote in 1949 that Indonesia was 94% Muslim, with about 90% of these really committed to Islam; of the remaining population, he estimated 1.5 million Protestants, 0.5 million Catholics, 1.5 million Buddhists in Bali, Lombok, and the lesser Sundas (what we would now identify as local Hinduism), with the remainder embracing forms of animism.[30] He also insisted that if Indonesia had any anti-religious or non-religious population, it was less than one-hundredth of a percent of the entire Indonesian population.[31]

The Ministry of Religion must have recognized that these wartime ideas were merely speculative. Hence, after independence was consolidated in 1950, the Ministry and its local branches made several attempts to take stock of the religious beliefs adhered to in each corner of the archipelago. This began with requests to the regency-level Offices of Religious Affairs in mid-1951, asking for reports of the religions practiced locally and their numbers.[32] Evidence of this process can be found even in documents from isolated areas such as rural Central Sulawesi,

28 Arsip Propinsi Naggroe Aceh Darussalam, Koleksi Lhok'nga, 1934–52, #88, letter from Bukittinggi (15 October 1948). No Hindu or Buddhist holidays were listed; there were additional secular national holidays on 1 January (New Year's), 17 August (Indonesian Independence), 5 October (Army Day), and 10 November (Heroes Day). Unlike the Islamic and Christian holidays when government offices would be closed for the full day, on 'Chinese' holidays, government offices would close after a half-day (except for important offices, which could stay open). Apparently Confucius's birthday was a listed public holiday at least through 1951, when another announcement from the Ministry of Religion was released on this point; see Arsip Propinsi Naggroe Aceh Darussalam, Koleksi Lhok'nga, 1934–52, #88, Maklumat Menteri Agama RI No. A.II/ 3/ 2918/a tentang lahirnya Kong Hu Tju (Hari Raya) tanggal 27 September 1951 (tahun 1951).

29 Helen Pausacker, 'The Sixth Religion' *Inside Indonesia* (Canberra, 14 July 2007), www.insideindonesia.org/the-sixth-religion (accessed 5 May 2017).

30 Abu Hanifah, *Soal Agama dalam Negara Modern* (n. 19), 21–2. Abu Hanifah does not give a total population figure, but we can assume that if the non-Muslim 6% was about 3.75 million people, the total population of Indonesia would have been roughly 62.5 million people.

31 Ibid., 53. Given the foregoing calculations, this would come to about 6,000 people, although it is highly doubtful that Abu Hanifah had thought these calculations through.

32 Arsip Propinsi Naggroe Aceh Darussalam, Koleksi Lhok'nga, 1934–52, #92, note from Zainuddin Lp, Kepala Nagri Lho'nga, to Bupati Aceh Besar (6 November 1951).

suggesting that the project was truly national not only in aspiration but also in action.[33]

Of particular interest in the assessment process were any local religions or beliefs that the offices identified. In 1951, the Ministry of Religion circulated among all offices a list of 'All Faiths and Beliefs outside Islam/Christianity-Catholicism-Protestantism'.[34] This list of seventy-three groups from Java alone is made up entirely of local religions (with no mention of Buddhism, Hinduism, and the like), usually local religions at some distance from a form of heterodox Islam. The range of beliefs had names like 'True Islam' ('Islam Sedjati', a group that believed in reincarnation but not the Qur'an), 'Humanitarianism' ('Pri-Kemanusiaan', one of several religions that incorporated Indonesia's national principles in their doctrine), 'the Just King' ('Ratu Adil', which was reported to have existed for several generations), and 'Brothers' Union' ('Serikat Abang', led by a couple of hajjis, with followers being mostly women in their twenties and thirties). This list from 1951 was not the last time the Ministry of Religion would attempt to document religious groups, especially those perceived as cults or sects. In 1954, the Ministry circulated a list (labeled 'Secret') of some 30 heterodox groups in the province of West Java alone,[35] and in 1955, the attorney general sent around a circular (labeled 'Top Secret') to all but two provinces, asking them to report about any 'streams of belief' (*aliran kepercayaan*, i.e., heterodox groups) or mystical movements in their regions.[36]

These inventories by the Ministry of Religion, which sought both general statistics about the number of followers of world religions as well as information about smaller religious groups in existence, did not result in any direct action. The local groups were not asked to register, and no nationwide program seems to have been run to 'recognize' any of these smaller religions, in line with the stipulations of the Provisional Constitution. However, the information on the wide variety of local beliefs did inform the Ministry as it turned to questions of regulation.

33 Private collection of Jennifer Nourse from Tinombo, Central Sulawesi, 'Daftar Agama jang dianut oleh penduduk Swapradja Moutong' (13 November 1951). This collection is composed of the files of a kecamatan (subdistrict office) saved through the 1980s and surrendered to Prof. Nourse for her research. I am thankful to Prof. Nourse for making this collection available to me.

34 Arsip Sulawesi Selatan, Koleksi Kantor Wilayah Departemen Agama Propinsi Sulawesi Selatan, Periode Tahun 1947–90, #111, Kementerian Agama, Kepala Bagian Politik dan Perkumpulan/Aliran-aliran Agama: Surat pengantar No. F/I/2655 tanggal 18 Pebruari 1952 tentang Daftar organisasi yang memakai dasar agama Tahun 1951 dan daftar aliran/ kepercayaan di luar Islam/ Kristen tahun 1951.

35 Private collection of Jennifer Nourse from Tinombo, Central Sulawesi, Circular Letter No: Polx/11/1/31 (11 February 1955). I am thankful to Prof. Nourse for making this collection available to me.

36 Arsip Propinsi Naggroe Aceh Darussalam, Koleksi Keresidenan Aceh, 1945–49 and 1951–55, #68, Surat Edaran Sangat Rahasia No. Plk.C/2615/589, from Kedjaksaan Agung pada Mahkamah Agung Indonesia (25 August 1955). The two excluded provinces were Maluku and Sunda Ketjil, perhaps because these were the only two provinces without a Muslim majority.

V. REGULATING RELIGION

A. *Regulating World Religions besides Islam*

It is undeniable that Islam was normative in the thinking of the Ministry of Religion. Every Minister of Religion in Indonesia's history has been a Muslim, and most are drawn from the major Islamic mass organizations of the country.[37] As the Ministry initially expanded its offices across the archipelago, Islam was usually the first religion represented in the office, even in majority Christian areas.[38]

Despite this normative bias, the Indonesian state never had any difficulties with recognizing Christianity, in both Protestant and Catholic forms, in the country, and with accommodating Christians as citizens. Abu Hanifah wrote in 1946: 'In living alongside in peace and prosperity, there is a happy future for Indonesia's children who are Muslim and who are Christian. … Even more so because both of these religions are religions of the East and believe in the One Almighty God who will protect the religious country.'[39] There was minimal regulation of Christianity in the early era; the Ministry happily recognized Christians' freedom of religion and was not concerned with creating extensive regulations for this minority community.

It was slightly harder for the Ministry to define and regulate traditional Balinese religion. This was a very well-established religious system that was practised more or less homogeneously throughout the island of Bali (thus largely isolated from other religious communities, although some practitioners of the Balinese religion had spread their faith to the islands immediately to the east and west of Bali). It was not, however, well-tied to a world religion. Over time, bureaucratic consensus (both on Bali and in Jakarta) consolidated around the idea that Balinese religion could be anchored to Hinduism. The categorization therefore changed from Balinese religion (*Agama Bali*) to Balinese Hinduism (*Agama Hindu Bali*) to just Hinduism (*Agama Hindu*) today, even though Balinese practice is certainly unlike the Hinduism recognized in India.[40]

One example of how other major world religions were respected and to some extent protected in the early independent state can be seen in a directive issued in the build-up to Indonesia's first national elections. The Ministry of Religion prepared and circulated several letters relating to the threat of religion-based conflict;

37 Azyumardi Azra and Saiful Umam (eds.), *Menteri-Menteri Agama RI: Biografi Sosial-Politik* (PPIM with INIS and Litbang Agama DepAg, 1998).

38 See a controversy about this pattern in Timor in Arsip Nasional Republik Indonesia, Koleksi Kabinet Presiden, #158, Resolution (15 January 1952) by Parkindo and Partai Katholik. In its letter of reply, the Ministry denied that this was the case, but the local Christian parties are, in my estimation, more reliable on this question.

39 Abu Hanifah, *Kita Berdjoang: Goebahan Kultur Politis* (Merdeka, 1946), 161.

40 Michael Picard, 'Balinese Religion in Search of Recognition: From Agama Hindu Bali to Agama Hindu (1945–1965)', *Bijdragen tot de Taal-, Land- en Volkenkunde* 167.4 (2011), 482.

these letters reached even the lowest levels.[41] One repeated message was that Indonesian Muslims should not accuse their electoral opponents of being *kafir*, or infidels, because this word for non-believers is not applicable and because the religious consequences for those who misapply it are dire. In an instruction of March 1954, the Secretary-General of the Ministry specifically addressed the special status of Catholics, Protestants, and Jews as protected communities under Islam law whose sincere beliefs should be respected (although no mention was made of other world religions that could be found in Indonesia, such as Hinduism, Buddhism, or Confucianism). This certainly did not prevent the use of *kafir* as an epithet during election season, especially against Communist atheists (though much less commonly against non-Muslim religious minorities). Still, the letter shows the Ministry's clear concern that this Islamic concept should not be used to alienate other religions.

This practice of restricting the use of *kafir*, however, highlights the fact that the government was most interested in regulating Islam and using regulations to protect the boundaries of Islam. This reflected the normative position of Islam as the key tradition for the Ministry of Religion and the pressure from both Islamic parties and mass Islamic organizations to promote the interests of orthodox and orthoprax Muslims in this era.[42]

B. Regulating Heterodox Groups Well Outside Islam

The Ministry's accommodative or even protective attitude was less often directed towards religious beliefs that were well outside the mainstream – in other words, beliefs that were distant from Islam, Christianity, and other world religions, and that were not in a position of local dominance. The case of the *Agama Djawa Asli Republik Indonesia* (Native Java Religion of the Republic of Indonesia) is a clear illustration of the government's attitude in the 1950s (arguably unlike today) of neither seeking to protect nor eliminate such heterodox beliefs.[43]

The *Agama Djawa Asli Republik Indonesia*, abbreviated ADJARI (which also means 'teach' in Indonesian), was a new religion that emerged during this period. During the Indonesian revolution against the Dutch in the late 1940s, two militia leaders in Central Java fasted for seven days – only drinking tea from 8 February to

[41] Several of the original letters can be found in Arsip Nasional Republik Indonesia, Koleksi Kabinet Presiden RI 1950–59, #91, Menteri Agama RI: Surat tanggal 17 Januari 1955 tentang tugas pegawai Kementerian Agama mengurangi ketegangan sosial, dengan lampiran. I have also found a copy of the Ministry's letter of April 1954 that was circulated by the Governor of Sulawesi among all local Religious Affairs Offices; a copy is in the private collection of Jennifer Nourse from Tinombo, Central Sulawesi, the Circular Letter of the Governor of Sulawesi, No. Aga/4/1/5 (11 May 1954). I am thankful to Prof. Nourse for making this collection available to me.

[42] On the position and influence of Islamic mass organizations and Islamic parties in this period, see Fogg (n. 5), chapters 3 and 4.

[43] The position of many religions outside the mainstream in Indonesia today was discussed in a special issue of *Gatra* magazine (20 July 2016) on 'Taman Sari Agama Indonesia'.

15 February 1946. At the end of this fast, they felt a divine calling to go in search of the 'revelation for the island of Java' (*Wahjunja Tanah Djawa*). They set off on peregrinations around the island, including visits to Borobudur, the Dieng Plateau and spiritual teachers in Surakarta; these peregrinations ended with their capture and imprisonment by the Dutch, and later detention (for unclear reasons) by Indonesian forces. While in detention in early 1950, the two leaders were praying in their cell when they heard a disembodied voice saying to them in Javanese that Sukarno, the president of the young Republic, was their prophet. Thus, on 13 November 1950, they formally founded their religion, ADJARI.[44]

The group tried repeatedly to convince the president that he was the prophet of ADJARI, and this is where the state's response becomes interesting. President Sukarno seemed very unwilling to receive this honour. The presidential secretary wrote several letters to the group asserting that the president did not want to be called a prophet and would not become involved with this group or meet with them, but that he recognized their right to freedom of religion. As reflected in ADJARI's letters to the president and government citing earlier correspondence, it seems that there was lip-service to the idea of freedom of religion and the right of these individuals to believe and practise what they wanted, but the government did not accommodate their requests to be treated on par with Islam as a religion represented in the state.[45] For example, no ADJARI believer did or could have become a functionary of the local Ministry of Religion, nor could ADJARI beliefs be taught during the time for religious instruction in state schools.

Thus, for heterodox groups that were at little or no risk of being confused with a major world religion, the government's position was hands-off and mildly negative. The state did not try to register, recognize, or regulate these religions, nor did it attempt to curtail the rights of followers to practise according to their beliefs; however, it also did not facilitate such small communities in the way it facilitated major faith communities. In this era, unlike in Indonesia today, citizens did not have to process official documents (other than marriage) in accordance with their religion. Hence, regulation of such heterodox communities was minimal, and the consequences of the government's mild negativity were also minimal.

C. *Regulating Groups on the Fringes of Islam*

ADJARI represented a minor local belief that was well outside the mainstream. The real test of the Ministry of Religion's commitment to the neutral regulation of religion lay in dealing with heterodox groups that were on the fringes of Islam or that claimed to be part of Islam. In this area, the government in the 1950s was willing to

[44] Arsip Nasional Republik Indonesia, Koleksi Konstituante, #300, Surat mengenai riwayat berdirinya Barisan Samadi Republik Indonesia (BASRI) dari Agama Jawa Asli.

[45] Arsip Nasional Republik Indonesia, Koleksi Konstituante, #307, Surat dari Agama Jawa Asli (ADJARI) kepada Presiden Soekarno mengenai anggapan bahwa Soekarno adalah nabinya.

allow only a narrow leeway for variations of beliefs under the label of 'Islam'; other practices could still exist, but they had to be outside the Islamic category.[46]

In 1954, a parliamentarian from a minor Islamic party explicitly raised the question of Muslim religious freedom with the Ministry of Religion. He reported that a member of the Naqshbandi Sufi brotherhood had been called into the local Office of Religious Affairs in West Sumatra and told that a permit was needed to practice with a Sufi brotherhood. This prompted strong assurances from the Ministry that this was not in line with policy, while a circular from the Ministry on religious freedom, dated 14 April 1954, was sent to all branches and offices across the country.[47] This letter, penned by the Secretary-General of the Ministry, Mohd. Kafrawi, opened with this sentence: 'One of the important duties of the Ministry of Religion is to ensure that every resident has the freedom to embrace their own religion and to practice it following their religion and beliefs.' (This echoes the Indonesian Constitution in its word choice.) He later stated: 'The issue of religion and religiosity has been recognized as a really very delicate issue, such that if there are any actions that are intemperate, especially on the part of governmental institutions, it can easily cause a person or community to feel offended.' He then reprinted as a reminder Article 18 and Article 43 of the Indonesian Constitution concerning, respectively, freedom of religion and state neutrality on religious issues, which could only be abridged (according to Article 33) to protect public safety and order. In closing, Kafrawi emphasized that 'the Ministry of Religion absolutely does not interfere in a religion's internal matters and does not support the propagandizing of a particular religious group'.[48] Hence, it seems that the government generally took an open and accepting position towards Sufi groups, which might not look like Arab orthodoxy but which belonged to a well-known and well-respected tradition in Islamic practice. The headquarters of the Ministry of Religion explicitly advised against regulatory interference in this practice.

In contrast, a different attitude was demonstrated toward the Ahmadiyyah at the time.[49] This became clear in the biggest case that the Ahmadiyyah brought before the Ministry of Religion, regarding religious slander. In 1948, while Indonesia was still in the throes of its national revolution and the nascent government was running on a shoestring budget in Jogjakarta, the Ministry of Religion published a book by

46 Compare this with the argument in Jeremy Menchik, *Islam and Democracy in Indonesia: Tolerance without Liberalism* (Cambridge University Press, 2015).

47 Arsip Sulawesi Selatan, Koleksi Kantor Wilayah Departemen Agama Propinsi Sulawesi Selatan, Periode Tahun 1947–90, #227, Kementerian Agama, Sekretaris Jenderal: Surat tanggal 14 April 1954 tentang Pedoman mengenai tugas menjaga kemerdekaan agama.

48 Ibid.

49 The question of the exact relationship between the Ahmadiyyah belief and Islam is much debated, but basically the Ahmadiyyah community accepts Islam as taught by Muhammad but with additional renewal or possibly revelation as shared by the 19th century Pakistani teacher Mirza Ghulam Ahmad. See Erni Budiwanti, 'Pluralism Collapses: A Study of the Jama'ah Ahmadiyah Indonesia and Its Persecution' (2009) Asia Research Institute Working Paper Series No. 117, www.ari.nus.edu.sg/docs/wps/wps09_117.pdf (accessed 1 March 2017).

the traditionalist Muslim author and activist H. Aboebakar titled *The History of the Qur'an* (*Sedjarah al-Qur'an*).[50] The book covered basic information about the Muslim scriptures in some 330 pages, including appendices. One of these appendices included a list of 'False Revelations' ('*Wahyu Buatan*') that named various offshoots of mainstream Islam. Number six on this list was the Ahmadiyyah.

When the Ahmadiyyah community realized that their beliefs were listed as a 'False Revelation', and particularly in a book published by the Republic of Indonesia's Ministry of Religion, they raised the issue at a joint meeting of the Central Leadership of the Ahmadiyyah Community in Indonesia and the Ahmadiyyah Moslem Missionaries of Indonesia. This joint meeting issued a resolution in early May 1951, renouncing in no uncertain terms the inclusion of 'Hazrat Mirza Gulam Ahmad and colleagues' in the list of 'False Revelations', saying that it 'greatly injured their honour' and violated the Indonesian Constitution, and that the government should 'protect and respect the beliefs of various groups in society on issues of ritual according to their religions and beliefs'.[51]

A delegation of Ahmadiyyah leaders delivered this resolution to the Ministry of Religion in late June, eliciting a response from the Minister, Wahid Hasjim (famous for being both a major leader of the mass organization Nahdlatul Ulama and the father of Indonesia's fourth president). His response is interesting for two reasons. First, Wahid Hasjim appeared open to the suggestion that H. Aboebakar could have been wrong in denouncing the Ahmadiyyah founder as a source of 'False Revelations'. Hasjim wrote: 'Although the Ministry of Religion was involved in the publication of the book that you gentlemen are protesting, we are not influenced by it. Truth is above all things.'[52] However, the main thrust of the letter also demonstrates Wahid Hasjim's misunderstanding of the Ahmadiyyah protest, which is the second interesting point. Wahid Hasjim offered to arrange a meeting between the Ahmadiyyah leaders and H. Aboebakar via a Ministry of Religion intermediary so that the Ahmadis and the book's author could try to overcome the misunderstanding about the nature of Ahmadiyyah beliefs. He did not grasp that the Ahmadiyyah leaders were not just upset by the contents of the book, but were also protesting the publication of such a book by the Ministry of Religion, which they believed should be neutral.

This misunderstanding by Wahid Hasjim was compounded by the Secretary General of the Ministry of Religion, Mohammad Kafrawi, who followed up with a letter on 16 August 1951. Kafrawi wrote that he had consulted with H. Aboebakar, who defended his book by pointing to the prominent scholars who were his

50 H. Aboebakar Atjeh, *Sedjarah Al-Qur'an* (Sinar Pudjangga, 1952). This is a later edition, but it seems nothing was removed from the offending appendix.

51 Arsip Nasional Republik Indonesia, Koleksi Kabinet Presiden, #163, Resolusi Rapat Gabungan Pengurus Besar Djema'at Ahmadiyah Indonesia dan para Ahmadiyah Moslem Missionary di Indonesia.

52 Arsip Nasional Republik Indonesia, Koleksi Kabinet Presiden, #163, Letter from Wahid Hasjim to Pengurus Besar Djema'at Ahmadiyah Indonesia (20 July 1951).

sources.[53] Following a mediated meeting (mediated, incidentally, by one of Indonesia's most anti-Ahmadi ulama, Hamka),[54] the government refused to apologize or withdraw the book but made the concession that the Ministry of Religion would not act as the publisher for future editions; instead, future editions would be published by a private publisher.

Hence, when it came to minority Islamic beliefs or heterodox beliefs that were close to Islam, the Ministry of Religion in the early 1950s wanted to preserve its power to regulate what was or was not proper Islam. Muslim officials of the Ministry had very little capacity to think outside of normative constraints about the definition of Islam, even as they demonstrated openness and receptiveness to other minority religions.

VI. CHANGES LEADING TO THE TIGHTER REGULATION OF RELIGION

By the end of the 1950s, Indonesia was leaving behind its period of liberal parliamentary democracy. It was also during this time that it started to shift away from a more open attitude toward the definition and regulation of religion. In the period between 1958 and 1965, the government adopted an increasingly rigid approach to religion, even as Muslim and Communist communities in the country grew more and more alienated from each other.

The increase in regulation was partially driven by the growing army influence in the state and the military's desire for clear definitions. This led the Ministry of Religion to decree by the end of the 1950s the necessary requirements for a religion: a God, a Prophet, and a Holy Book. This was soon followed by a directive from the head of the army for East Java, which was later taken up and circulated by the Ministry of Religion, declaring that only Islam, Protestantism, Catholicism, and Balinese Hinduism were recognized religions for the government.[55] This list of religions seems to be the first official list of 'recognized' religions in Indonesia, thus fulfilling the vague constitutional standard of Article 43. The number of religions listed – four – is the lowest in Indonesia's history; following the addition of Buddhism in the 1970s, Indonesia long has since had five recognized religions to match the *Pancasila* or the Five Principles of the national ideology.[56]

[53] Arsip Nasional Republik Indonesia, Koleksi Kabinet Presiden, #163, letter from the Ministry of Religion to Pengurus Besar Djema'at Ahmadiyah Indonesia (16 August 1951). The specific authors he lists are Adnan Lubis and Abdul Karim Amrullah, the latter being the father of the famous polemicist Hamka, who appears again in the text accompanying n. 54.

[54] On Hamka's anti-Ahmadi position, see Karel Steenbrink, 'Hamka (1908–1981) and the Integration of the Islamic Ummah of Indonesia', *Studia Islamika* 1.3 (1994), 119.

[55] Arsip Sulawesi Selatan, Koleksi Kantor Wilayah Departemen Agama Propinsi Sulawesi Selatan, Periode Tahun 1947–90, #223, Penguasa Perang Daerah Swatantra Tingkat I, Jawa Timur: Surat keputusan No. KP/2-33/7/1959 tanggal 4 Juli 1959 tentang Agama yang telah diakui oleh pemerintah.

[56] The introduction of Confucianism in the Reformasi Era brought this number up to six. In spite of occasional presidential suggestions that religions did not need to be formally recognized and Ministry of Religion overtures to possibly add other faiths (in particular Bahai'ism), the list remains at six today.

In the 1960s, officers in the Ministry of Religion were more likely to work on instilling religion in the Indonesian people than to serve and support the religions that citizens had already embraced. In many cases, they even identified 'Not Yet Religious' groups in society as potential objects of Islamic proselytization.[57] This trend intensified even more after 1965. After a supposed attempted Communist coup and an immediate army counter-coup that demonized Communism and led to nation-wide purges of suspected Communists, the practice of religion became a state requirement. In an environment where religion was mandatory, large numbers of previously unaffiliated or only loosely affiliated individuals joined organized religion in droves. Many became Muslims, a process aided by direct bureaucratic facilitation of such decisions, but many others who felt antagonistic toward Islam because of previous persecution of religiously heterodox groups thought they might have better luck as Christians. In Central Java, churches resorted to baptizing crowds by hose in order to accommodate the huge numbers.[58] Christian foreign missionaries across Indonesia reported incredulously their great success at conversion in the late 1960s, not realizing that this had little to do with their outreach techniques or their message but was due to the new social imperative of affiliating oneself with a religion and the perceived benefit of being outside the control of the Islamic functionaries of the Ministry of Religion.[59]

In the 1970s and 1980s, the bureaucratizing impulse of the Ministry of Religion was facilitated by the strength of Suharto's New Order regime. The tight regulation of religious definitions and religious groups showed Suharto's instinct to mandate religion (as a bulwark against Communism), but only when religion was narrowly defined and tightly regulated.[60] Religion was introduced as a mandatory category on Indonesian state identity cards, where the only options were a list of five religions.[61] Any deviant beliefs had to be hidden or could be swiftly shouted down with accusations of irreligion and thus Communism.

Even today, after the democratization reforms of 1998 and the consolidation of democracy in the intervening years, Indonesia has struggled with defining and regulating religion in a way that reflects the beliefs of its citizens. When the current Minister of Religion proposed in 2014 to recognize Baha'i as a religion for state purposes, the idea died on the desk of the Minister for

57 For example, this was already the attitude displayed in the following document: Arsip Sulawesi Selatan, Koleksi Kantor Wilayah Departemen Agama Propinsi Sulawesi Selatan, Periode Tahun 1947–90, #293, Kantor Urusan Agama Propinsi Sulawesi, Kepala Bahagian Sekretariat: Surat tanggal 13 Maret 1952 tentang Laporan Politik dan perkumpulan aliran agama dalam Propinsi Sulawesi.

58 Author's personal communication with Mujiburrahman (17 November 2016).

59 Ricklefs (n. 12), 135–46; Audrey R. Kahin, *Islam, Nationalism and Democracy: A Political Biography of Mohammad Natsir* (NUS Press, 2012), 167–71.

60 Robert W. Hefner, *Civil Islam: Muslims and Democratization in Indonesia* (Princeton University Press, 2000), 79–85.

61 Luthfi Assyaukani, 'Muslim Discourse of Liberal Democracy in Indonesia', in *Muslim Politics and Democratisation in Indonesia* (Monash Asia Institute, 2008), 18.

Home Affairs (who oversees the issuing of identity cards and thus would have to implement such a decision).[62]

VII. CONCLUSION: DEFINING AND REGULATING RELIGION IN INDONESIA TODAY

The disagreement between different ministries over the definition of religion continues to slow down Indonesian government processes today. The Bill on the Protection of Religious Communities shows some of the disagreements between those who want to serve all religious beliefs in Indonesia (under the umbrella of promoting social harmony among communities) and those who would like to promote specific types of orthodoxy by limiting the definition of religions. This Bill is still being formulated by the Ministry of Religion (in consultation with other offices) and is slated for debate in the Indonesian parliament in 2017.[63]

In contrast with previous practices during the Suharto era, there is now much wider scope – on paper – for religious minority communities to have basic documents like birth certificates and burial permits processed by their local governments without having to falsify or change their religion. However, this process remains very difficult for religious communities to access. An updated definition of religion in Indonesia would thus greatly help believers of minority or local religions.[64]

Within the government, expectations of the forthcoming Bill vary widely, especially where it relates to definitions of religion. The former Minister of Education and Culture, Anies Baswedan, has called on the government to fully protect the widest freedom of religion and belief while noting that this protection has been included in Indonesia's constitutions and has never been subject to amendments. The Ministry of Education and Culture also holds the widest and most open list of beliefs in the government, with 182 groups listed at the national level and 937 in the regions.[65] In contrast, the Minister of Home Affairs, Tjahjo Kumolo, seeks to limit recognized religions and still wants to use the government to promote certain normative positions. He has said: 'There are some who say they are being hampered [in their practice of religion], although they are not being hampered, but we just need clarification. Is your belief misguided or not?'[66] By retaining the possibility

62 Camelia Pasandaran, 'New Religious Affairs Minister Supports State Recognition of Baha'i Religion', *The Jakarta Globe* (25 July 2014).

63 'Kemenag Targetkan RUU Perlindungan Umat Beragama Dibahas di DPR 2017' *Kompas* (Jakarta, 23 February 2016), http://nasional.kompas.com/read/2016/02/23/16234821/Kemenag.Targetkan.RUU.Perlindungan.Umat.Beragama.Dibahas.di.DPR.2017 (accessed 1 March 2017). See also 'Menag: RUU PUB Dalam Tahap Pendalaman' Ministry of Religious Affairs of the Republic of Indonesia (21 June 2016), www.ropeg.kemenag.go.id/index.php?a=berita&id=379280 (accessed 1 March 2017).

64 'Ini Pekerjaan Rumah Kita: Wawancara dengan Tjahjo Kumolo', *Gatra* (Jakarta, 20 July 2016), 42–5.

65 'Secara Prinsip Hak Telah Terpenuhi: Wawancara dengan Anies Baswedan', *Gatra* (Jakarta, 20 July 2016), 83.

66 'Ini Pekerjaan Rumah Kita' (n. 64), 44.

that government regulations could prohibit certain practices for being misguided, Kumolo would promote orthodoxy by limiting the opportunity for local and minority religions to gain recognition. The Majelis Ulama Indonesia (MUI), a quasi-official board composed of representatives of Indonesia's major Islamic organizations, takes an even stronger line; it opposes this Bill on the grounds that it could pave the way for new beliefs or religions to be recognized. Its members strongly seek to promote only mainstream Islamic orthodoxy and want to clamp down on any local or heterodox offshoots that are related to Islam.[67] The vice-chairman of the MUI has publicly said that if minority beliefs like the Ahmadiyyah 'are protected, this poses a risk to the entire Islamic community'.[68] The Minister of Religion has tried to hold a middle position in public by recognising the need for a definition that more accurately reflects Indonesia's diversity, while also trying to avoid offending his backers among the conservative Muslim community.[69]

In these different responses, one can see both the continuing importance of defining religion as the first step towards regulating religion and the ongoing influence of the early era of Indonesian independence in these processes. Priorities such as protecting beliefs, supporting social harmony, and channelling beliefs into certain acceptable streams still inform the process of definition. In the current debate, though, it is useful to remember that the Indonesian state did not always limit itself to a small list of acceptable categories (as popular memory would suggest). It also bears remembering that the initial legislative impetus was to protect freedom of belief and freedom of conscience in their broadest possible meaning.

67 'MUI Keberatan jika RUU PUB Beri Peluang Munculnya Aliran Sesat dan Agama Baru', *Kompas* (Jakarta, 19 March 2016), http://nasional.kompas.com/read/2016/03/19/21050031/MUI .Keberatan.jika.RUU.PUB.Beri.Peluang.Munculnya.Aliran.Sesat.dan.Agama.Baru (accessed 1 March 2017).

68 'Kemenag Telah Siapkan RUU Perlindungan Agama', *IslamPos* (Jakarta, 21 February 2015), www .islampos.com/kemenag-telah-siapkan-ruu-perlindungan-agama-165383 (accessed 1 March 2017).

69 'Mendefinisikan Agama Tidak Sederhana' (n. 1).

PART II

Regulating Religion: State Practice and Legal Norms

6

Principled Pluralism, Relational Constitutionalism and Regulating Religion within Singapore's Secular Democratic Model

Thio Li-ann

I. INTRODUCTION

Law and religion are both normative, regulatory orders which govern human conduct and the communal life of the political community and the community of faith. The prospect of conflict from competing demands of loyalty is present, given the monist conception of the modern state, where the law claims ultimate authority as 'a common framework'[1] for all citizens within a unitary system hostile to non-state normative orders in the form of religious laws. This speaks to a 'foundational power struggle' between 'the earthly, human-enacted constitution and the claim to speak in a vernacular of a revealed or divine authority'.[2] The focus of this volume, as it were, on the idea of 'regulating religion', necessarily assumes the coexistence of religion and the state within the same legal order, rather than operating dualistically in separate realms as 'sphere sovereigns'.[3] Religion is not 'sovereign' in the sense of occupying 'a sacred realm operating over and above human-made law', insulated from the decisions of secular authorities such that there is 'no balance of powers'.[4]

However, regulation has its limits and an accommodation between state and religion is reflected in constitutional settlements. State power must be exercised in a manner compatible with fundamental principles, such as liberty of religion and conscience and legal pluralism. In turn, this might require the limited operation of religious laws administered by religious institutions. In terms of religious freedom, international human rights law recognizes the *forum internum* (freedom to profess faith) as inviolate while acknowledging reasonable or proportionate limits upon the

1 Mariano Croce, 'What Is Legal Pluralism All About? The Disquieting Effect of Deconstructing Narratives', *XI Jura Gentium* (2014), 164, 176.

2 Ran Hirschl and Ayelat Shachar, 'The New Wall of Separation: Permitting Diversity, Restricting Competition', *Cardozo Law Review* 30(2009), 2535, 2537.

3 Johan D. van der Vyver, 'Equality and Sovereignty of Religious Institutions: A South African Perspective', *Santa Clara Journal of International Law* 10 (2012), 147.

4 Jonathan Seglow, 'Religious Sovereignty and Group Exemptions', *Netherlands Journal of Legal Philosophy* 44.3 (2015), 231.

right to 'manifest' religious belief, individually or in community, in worship, observance, practice and teaching.[5] Religious groups' rights to manage their own affairs can also act as a jurisdictional principle of structural restraint, delineating spheres of human activity where the state may not intrude, or must show compelling reasons for regulatory intervention.

In this chapter, I propose the idea of 'principled pluralism' as a controlling norm for regulating religion. Principled pluralism takes the constitutional norms of religious freedom and secularity and the social fact of religious diversity seriously. It posits that the important democratic values of viewpoint diversity and free conscience are best secured by a government agnostic towards religious orthodoxy, without oppressive laws regulating apostasy, blasphemy, heresy and religious propagation, a form of free speech. In preserving free conscience, it is argued that religion – or more precisely, religious freedom – complements, rather than undermines, democracy.[6] A commitment to these freedom values does not obviate the need to instrumentally regulate certain religious freedoms to serve the public interest. What matters is how to strike a balance so that neither side of the equation is rendered nugatory or unjustly discounted.

Consequently, principled pluralism rejects three extreme positions. First, it rejects theocratic rule or clerocracy, where divine sanction or ecclesiastical authority underwrites political authority. As such, within secular constitutional orders, public power flows from popular, not divine sovereignty. Secondly, it rejects militant secularism, a brand of antitheistic illiberal secularism which seeks the religious cleansing of public spaces in favour of a preferred humanistic ideology; in marginalising religion, it tends to trivialise religious freedom and insofar as it does so, is inimical to democracy. Thirdly, it rejects a radical form of multiculturalism which embraces an extreme cultural and ethical relativism which robs society of the ability to make authoritative judgements on unjust cultural or religious practices.[7]

Within religiously diverse communitarian polities like Singapore, this involves the negotiation of religious liberty, religious pluralism and religious harmony as a facet of public order and relational solidarity.[8] Pluralism implies that people must accept limits for the sake of living together and engage with each other to build partnerships which serve the common good. In the interests of securing social harmony, the approach of relational constitutionalism is sometimes applied, which seeks to ensure a form of sustainable democracy and relational health rather than intergroup antagonism, through promoting dialogue, public rituals of

5 Article 18, Universal Declaration of Human Rights, GA Res 217A (III), UN Doc A/810 at 71 (1948).

6 This is with the caveat that 'religion' is not a monolithic or agreed on category and the appreciation that some religions, especially those supporting free conscience, are more 'democracy friendly' than others.

7 Richard Neuhaus, *The Naked Public Square: Religion and Democracy in America*, 2nd edn (Eerdmans, 1968), 374.

8 Li-ann Thio, 'Relational Constitutionalism and the Management of Inter-Religious Disputes: The Singapore "Secularism with a Soul" Model', *Oxford Journal of Law and Religion* 2(2012), 446.

reconciliation in the event of disputes, while maintaining freedom of religious choice and the non-involvement of the state in religious doctrine, as a matter of fundamental principle.

This chapter examines the extent to which the values underlying principled pluralism have affected government approaches towards regulating religion in Singapore. The Singaporean experience is interesting, as it is a secular state with a religious society, where 80% of its population bears a religious affiliation, and has been described as the world's most religiously diverse country.[9] This chapter first unpacks the core values that inform a principled pluralism approach and relates this to the constitutional and legal framework ordering state and religion. It then identifies and evaluates five broad postures the government has adopted in relation to religiously related activities (Controller, Cooperative Partner, Consultative Leader, Constant Calibrator and Culture War Manager). Lastly, this chapter offers concluding observations, noting that a chief criterion for measuring whether state and religion have been optimally accommodated is the extent to which there are healthy prospects for nurturing and sustaining 'Religion Freedom-Friendly Democracy and Democracy-Friendly Religion';[10] this is foundational to a just and stable religiously plural polity, where distinctive identities and national integrity are both secured.

II. CORE VALUES OF PRINCIPLED PLURALISM AND THE SINGAPORE CONSTITUTIONAL ORDER

A. *Unpacking Principled Pluralism*

Principled pluralism, as an approach, implicates the proper relationship between state and religion, between models of secularism, religious freedoms and the plural religious affiliations of citizens. Various principles or core values associated with principled pluralism can be identified.

First, principled pluralism is built on the recognition that free conscience as a facet of personal integrity is inviolate, protecting a voluntarist understanding of religious identity and affiliation. It values religious liberty on the basis that individual free conscience and the communal autonomy of religious groups guards against organicist states which dictate citizen beliefs and seek to control every area of civic life. Where religious liberty is robustly protected, among other liberties,

9 "Of the 232 countries in the study, Singapore – an island nation of more than 5 million people situated at the southern tip of Malaysia – has the highest score on the Religious Diversity Index. About a third of Singapore's population is Buddhist (34%), while 18% are Christian, 16% are religiously unaffiliated, 14% are Muslim, 5% are Hindu and <1% are Jewish. The remainder of the population belongs to folk or traditional religions (2%) or to other religions considered as a group (10%)." Pew Research Center, 'Global Religious Diversity' (4 April 2014), www.pewforum.org/2014/04/04/global-religious-diversity/ (accessed 23 May 2017).

10 Tony Blair, 'Protecting Religious Freedom Should Be a Priority for All Democracies', *Review of Faith and International Affairs* 10.3 (2012), 5.

government does not become the totality of society, but merely one institution in society, coexisting with groups like families, businesses, societies and faith communities, each with their respective spheres of competence and authority. Furthermore, principled pluralism sees religious liberty as grounding political liberty, and this secures the freedom of citizens to determine their priorities and choices and to collectively shape society. Religious liberty helps preserve limited government and social resilience insofar as the state does not alienate religious communities through oppressive measures or enforce a coercive public secularist ideology.

Second, the state must recognise deep religious differences and the desire of citizens to lead authentic lives based on their cherished religious convictions. It must be officially impartial or neutral between religious faiths and secular humanist ideologies, treating these in an even-handed manner as far as possible.

Third, in enacting general laws relating to employment or public service, the state may apply a principle of 'reasonable accommodation' of differences through providing exemptions, particularly where conscience is implicated or where laws negatively and disproportionately impact certain categories of people. While dissenters must not suffer political disadvantage, exemptions cannot undermine basic civil rights. In applying an approach of reasonable accommodation, courts must seek a judicious balance between expressive freedoms and threats to social harmony or the civil duty of solidarity, expressed through observing equal respect for the public dignity of religion and religious minorities.

Fourth, the public square is to be kept open to the fullest expression and testing of a diverse range of viewpoints, including the assertion of public truth-claims, which is compatible with the essential obligations of citizenship. It must neither be a 'sacred' public square which requires conformity with preferred religious dogma, nor a 'naked' public square, shorn of religious views, which deprives society of an important normative resource of knowledge and meaning. Citizens of whatever theological or philosophical persuasion enjoy equal rights to participate in democratic processes and to persuade their peers; this should be accomplished preferably through elevated debate, disciplined by a commitment to reason-giving, civility and a good faith orientation towards the common good, rather than a myopic preoccupation with single-issue agendas. In a 'civil' public square, no one faith is comprehensively normative though all faiths may be freely expressed.[11]

Furthermore, a commitment to deliberation and mutual restraint in not gratuitously giving offence to the convictions or practices other citizens value is required for relational health and sustainable democracy. This view appreciates that the objective of free speech is not primarily 'to protect the bare agency of a speaker, abstracted from all social relations',[12] but to facilitate and not thwart communication.

[11] Neuhaus (n. 7).

[12] Jonathan Chaplin, 'Liberté, Laïcité, Pluralité: Towards a Theology of Principled Pluralism', *International Journal of Public Theology* 10(2016), 354, 378.

Fifth, some 'give-and-take' is needed between the state and religious communities: while the state cannot impose ultimate truths or arrogate the power to determine 'true' religion, all religious and secular citizens 'should renounce any aspiration to the monopolization of the polity by their own faith or worldview'.[13] Principled pluralism seeks to secure space for deep diversity because of 'its commitment to the search for universal truth'; this rejects 'monopolistic claims on the part of the gatekeepers of the public realm'[14] to determine what public truth is and thereby marginalise dissent.

Sixth, the government is obliged to protect and respect the autonomy of religious groups as one of many social institutions distinct from government. It must recognise that the communal dimension of religious freedom entails not merely religious belief but religious relationships, and maintain 'a community of faith that shares a common understanding'.[15] It must also adhere to the jurisdictional limits of its own power, grounded on the distinction between civil and religious authority, and appreciate the relational dimension of human beings as citizen-members of a polity, members of families, faith and professional communities. This militates against a fusion of shared religious and political unity; instead, the state's role is to preserve civic peace and to facilitate the pacific coexistence of beliefs within the same territorial space. Principled pluralism is supported by a cooperationist model of state–religion relations, where religious groups may 'manifest' their faith through offering public services in the form of medical, educational and social services in their own distinctive manner.

These values of principled pluralism operate within a context where minimum expectations of modest standards of 'good citizenship' are observed, such as the ready acceptance of democratic decisions, paying taxes, being law-abiding and the practice of fundamental political virtues like a commitment to peaceful coexistence with ideological rivals and civil deliberation.

B. *Principled Pluralism and the Singapore Constitutional Order*

On seceding from the Malaysian Federation on 9 August 1965, the Singapore government had to formulate an approach and policy towards religion, and managing social tensions arising from conflicts within a multireligious, ethnically diverse polity. Parliament convened on 22 December 1965 to settle the formalities consequent to Singapore's new status as an independent sovereign republic, presenting a key 'constitutional moment' for Singapore to define its own identity as an independent Republic.

The path taken at inception was both one of continuity and rupture, fuelled by principled and pragmatic instrumentalism. The pragmatism was evident in the

13 Ibid., 368.
14 Jonathan Chaplin, 'The Point of Kuyperian Pluralism' *Comment Magazine* (1 November 2013).
15 *Alberta v. Hutterian Brethren of Wilson Colony* [2009] SCC 37 [180]–[182].

nature of the first Independence Constitution. This was not a product of grand design but a serviceable instrument composing a patchwork quilt of various instruments, adapting the 1958 State Constitution, borrowing selectively from the Malaysian Federal Constitution, modifying nomenclature and making necessary adjustments to reflect Singapore's status as a sovereign state.

Reflecting aversive constitutionalism, the Singapore Constitution diverged in principle from the Malaysian one in three key aspects. First, the Constitution does not 'confess' an official religion, contrary to the Malaysian Article 3.[16] Instead, it founds a secular democratic order which does not identify with any religion. Unlike Malaysia, no Singapore government agencies protect religious orthodoxy or prosecute deviationist groups.[17] The government holds 'no theological views' on what constitutes heresy;[18] it does not take action against religious bodies on grounds of religious doctrine or because it considers it a 'cult'[19]; it acts when general law is contravened, such as when a registered (religious) society participates in an unlawful assembly.

Second, it did not import the Malaysian Article 11(4), which authorises legislation to prohibit propagating another faith to Muslims, because giving such 'special treatment' to any religion was contrary to a democratic secular order.[20] Third, it refused to conflate ethnicity (Malay) and religious faith (Islam), as the Malaysian Article 160 does.

The last two points reflects Singapore's approach towards religious identity and affiliation, which is based on personal self-determination. The Court of Appeal confirmed this voluntarist approach in *Nappalli v. Institute of Technical Education*, noting that 'protection of freedom of religion under our Constitution is premised on removing restrictions to one's choice of religious belief', which was described as 'accommodative secularism'.[21] Furthermore, no person is required to participate in religious ceremonies or receive religious instruction in relation to a religion he does not subscribe to: Article 16(3).

While Article 15(1) protects the right of every person to 'profess and practise his religion, and to propagate it', this may be regulated by 'any general law relating to public order, public health or morality': 15(4). Religious groups have the right to manage their 'own religious affairs' under Article 15(3) and to establish and maintain

16 Article 3 of the Federal Malaysian Constitution identifies Islam as the 'religion of the Federation'.

17 Restricting the propagation of religious doctrine to Muslims under Article 11(4) of the Constitution is to protect Islam from exposure to other religions or certain Islamic schools of thought: *Lina Joy* [2004] 2 MLJ 119 (CA) 131.

18 This was stated in rejecting a request in 1994 to ban Al Arqam which Muslim leaders considered a deviant sect. 'Certain Controls Necessary to Keep Peace', *Straits Times, Sunday Review* (Singapore, 10 December 1995), 4.

19 This was stated in relation to the Falun Buddha or Falungong society: Singapore Parliament Reports 6 March 2000, col 1141.

20 Constitutional Commission, *Report of the Constitutional Commission* (Singapore Government Printers, 1966), para 38.

21 [1999] 2 SLR 569 (CA) [28].

educational institutions, including the provision of religious instruction under Article 16(2). In comparison, reflecting a protectionist approach towards Islam, Article 12(2) of the Malaysian Constitution makes it lawful for the government to maintain Islamic institutions or underwrite Islamic instruction. Thus, the Singapore approach is more closely aligned with a 'free marketplace' attitude towards religious competition, with the government not endorsing or promoting any one religion, and generally refusing to get entangled in matters of religious orthodoxy.[22]

The Singapore Constitution does not have an anti-establishment clause and does not prohibit the 'establishment' of any religion.[23] Article 15(2) protects a person from paying taxes whose proceeds go to 'the purposes of a religion other than his own'. Indirect support is given to the religion of Islam on the basis of an indigeneity clause in Article 152(2) which requires the government to recognise the 'special position of the Malays' and to promote their interests, including religious interests. The reason Islam gets some special treatment is because more than 99% of Malays are Muslims[24] as a matter of fact. This does not extend to state propagation of Islam to non-Muslims,[25] but rather, to supporting Malay-Muslim communal life. For example, the collection of religious tithes or *zakat* is facilitated by access to government machinery in relation to the Central Provident Fund, a privilege not extended to other religious groups.[26] Article 153 authorised the enactment of the Administration of Muslim Law (AMLA) Act (Cap 3) which regulates Muslim religious affairs and constitutes the Islamic Religious Council (MUIS) which advises the President. AMLA contains norms concerning personal laws relating to marriage, divorce, testamentary disposition, as well Muslim-specific offences like cohabitation outside marriage. It establishes religious courts and empowers MUIS to regulate Islamic religious schools (*madrasashs*), the Mosque building fund, *halal* certification, Mecca pilgrimages and to maintain a registry of converts. Government policy also ensured that when Malays were resettled in new towns as part of the urban resettlement programme, a site for building a mosque (underwritten by the Muslim community) would be guaranteed.[27]

22 Although the Muslim Affairs Minister has stated that the Islamic State was a 'deviant group' which was 'basically not Islam'. Olivia Siong, 'PM Lee Holds Dialogue with Religious, Community Leaders on Islamic State Threat', *Channel News Asia* (Singapore, 29 November 2014).

23 *Chan Hiang Leng Colin v. Public Prosecutor* [1994] SGHC 207, [1994] 3 SLR(R) 209 [53].

24 The 2010 Census of Population reports that 98.7% of Malays were Muslim: www.singstat.gov.sg/-/media/files/publications/cop2010/census_2010_release3/indicators.pdf (accessed 15 September 2018).

25 In contrast, the Malaysian government implements programmes designed to assimilate indigenous Orang Asli into mainstream society through conversion to Islam, by offering financial inducements. Toshihiro Nobuta, 'Islamization Policy Towards the Orang Asli in Malaysia', *Bulletin of the National Museum of Ethnology* 31.4 (2007), 479–95.

26 Contributions from Hindus for Temples etc. and Monies from Muslims for Mosques etc., *Singapore Parliament Reports* (3 December 1982), col 309, 311.

27 Ministerial Statement, *Singapore Parliament Reports* (29 June 1977), col 62 (Mosque Building Fund Scheme).

The government propounds the view that in a multiracial, multireligious setting where the population has no shared past, a common future grounded on shared values, built from some form of constitutional patriotism perhaps of the communitarian variety, is needed for nation-building and cultivating solidarity. As transcendence abhors a vacuum, the place assumed by a common religion is replaced by an *ersatz* political substitute or a constitutional 'civil religion' of sorts, comprising core principles which shape public governance and duties of citizenship. This departs from the belief that political unity depends on a shared religious vision which must be enforced to secure civic peace; rather it rests on a commitment to freedom for all faiths, ensuring that plurality becomes a source of national resilience, not social unrest.

As the Constitution is largely silent on normative values, the contents of this 'civil religion' may be gleaned from sources of 'soft constitutional law'[28] which, while not legally binding, has some legal effect and create expectations of adherence amongst constitutional actors. Such norms relevant to regulating religion are found in various white papers relating to shared values (1990),[29] maintenance of religious harmony (1989), Jemaah Islamiyah terrorist threat (2001) and in non-binding instruments such as the 2004 Declaration of Religious Harmony.[30] These norms are given written expression and confirmed or modified by subsequent practice where they are invoked as normatively in terms of how constitutional actors should behave.

These norms include secularism, treating other religious groups respectfully and not inciting hostility or violence inter se, non-denigratory approaches in evangelism in deferring to religious sensitivities within a multireligious setting. They foster pragmatic goals such as maintaining racial and religious harmony;[31] however, they are also grounded on principle, as these soft norms exhort all to respect the rights of individuals 'to accept or not to accept any religion',[32] consistent with Article 15(1). If there is a deity, this cannot be revealed through state *diktat,* only individual conscience. *Libertas ecclesiae*, or the freedom of religious institutions from secular jurisdiction, begat free conscience.

Secularism thus operates as a principle of limited government where the state recognises the limits of its own capacity; the Singapore model of secularism is antitheocratic, not antireligious.[33] Prime Minister Lee has observed that as a

28 Li-ann Thio, 'Soft Constitutional Law in Nonliberal Asian Constitutional Democracies', *ICON* 8.4 (2010), 766.

29 The values declared support communitarianism in the form of norms favouring consensus over contention, the family as the basic unit of society and placing nation over community and society over self as well as racial and religious harmony. The courts have also identified 'communitarian values' as shaping public law: *Public Prosecutor v. Kwong Kok Hing* [2008] SGCA 10, [2008] 2 SLR (R) 684 [17].

30 For an analysis of these norms and how they operate, see Thio (n. 8), 1–24.

31 'Pragmatic pluralism' defends pluralism on grounds of social harmony: see Rex Adhar and Ian Leigh, *Religious Freedom in the Liberal State*, 2nd edn (Oxford University Press, 2013), 109–12.

32 *Maintenance of Religious Harmony White Paper* (Cmd 21, 1989), para 18.

33 For an examination of Singapore's secular constitutional practices, see Jaclyn L. Neo, 'Secular Constitutionalism in Singapore: Between Equality and Hierarchy', *Oxford Journal of Law & Religion* (2016), 431.

whole, religion was a 'good thing', as a 'godless society' would 'have many other problems' as the communists found out.[34] Secularity within Singapore is thought essential to accommodate diverse spiritual beliefs, where the state is not 'antagonistic' towards religious beliefs, and treats all religious groups in an even-handed manner.[35]

III. REGULATING RELIGION: FIVE POSTURES

The secular orientation of the Singapore government is such that it has no interest in upholding religious orthodoxy, only the pragmatic concern of maintaining social harmony. It appreciates that unlike homogeneous societies where settled customs and unwritten expectations are enforced by peer pressure, the rule of law which makes expectations transparent is more important in non-homogeneous societies. In plural societies with people of different cultural backgrounds, the prospect of conflict is enhanced such that '[h]armony in a diverse society cannot be achieved with a laissez-faire system'.[36] Different communities have their own religious beliefs and moral values and without observing the rule of law as the basis for general law, conflict will ensue. Thus, all must respect the law in accordance with 'common ground rules of engagement and conflict resolution, and to secure a large common secular space which belongs to all citizens regardless of race, language or religion'.[37] The rule of law is thus linked not only to public order but also to 'racial and religious harmony'.[38] This reflects a concern with relational constitutionalism, the health of social relationships beyond bare social order.

Given the 'primordial pulls' of race, religion and language, the government believes that 'social harmony must be sustained by human endeavour'.[39] In taking a 'pragmatic approach', the government seeks to expand 'common spaces and experiences for all citizens', while recognising the need for a separate domain 'sensitive to the needs of every community'.[40] Some degree of autonomy is recognised with respect to the Muslim community whose personal laws and customs are set out in AMLA and administered by the religious institutions (the Syariah Court and MUIS) it establishes. Although originating from divine sources, AMLA norms are not non-state laws but statutorily 'restated' secular laws. These provisions co-exist in tension with other constitutional protections and human rights obligations, such

34 'We Welcome Criticism within Constraints, Says Singapore Prime Minister Lee Hsien Loong', *Channel NewsAsia* (Singapore, 23 July 2015).
35 *Maintenance of Religious Harmony White Paper* (n. 32), para 5.
36 DPM S Jayakumar, 'Keynote Address' (19 October 2007), IBA Rule of Law Symposium, www.mlaw.gov.sg/news/speeches/keynote-address-by-dpm-prof-s-jayakumar-at-the-iba-rule-of-law-symposium.html para 17 (accessed 15 September 2018).
37 Ibid., para 18.
38 Ibid., paras 17–19.
39 Ibid.
40 Singapore National Report, *Universal Periodic Review* (28 October 2015), A/JRCWG.6/24/SGP/1, para 6.

as gender equality. Thus, Singapore attached reservations when it acceded to the Convention for the Elimination of All Forms of Discrimination against Women 1995.[41] This insulates statutory norms which embody Islamic religious laws that discriminate against women – e.g., as in terms of testamentary disposition and permitting polygamy. Nonetheless, the state determines which general laws religious law should enjoy exemption from, and civil courts do maintain a degree of supervisory jurisdiction over religious courts, such as requiring them to observe natural justice principles.[42]

Five broad postures have been adopted by the state, in relation to various forms of religiously related activities, which is explored in the text that follows with a view to seeing how successfully the concerns of principled pluralism – the recognition of diversity and pacific coexistence and the robust protection of religious freedoms by an impartial state – are realised. It employs both obligatory 'hard' law and persuasive soft constitutional law norms in regulating religion, whether as an external or coregulator, or in urging self-regulation to avoid the appearance of being over-intrusive with respect to religious freedom.[43]

A. *Controller*

Singapore has been characterised as a 'soft authoritarian' state where economic liberalisation took place without political liberalisation – political liberties were curbed when seen to threaten political stability, a precondition to attracting foreign investment and trade. However, in a repoliticised, post-deferential landscape today, contemporary governance is more consultative in nature. The government styles Singaporeans as 'co-authors' of the next chapter of the Singapore story where 'every voice counts'.[44] Nonetheless, a premium is still placed on public order[45] and national survivability, where the government adopts the role of 'controller', who acts to preserve racial and religious harmony.

Regulatory legislation is both preventative and punitive in nature. First, in pre-emptive terms, Section 8 of the Maintenance of Religious Harmony Act (MRHA) (Cap 167A) permits the Minister to issue 'restraining orders' against religious leaders

[41] Li-ann Thio, 'She's a Woman, But She Acts Very Fast: Women, Religion and Law in Singapore', in Carolyn Evans and Amanda Whiting (eds.), *Mixed Blessings: Law, Religions, and Women's Rights in the Asia-Pacific Region* (Brill, 2006), 241–77.

[42] *Mohamed Ismail bin Ibrahim v. Mohammad Taha bin Ibrahim* [2004] SGHC 210, [2004] 4 SLR (R) 756.

[43] *Jemaah Islamiyah Arrests and the Threat of Terrorism* (Cmd 2, 2003) 22, the government noting that efforts to identify and neutralise radical teachers and foreign terrorist operatives must not 'disrupt the legitimate practices and peaceful activities of the local Muslim community'. It urged the Muslim community to develop 'a comprehensive self-regulatory system to monitor religious education'.

[44] Prime Minister Lee Hsien Loong, 'Speech at Swearing-in Ceremony on 1 October 2015', www.pmo.gov.sg/mediacentre/transcript-speech-prime-minister-lee-hsien-loong-swearing-ceremony-1-oct-2015 paras 22, 25 (accessed 15 September 2018).

[45] *Chee Siok Chin v. MHA* [2005] SGHC 216, [2006] 1 SLR (R) 582 [135].

on various grounds, which gags the object of the order from addressing any religious groups orally or through religious publications. These grounds include 'causing feelings of enmity, hatred, ill-will or hostility between different religious groups', promoting political causes, subversive activities or exciting disaffection against the government under the guise of propagating religious beliefs. Section 9 captures conflict entrepreneurs who incite religious groups to commit any of these acts.

MRHA has never been deployed, as the government prefers to give warnings to possible 'transgressors', such as religious leaders who criticise other faiths or who mix religion and politics – e.g., when an Islamic leader urged Muslims to vote for Muslim candidates in the 1991 General Elections.[46] These open-ended provisions confer broad discretion on the Minister to determine what constitutes 'religion' and 'politics' and when they may not be mixed, thereby defining the parameters of permissible behaviour. Insofar as this preserves the social order, it protects the pacific coexistence of plural faiths; however, restraining orders do constitute a limit on religious freedom and some measure of accountability is needed to guard against abuses. Judicial review is precluded under Section 18, replaced by political checks in the form of the elected President and the Presidential Council of Religious Harmony who may, if ad idem, effectively 'veto' a restraining order. Terrorists acting in the name of religion, such as the Jemaah Islamiyah terrorists who planned several failed bomb attacks in the early 2000s, may be preventively detained under the Internal Security Act (Cap 143). This extraordinary power which limits personal liberty protected under Article 9 is authorised by Article 149, under which draconian laws are enacted to deal with national security threats, as society is not a suicide club.

Secondly, law has a 'major capacity for coercion'[47] and this is reflected in the punitive legal sanctions imposed for offences under the Penal Code (Cap 224). Section 298 criminalises wounding religious feelings by word or sound, and Section 298A addresses promoting 'disharmony or feelings of enmity, hatred or ill-will between different religious or racial groups'.

Thus, the accused in *Public Prosecutor v. Amos Yee Pang Sang*[48] was convicted of a Section 298 offence by uploading a YouTube video slurring the late former prime minister Lee Kuan Yew and Christian priests as power hungry, malicious and manipulative. The judge found the derogatory comments offensive to Christians, which was tantamount to wounding religious feelings. The acute sensitivity the law has towards social harmony is reflected in that impact is irrelevant to liability, and what matters is instead whether the publisher had deliberate intent to cause offence. The imposition of deterrent and retributive imprisonment sentences indicates the state's intolerance of potential threats that pejorative remarks pose to social disorder.

[46] 'Government Reins in Religious Leaders', *Straits Times* (Singapore, 12 May 2001), 1.

[47] Francesco Viola, 'The Rule of Law in Legal Pluralism', in T. Gizbert-Studnicki and J. Stelamach (eds.), *Law and Legal Cultures in the 21st Century: Diversity and Unity* (Oficyna, 2007), 107.

[48] [2015] SGDC 215.

Existential threats to national security and communal peace posed by religion or the exploitation of religion may also be sanctioned under the Sedition Act (Cap 290) which forms part of the 'strong legal framework' designed to deter anyone from 'attempting to cause racial and religious conflict'.[49] Sedition is statutorily defined under Section 3 not only as exciting disaffection against the government, but extends unusually to promoting 'feelings of ill-will and hostility between races or classes of the population of Singapore'. 'Races and classes' have been broadly defined to include religious groups, particularly Malay-Muslim groups, as in *Public Prosecutor v. Koh Song Huat Benjamin*,[50] where a blog post placing a pig's head next to a halal logo and comparing Islam to Satanism was held to be seditious, given the threat posed to especially sensitive race and religion issues. Similarly, in *Public Prosecutor v. Ong Kian Cheong*,[51] a Christian couple was fined and imprisoned under the Sedition Act for placing tracts entitled 'The Little Bride' or 'Who is Allah' in mailboxes with Malay sounding names, as this was likely to case feelings of enmity, ill-will or hostility between Christians and Muslims.[52] The judge observed the couple could not be ignorant of racial and religious sensitivities and prudential rules that evangelism within Singapore had to be 'constrained by sensitivity, tolerance and mutual respect for another's faith'.[53]

Such restrictions on constitutionally guaranteed expressive freedoms are justified on grounds of preserving the integrity of the multiracial and multireligious state. However in protecting wounded 'feelings' which generate pain through speech restrictive laws, truth is sometimes sacrificed at the altar of civil peace, and the emotional person voicing his distress may displace the disposition of the rational person who values dissent and viewpoint diversity as a common good.[54] This has been framed as a balancing act between free speech and freedom from offence, insults and harassment (which is not constitutionally guaranteed). Evaluating when speech warrants curtailment will involve difficult but necessary line-drawing exercises between speech which is and is not legitimately offensive, as informed by local particularities.[55] In *Benjamin Koh*, reference was not made to a constitutional right of freedom from offence, but to the 'appropriate social behavior, independent of any legal duty' of all Singaporeans to adhere to basic grounds, so as not to 'plunge the country into strife and violence' by what one might say or do.[56] Expressive freedoms

49 Singapore National Report (n. 40), para 97.

50 [2005] SGDC 272.

51 [2009] SGDC 163.

52 See further Jaclyn L. Neo, 'Seditious in Singapore! Free Speech and the Offence of Promoting Ill-Will and Hostility between Different Racial Groups', *Singapore Journal of Legal Studies* (2011), 351.

53 [2009] SGDC 163 (n. 51) [82].

54 Daniel Statman, 'Hurting Religious Feelings', *Democratic Culture* 3 (2000), 199, 211 (arguing that as a matter of dignity, to avoid acting like 'weeping children appealing for pity', a religious group should make claims not on the basis of feelings, but on the reasons for the bad feelings, save where there is a deliberate intent to offend or disrespect the victim).

55 *Chee Siok Chin* (n. 45) [136]. *PP v. Benjamin Koh* [2005] SGDC 272 [8].

56 *PP v. Benjamin Koh* [2005] SGDC 272 [8].

are expressly subject under Article 14 to eight permissible grounds of derogation, including 'public order', as Parliament deems 'necessary or expedient'. Although the courts appear to peg the test implicitly at whether a government official was acting reasonably in undertaking speech restrictive action,[57] what is 'reasonable' in a communitarian context that valorises civil peace often translates practically to tipping the scale in favour of justifying the restriction.

While the right to religious propagation is an expression of constitutional guarantees of free speech and religious freedom which seek to advance truth claims by respectful persuasion, there are laws regulating this liberty. Propagation is moderated not for content but for style and impact – one of the dangers MRHA was enacted to control is that of 'aggressive proselytization', which can breed ill-will between religious groups and so constitute sedition as in *Ong Kian Cheong*, or be the subject of an MRHA order. Aside from this form of legal regulation, the government seeks to regulate propagation informally by stressing the importance of refraining from propagation in a manner which insults or denigrates the religious beliefs of others. This soft constitutional norm is contained in the Maintenance of Religious Harmony White Paper[58] and has been reiterated by government ministers after disquiet arises between religious groups, such as in the Lighthouse Evangelism case where a video put up by a Christian pastor on his church website upset some Buddhists and Taoists.[59] The pastor took the video down after the Internal Security Department issued him a warning; Buddhist and Taoists leaders accepted the pastor's personal apology and issued media statements urging interfaith understanding. Thus, the incident was diffused publicly by the actions of the private parties; the government took more of a background role in affirming the responses of the respective parties.[60]

Despite the indirect control the government exerted here, it is clear that if the parties had not acted to de-escalate things, the government would have had to step in, which is itself risky as that can heighten tensions and place entire religious communities under siege. The government thus supports a relational approach that seeks to restore relationships between religious groups, rather than stepping in with heavy-handed punitive measures. After the Taoists and another church had a run-in and made up, the Taoist Chief and a church deacon performed a duet at the Taoist Federation 20th Anniversary dinner, with no less august a guest than Prime Minister Lee Hsien Loong gracing the occasion and giving his stamp of approval to their reconciliation.[61]

57 *Chee Siok Chin* (n. 45) [123].

58 *Maintenance of Religious Harmony White Paper* (n. 32), para 13.

59 Yen Feng, 'ISD calls up Pastor for insensitive comments', *Straits Times* (9 February 2010); Grace Chua, 'Leaders of Buddhists Taoist Groups Urge Restraint', *Straits Times* (9 February 2010).

60 Thio Li-ann, 'Contentious Liberty: Regulating Religious Propagation in a Religiously Diverse Secular Democracy', *Singapore Journal of Legal Studies* (2010), 484.

61 'Song of Friendship', *Straits Times* (4 December 2010).

Thus, the state as controller has a limited mandate and neither interferes with the personal selection of religion nor imposes orthodoxy. It confines its role to regulating the external expression of religious liberty while seeking to be fair and neutral – 'We hold the ring so that all groups can practice their faiths freely without colliding with one another in Singapore.'[62]

B. Constant Calibrator: From Categorical Trump to Genuine Balancing

Interpreting religious freedom clauses, which embody constitutional bargains, involves balancing liberties against competing interests. In earlier decisions, Singapore courts have upheld state determinations of what the public interest requires without critically scrutinising the justifications for restricting a liberty. This is best exemplified in the 1994 High Court decision of *Colin Chan v. Public Prosecutor*[63] which concerns the religious and associational freedoms of the Jehovah's Witnesses, a minority religious sect which is pacifist and opposes compulsory military service. Because of this belief, the sect was deregistered in 1972 under Section 24(1) of the Societies Act (Cap 311) as being prejudicial to public welfare and good order in Singapore. All publications by their publishing arm were prohibited by Order 123 issued under Section 3 of the Undesirable Publications Act (Cap 338). The constitutionality of Order 123 against the Article 15 religious freedom clause was unsuccessfully challenged.

The approach towards constitutional interpretation was notable in various ways. First, although the interpretive method adopted was framed as 'balancing', which involves giving due consideration to both sides of the equation, it actually was categorical in applying a 'trump' of public order. The High Court declared an unwritten 'paramount mandate' in the form of the 'sovereignty, integrity and unity' of Singapore, against which anything 'including religious beliefs and practices' which 'tend to run counter to these objectives' must be restrained.[64] Second, the court conferred the status of 'fundamental tenet'[65] to the government policy of military service, which was regulated by statute rather than the Constitution. Third, in evaluating whether public order was threatened, the court discounted contextual considerations such as the small size of the Jehovah's Witnesses and insisted that anything other than a blanket ban on anything the Jehovah's Witnesses published was administratively unworkable.[66] Last, rather than a contextual evaluation of the relevant factors, the High Court was content to justify its decision by way of abstract statements such as locating the basis for de-registration in an overstatement: 'the

62 Prime Minister Lee Hsien Loong, 'National Day Rally Speech' (2009), www.pmo.gov.sg/newsroom/prime-minister-lee-hsien-loongs-national-day-rally-2009-speech-english (accessed 23 May 2017).

63 [1994] 3 SLR (R) 209 (HC).

64 Ibid. [64].

65 Ibid. [37].

66 Ibid. [72].

danger of allowing absolute freedom of religion which might create a complete denial of a government's authority and ability to govern'[67] religious groups and individuals.

Clearly, where the issue in question relates to an 'immovable' government policy (e.g. national service) and the non-recognition of any exemptions, a deferential court that is more concerned with bureaucratic considerations rather than protecting liberties is unlikely to read a right of conscientious objection into Article 15. Article 15(4) permits restrictions on the basis of 'public order' considerations, which in *Colin Chan*, were elevated to something 'prejudicial to national security';[68] once that category is invoked, balancing ends.

However, indications from more recent twenty-first century cases are that a more calibrated approach is taken with respect to exercises of religious liberties not rising to the level of a 'national security' threat, in both the political and legal realms. In the political realm, the 2002 '*tudung* controversy' and 2013 'hijab controversy' reflect periodic expressions of disquiet over restrictions on wearing Islamic religious dress in specific public spaces such as schools and public sector workplaces (nurses, police and military personnel).[69] None of these issues have been litigated; rather they have been diffused by political dialogue. With respect to the *tudung* controversy concerning the uniforms policy in public primary schools, the government responded to critics by explaining the need to create a 'common space' in schools to promote integration and social cohesion. The mufti issued a statement urging the parents of the schoolgirls who were banned from wearing *tudung* to send their children back to school.[70] The government did not dismiss the possibility of future policy changes when a successful multiracial society was attained and when attitudes have changed, urging constructive dialogue, good-will and sensitivity towards how other communities might view the pressing of this concern in the interim.[71]

There are clearly limits to religious accommodation. For example, when public officials like school principals go too far in banning non-halal food from public school canteens, reflecting attempts to assert religious privilege, the government will and has stepped in to calibrate the situation. The Ministry of Education required that a mix of halal and non-halal food suitable for children of all religions be made available. This serves the policy of maintaining schools as common spaces where

67 Ibid. [78].

68 Ibid.

69 This is not a blanket ban; headscarfs are worn in universities; Madam President Halimah Yacob wears hijab and also wore in in her term as the Speaker of the House.

70 'Heed Mufti's Advice – Mohd Maidin to Parents of *Tudung*-Wearing Girls', *Channel NewsAsia* (7 February 2002).

71 'PM Firm on *Tudung* Issue', *Straits Times* (3 February 2002). For further analysis, see Thio Li-ann, 'Recent Constitutional Developments: Of Shadows and Whips, Race, Rifts and Rights, Terror and Tudungs, Women and Wrongs', *Singapore Journal of Legal Studies* (2002), 328, 336–7. See 'Allowing Hijab Problematic for Some Jobs: Yaacob', *Today Online* (1 November 2014); 'PM Lee Meets MPs Over Headscarf Issue', *Straits Times* (5 November 2013), A3.

students can interact, rather than discriminatory 'halal zones',[72] and ameliorating parental concerns.

The conditions regulating the conduct of Thaipusam religious street processions celebrated by the minority Hindu community has been challenged in judicial review proceedings in *Vijaya Kumar s/o Rajendran v. Attorney General*.[73] The case of *Colin Chan* was cited, affirming that the test was not the American one of 'clear and immediate danger' and that the concept of public order was 'not dissimilar to the notion of public peace, welfare and good order' under Section 24(1)(a) of the Societies Act. Fortunately, no 'sovereignty, unity and integrity' trump was mentioned. Instead, the High Court embarked upon an authentic, contextualised balancing of the competing interests, transparently identifying the relevant considerations entering the balancing process, which nurtures a culture of reasoned decision-making.

In general, all religious processions must receive police authorisation to play music or musical instruments in public under regulation 8(2) of the Public Order Regulations 2009, flowing from 'communal sensitivities and the potential for communal disturbance and strife'. The general policy is not to allow this; thus, the Thaipusam procession received more favourable treatment than other religious processions; the Court found that the police had 'nuanced its approach over time in response to dialogue with the Hindu community'. From a complete ban of musical instruments in 1973, the police had gradually allowed the singing of hymns and music playing. The conditions in question allowed religious hymns to be sung during the procession and the broadcasting of music from three points near temples.

The court found that the risks of 'communal disturbance' in Singapore were not 'unreal' and the 'magnitude of public order considerations arising from crowd build-ups, traffic congestion, unhappiness and conflicts among participants' should not be under-estimated. The facts received detailed scrutiny – the scale and religious nature of the procession involving 'about 9000 to 10,000 devotees carrying kavadis or milk pots along a route of about 3 km'. This procession lasted for more than 24 hours and had thousands of supporters and spectators. The conditions in the permit, such as requiring the music to be at 65 decibels, to be played only between 8 a.m. and 8:30 p.m., were 'clearly linked to legitimate public order considerations', based on police assessments of ground conditions in consultation with temple organisers, security providers, the traffic police, the Land Transport Authority and the Hindu Endowments Board. The courts refrained from reviewing the merits of the decision given the polycentric considerations involved but noted that the policy was regularly adjusted, calibrated and thus reasonable; it upheld the police permit conditions noting that the 'calibrated approach to the music showed that the police

[72] 'All Schools Must Have Mix of Halal and Non-Halal Food', *Straits Times* (6 February 2008).
[73] [2015] SGHC 244.

had due regard for the applicants' rights in Article 15(1) even as it sought to balance those rights against the exigencies of public order'.[74] A forty-two-year-old policy was 'not being applied as strictly as the years gone by in order to accommodate new realities';[75] the police authorities regularly engaged in dialogue with concerned parties, demonstrating willingness to moderate policy. Thus, the court struck a balance in recognising police expertise, while requiring police policy to be made and applied reasonably, which requires sufficient flexibility to modify policy as appropriate, including giving due weight to constitutional liberties.

A broader point is that while regulating religious processions, the state seeks to ensure the enjoyment of corporate expression of religious liberties, with an eye to public order considerations. This indicates some degree of official openness towards religious expressions in public, rejecting the view that a rational secular state is menaced by public expressions of faith. It favours accommodation, which requires constant calibration, over dogmatic exclusion.

C. *Cooperative Partner*

In addition, the Singapore government sees religion as a potentially 'constructive social force'[76] not only as a source of 'spiritual strength and moral guidance'[77] to adherents but generally, in relation to religious philanthropy, welfare services and prison rehabilitation.[78] As mediating institutions, religious groups promote social weal and human flourishing as public rather than political entities, as when the Methodist Church raised $3 million to help families struggling with debt as part of Singapore's Golden Jubilee celebrations in 2015.[79]

The state assumes the posture of a cooperative partner, reflecting the cooperation of state and religion, in facilitating a diversity of faith-based providers which meet professional standards fields such as education and health care. This gives substance to the corporate right of religious groups to manifest their belief 'by offering a distinctive form of public service from a position of institutional independence'.[80] For example, Buddhist free clinics offer free alternative Chinese medical care, serving all patients 'irrespective of sex, race and creed' in a manner aligned with Buddhist morality such that clinics 'do not treat patients with venereal or infectious

74 Ibid. [38].
75 Ibid. [51].
76 *Shared Values White Paper* (Cmd 1, 1990), para 45.
77 *Maintenance of Religious Harmony White Paper* (n. 32), para 6.
78 Religious volunteers are able to teach religious tenets to prison inmates as part of the rehabilitative aim of imprisonment, subject to prison policy such as the hair grooming policy which a Sikh religious counsellor opposed in *Madan Mohan Singh v. AG* [2015] 2 SLR 1085 (HC) [57].
79 'S$3.07 Million Raised to Help Families Break out of Debt', *Channel NewsAsia* (15 August 2015), www.channelnewsasia.com/news/singapore/s-3-07-million-raised-to/2052344.html (accessed 23 May 2017).
80 Neuhaus (n. 7), 373.

diseases or patients injured or wounded because of fighting'.[81] Faith-based public schools such as the Catholic St Joseph's Institution (SJI) accommodates itself to multireligious realities, as the prime minister noted, by accepting non-Catholic students; many Malay SJI students attend Friday prayers at the nearby Ba'alwi Mosque in their school uniforms which SJI, the mosque, the students and the prime minister thought was 'fine'.[82]

The government partners with religious groups delivering welfare services by giving tax exemptions or grants for setting up nursing homes; a certain percentage of beds are reserved for Ministry of Health referrals, depending on the grant size.[83] It draws upon the 'special resources, moral energies and insights of plural faith communities for the sake of the common good'.[84]

Mainstream religious groups and the government share a cordial relationship: representatives from major world religions are invited to offer benediction at state-sponsored public events such as the annual Racial Harmony dinner; Buddhist sects such as the Soka Gakkai, which celebrates rather than challenges national goals, are the only religious group privileged to march in the National Day Parade.[85] Singapore secularism is pragmatic rather than dogmatic and separationist, where government ministers mix easily with religious leaders at national mourning events[86] or celebratory occasions, such as the jubilee religious thanksgiving services of Protestants, Catholics, Buddhists and breaking fast with Muslims.[87] This state of affairs allows both the promotion of a national identity and respect for particular religious identities.

D. *Consultative Leader: An Inclusive Public Square*

Within a multireligious democratic setting, the question of the legitimate role and limits of religion in the *res publica* is urgent and compelling. The Singapore government rejects the brand of militant secularism which seeks to illiberally

81 Kuah-Pearce Khun Eng, 'The Poetics of Religious Philanthropy: Buddhist Welfarism in Singapore', in Bryan Turner (ed.), *Religious Pluralism and Civil Society: A Comparative Analysis* (Bardwell Press, 2008), 167, 176.

82 Lee Hsien Loong (n. 62).

83 See Li-ann Thio, 'The Cooperation of Religion and State in Singapore: A Compassionate Partnership in Service of Welfare', *Review of Faith & International Affairs* (2010), 33, 41.

84 Neuhaus (n. 7), 373.

85 Juliana Finucane, 'Proselytizing, Peacework and Public Relations: Soka Gakkai's Commitment to Interreligious harmony in Singapore', in Juliana Finucane and R. Michael Feener (eds.), *Proselytizing and the Limits of Religious Pluralism in Contemporary Asia* (Springer Science +Business Media, 2014), 103, 113.

86 For example, the 1997 Silkair airplane crash in Sumatra or the December 2004 Tsunami disaster.

87 'Buddhist Community Sets Tone of Tolerance and Acceptance of Other Faiths', *Channel NewsAsia* (15 May 2015); '10,000 Catholics and Guests Celebrate SG50 at Thanksgiving Mass Attended by PM', *Straits Times* (4 July 2015); '51,000 Christians Gather at Sports Hub to Mark SG50; PM Lee Thanks Community for Helping Build S'pore', *Straits Times* (5 July 2015); 'PM Lee Joins 400 Muslims Breaking Fast at Al-Ansar Mosque', *Today* (13 July 2015).

exclude citizens with religiously influenced convictions in public debates. A plurality of views is to be expected in any modern democracy; democracy is facilitated where a discerning citizenry is exposed to and may critically scrutinise a broad range of views compatible with fundamental norms of citizenship.[88] The official approach seeks not to discriminate between citizens on the basis of their 'religious' or 'secular' convictions, as both sustain comprehensive worldviews and neither is 'neutral'. The issue is not whether morality should be legislated, as all laws have a moral basis, but what moral values should be embodied in legislation.

Principled pluralism is upheld where the government facilitates free and robust debate from all citizens, within an inclusive public square which treats religious views as unexceptional, like any other comprehensive worldview. This vindicates free speech, freedom of religion and equal citizenship, all aspects of the normative constitutional order.

The government observed in another context that it is 'neither possible nor desirable to compartmentalise completely the minds of voters into secular and religious halves, and ensure that only the secular mind influences his voting behaviour'.[89] The same applies equally to citizens engaged in public policy debates. While the government urges religious leaders to be circumspect in preaching their political views from the pulpit, no such restraint exists for citizens with religious or indeed, secular faiths. The government recognises that 'religious groups are free to propagate their teachings on social and moral issues' and have done so in relation to organ transplants and matters of public sexual morality. It recognises that 'in Parliament we have people of all faiths and in Cabinet too'. However, public debate cannot be based on the veracity of religious views but 'on secular rational considerations, public interests – what makes sense for Singapore'.[90]

Public reasoning does not entail privileging a humanistic epistemology which is not universally accessible or self-evident to those who access knowledge through both reason and revelation; there is no need to subscribe to the particularistic Enlightenment liberal view of a neutral 'universal reason' abstracted from history and context. Rather, the focus should be on communication, on articulating persuasive arguments that fellow citizens can understand and evaluate on the basis of fair hearing and collective deliberation. Through dialogue, principled pluralism is oriented towards cultivating a working consensus on broad political objectives, rather than to seek agreement on theological or philosophical questions. One may learn to appreciate the views of others without giving up one's own values. The current Singapore approach conduces to this orientation.

88 This would include the duty to uphold the civic order, not calling for the destruction of the state and a commitment to civil, reasoned discussion, not bare emotive 'shouting' that fails to contemplate the common good or make a reasoned case.

89 *Maintenance of Religious Harmony White Paper* (n. 32) para 24.

90 Lee Hsien Loong (n. 62).

Faith-based convictions may not need to be expressed in an openly theological voice, though this should be an option if desired.[91] For example, MUIS gave both 'religious' and 'secular' reasons for opposing a casino in Singapore when the issue was being debated nationally in 2005. Both were easily accessible to citizens. In religious terms, Islam opposed gambling as it teaches that a living should be made through hard, honest work, rather than chance. In social terms, MUIS was concerned with the high social costs of gambling, its addictive nature and deleterious effects on youth and the lower income groups.[92] These are reasons that can be weighed and there is the added value of appreciating the views of a religious minority on a matter of national importance – this is more inclusive than requiring a person with a religious identity to excise that identity when speaking about public matters, which privileges irreligious persons and humanistic ideologies like Marxism or liberalism. 'Democracy-friendly' religion requires religious (and indeed, humanistic) citizens in the public square not only to express their religious perspectives but to speak in the tone of persuasion, not dictation, framing arguments based on reasons that all may understand, even if there is disagreement over public values and the common good.

Though parliamentarians rarely confess their religious identity as a preface before engaging in debate before Parliament, many did so during the 2005 casino debates.[93] Presumably this was to show citizens that religiously influenced considerations were not discounted but agonised over, that parliamentarians were truly representative in demonstrating cognisance of concerns. The government makes it a practice to broadly consult interested stakeholders, including religious communities, on contentious matters such as whether to have a casino. This shows appreciation of the social dimension of religious faiths.

The government consults, but makes the final decision. After all views are articulated, the government is elected to drive law and policy, as it did in making the decision to have two casinos in Singapore for economic reasons, religious opposition and divided views within the cabinet notwithstanding. However, the prime minister struck a conciliatory tone in noting dissent and expressing respect for religious teachings and the hope that religious groups would continue to work with the government 'to help build strong families' and social resilience, and to continue to help fellow citizens in need, including gambling addicts.[94]

91 For example, banking reform proposals 'will not normally require advocates or opponents to make explicit that they are most deeply motivated by, say, a libertarian philosophy of freedom, an Islamic conception of usury or a Catholic personalist understanding of "the priority of labour over capital"': Jonathan Chaplin, 'Liberté, Laïcité, Pluralité: Towards a Theology of Principled Pluralism', *International Journal of Public Theology* 10 (2016), 354, 372.

92 'MUIS Against Having a Casino', *Straits Times* (11 February 2005), H7.

93 Singapore Parliament Reports, *Proposal to Develop Integrated Resorts*, 18–21 April 2005, col 54-535.

94 Prime Minister Lee Hsien Loong, 'Statement by Prime Minister Lee Hsien Loong on Integrated Resort on Monday, 18 April 2005 at Parliament House' (18 April 2005), www.mti.gov.sg/MTIInsights/Documents/Ministerial%20Statement%20-%20PM%2018apr05.pdf (accessed 20 April 2017).

E. 'Culture War' Manager: Politics, Plurality and Polarisation

In 2004, the government exhorted the citizenry to engage in 'fruitful' public debate over national issues 'rigorously and robustly' in a manner which was 'issued-focused, based on facts and logic and not just on assertions and emotions' with the view to reaching 'correct conclusions' on 'the best way forward for the country'. It signalled that not all critics would be viewed as 'adversaries', where the criticism sought to improve policies as opposed to scoring political points. It indicated it would 'pull back from being all things to all citizens' and on questions of 'public morality and decency' would be increasingly guided by the community's consensus views. Rather than being advocates engaged in 'crusading journalism'; which slanted news coverage and emphasis 'to campaign for personal agendas', the media should 'report news accurately and fairly' to inform, rather than misinform the public.[95]

A consequence of this more relaxed attitude towards public debate has been the advent of what has become known as the 'culture wars between the extreme liberals and conservatives that are going on in the US'.[96] Civil society groups have become more organised in lobbying for favoured causes, often bypassing opposition politicians.

The 'culture war' relates to a struggle over public values and morally contentious issues, which has erupted over threats to traditional or family values posed by the homosexualism agenda advanced by liberal rights advocates. This espouses erotic liberty, seeks to mainstream homosexuality by asserting its moral equivalence with the heterosexual norm and challenges traditional conceptions of marriage and family. The latter is staunchly defended by social conservatives, including those whose moral convictions are shaped by religion. Effectively, they are supporting rather than opposing existing laws and government views on what constitutes the family – 'one man, one woman, marrying, having children and bringing up children within that framework of a stable family unit'.[97] This is anathema to alternative lifestyle liberationist activists who radically challenge the status quo.

This new brand of politics, engaging different sectors of civil society, is fraught and acrimonious, with many liberal advocates favouring a brand of militant secularism. They often invoke the myth of the 'neutral' state to argue for the privatization of religion, and thereby, the silencing of religiously shaped views that stand in the way of their agenda. To that end, mischievous voices use misleading terms such as 'creeping theocracy' or 'don't mix religion and politics' to insinuate the overreaching

95 Deputy Prime Minister Lee Hsien Loong, 'Building a Civic Society' (6 January 2004), Harvard Club Speech, http://unpan1.un.org/intradoc/groups/public/documents/APCITY/UNPAN015426.pdf (accessed 23 May 2017).

96 '*Today* (Singapore) interview with Deputy PM Wong on the Government's Position on Homosexuality', *Channel NewsAsia* (14 May 2009). For an extended analysis of the culture war over the 'AWARE' incident where the government noted liberal media bias, see Thio Li-ann, 'Between Eden and Armageddon: Navigating "Religion" and "Politics" in Singapore', *Singapore Journal of Legal Studies* (2009), 365.

97 Prime Minister Lee Hsien Loong, 83 *Singapore Parliament Reports* (23 October 2007), Vol. 83, col 2354ff.

of religious groups in the public sphere. This detracts from the issue at hand, which is not about the replacement of a secular democracy with a theocracy, but over what public values should be normative. Clearly, the accepted practice is that all Singaporeans may participate in debates over public issues, which recognises the plurality of extant views and the need for the principled protection of expressive freedoms. It is important to recognise that secularism is itself a political project with a set of normative claims; militant secularism which seeks to disqualify or suppress the expression of certain views embodies a form of 'creeping cultural totalitarianism' inimical to anti-totalitarian constitutionalism.

The aggressive brand of advocacy adopted by homosexualism agenda activists poses a new threat to social harmony. The Hard Left sees its vision of left-wing politics not only as a view, but as virtue itself. This justifies its tactics, which include casting the beneficiaries of their agenda as 'victims' and those who oppose their agenda as 'oppressors', while demonising and intimidating those who dissent with abusive invective and spiteful death threats.[98] The uncivil methods of argument by insult, harassment and bullying adopted by certain secular fundamentalists may have a horizontal chilling effect[99] on speakers holding dissenting views, terminating rather than starting conversations. Where speech is excluded or chilled, deliberative, sustainable democracy, which is contingent on a collective political culture of reciprocal civil tolerance for diverse views and free speech, is imperilled. This exemplifies illiberal tolerance. Emotive sloganeering, name-calling and character assassination do little to promote informed, intelligible public debate based on reason-giving and persuasion, civil peace and the democratic virtue of compromise.

Given this repoliticised landscape, the government affirms the expressive rights of all citizens while declaring new rules of engagement to address militant secularist tactics. It notes that 'the need for all groups to practise tolerance, respect and mutual restraint' which used to be the prescription for inter-religious harmony, now extends not only to religious groups operating in the secular domain, but 'also to secular groups which want to strong push their views and change our social norms'.[100] Issues such as those pertaining to homosexualism create a fraught, acrimonious environment and the government recognises the intransigent, polarised nature of this debate. It notes that on matters like same-sex marriage, consensus is impossible given the 'very entrenched views' such that 'the more you discuss, the angrier people get'.[101]

Citizens now actively articulate their views over controversial issues in a polemical fashion in print media and online forums – for every petition, there is a counter-petition;[102] for every letter complaining about allowing books with homosexual

[98] Andy Ho, 'Identity Politics: There Are Gays, and There Are Gays', *Straits Times* (10 November 2007).

[99] Thio Li-ann, 'The Virtual and the Real: Article 14, Political Speech and the Calibrated Management of Deliberative Democracy in Singapore', *Singapore Journal of Legal Studies* 25 (2008), 54–6.

[100] President SR Nathan, Opening of Parliament (18 May 2009).

[101] 'Conservative S'pore "Not Ready for Same-Sex Marriage"'. *Today* (6 June 2015).

[102] For example, there were petitions and counter-petitions calling for a review of a FAQ by the Health Promotion Board which contained one-sided, ideological opinions about homosexuality: 'Phobia

themes in the children's section of the national library, there is a letter expressing contrary views;[103] in response to attacks on an academic's critical views on lesbianism impugning his character and threatening academic freedom, there are supportive responses.[104] This indicates a permanent rift, based on political ideology and a predictable response-counter response scenario. Furthermore, 'constituencies' are no longer monolithic; government parliamentarians are critical of the implementation of certain government policies, such as the Health Promotion Board's one-sided FAQ on sexuality; Open Letters asking probing questions are addressed by religious groups towards government ministers,[105] representing demands for forms of accountability within and without official forums. This is a healthy democratic development. Differing perspectives exist within the Muslim community beyond that of the 'official' statutory body, MUIS. For example, in 2014, some churches and Muslim groups developed an alliance in promoting the 'Wear White' campaign which was seen to oppose the pro-homosexual 'Pink Dot' event. While MUIS urged mosques not to take confrontational stances against the LGBT lifestyle, Muslim teacher Ustaz Noor Deros spearheaded a grassroots initiative urging Muslims to avoid Pink Dot, to wear white as a symbol of purity in attending Ramadan evening prayers on the same day Pink Dot was scheduled, signalling 'the Muslim community's opposition to homosexuality'.[106]

Comments in HPB's FAQ Should Be Removed', *Today* (9 February 2014); 'HPB's Sexuality FAQ Undermine Family', *Mypaper* (6 February 2014), 'FAQ an Educational Tool That Should Remain in Its Original Form', *Today* (13 February 2015). Government MPs also criticised this FAQ before Parliament: 91 Singapore Parliament Reports (Health Promotion Board FAQ Segment for Same-Sex Relationships), 17 February 2014 [54] (Mr Lim Biow Chuan, Mr Gan Kim Yong). Critical Open Letters, such as that directed at the Health Minister by LoveSingapore Chairman Pastor Lawrence Khong, are now the norm: Lawrence Khong, 'An Open Letter' (26 February 2014), www.lovesingapore.org.sg/OpenLetter_HealthMin_26Feb2014.pdf (accessed 23 May 2017).

103 'NLB Removes Two Childrens' Title After Complaint That They Are Not "Pro-Family"', *Straits Times* (8 July 2014); 'NLB "Saddened By" Reaction Over Its Removal of Three Books with Homosexuality Themes, Says Chief Executive', *Straits Times* (13 July 2014).

104 'NUS Prof's Comments on Lesbians Spark Protests from Past and Present Students', *Straits Times* (28 February 2014); 'FMSA Official Statement on Matter of Letter of Concern to NUS Provost on A/Prof Dr Syed Muhd Khairudin Aljunied' (3 March 2014), http://rilek1corner.com/2014/03/03/fmsa-issues-statement-to-nus-provost-in-support-of-prof-syed-khairudin-aljunied (accessed 23 May 2017).

105 Government MPs also criticised this FAQ before Parliament: 91 *Singapore Parliament Reports* (Health Promotion Board FAQ Segment for Same-Sex Relationships), 17 February 2014 [54] (Mr Lim Biow Chuan, Mr Gan Kim Yong). This was in relation to the use of an ideologically loaded attack word like 'homophobia', which slurs people who do not think homosexuality should be mainstreamed or consider it morally repugnant, as having a phobia or mental disease, as the remit of the Health Promotion Board is health, not ideology. Critical Open Letters, such as that directed at the Health Minister by LoveSingapore Chairman Pastor Lawrence Khong, are now the norm: Lawrence Khong (n. 105). Islamic groups like PERGAS also considered the FAQ insensitive and disappointing: 'Islamic Association Calls HPB's FAQ Insensitive to Prevailing View on Homosexuality', *Today Online* (15 February 2015).

106 'Govt Leaders Must Draw "Clear Line" on LGBT Issue: Pastor', *Today* (28 June 2015); 'Church Network Joins Muslim Group in Stand Against Pink Dot', *Singapolitics* (20 June 2014); 'MUIS Urges Mosques Not To Take Confrontational Stand on LGBT Lifestyles', *Today* (21 June 2015).

In this brave new world, the government positions itself between two polarised camps; with respect to the homosexualism agenda, a minister stated: 'This is a complex issue with diverse views. The government is in the middle, seeking to manage the different viewpoints, interests.'[107] The prime minister notes that Singapore is 'basically a conservative one' which rejects the prospect of the LGBT community setting 'the tone for Singapore society'. While plural views existed and there was 'space for the gay community', activists are advised not to 'push the agenda too hard', as 'very strong pushback' would be elicited, including from religious groups reacting against a radical agenda, which was 'completely understandable'.[108] As a 'culture war' manager, government actions often frustrate both sides; for example, a voluntary welfare organization chaired by a Christian pastor, who is vocal against the homosexualism agenda while affirming the dignity of all persons was denied a licence to hold a 'Red Dot Family Moment' on the Padang the same day Pink Dot was to meet at a different venue in June 2014.[109] Presumably, this was motivated by a desire to avoid escalating social conflict, though conflicting signals were sent. Where government action appears to contravene government policy, these are publicly queried, eliciting official answers. For example, the government has affirmed that foreign corporate bodies are not allowed to intervene in the domestic affairs of Singapore by sponsoring any lobby group and were not to publicly advocate causes, such as Pink Dot, which sowed discord among Singaporeans.[110]

On questions of value, reasonable people will reasonably disagree. Intransigent positions over controversial issues implicating questions of public morality cause friction, which the government considers must be 'managed without fracturing society' by allowing the 'conservative population'[111] to decide these issues 'collectively' rather than letting the government decide.[112] By refusing to take the lead on these questions or to impose an authoritarian *diktat*, liberal activists and social/religious conservatives with disparate views will continue to use the internet and other mediums to state their positions and counter-positions in an attempt to shape public discourse and influence law and policy. Principled pluralism minimally requires that all views be advocated robustly and examined closely, and avoids the hegemonic imposition of a totalising homogenising dogma by the state or by civil society actors through a political correctness code which shields certain ideologies from scrutiny. For democracy to be sustainable, democratic dialogue should be civil, and oriented towards the common good rather than single-issue agendas, in the hopes of creating community within the larger polity. Social stability does not

107 'Shanmugam Meets Gay Activists', *Straits Times* (5 January 2013), B16.

108 'Conservative S'pore "Not Ready for Same-Sex Marriage"' (n. 101).

109 'Christians to Don White for Services as Hong Lim Park Hosts Pink Dot', *Straits Times* (12 June 2015).

110 'Foreign Firms in S'pore Must Respect Cultural Norms: Chan Chun Sing', *Today* (3 May 2015).

111 In a 2014 Institute of Policy Studies survey, 78.2% of participants considered same-sex relations wrong: 'Singaporeans Still Largely Conservative, IPS Survey Finds', *Straits Times* (28 January 2014).

112 Transcript, PM Lee's Dialogue at Ho Rih Hwa Leadership in Asia Public Lecture Series, 30 June 2015.

require a unified moral community as this is unrealistic. Instead, principled pluralism views a plural society as a nation of different secular and theistic faith communities, all of which have a place at the table of public discourse, and commit to adhering to the democratic rules of the game. This includes accepting the outcome of processes, within an open system where change is always possible and where proposed changes may always be resisted.

V. CONCLUSION

Political ideologies, like religion, may assume an 'idolatrous character, and like all idols, are unwilling to share power with others'.[113] If politics is the art of the possible and religion is the pursuit of the ideal, when both worlds collide, can a *via media* be maintained?

The regulation of religion by the state may assume a hierarchical relationship of dominance and subordination, though the approach of principled pluralism defies this binary ordering. It seeks to occupy a third space between an overweening, antitheistic secularist statism which seeks to occupy all social political space, and a theocracy where religious and political authority is fused, and accords primacy to neither; it thus neither establishes religion nor enforces secular humanism with its relativistic precommitments in public life. It tries to avoid both 'hierarchical authoritarianism' and the 'balkanizing atomism of modernity'[114] in seeking equilibrium between religious freedom and national solidarity.

Rather than domineering control, it prefers the metric of autonomy, conciliation and respectful coexistence without compromising deep convictions, as a response to the fact of religious diversity. It recognises the role played by individual and corporate rights to religious freedom, beyond the freedom to worship, in combatting totalitarianism of any sort, and the simultaneous need to nurture and sustain a basis for common citizenship. This makes a demand on religious groups to hold any totalising messianic or comprehensive utopian visions in abeyance (short of divine intervention) in the interest of a 'democracy friendly' vision of Religion; on this basis a secular democracy can uphold religious freedom and pluralism which buttresses the common framework for sustaining *le vivre ensemble*.

State unity is not grounded on a singular religious vision but has to be grounded in the basic constitutional framework and common commitments, such as a commitment to religious freedom and free conscience, to racial and religious harmony, and religious pluralism. As a matter of equity, the social dimension of religion beyond personal spirituality is recognised, as religion encompasses moral prescriptions for life and living. It would not be 'reasonable or practical' to expect religious people 'to

113 David T. Koyzisk, 'What Would Kuyper Do? Idolatry and the Limits of Pluralism', *First Things* (23 January 2015).

114 Max L. Stackhouse, 'Public Theology and Democracy's Future', *Review of Faith and International Affairs* 7.2 (2010), 49.

act in the public realm without reference to their deeply held, religiously based moral convictions'.[115] This would fail to take religion seriously and thwart the objective of nurturing democracy-friendly religion and religion-friendly democracy.

Democracy is pluralistic in treating people of all faiths equally; it is inherently secular, based on the popular will, even if the people are profoundly religious, which will affect the public decision-making process. As EW Barker noted, 'a nation based on one race, one language and one religion, when its people are multi-racial, is one doomed for destruction'.[116] To this, one might add, a nation based on one imposed ideology is insalubrious, where viewpoint diversity is a fact and desideratum. Rather than conflict resolution, seeking reasonable accommodation is a better goal, as some differences are irreconcilable. Democratic consensus is periodically refreshed and in civilised dialogue between interested parties, conflict is contained as this entails a 'two way discourse that is essential to relationship, not domination … the language of mutuality, not of power'.[117]

Secular and religious fundamentalisms which seek absolute political power to impose their agendas are both anti-constitutionalist and anti-models. Within a constitutional order, religious freedom resists totalising power; the government has no authority over what true religion is or to compel adherence to any faith, but has legitimate authority to regulate external manifestations of religious liberty where these contravene the general law which upholds civil order and promotes the common good and basic duties of citizenship. Again, the perennial tension between liberty and public order and other public goods like relational health is evident.

Current government policy in regulating religion broadly reflects an awareness of these tensions that 'principled pluralism' realistically apprehends, and idealistically seeks to manage. 'Principles' refer to maintaining respect for constitutional religious freedoms and celebrating religious diversity or pluralism. It recognises that 'religion' and the 'political/public' are not hermetically sealed spheres, though there are different realms of jurisidictional competence; secularity, as a principle of limited government, appreciates the need to limit power to ensure it is not concentrated in the hands of any state or non-state elite. 'Pluralism' transcends the fact of religious diversity; within a democracy, it values the expression of diverse viewpoints which can correct and refine views by bringing competing reasoned perspectives to bear. It speaks to the project of creating a common society from plurality, while taking religious faith seriously by engaging with it and respecting the limits of that engagement.

Within Singapore, a secular state with a religious society, a 'principled pluralism' approach may be the surest foundation for a stable, sustainable democracy. In a

115 George Marsden, *The Twilight to the American Enlightenment: The 1950s and the Crisis of Liberal Belief*, 1st edn (Basic Books, 2014), 158.

116 Minister for Law and National Development E. W. Barker, *Singapore Parliament Reports* (22 December 1965).

117 Diane Eck, *Encountering God: A Spiritual Journey from Bozeman to Banaras* (Beacon Press, 1993), 19.

world where few, if any homogeneous nations exist, it remains a worthy experiment: it seeks to attain social cohesion within a polity where citizens share sufficient allegiance to their country to have enough good-will and confidence to tolerate or even celebrate their religious differences, as an expression of the private right and public good of religious liberty.

7

Legal Regulation of Religion in Vietnam

Bui Ngoc Son

I. INTRODUCTION

Vietnam is home to different religions which are all subject to state regulation. According to the 2009 Census, Vietnam has thirteen officially recognized religions, with the breakdown of believers as follows: Buddhism (6,812,318); Catholicism (5,677,086); Protestantism (734,168); Hòa Hảo (1,433,252); Cao Đài (807,915); Islam (75.268); Bahai Faith (731); Pure Land Buddhist Home Practice (11,093); Four Debts of Gratitude (41,280); Threefold Enlightened Truth Path (366); Threefold Southern Tradition (709); Way of the Strange Fragrance From the Precious Mountain (10,824); Brahmin (56,427).[1] Recently, Mormon became the fourteenth religion to be recognized by the state. According to the 2015 report by the Ministry of Internal Affairs, there are 36 state-recognized religious organizations with 24 million followers (27% of the total population of around 91.9 million people), and more than 70 religious organizations and groups that have not been officially recognized by the state.[2]

Vietnam is a highly regulatory state. The state uses legal instruments to regulate almost every aspect of society. The regulatory sphere is not limited to the economy, but also extends to the spiritual and social sphere, and specifically to the area of religion. This chapter discusses how and why the state in Vietnam uses legal instruments to regulate religion. This study is epistemologically connected to relevant literature on regulation, in particular, legal regulation. My methodology relies mainly on the formal laws regulating religion in Vietnam, while the actual regulation of religion and the practice of the right to religious freedom are only occasionally mentioned. I also rely on sources in the Vietnamese language.

The structure of my argument is as follows. The Vietnamese state uses formal laws to comprehensively and stringently regulate religion. This regulatory framework for

1 The report can be found on the website of the General Statistics Office, www.gso.gov.vn

2 Ministry of Internal Affairs, 'Báo cáo Tổng kết 08 năm thự c hiện Pháp lệnh tín ngưỡ ng, tôn giáo' [Synthetic Report on 8 Years Implementing the Ordinance on Belief and Religion] (2015).

religion is situated within broader institutional settings defined by four fundamental socialist attributes: the socialist regime, the ideology and strategy of 'great unity', the principle of socialist legality, and statist human rights. Owing to growing domestic social complexity and the growing pressure to comply with the internationally recognized human right to religious freedom, the institutional space for religion in Vietnam has been incrementally expanded. This study therefore has implications for other Asian socialist states such as China, Laos, and North Korea, all of which share with Vietnam socialist attributes that shape the regulatory framework for religion.

The chapter contains four parts. Part I sets out the conceptual framework. Part II describes the regulatory framework for religion in Vietnam. Part III analyses the institutional factors that shape this regulatory framework. Part IV concludes by briefly touching on the question of legitimacy.

II. CONCEPTUAL FRAMEWORK

The language of 'regulation' (*điều chỉnh* or *quy định* in Vietnamese) is prevalent in Vietnamese legal discourse and practice. To illustrate, Vietnamese textbooks on 'general theory on law and state' conceive of regulation as the nature of law.[3] The language of regulation is also prevalent in the making of formal law. For example, the first article of a law is normally about the 'scope of regulation'. Given this reality, it is reasonable to situate the legal framework for religion in Vietnam within international regulatory scholarship.

Regulation has emerged as a separate area of scholarly inquiry in the last few decades. Regulatory scholars in different disciplines (law, business, economics, sociology, etc.) have provided different definitions of regulation.[4] However, in a recent study, Chritel Koop and Martin Lodge analysed the conceptions of regulation put forth in 109 articles since 1970 and concluded that 'there are shared conceptions across disciplines'.[5] These scholars propose a broad distinction between *essence-based* and *pattern-based* definitions of regulation.[6] The former essentially defines regulation as '*intentional intervention in the activities of a target population*'.[7] Three elements define the essence of regulation: intentionality, intervention, and target population, thus distinguishing it from other forms of social control such as cultural and social norms.

3 See, for example, Lê Minh Tâm (ed.), *Giáo Trình Lý Luận Nhà Nước Và Pháp Luật* [*Textbook on General Theory on Law and State*] (People's Public Security Publishing House, 2009).

4 See generally, Robert Baldwin, Colin Scott, and Christopher Hood, *A Reader on Regulation* (Oxford University Press, 1998).

5 Chritel Koop and Martin Lodge, 'What Is Regulation? An Interdisciplinary Concept Analysis', *Regulation & Governance* 1 (2015), 196.

6 Ibid., 104.

7 Ibid. (original italic).

Intentional intervention indicates that 'regulation implies governed, guided, controlled interference'.[8]

Despite these identities, regulation may be confused with other phenomena such as policy.[9] This, therefore, requires the pattern-based definition, which is concerned with the manifestations of regulation.[10] Accordingly, regulation is defined as '*intentional intervention in the activities of a target population, where the intervention is typically direct – involving binding standard-setting, monitoring, and sanctioning – and exercised by public-sector actors on the economic activities of private-sector actors.*'[11] In this pattern-based definition, regulation is treated as a 'radial' concept with core prototypical features such as direct intentional intervention, public regulators regulating private regulates, and economic activity being the main subject of regulation; while leaving open the possibility of peripheral types of regulation which share the core features while also containing additional elements such as indirect intervention, private regulators, and non-economic activity being the subject of regulation.[12]

In this study, I adopt the pattern-based definition of regulation as it characterizes regulation as a distinctive phenomenon. However, I contend that a pattern-based conceptualization of regulation does not necessarily lead to a radial (or core-periphery) approach. This is because the manifestations of regulation are embedded in 'the political and constitutional context'.[13] In particular, the position of economic activity as the main subject of regulation must be qualified. Regulatory scholarship has mainly developed based on the experience of democratic market economies. Theories and practices of regulation have emerged primarily in response to the necessary intervention of the state into the market to rectify its failures, particularly in the areas of financial crisis, environmental disasters, and the safety of food and medicine.[14] One conceptual consequence is the focus on economic activity as a core feature of regulation. Another consequence is the marginalization of regulation in other institutional settings. For instance, one critique of Bronwen Morgan and Karen Yeung's work on regulation is that they agree on the embeddedness of regulation in 'macro-political linkages' but concentrate on 'the democratic market economy that characterizes most western industrialized countries, rather than considering other forms of political economy such as developing, socialist, and Islamic states'.[15]

8 Barry M. Mitnick, *The Political Economy of Regulation: Creating, Designing, and Removing Regulatory Forms* (Columbia University Press, 1980), 3.
9 Koop and Lodge, 'What Is Regulation?', 104.
10 Ibid.
11 Ibid., 105.
12 Ibid.
13 Bronwen Morgan and Karen Yeung, *An Introduction to Law and Regulation* (Cambridge University Press, 2007), 4.
14 Koop and Lodge, 'What Is Regulation?', 95.
15 Ibid., 98–99.

However, regulation is a global phenomenon, and a Western-centric approach will limit our understanding of the kaleidoscopic manifestations of regulation in different political and constitutional corners of the globe. In developing, non-democratic milieus which feature many Asian states, including Asian socialist states like China, Vietnam, and Laos, regulation of the economy is important but may not be the sole focus, as the regulation of social activities is also of equal concern to the state. In such settings, human rights and individual freedoms, including religious freedom, are subject to the state's regulation alongside the market.

Regulation of religion therefore can be defined as the state's intentional intervention into the religious activities of the target believers and followers and their organizations and groups. In institutional settings where there is no culture of limited government dominating constitutional politics, there is likely to be greater space for the state/government to regulate religious activities.[16]

As mentioned earlier, this study addresses two questions: how and why does the state regulate religion in Vietnam? The 'how' question concerns several instruments and techniques of direct intervention, such as command, and these of indirect intervention, such as consensus, communication, and code with the state as the architect of the code.[17] Given the space constraints, this study focuses more on direct interference by command, which involves the state's promulgation of legal rules (binding standard-setting), followed by the state monitoring the implementation of these rules (monitoring), backed by coercive sanctions (sanctioning) of non-compliance.[18] More specifically, I will examine how the Constitution, legislation, and administrative legal instruments regulate religion in Vietnam.

The 'why' question examines the factors behind the legal regulation of religion. Morgan and Yeung have proposed three theories of regulation: public interest theories, private interest theories, and institutional theories.[19] The interest-based theories (whether public or private) may be more relevant to explaining the regulation of economic activities. The institutional theories are more general, which can be useful in explaining the regulation of both economic and non-economic activities. Generally speaking, the institutional theories do not focus on the actors and their interests but on institutional factors.[20]

My explanation of the regulatory framework for religion in Vietnam is informed by the institutional approach. In particular, I draw on the theory of 'regulatory space' to explain the institutional factors behind the regulation of religion in Vietnam.

[16] Pitman B. Potter, 'Belief in Control: Regulation of Religion in China', *The China Quarterly* (2003), 317; James T. Richardson (ed.), *Regulating Religion: Case Studies from Around the Globe* (Springer Science+Business Media, 2004); Yuksel Sezgin and Mirjam Künkler, 'Regulation of "Religion" and the "Religious": The Politics of Judicialization and Bureaucratization in India and Indonesia', *Comparative Studies in Society and History* 56 (2013), 448.

[17] Morgan and Yeung, *An Introduction to Law and Regulation*, 80.

[18] Ibid., 80.

[19] Ibid., 16.

[20] Ibid., 53.

The theory of 'regulatory space' focuses on 'the space where regulation occurs, almost a kind of physical arena which influences the practices that happen'.[21] It emphasises that the 'actions and intention of regulatory actors are embedded in larger systems and institutional dynamics'.[22] The theory of regulatory space is well-developed by Hancher and Morgan in their 1989 book *Organizing Regulatory Space*.[23]

The concept of 'regulatory space' is a useful analytical tool for understanding the factors influencing the regulation of religion in Vietnam. The concept of space has several implications. First, space suggests an area that 'is available for occupation'.[24] Second, a space can be divided into major and minor occupants.[25] Third, 'just as we can identify a general concept of regulatory space in operation in a particular community we can also speak of specific concepts of regulatory space at work in individual sectors'.[26] Along these lines, we can speak of 'regulatory space' operating specifically in the context of religion. The state institutions and religious actors are the occupants of the regulatory space. These occupants enjoy a major status, while others have to be satisfied with a minor status. Understanding the regulatory space also requires us to examine the relationship between these occupants.[27] However, the idea of space also directs us to 'examine the characteristics of the excluded'.[28] Therefore, 'understanding who is in, and who is out' is crucial to analysing the regulatory space.[29] This means that the concept of regulatory space requires us to examine not only the inclusion of religious actors in the space but also the exclusion of certain religious actors from the space. My explanation will therefore focus on the institutional space that shapes the legal regulation of religion in Vietnam.

III. THE LEGAL REGULATORY FRAMEWORK FOR RELIGION

A. *Binding Standard-Setting*

The Vietnamese state uses law to regulate religion. This first involves the promulgation of legal rules that establish binding standards for religious activities. There are three types of legal instruments that regulate religion: the Constitution, legislation, and administrative legal instruments. Article 24 of the 2013 Constitution states: 'The State respects and protects freedom of belief and of religion. No one has the

[21] Ibid., 59.
[22] Ibid.
[23] L. Hancher and M. Morgan, 'Organizing Regulatory Space', in Robert Baldwin, Colin Scott, and Christopher Hood (eds.), *A Reader on Regulation* (Oxford University Press, 1998), 148–72.
[24] Ibid., 153.
[25] Ibid.
[26] Ibid.
[27] Ibid., 154.
[28] Ibid.
[29] Ibid.

right to infringe on the freedom of belief and religion or to take advantage of belief and religion to violate the laws.'[30] The Constitution therefore provides for religious freedom but also establishes a base for the subsequent detailed regulation of religion by legislation and administrative legal instruments. Thus, it can be seen that the practice of religious activities is situated within a regulatory framework.

The most important legislation that regulated religion in Vietnam during the last decade is the Ordinance on Belief and Religion, enacted in 2004 by the National Assembly's Standing Committee. The preamble states: 'This Ordinance regulates religious and belief activities.' Its main concern is to guide and control religious activities in accordance with certain directions. The Ordinance's first chapter on 'General Provisions' reconfirms the constitutional right to religious freedom and states that the purpose of regulating religion is to ensure that religious activities will be 'consistent with the regulation of law', Vietnamese culture and moral values, and the tradition of 'great solidarity'.[31] The Ordinance contains a series of prohibitions, including prohibiting the abuse of the right of belief and religious freedom 'to undermine peace, national independence and unification; incite violence or propagate wars, conduct propagation in contravention of the State's laws and policies; divide people, nationalities or religions; cause public disorder, infringe upon the life, health, dignity, honor and/or property of others, or impede the exercise of civic rights and performance of civic obligations; conduct superstitious activities or other acts of law violation'.[32]

Chapter 2 of the Ordinance regulates 'religious activities'. According to the law, annual programs for religious activities must be approved by local governments. Conducting ad hoc religious activities beyond the registered and approved program requires the approval of local authorities. The Ordinance also establishes a wide range of circumstances in which religious activities can be suspended, such as when the activities allegedly infringe on national security; seriously affect public order or the environment; adversely affect the people's unity; adversely affect fine national cultural traditions; infringe on the life, health, dignity, honor, or property of other persons; and/or involve other serious violations of the law.[33]

Chapter 3 of the Ordinance regulates religious organizations. Accordingly, legal religious organizations must be officially recognized and registered. The Ordinance lists several requirements for registration, including among other things, having religious tenets, principles, and rites which are not contrary to the nation's fine traditions, customs, and interests; having a charter or statute being closely associated with the nation and not contrary to legal provisions; and having registered religious activities (Article 16). The establishment, division, separation, merger, or amalgamation of religious organizations at different levels must be approved by government

[30] The previous 1992 Constitution had similar provision (Article 70).
[31] Article 5 of the Ordinance.
[32] See Article 8 of the Ordinance.
[33] See Article 12 of the Ordinance.

authorities at respective levels (Article 17). Conferences or congresses of religious organizations must also be approved by the authorities (Article 18). The Ordinance also requires religious organizations to register the ordained, order-bestowed, appointed, elected, or honorary nominated persons to state authorities (Article 22). Moreover, the establishment and operation of schools for training professional religious activists must be approved by state authorities (Article 24).

Chapter 4 deals with the assets of believers and religious organizations. Registered religious organizations are allowed to use lands related to religious bodies (such as pagodas, churches, sanctuaries, chancels, monasteries, and religious schools) in 'a stable and long-term manner' while complying with the provisions of land legislation (Article 27). Belief establishments and religious organizations may raise funds, and the local government must be notified in advance of the fundraising (Article 28). The publication of religious materials 'must comply with law provisions' (Article 32). These provisions allow the state to control religious assets.

Chapter 5 regulates the international activities of religious organizations. Accordingly, these international religious activities must be approved by the central government. As Article 35 sets out, international religious activities include 'inviting foreign organizations or foreigners into Vietnam or organizing the execution of undertakings of foreign religious organizations in Vietnam; participating in religious activities or sending persons to join religious training courses overseas'. These provisions facilitate international engagement of religions but at the same time allow the state to control international activities of religious organizations to make sure that international engagement would not invite challenges to the socialist regime by, for example, disseminating believes that challenge socialist ideology.

The final chapter contains implementation provisions. It prescribes how the Government should detail and guide the implementation of this Ordinance (Article 41). Following that prescription, the Government enacted a decree in 2005, which was later replaced by another decree in 2012, No. 92/NĐ-CP.[34] The 2012 decree regulates in detail the different types of religious activities and their registrations; the complex procedures and requirements for the registration and approval of religious organizations; the establishment, division, separation, merger, or amalgamation of religious organizations; the registration and approval of programs for their activities; their internal ordainment and appointment; their assets, and their international activities.

Recently, the National Assembly passed a Law on Belief and Religion on 18 November 2016 to replace the Ordinance. According to the Minister of Internal

[34] Among other things, the latter introduced new provisions on the international aspects of religions (e.g., foreigners studying in religious schools in Vietnam). For more details, see Nguyễn Thanh Long, 'Nghị định 92/2012/NĐ-CP, Sửa Đối Đề Phù Hợp Với Thự c Tế', [Decree No. 92/2012/NĐ-CP, Amendments Inconsistence with the Reality], (*Ban Tôn giáo Chính phủ*], http://btgcp.gov.vn/Plus.aspx/vi/News/38/0/240/0/3548/Nghi_dinh_92_2012_ND_CP_sua_doi_de_phu_hop_voi_thuc_te (accessed 31 July 2017).

Affairs, the institution proposing the bill, there are five official reasons for enacting this law: (1) to detail the Party's opinion and the provisions of the 2013 Constitution pertaining to religious freedom; (2) to update and correct the current legal framework on belief and religion; (3) to allow for a more transparent and open legal process for the practice of religious freedom and to limit state interference into the internal activities of religious organizations; (4) to consolidate the 'national great solidarity'; and (5) to contribute to the implementation of the party and state's international policies to 'figh[t] against the abuse of religion to oppose the Party and State'.[35]

In 2015, the drafting board, mainly consisting of senior government members, held several conferences and workshop to discuss the bill with officials, experts, and religious persons.[36] The bill was then presented for debate in the National Assembly's Standing Committee and the National Assembly's specific committee for cultural and educational affairs. The National Assembly discussed the bill at its plenary meeting on 13 November 2015 and approved the bill on 18 November 2016, nearly one year later, after the second discussion.[37]

When the bill was first presented and discussed in the National Assembly's Standing Committee in mid-August 2015, many members of the Committee agreed on the need for the new law but criticized the bill for introducing onerous administrative procedures for registration and permits that failed to limit state interference in religious activities.[38] Member Trương Thị Mai, for example, lamented that the draft law 'lets the state do so many things. There are registrations and permissions everywhere'.[39] Member Nguyễn Kim Khoa even argued that the bill 'focused on management [and] creates such conditions that fail to meet with the requirements of protecting religious freedom established by the Constitution'.[40]

At the plenary meeting of the National Assembly in late 2015, several deputies again raised the issue of the state's interference in religious activities through the imposition of cumbersome administrative instruments.[41] Deputy Công Lưu Thành Công, for instance, stated: 'In the bill, there are 20 references to the fact that religious organizations must ask for permission from the state. There are few protective provisions that allow for open space and transparency and ensure the

35 Phóng viên Cổng thông tin điện tử Bộ Nội vụ, 'Phỏng vấn Bộ trưởng Lê Vĩnh Tân về Luật tín ngưỡ ng, tôn giáo' ['Interview with Minister Lê Vĩnh Tân on the Law on Belief and Religion'] (*Cổng thông tin điện tử Bộ Nội vụ* 13 December 2016), www.moha.gov.vn/tin-noi-bat/phong-van-bo-truong-le-vinh-tan-ve-luat-tin-nguong-ton-giao-28534.html (accessed 30 December 2016).

36 It is common to have such public consultation on proposed laws in Vietnam.

37 For details in the law-making process, see Ibid.

38 Chung Hoàng, 'Lần đầu bàn luật Tín ngưỡng, tôn giáo' ['The First Discussion on the Law on Belief and Religion'] (*Vietnamnet*, 14 August 2015), http://vietnamnet.vn/vn/thoi-su/lan-dau-ban-luat-ti-n-nguo-ng-ton-gia-o-256499.html (accessed 30 December 2016).

39 Ibid.

40 Ibid.

41 Thu Hằng, 'Không can thiệp hành chính vào nhân sự tôn giáo' ['No Administrative Interference into Religious Personnel Affairs'] (*Vietnamnet*, 20 November 2015), http://vietnamnet.vn/vn/thoi-su/khong-can-thiep-hanh-chinh-vao-nhan-su-ton-giao-274469.html (accessed 30 December 2016).

right to everyone's right to freedom of belief and religion.'[42] To illustrate, he suggested that religious organizations should have the right to ordain and appoint leaders (or members?) without the interference of the state through administrative commands.[43] Another deputy, Võ Thị Dung, suggested that as belief is a need of the people that is protected by the Constitution, 'there should not be extensive regulations; there should not be too many administrative resolutions'.[44] Deputy Lê Văn Tấn also proposed that separation of religious organizations is their internal affairs, and they should notify the state authorities but should not be required to seek permission.[45]

In October 2016, when the National Assembly was discussing the draft law, fifty-four religious bodies and civil society organizations led by the Committee on Human Rights and Christian Solidarity Worldwide sent a letter to National Assembly President Nguyễn Thị Kim Ngân to criticize the bill and call for substantive revisions of the draft. The letter also stated:

> The 9-chapter draft law contains some improvements, but also continues to place unacceptable restrictions on the right to freedom of religion or belief and other human rights. Specifically, basic guarantees of the right to freedom of religion or belief continue to be undermined by onerous registration requirements and excessive state interference in religious organizations' internal affairs. Indeed, this and the previous versions of the law inherit from previous rules and regulations this emphasis on government control and management of religious life which is contrary to the spirit and principle of the right to freedom of religion or belief.[46]

The law was eventually adopted by 417 of 439 members (84.7 per cent).[47] The law has come into force since 1 January 2018 and replaces the Ordinance. The Government has also issued new administrative regulations to implement this law.

After the law was passed, it was criticized by religious activists and some international organizations.[48] Human Rights Watch, for example, claimed that the law 'allows authorities to single out and persecute religious groups they dislike'.[49] Domestic official media, in contrast, acclaimed the law. One newspaper, for instance, said:

42 Ibid.

43 Ibid.

44 Ibid.

45 Ibid.

46 The letter is available at: http://hrwf.eu/vietnam-open-letter-to-the-president-of-the-vietnam-national-assembly-on-vietnams-draft-law-on-belief-and-religion/

47 The law is composed of nine chapters divided into sixty-eight articles: Chapter I, general provisions; Chapter II, the freedom to belief and religion; Chapter III, belief activities; Chapter IV, registration of religious activities; Chapter V, religious organizations; Chapter VI, religious activities concerning publication, education, medicine, and others; Chapter VII, religious assets; Chapter VIII, state management and punishment of legal violations in the area of belief and religion; Chapter IX, implementation provisions.

48 Luke Hunt, 'People in Vietnam Think a Controversial New Law Is Just a Smokescreen for Government Repression', *Business Insider* (3 December, 2016), www.businessinsider.com/vietnam-religion-law-government-repression-2016–12?IR=T&r=US&IR=T (accessed 30 December 2016).

49 Ibid.

> Religious dignitaries told the National Assembly that the approval of the law was a turning point in Vietnam's religious policy which encourages religious followers to promote the values of religions and patriotism and combat hostile forces' intention to sabotage socialism.[50]

My views about this law are as below. Despite the new form of codification, the substance of how religion is regulated by law remains intact. The regulatory tone features strongly in the law, as is most evident in the first Article titled 'scope of regulation and applied subjects'. The Article states: 'This Law regulates the freedom to belief and religion; belief and religious activities; religious organizations; the rights and duties of institutions, organizations, and individuals pertaining belief and religious activities.'

The law retains the substantive provisions on prohibited religious activities; the registration of religious activities; the procedures and requirements of registration and approval of religious organizations; the establishment, division, separation, merger, or amalgamation of religious organizations; and the registration and approval of programs for their activities, their assets, and their international activities. Retaining these regulatory features is consistent with the state's concern with consolidating the 'national great solidarity' and 'fighting against the abuse of religion to oppose the Party and State'. Many of the changes can thus be said to be relatively minor, such as a shift in the style of expression and adjustments to the registration procedure and the role of the authorities in registering and approving religious activities and religious organizations.

Yet, there are some notable changes. First, a separate chapter on the freedom of belief and religion was introduced, aiming to emphasize the state's commitment to respect and protect the right to religious freedom as a human right of 'everyone', not merely a right that comes with being a citizen. This is consistent with the new provision on religious freedom in the 2013 Constitution that 'Everyone shall enjoy freedom of belief and of religion .... The State respects and protects freedom of belief and of religion' (Article 24). In theory, this chapter indicates that the law is not merely about the state's regulation of religious activities but also about the facilitation of religious freedom. Second, the new law makes the recognition of religious organizations easier and quicker by shortening the requisite time for recognizing a new religious organization from twenty-three years to five years of continued recognized religious activities. Third, the right to religious freedom of foreigners legally residing in Vietnam is now more fully recognized. This includes the right to be nominated, appointed, or elected to a religious post in Vietnam. Fourth, the law limits state interference in the internal affairs of religious organizations to some extent, by replacing the requirement of registration with notifying state authorities of the ordained, order-bestowed, appointed, elected, or honorary nominated persons

50 'Vietnamese Law in Line with International Norms of Religion and Belief', *The Voice of Vietnam* (3 December 2016), http://english.vov.vn/Print.aspx?id=338411 (accessed 30 December 2016).

who are not leaders of religious organizations working across provinces or leaders of religious schools. Fifth, religious organizations are now recognized as 'legal entities', thus allowing them to enter into civil transactions according to civil law.

However, as the law expressly states in its first Article on the 'scope of regulation', this law regulates religious freedom, religious activities, and religious organizations. Regulation means intentional interference by governing, guiding, and controlling. Therefore, the law is a regulatory framework for state management and control of religion. Even though it does not contain many substantive changes, the state enacted the law to replace the Ordinance because of the significance of the formal and procedural changes to the regulatory framework. First, the codification in a statute of the legal rules pertaining to religion provides a comprehensive and unified framework for the state to regulate religion. Second, the law has gained greater legitimacy due to its compliance with the new Constitution, which provides that human rights, including the right to religious freedom, can be limited only by statute by the National Assembly. The enactment of the law, therefore, limits the possible restriction of religious freedom through the avenue of administrative regulations.

Third, the legitimacy of the regulatory framework has also been enhanced as the law was enacted by the National Assembly, a popularly elected institution, through a relatively open deliberative process. There appeared to be tension between the National Assembly and the Government during the deliberative process. The Government, as an institution of management, was more concerned with managing and controlling religion, while the National Assembly, which tends to be more reflective of the popular will, sought to protect the constitutional right to religious freedom from administrative interference. The legislative deliberations were helpful to some extent in removing some provisions that allowed for administrative interference in religious activities, although these deliberations ultimately failed to create substantive deregulation of religion due to the state's concerns. I contend that the deliberative process conferred more legitimacy on the new regulatory framework, although there are no substantive changes in the new law.

B. Monitoring

Monitoring concerns the institutions responsible for implementing the promulgated legal rules. The monitoring institutions that enforce the regulatory framework for religious activities in Vietnam are highly intricate. One key institution comprises the central government and the local governments at all levels, as the legal framework allows state authorities at different levels to monitor religious activities through the approval of programs for religious activities, the recognition of religious organizations, and the issuing of different types of permits.

There are also hierarchical institutions that are specifically responsible for monitoring religious activities. These comprise the Government Committee for Religious Affairs at the central government level and the committees for religious affairs at the provincial government level. The Government Committee for Religious Affairs is a body of the Ministry of Internal Affairs. The prime minister defines the detailed functions of this committee. The most recent relevant regulation, Decision No. 06/2015/QĐ-TTg issued on 12 February 2015, lists the nineteen functions of this committee. Its most notable functions for the purpose of monitoring religious activities include: informing, propagandizing, guiding, and supervising the practice of the state and party's policies on religion; examining the profiles of applicants for the recognition of religious organizations and submitting reports to the relevant authorities for approval; mobilizing the people to practice the state and party's policies on religion; centrally managing the publication of religious materials; instructing religious organizations and followers in international religious activities; and educating and training state officials responsible for religious affairs at different governmental levels. Local governments at the provincial level also create similar committees for religious affairs with relatively similar functions to the Government Committee. These local committees are under the unified control and guidance of the central committee, hence indicating that the monitoring mechanisms are highly centralized.

Another important mechanism for monitoring religious activities is inspection. A recent regulation issued by the Ministry of Internal Affairs, Circular No. 04/2016/TT-BNV, allows the Government Committee for Religious Affairs and the departments of internal affairs at the provincial government level to inspect or to examine in detail whether there is something wrong or illegal in these areas: the registration of religious activities and the recognition of religious organizations; the division, separation, merger, or amalgamation of religious organizations; the registration of religious societies, religious orders, monasteries and other collective religious practice organizations; the creation, management, and dismissal of religious schools; the ordainment, bestowal of orders, appointment, election, or honorary nomination in religions; the transfer of religious dignitaries, priests, or monks to other areas of operation; the registration of annual programs of activities; conferences of religious organizations; publication of religious materials; and others. Thus, the inspecting institutions can closely examine different aspects of religious activities.

C. *Sanctioning*

The Government Committee for Religious Affairs has published an article on its website which expressly states that 'the law on belief and religion lacks sanction'.[51] This means that there are no formal mechanisms to punish unregistered religious activities, unregistered religious organizations and groups, and other religious

[51] Minh Anh, 'Văn bản pháp luật về tín ngưỡng, tôn giáo ở Việt Nam hiện nay, kết quả và bất cập' ['Law on Belief and Religion in Today's Vietnam: Achievements and Shortcomings'] (*Government Committee for Religious Affairs*), http://btgcp.gov.vn/Plus.aspx/vi/News/38/0/240/0/7170/Van_ban_phap_luat_ve_tin_nguong_ton_giao_o_Viet_Nam_hien_nay_ket_qua_va_bat_cap (accessed 30 December 2016).

activities that are not approved by the state. However, religious dissidents, international organizations, and foreign governments often refer to informal sanctions that applied in practice, such as the authorities' harassment of unregistered groups.[52] This might change with the new Law on Belief and Religion, which authorizes the Government to use this law and the Law on Handling of Administrative Violations (2012) to provide for administrative offences in the area of belief and religion. Whether this change will take place remains to be seen.

Without formal administrative sanctions, the regulatory framework of religion in Vietnam is largely backed by criminal sanctions. The Penal Code, which was last revised in 2015, includes a separate provision that protects the right to religious freedom (Article 164) in that those who infringe upon others' right to freedom of belief and religion may be imprisoned for up to five years. In contrast, the Penal Code does not spell out specific crimes for religious dissidents but contains a wide range of general crimes that can be applied to dissidents, including 'activities aimed at overthrowing the people's administration' (Article 109, with a maximum penalty of capital punishment), 'undermining the unity policy' (Article 116, with a penalty of up to fifteen years in prison), 'conducting propaganda' against the state (Article 117, with a penalty of up to 20 years in prison), 'disrupting security' (Article 118, with a penalty of up to fifteen years in prison), 'fleeing abroad or defecting to stay overseas with a view to opposing the people's administration' (Article 121, with a penalty of up to twelve years in prison), 'causing public disorder' (Article 318, with a penalty of up to two years in prison), and 'abusing democratic freedoms to infringe upon the interests of the State, the legitimate rights and interests of organizations and/or citizens' (Article 331, with a penalty up to seven years in prison). In practice, these criminal provisions have become the basis for sanctioning religious activists. For example, in July 2011, fifteen Vietnamese religious activists were arrested for carrying out subversive activities.[53]

In short, the Vietnamese state uses the Constitution and other laws to comprehensively and stringently regulate nearly all aspects of religious activities. The legal rules regulating religious behaviour are monitored by centralized and hierarchical institutions and backed by the strong deterrent power of serious criminal sanctions.

IV. THE SOCIALIST INSTITUTIONAL SPACE FOR RELIGION

Four institutional factors explain the regulatory framework for religion in Vietnam: the socialist regime, the ideology of 'great unity', the socialist view of legality, and the statist human rights regime. The first two factors explain the purposes of regulation, while the next two factors explain the degree and manner of regulation. However,

[52] See, for example, US Department of State, *Vietnam 2015 International Religious Freedom Report* (2015).

[53] Human Right Watch, 'Vietnam: Free Religious Activists Immediately', *Human Rights Watch* (30 September 2011), www.hrw.org/news/2011/09/30/vietnam-free-religious-activists-immediately (accessed 30 December 2016).

this distinction between the two types of factors is noted here only for analytical purposes. The reality is complex; the different factors interact with each other to shape the regulatory framework for religion.

A. *The Socialist Regime and Religion*

One distinctive feature of the general institutional space for religion in Vietnam is that this space is predominantly occupied by the socialist state. More importantly, the socialist state has the power to decide who is inside and who is outside this space. The top concern of the state in making such decisions is whether prospective new occupants are aligned with or pose a threat to the socialist regime. This logic is also applied to regulating religion. Through regulatory methods of registration and approval, the state decides which religions, religious activities, religious figures, and religious organizations are included within or excluded from the institutional space by considering whether they are aligned with or pose a threat to the socialist regime. The state carefully regulates religions to protect the existing socialist regime, which is defined by the single leadership of the Communist Party, the dominant ideology of Marxism-Leninism, and the Leninist unitary government.

In and of themselves, religions already present a challenge to the socialist regime in Vietnam. First, the existence of diverse religions in Vietnam challenges one precept of the ideological base of the socialist regime, namely Marxist-Leninist atheism. The state carefully manages religions to ensure that Marxist-Leninist atheism remains the dominant belief in not only the party and state but also in the entire society, though supernatural beliefs are still tolerated. Second, the government in Vietnam associates religion with the change of the socialist regime. A party commentator states: 'Imperialism and enemy forces consider religions in Vietnam [to be] a political force capable [of] "counter[ing]" . . . the Communist Party of Vietnam and are supporting religious opponents financially and spiritually, [as part of a plot to use] religion as a force to foster the process of "democratization" so as to change the political regime in Vietnam.'[54] Given this perception of the power of religion, the state thus stringently regulates religions to avoid regime change. Third, the state's careful regulation of religion to protect the unitary socialist state is also motivated by religion-based separatism advocating for the creation of ethnically based states that are independent of the socialist state. One example is the Protestant mobilization for the creation of a 'Degar Republic' for the Degar people, the indigenous people of the central Highlands of Vietnam.[55]

[54] Bùi Đình Bôn, 'Lợi dụng vấn đề tôn giáo để chống phá Việt Nam' ['Appropriating Religion to Oppose Vietnam'] (*Báo Lao Động*, 20 November 2010), http://laodong.com.vn/chinh-tri/loi-dung-van-de-ton-giao-de-chong-pha-viet-nam-39334.bld (accessed 30 December 2016).

[55] Nguyễn Văn Minh, 'The Creation, Aim, and Activities of the So-called "The State of Degar Republic"', *Journal of Anthropology* 4 (2006), 60.

Because the Vietnamese state is acutely aware of the challenge posed by religion to the existing socialist regime, it comprehensively regulates religions to allow into the existing space new religious occupants that are aligned with the regime, while excluding potential religious opponents. The state's regulation of Buddhism illustrates that well. The Vietnam Buddhist Church (VBC) (*Giáo hội Phật giáo Việt Nam*, formed in 1981), is officially recognized and strongly supported by the state as it is committed to promote 'Dharma, Nation, and Socialism'.[56] A VBC dignitary has expressly proclaimed that 'real experience indicates that Buddhism is not far from socialism'.[57] In contrast, the Unified Buddhist Sangha of Vietnam (UBSV) (*Giáo hội Phật giáo Việt Nam Thống nhất*, founded in 1964) is banned in Vietnam and operates in exile, as it has a history of promoting anti-Communism during the Vietnam War. After the 1975 unification of Vietnam, most of the UBSV leaders were punished by the socialist state.[58]

The state adopts similar approaches in regulating Catholicism. As Peter Hansen notes: 'The relationship between Catholicism and the state [in Vietnam] has through the *long duree* of almost 400 years, been fraught with conflict, mutual suspicion, antipathy, anti-Catholic persecution and martyrdom.'[59] The fraught nature of the relationship between Catholicism and the state can partly be attributed to the antipathy of Catholicism to the existing socialist/communist regime. For instance, during the 2013 constitution-making process, the Catholic Bishops' Conference of Vietnam addressed a letter to the Constitutional Amendment Commission, challenging the core of the socialist regime. The letter called for religious freedom and also for the removal of the entrenchment of the leadership of the Communist Party of Vietnam and its ideology, Marxism-Leninism and Ho Chi Minh's Thought, from the Constitution.[60] Although Catholicism is still tolerated, the state remains a contentious, stringent regulatory space for the Catholic community. The state has also sanctioned, through criminal means, Catholic

56 Nguyễn Phúc Nguyên, 'Giáo hội Phật giáo Việt Nam 30 năm thự c hiện đường hướng: Đạo pháp – Dân tộc- Chủ nghĩa xã hội' ['Vietnam Buddhist Church's 30 Implementation of the Program: Dharma, Nation, and Socialism'] (*Ban Tôn giáo Chính phủ*), http://btgcp.gov.vn/Plus.aspx/vi/News/38/0/240/0/2402/Giao_hoi_Phat_giao_Viet_Nam_30_nam_thuc_hien_duong_huong_Dao_phap_Dan_toc_Chu_nghia_xa_hoi (accessed 30 December 2016).

57 Ibid.

58 Zachary Abuza, *Renovating Politics in Contemporary Vietnam* (Lynne Rienner, 2001), 192.

59 Peter Hansen, 'The Vietnamese State, the Catholic Church and the Law', in John Gillespie and Pip Nicholson (eds.), *Asian Socialism & Legal Change: The Dynamics of Vietnamese and Chinese Reform John* (ANU E Press; Asia Pacific Press, 2005), 310.

60 'Thư của Hội đồng Giám mục Việt Nam gửi Ủy ban Dự thảo sửa đổi Hiến pháp năm 1992 nhận định và góp ý sửa đổi Hiến pháp' ['Catholic Bishops' Conference of Vietnam's Letter to the Commission for Amending the 1992 Constitution Concerning Assessments and Comments on Constitutional Amendments'], available at: http://hdgmvietnam.org/thu-cua-hoi-dong-giam-muc-viet-nam-nhan-dinh-va-gop-y-sua-doi-hien-phap/4750.116.3.aspx

dissidents who dare to go beyond the acceptable space by engaging in subversive activities.[61]

B. The 'Great Unity' and Religion

The institutional space for religion in Vietnam is also shaped by the ideology and strategy of 'great unity' (*đại đoàn kết*). The concept of 'great unity' was originally developed by Ho Chi Minh as a strategy to unify all social forces in Vietnam to carry out a communist revolution to overturn colonialism; this was captured in his motto 'Unity, Unity, Great Unity' and 'Success, Success, Great Success'.[62] The ideology of 'great unity' is a mixture of the Vietnamese tradition of patriotism and communist ideology. The tradition of patriotism is the 'common denominator' unifying all social forces.[63] At the same time, the communist ideology suggests that social forces lie at the root of the 'great unity', namely 'the workers, the peasants, and other working classes',[64] whose leadership over other social classes is a guarantee of the movement towards socialism and subsequently communism. There remains, however, a distinction between the tradition of patriotism and communist ideology. One consequence of the distinction is the revolutionary approach to social relationships that is characterized by an antagonistic attitude towards 'enemies', who include not only foreign invaders but also domestic capitalists and other social actors.

The Vietnamese political leadership now considers the great national unity 'a strategic policy, a source of power, a major motivation and a factor crucial to [the] victory of the Vietnamese revolution'.[65] After the communist revolution of August 1945, the ideology of 'great unity' has been applied to different aspects of society:

> Since the August Revolution, the Party and State have issued a number of policies and laws on ethnic and religious affairs, youths, women, workers, farmers, intellectuals, artists and Vietnamese nationals abroad, with a view to upholding the power of great national unity in the national construction, defence and development.[66]

61 Human Rights Watch, 'Vietnam: Release Convicted Activists, Drop Charges Against Blogger Le Quoc Quan, Human Rights Watch', *Human Rights Watch* (9 January 2013), www.hrw.org/news/2013/01/09/vietnam-release-convicted-activists (accessed 30 December 2016).

62 'Ho Chi Minh Thought on Great National Unity and Religions', *VOV Vietnam* (27 May 2006), http://english.vov.vn/world/ho-chi-minh-thought-on-great-national-unity-and-religions-34666.vov (accessed 30 December 2016).

63 Đoàn Minh Duệ, 'Tư tưởng Hồ Chí Minh về đại đoàn kết dân tộc và sự vận dụng của Đảng ta trong công cuộc đổi mới' 2007 (1) *Tạp chí Triết học*, http://philosophy.vass.gov.vn/nghien-cuu-theo-chuyen-de/Triet-hoc-Mac-Lenin/Tu-tuong-Ho-Chi-Minh-ve-dai-doan-ket-dan-toc-va-su-van-dung-cua-Dang-ta-trong-cong-cuoc-doi-moi-369.html (accessed 30 December 2016).

64 Ibid.

65 'President underscores great national unity in development', *Vietnam Pictorial* (1 September 2016), http://vietnam.vnanet.vn/english/president-underscores-great-national-unity-in-development/259599.html (accessed 30 December 2016).

66 Ibid.

In other words, the 'great unity' is the ideological base for the state's regulation of various sectors, including religion.

The state comprehensively regulates religion to ensure that religion will not create serious divisions that might undermine the 'great unity'. Why does the state need to regulate religion to protect the 'great unity'? One possible explanation could be that religious diversity may result in religious conflicts in society that may undermine the 'great unity'. In fact, although Vietnam is home to different religions, serious religious conflicts have not arisen in the country. Vietnamese history can attest to a long tradition of harmonious existence among different religions.[67] Because Vietnam is not a religiously divided society and religious conflicts do not present an ostensible threat to the 'great unity', it can be argued that the state need not comprehensively and stringently regulate religion to avoid such conflicts.

However, the threat posed by religion to the 'great unity' does not arise in the conflicts among religions but in the conflict between religion and the state. State–religion conflicts are officially recognized as indispensable in Vietnam.[68] The conflicts do not just surface between Marxist-Leninist atheism, 'historic materialism' and religious convictions in transcending spiritual forces;[69] there are also conflicts between the state and specific religions with regard to their distinctive visions on human nature, a just society, and political order. For example, some religions – such as Christianity – 'embody the insistence that there are inherent limits to state power', a proposition that conflicts with the communist government's principle of 'dictatorship of the proletariat'.[70] Consequently, the state comprehensively regulates religion to maintain the 'unity' between the secular ruling classes (the workers, the peasants, and other working classes) of the socialist state and religious followers, which would contribute to the 'great unity'.

The revolutionary spirit within the ideology of 'great unity' is reflected in the regulatory space for religion. The socialist state in Vietnam conceives of communist revolution as a process taking place in multiple phases, such as gaining national independence and constructing the socialist state.[71] By its own count, the socialist

67 Lê Anh Dũng. 'The Tradition of Unity of Three Religions in the Vietnamese Nation During Different Periods', *Nhịp Cầu Giáo Lý* (1 June 2004), www.nhipcaugiaoly.com/post?id=142 (accessed 30 December 2016).

68 Hà Quang Trường, 'Công tác quản lý nhà nước về tôn giáo hiện nay (State's Management of Religion Today'), *Tạp chí Lý luận chính trị* 12 (2015), http://lyluanchinhtri.vn/home/index.php/nguyen-cuu-ly-luan/item/1648-cong-tac-quan-ly-nha-nuoc-ve-ton-giao-hien-nay.html (accessed 30 December 2016).

69 Ibid.

70 Samuel Gregg, 'Corruption, Communism, and Catholicism in Vietnam', *Acton Institute* (11 August 2009), www.acton.org/pub/commentary/2009/08/12/corruption-communism-and-catholicism-vietnam (accessed 30 December 2016).

71 Nguyễn Viết Thảo, 'Quá Trình Cách Mạng Việt Nam: Nhữ ng Thành Tự u Vĩ Đại Và Ý Nghĩa Lịch Sử' ['The Process of Revolution in Vietnam: Great Achievements and Historic Meanings'], *Báo Điện tử Đảng Cộng sản Việt Nam* (30 September, 2015), http://dangcongsan.vn/tu-lieu-van-kien/tu-lieu-ve-dang/sach-ve-cong-tac-dang/doc-2930201510473746.html (accessed 30 December 2016).

state is now in the process of revolution. Accordingly, the revolutionary approach still informs the state's regulation of different sectors of society, including religion, in Vietnam today. This revolutionary approach to regulation is characterized by an antagonistic distinction between the ruling classes and the ruled. Within this regulatory approach, those who present a threat to the 'revolutionary mission' or the construction of the socialist state are treated as state 'enemies' to be severely punished. It is in this revolutionary context that the state comprehensively regulates religions and seeks to punish religious actors who present a danger to the 'revolutionary mission' by undermining the 'great unity'.

In short, the ideology of the 'great unity' shapes the institutional space for religion in Vietnam. Whether certain religious activities and religious organizations are included inside or excluded from the regulatory space depends on the state's assessment of whether they are constructive or destructive to the state's 'great unity'.

C. *Socialist Legality and Religion*

The concept of socialist legality, advanced by V. I. Lenin, is characterized by the state's use of formal law as an instrument to strictly regulate society to achieve socialist goals.[72] Like Western legal positivism, socialist legality treats the nature of law as being closely associated with the state's formal promulgation. What then is distinctively socialist about socialist legality? Socialist legality has two main characteristics: (1) the unanimous observation of the law by citizens; and (2) the state's strict handling of legal violations committed by citizens in order to protect the state's interests and other collective interests.[73] The principle of socialist legality thus disregards the employment of the law by citizens to challenge state authorities, while emphasizing the employment of the law by state authorities to deal with citizens.

The principle of socialist legality has been adopted in Vietnam and it informs the regulatory framework of various social sectors, including religion. Socialist legality explains in particular the formality and the degree of comprehensiveness of religious regulation in the country. In line with this principle, religions are comprehensively and stringently regulated by formal law. Religious actors are required to unanimously observe the formal laws that regulate their behaviour. The formal laws are predominantly concerned with providing instruments and mechanisms for the state to manage religions. The state deals strictly with religious followers who violate the regulatory framework in order to protect the state's interests and other collective

72 Đỗ Ngọc Hải, 'Bàn về pháp chế xã hội chủ nghĩa trong điều kiện xây dự ng và hoàn thiện nhà nước pháp quyền xã hội chủ nghĩa Việt Nam' (Commenting on Socialist Legality in the Context of building and Perfecting Vietnamese Socialist Rule of Law State), *Tạp chí Tổ chức Nhà nước* 12 (2009), http://tcnn.vn/Plus.aspx/vi/News/125/0/1010067/0/5042/Ban_ve_phap_che_xa_hoi_chu_nghia_trong_dieu_kien_xay_dung_va_hoan_thien_nha_nuoc_phap_quyen_xa_hoi_chu (accessed 30 December 2016).

73 Ibid.

interests. At the same time, the principle of socialist legality also explains the limited institutional scope given to religious actors to challenge the state's actions. Generally, the mechanism of judicial review is absent in Vietnam, which means that religious actors cannot challenge the legislation, administrative regulations, and state authorities' actions in court for violating their constitutional right to religious freedom. The new Law on Belief and Religion, however, contains one article which allows religious actors to initiate administrative litigation to protect their rights and interests (Article 63). How this article will play out in practice remains to be seen.

D. *Statist Rights and Religion*

The regulatory space for religion is also shaped by the human rights regime in Vietnam, which is dominated by the statist approach to rights.[74] The statist approach to human rights in Vietnam has fostered a regulatory framework for religion. The Constitution grants the right to religious freedom to citizens and requires that the practice of this right must be consistent with the law. In this way, the Constitution allows the law to regulate the practice of the right to religious freedom. Religious actors may be granted the right to religious freedom, but this right can be controlled and withdrawn by the state according to the state's privileged interpretation.

E. *Expanding the Institutional Space for Religion*

As this chapter has demonstrated, the regulatory framework for religion in Vietnam has expanded over time. The new Constitution tries to present a universal concept of human rights in general and the right to religious freedom in particular. Accordingly, the Constitution and the new Law on Belief and Religion both seek to recognize the right to religious freedom as a right that a person possesses by virtue of being a human being, rather than a right that a citizen is granted as a subject of the state. In practice, the state has also recognized new religions and religious organizations.[75]

In his recent thoughtful article on religious freedom in Vietnam, Professor John Gillespie argues that 'government officials swiftly suppress the political mobilization of religion – a phenomenon that understandably attracts international media attention – but have privatized religious worship by incrementally loosening controls over religious beliefs and practices'.[76] This 'liberalization' is possible because party

[74] Christopher Osakwe, 'The Theories and Realities of Modern Soviet Constitutional Law: An Analysis of the 1977 USSR Constitution', *University of Pennsylvania Law Review* 127 (1979), 1390–5.

[75] See generally, Chung Van Hoang, *New Religions and State's Response to Religious Diversification in Contemporary Vietnam* (Springer Science+Business Media, 2017).

[76] John Gillespie, 'Human Rights as a Larger Loyalty: The Evolution of Religious Freedom in Vietnam', *Harvard Human Rights Journal* 47 (2014), 145.

leaders now accept religious communities that were previously excluded from the 'great unity'.[77] Gillespie argues that the expansion of the regulatory framework for religion can be attributed to the 'changing [of] the Vietnamese government's inward-looking, relativist views of human rights into cosmopolitan, universal perspectives',[78] which in turn is conditioned by modernization and globalization.[79] The argument here is that modernization and globalization create social complexity (in the form of a growing number of public interest advocates; an increase in transnational human rights discourse, public demonstrations, and diverse views in public discourse on religious freedom), which compels the government to expand its outlook and be more inclusive towards various forms of religious worship.[80] Gillespie rightly captures the significance of the domestic contextual factors that have positively reshaped the regulatory framework for religion in Vietnam. To complete the picture, more attention needs to be paid to the impact of external factors. Gillespie has already discussed some external factors (such as the global diffusion of new knowledge and transnational human rights discourse) in the context of their contribution to the creation of domestic social complexity. However, one key external factor that must be considered is the influence of international factors in socializing the Vietnamese state's behaviour towards human rights.[81]

The mechanism of 'socialization' or 'acculturation' has undoubtedly played a part in the expansion of the regulatory framework for religion in Vietnam. Acculturation refers to the general process of adopting the beliefs and behavioural patterns of the surrounding culture, where behavioural change is induced through 'pressures to assimilate – some imposed by other actors and some imposed by the self'.[82] This mechanism of acculturation influences the behaviour of not just individuals and social organizations but also of states. According to Goodman and Jinks, numerous empirical studies now suggest that 'states are significantly shaped and legitimated through their broader organizational environment', as states are highly legitimated actors in world society and their formal structures like administrative bodies and policy commitments 'substantially derive from institutionalized models promulgated at the global level'.[83] States also emulate standardized models of human rights to socialize themselves into 'world society'.[84] One consequence of acculturation is 'incomplete internationalization'.[85] As Goodman and Jinks explain:

77 Ibid.
78 Ibid., 112.
79 Ibid.
80 Ibid.
81 Ryan Goodman and Derek Jinks, 'How to Influence States: Socialization and International Human Rights Law', *Duke Law Journal* 54 (2004), 638.
82 Ibid.
83 Ibid., 647–8.
84 Ibid., 648. See also Benedikt Goderis and Mila Versteeg, 'The Diffusion of Constitutional Rights', *International Review of Law and Economics* 39 (2014), 1.
85 Goodman and Jinks, 'How to Influence States', 642.

> Acculturation occurs not as a result of the content of the relevant rule or norm but rather as a function of social structure—the relations between individual actors and some reference group. Acculturation depends less on the properties of the rule than on the properties of the relationship of the actor to the community. Because the acculturation process does not involve actually agreeing with the merits of a group's position, it may result in outward conformity with a social convention without private acceptance or corresponding changes in private practices.[86]

Hence, with regard to human rights, when states adopt a human right as a matter of socialization due to the pressure to comply with internationally legitimized standards instead of being motivated by local pressure and local capacity, one can expect some discrepancies between structural isomorphism and real practices.[87]

In Vietnam, the state's expansion of space for religion is not just due to domestic pressure, as Gillespie has argued, but also due to the influence of acculturation. In particular, acculturation can be seen in the pressure to comply with international standards of human rights in general and the right to religious freedom in particular. This external pressure comes from several sources: Vietnam has adopted major international human rights treaties, while the country has faced serious criticism by international nongovernmental organizations, international organizations, and foreign governments for violations of human rights and religious freedom in particular. Socializing the socialist state into civilized global society by adopting an internationally legitimatized model of human rights is therefore a mechanism to gain more international legitimacy, which is also instrumental to consolidating domestic legitimacy. The consequence, therefore, is the state's adoption of the universal language of human rights and religious freedom, and the expansion of the sphere for religious worship.

On the other hand, one consequence of acculturation is that the state's internalization of the international standard of religious freedom is incomplete. The incomplete internalization is reflected in the formal laws regulating religion and in the state's actual management of religion. First, while the provision on religious freedom in the Constitution and the new Law on Belief and Religion express a universal outlook towards religious freedom, the entire regulatory framework of religion is still dominated by the statist model. Religious activities must not threaten the socialist regime, the 'great unity', and the state's interests. Moreover, as mentioned earlier, there are still a number of requirements to be met in order to obtain state approval and recognition of the formation and operation of religious organizations. Hence, the formal regulatory framework contains competing cosmopolitan and statist approaches to religious freedom: the state recognizes – but does not grant – the universal right to religious freedom which everyone enjoys as a member of the human community (not as a subject of the state); but at the same

[86] Ibid., 643.
[87] Ibid., 652.

time, the state has not abandoned comprehensive and stringent control over the practice of this right, in order to protect the regime, the 'great unity', as well as the state's and other collective interests. Thus, the adoption of the international standard of religious freedom through the acculturation mechanism creates ambiguity and internal contradiction in the regulatory framework for religion.

Second, the acculturation mechanism also creates complexity, ambiguity, and contradiction in the state's actual management of religion. Thomas J. Reese, S.J. and Mary Ann Glendon, members of the U.S. Commission on International Religious Freedom, recently reported:

> The situation on religion in Vietnam is complex and at times confusing. On the one hand, Catholic churches are packed and vocations plentiful; the government recently granted Catholics permission to found a university-level institute of theology in the South. Catholics can even hold government jobs, and it is not uncommon for party members to send their children to Catholic preschool programs or to Catholic universities in the United States. On the other hand, we heard credible reports corroborating the commission's past findings that police often harass and assault religious followers from independent, unregistered religious organizations, including many Protestant churches.[88]

This complex and ambiguous situation can be attributed to, among other things, the influence of the acculturation mechanism on the Vietnamese state's attitude towards religious freedom. Further, the incomplete internalisation of the internationally standardized model of religious freedom has led to the situation in which the state respects the right to religious freedom in certain circumstances but tightly manages the practice of the right in other contexts.

V. CONCLUSION

This chapter concludes with a brief discussion of the legitimacy of the regulatory framework for religion in Vietnam. My contention is that the source of regulatory legitimacy stems more from the state's actual performance than from the formal regulations. Consequently, it is the state's performance that lends legitimacy to the formal regulatory framework.

The incremental move towards a universal model of religious freedom, which informed the new constitutional provision on religious freedom and the new Law on Belief and Religion, has conferred some legitimacy on the formal regulatory framework. Moreover, the fact that the law was drafted with a relatively open process that included some level of public deliberation also legitimatizes the formal regulatory framework to some degree. However, as the regulatory framework retains substantial

88 Thomas J. Reese, S.J. and Mary Ann Glendon, 'Report from Vietnam: The struggle between government and religion', *America Magazine* (29 February 2016), www.americamagazine.org/issue/report-vietnam (accessed 30 December 2016).

provisions that allow the state to comprehensively and stringently control the formation and operation of religious organizations, the source of the legitimacy cannot be said to arise mainly from the formal regulatory framework.

Hence, it can be said that the legitimacy of regulating religion in Vietnam rests mainly on the state's actual performance. In fact, the state mainly refers to its positive performance to justify its regulatory actions. Positive performance in the eyes of the state is reflected in the betterment of religious freedom in Vietnam.[89] This performance-based legitimacy comes from the slow but real expansion of institutional space for religion, thereby fostering the formal recognition of new religions, religious organizations, and religious activities, and the state's tacit toleration of unregistered religious organizations and religious activities.

[89] Ministry of Internal Affairs, 'Báo cáo Tổng kết 08 năm thự c hiện Pháp lệnh tín ngưỡ ng, tôn giáo' [Synthetic Report on 8 Years Implementing the Ordinance on Belief and Religion] (2015).

8

Regulating Buddhism in Myanmar

The Case of Deviant Buddhist Sects

Nyi Nyi Kyaw

I. INTRODUCTION

In the international domain, Myanmar has been a notorious state in terms of violations of human rights. This is so even after 2016, when the National League for Democracy (NLD) party chaired by Daw Aung San Suu Kyi came to power. Myanmar's inclusion as a Country of Particular Concern (CPC) in the United States Commission on International Religious Freedom's (USCIRF) annual reports throughout the 1990s and 2000s shone the spotlight on violations of the right to freedom of religion in the country. The US Department of State's annual reports consistently adduced evidence of violations of the right to religious freedom of minorities, such as Christians and Muslims – often highlighting the Myanmar military and state's favoritism towards Buddhism and Buddhists. The only occasion Buddhists, or Buddhist monks to be more exact, received attention in the context of the violation of religious freedom was when so-called 'politically educated'[1] or dissident monks were repressed by the state before, during, and after the Saffron Revolution of September 2007.

As a Theravāda Buddhist majority country, Myanmar has been known for violating religious freedom rights of adherents of minority religions – Islam and Christianity in particular.[2] The cases of the Rohingya and other non-Rohingya Muslims, and ethnic minority Christians such as the Chin and the Naga, have consistently been cited to support the claim that Buddhist Myanmar persecutes

[1] Christina Fink, 'Burma 2007: The Moment of the Monks', in Adam Roberts and Timothy Garton Ash (eds.), *Civil Resistance and Power Politics: The Experience of Non-violent Action from Gandhi to the Present* (Oxford University Press, 2009), 355; Bruce Matthews, 'Buddhism under a Military Regime: The Iron Heel in Burma', *Asian Survey* 33.4 (1993), 408–23; Mikael Gravers, 'Monks, Morality and Military: The Struggle for Moral Power in Burma – and Buddhism's Uneasy Relation with Lay Power', *Contemporary Buddhism* 13.1 (2012), 1–33.

[2] Bruce Matthews,. 'Religious minorities in Myanmar – Hints of the shadow', *Contemporary South Asia* 4.3 (1995), 287–308.

religious minorities. Up until April 2016 (when the new government was formed by the NLD), the militarized state was usually 'named' and 'shamed' as principals and agents of persecution. After April 2016, the state in present-day Myanmar is not as militarized as before. However, the state has continued to regulate religion. In this context, even after the NLD government of de facto leader State Counselor Daw Aung San Suu Kyi came to power, accusations were again made by the USCIRF that Myanmar is a CPC that continues to violate minorities' right to religious freedom.[3]

In all these international discourses about religious freedom in Myanmar, the case of Buddhism and how it is regulated by the state is understandably missing. Much attention has been paid to minority religions, which has resulted in the cases of illegal Buddhist sects, ideologies, and practices being overlooked. Moreover, the role of the supreme Sangha body established in 1980 – namely the *Naing-ngan-to Sangha Maha Nayaka Apwe* or State Sangha Maha Nayaka Committee (*Ma Ha Na*) – in declaring those sects, ideologies, teachings, and practices as evil or deviant has not been examined. Also missing in the literature is how *Ma Ha Na* has worked with the state in regulating and punishing illegal Buddhist sects. Tin Maung Maung Than[4] traces the development of the state-sponsored regulatory system in 1980 but does not discuss the details of deviancy cases. The only rather complete account is provided by Janaka Ashin and Kate Crosby,[5] who define it as a *legal* issue involving a Buddhist religious court system. They also provide a detailed case discussion of how and why each of the sects, ideologies, teachings, and practices has been declared as deviant by *Ma Ha Na* and special courts (that were formed by the council for such purposes). This chapter will argue that *Ma Ha Na*, courts, and decisions handed down against parties accused of deviancy are part of a 'political pact' between the state and the Sangha. Through this pact, outlier unorthodox groups have been regulated, disciplined, and 'punished' (as in the case of Moepyar U Nyana). This chapter will then point out that *Ma Ha Na*'s actions against these outlier groups have– intentionally or unintentionally – violated these groups' right to freedom of religion; and this is a story that has not been reported in any international human rights literature focused on the issue.

This chapter is organized as follows: it first looks at how Theravāda Buddhism is regulated in Myanmar. Then, it analyzes how deviance is defined according to Theravāda Buddhist orthodoxy, and discusses how *Ma Ha Na* has judged certain

3 United States Commission on International Religious Freedom, 'USCIRF Welcomes CPC Designations: Urges Additional Designations and Actions' (20 April 2016), www.uscirf.gov/news-room/press-releases/uscirf-welcomes-cpc-designations-urges-additional-designations-and-actions (accessed 24 September 2018).

4 Tin Maung Maung Than, 'The "Sangha" and "Sasana" in Socialist Burma', *Sojourn: Journal of Social Issues in Southeast Asia* 3.1 (1988), 26–61.

5 Janaka Ashin and Kate Crosby, 'Heresy and Monastic Malpractice in the Buddhist Court Cases (Vinicchaya) of Modern Burma (Myanmar)', *Contemporary Buddhism* 18.1 (2017), 199–261.

sects to be deviant. The special case of Moepyar U Nyana is also traced and analyzed, followed by a concluding discussion.

II. HOW THERAVĀDA BUDDHISM IS REGULATED IN MYANMAR

The present Constitution of the Republic of the Union of Myanmar recognizes Buddhism as the predominant religion in the country.[6] However, it does not define or qualify the generic term 'Buddhism'. Buddhism encompasses a variety of beliefs and practices. Broadly speaking, there are at least three schools of Buddhist thought and practice – Mahayana Buddhism, Theravāda Buddhism, and Vajrayana (or Tibetan) Buddhism. While the text of the constitution does not specify the brand of Buddhism that is widely practiced in Myanmar, social context tells us that it is in fact Theravāda Buddhism, which is also a majority religion in three Southeast Asian countries – Thailand, Cambodia, and Laos – and one South Asian country, Sri Lanka.

Lexicologically, Theravāda is a combination of *Thera* and *Vāda*. *Thera* means the elder(s) and *Vāda* means doctrine; Theravāda, therefore, means the Doctrine of the Elders. The Elders refer to the elderly monastics who *met* Buddha when the latter was alive and teaching. Hence, the Doctrine of the Elders is believed by adherents of Theravāda Buddhism to be pure, original, and authentic teachings (Tipitaka).[7] Theravāda Buddhist chronicles composed in Pali were guarded orally by monks for about four and a half centuries after Gautama Buddha's death, until they were committed to writing. The chronicles trace the origin of the Theravāda Doctrine to the time of Buddha's death. On Buddha's passing, an elderly monk by the name of Bhikkhu Subhadra told his fellow bereaved monks that they should be delighted at their freedom from the rules set by Buddha. These rebellious remarks came to the attention of Bhikkhu Mahakasyapa – one of Buddha's principal disciples – who then suggested to other monks who were attending Buddha's funeral that they should communally recite all the Master's teachings and rules to preserve them. The First Buddhist Council or Synod was thus held approximately three months after Buddha's death. At the Synod, five hundred monks recited the whole body of Buddhist scriptures for seven months. This resulted in the laying down of three fundamental principles of Theravāda Buddhism: monks shall not make rules that

[6] Constitution of the Republic of the Union of Myanmar, Section 361.

[7] On the subject of the pure, original doctrine of the elders who *met* Buddha in person and preserved his teachings, one can draw an interesting analogy between the ontological bases of Theravāda Buddhism and Salafist Islam – although they are rarely or never compared. Believers of Salafist Islam also claim that they preserve the original teachings and practices of the *salaaf* or forefathers who met and learned from Prophet Muhammad when he was spreading the message of Islam. While there may be lexical and semantic problems in comparing Theravāda Buddhism and Salafism, the ontological similarity in the efforts to preserve the originality, purity, and authenticity of both religions by referring to the elders or forefathers is striking indeed.

were not imposed by Buddha; monks shall not revoke rules that were imposed by Buddha; and monks shall abide by all the rules imposed by Buddha.[8] These three rules define the Theravāda Doctrine or School.

Definitions of Theravāda Buddhism that can be found in other Myanmar legal documents also stipulate that the school is one of *textual* purity or orthodoxy. For example, Section 2(d) of the Law Relating to the Sangha Organization (1990) defines Theravāda as 'the Pitaka [also known as Tripitaka or Tipitaka [Three Baskets] Theravāda Buddhist scriptures or canons] such as Pali [the Pali original text of the scriptures], Atthakatha [commentaries] and Tika [sub-commentaries] which have been submitted to and been reviewed by the Six Buddhist Councils commencing from the First Buddhist Council to the Sixth Buddhist Council'.[9] This definition is *wholly* textual or canonical; it effectively neglects the role of religious practices by Buddhists around the world throughout the approximately 2,500-year history of Buddhism. More specifically and importantly, this definition neglects the existence of various 'Buddhist' ideologies and practices in Myanmar for more than a millennium – at the very least, since the eleventh century, which is when Theravāda Buddhism is thought to have become a mass religion after King Anawrahta (reign: 1044–77) converted to Theravāda Buddhism in Bagan. What this definitional discussion tells us is that senior Buddhist monks of Myanmar try to preserve orthodox Theravāda teachings as contained in the Tipitaka, in a manner similar to their counterparts in Sri Lanka, Thailand, Cambodia, and Laos, albeit in differing degrees. Such preservation, with the official backing of the state, has resulted in several cases in Myanmar since 1980 where certain ideologies, interpretations, and practices were considered vis-à-vis the Tipitaka text and adjudged to be non-Theravāda by the state-recognized and -backed senior monks. An account of these allegedly unorthodox ideologies, interpretations, and practices is the focus of this chapter.

The main agent in outlawing unorthodox or deviant sects, *Ma Ha Na* was regularly accused of being an accomplice to the state in the 1990s and 2000s whenever there was outright repression of certain political monks by the military regime (the State Law and Order Restoration Council/State Peace and Development Council [1988–2011]). This discourse reflected the political atmosphere in the country under the military.

8 State Sangha Maha Nayaka Committee, *Shin Nyana U-saung-thaw Mo-pya-gaing-tha-do-e Ayuvada Apaw Dhamma-Adhamma A-nyin-pwa-hmu-gin Son-pyat-chet* [Decision on the Dhamma-vs-Adhamma Controversy relating to the Ideology of Followers of the Mopyar Sect] (Ministry of Religious Affairs Press, 2011), 2–3.

9 The monks-only Buddhist Council, which was convened to preserve the *original* and *authentic* teachings of Buddha as handed down for generations of Buddhist monks, has been held six times in history. The first council was held in approximately 483 BCE, three months after Buddha's passing; the second council was held some time in 334 BCE; the third council was held some time in 250 BCE; the fourth in 25 BCE; fifth in 1871; and the final or sixth in 1954–56. The Pitaka, which had been orally preserved by monks at the previous councils, were written down only at the third council held in Sri Lanka. Notably, the last two councils were held in Burma or Myanmar.

However politically reasonable and factually founded all those accusations and condemnations were, they were still ill-informed statements that stemmed from a lack of understanding of how the regulation of Buddhism and Buddhist Sangha works or is supposed to work alongside an orthodox interpretation of the monastic code. This section will now describe and explain how the present regulatory system works.

Different epochs in Myanmar's history (from the Burmese Buddhist kingdoms before colonization, to British colonization from 1886 to 1948, and the parliamentary period from 1948 to 1962) were characterized by different regimes set up to regulate the Sangha. Whereas the Buddhist kings acted as patrons of the Sangha and facilitated the Sangha's work in cooperation with the office of the *Thathanapaing* (Buddhist Primate), the British generally stayed aloof and avoided direct regulation of the community. The British once tried to reinstall the *Thathanapaing's* office without recognizing his authority as being on a par with the lay judiciary. The *Thathanapaing* mostly had jurisdiction in upper Burma with little oversight of lower Burma, which had been under British control since 1852. In short, whatever authority the primate had was not extensive. The British experiment was not much of a success, as the office was eventually abolished after the last primate, Taunggwin Sayadaw Visuddha Silacaraha, died in 1938. Thereafter, lay legislation was used to punish Buddhist monks who committed political and non-political crimes.[10]

This created a wide regulatory vacuum because lay legislation was not supposed to be used to adjudicate disputes amongst monks or between monks and laypeople, on monastic properties, ideologies, practices, and the like. Subsequently, after independence was obtained in 1948, the U Nu government passed the Year 1311 (ME) Vinasaya Hta-na Act (1949), the Provisional Vinasaya Hta-na Act (1951), and the Year 1316 (ME) Vinasaya Hta-na (Amendment) Act (1955)[11] to create courts and/or tribunals in which monks sat as judges and adjudicated cases involving monks that should, in theory, be decided according to the Vinaya[12] or Monastic Code of Conduct. Indeed, these acts providing for ecclesiastical courts and their (such as

10 E. Michael Mendelson, *Sangha and State in Burma: A Study of Monastic Sectarianism and Leadership*, edited by John P. Ferguson (Cornell University Press, 1975), 179–93. For a rather detailed account of the British policies towards Buddhism and the Sangha, see Donald Eugene Smith, *Religion and Politics in Burma* (Princeton University Press, 1965), 38–80.

11 A rather detailed discussion of the three Acts can be found in Mendelson (n. 10), 239–45. Mendelson translates the Burmese term *Hta-na* as court. The three Acts contain this term in their titles but do not provide a definition. *Hta-na* literally means place, location, or office. Owing to *hta-nas*' formation with monks sitting as judges and adjudicating cases relating to the Vinaya, Mendelson might have interpreted this to refer to a monastic or ecclesiastical court. The Provisional Vinasaya Hta-na Act was passed in 1951 to provide for the formation of provisional monastic courts, when proper courts could not be formed according to the Vinasaya Hta-na Act. The Year 1363 (ME) Vinasaya Hta-na (Amendment) Act – which changed the title of the Year 1311 (ME) Vinasaya Hta-na Act into the Year 1311 (ME) Vinasaya Hta-na and Tribunal Act – was drafted to reduce lay involvement and create certain favorable conditions, such as allowing monks to form their own tribunals.

12 Vinaya (Discipline) constitutes part of the Tripitaka or one of the three baskets, the other two being Abhidhamma (Doctrine) and Sutta (Discourse).

the Year 1311 [ME] Vinasaya Hta-na Rules) laid out a detailed architecture of a Buddhist monastic judiciary. However, this judiciary faced its own share of controversies in the politically volatile 1950s when it was caught between different political sides and monastic groups as well. In short, it was short-lived.[13]

After General Ne Win mounted a coup and took power in 1962, he tried to reform the Year 1311 (ME) Vinasaya Hta-na and Tribunal Act but was met with strong opposition from some sections of the Sangha. Hence, he allowed the continued use of the Act until 1965, when his coup regime repealed it. Subsequently, Ne Win generally sidelined the issue because he assumed that the increasing religionization and Buddhicization of the U Nu government in the 1950s and early 1960s[14] – which eventually resulted in the 1961 amendment (the 1961 Constitution [Third Amendment] Act) to the first constitution[15] that made Buddhism the state religion – had been one of the causes of unnecessary political instability. It must be stated that the third amendment, which declares Buddhism as the state religion of Burma and stipulates that the state shall provide for the Buddhist faith and protect it from blasphemy and wrongful accusations, has often been, rather erroneously, highlighted as a major cause of animosity between the Buddhist majority and religious minorities such as Christians and Muslims. It would not do justice to U Nu if it is not stated here that there was a subsequent constitutional amendment (the 1961 Constitution [Fourth Amendment] Act) which protected minorities' right to religious education and gave these minorities state protection from blasphemy and wrongful accusations. In other words, although the 1961 constitutional declaration – that Buddhism was the state religion in Burma – has often been interpreted as a negative development, it actually came with a benefit. Never in the history of independent Myanmar had the protection of religious minorities been written into the constitution. However, 'minorities' still did not include Buddhist minorities such as smaller unorthodox sects.

After accusing U Nu of using religion for political ends, Ne Win generally turned a blind eye to the issue of regulating the Buddhist Sangha throughout the 1960s and 1970s. However, he did try to regulate the Sangha once. In 1965, he helped to organize a Sangha assembly from 17 to 19 March to decide on the regulation and punishment of immoral, corrupt, and unorthodox members of the Sangha. However, no agreement was reached and the issue floated around unresolved. As a result, the problem of bogus, nonorthodox, or corrupt monks and cults emerged in the 1970s, and this was also supposedly caused by the lack of a centralized administration among the Sangha themselves.[16] The political climate had also grown favourable to

13 Mendelson (n. 10), 239–45.

14 For details of this period, see Donald Eugene Smith, *Religion and Politics in Burma* (Princeton University Press, 1965), 140–85.

15 The first constitution – known as the Constitution of the Union of Burma – was in operation from 1948 to 1962 until the coup suspended it.

16 Aung Kin, 'Burma in 1980: Pouring Balm on Sore Spots', *Southeast Asian Affairs* 93 (1981), 103–25; Tin Maung Maung Than, 'The "Sangha" and "Sasana" in Socialist Burma', *Sojourn: Journal of Social Issues in Southeast Asia* 3.1 (1988), 26–61.

regulation by the 1970s. The coup regime, the Revolutionary Council (RC), ruled by decree between 1962 and 1974 without a constitution in operation. This was before it gradually transformed itself into a socialist cadre party – the Burma Socialist Programme Party (BSPP) – to which power was transferred in 1974, after the adoption of the Constitution of the Socialist Republic of the Union of Burma. There was little political dissidence, and ideological and ethnic insurgencies were not as challenging a problem as before. In this context, Ne Win became interested in the regulation and punishment of unorthodox and bogus teachings and practices by monks and laypersons as well. By that time, senior orthodox sections of the Sangha appeared to have grown disgruntled with the degradation and corruption of their faith.[17] Younger and more active sections, which tended to be more rebellious, had also grown less powerful and been made to be more obedient to their seniors and, more importantly, to the state. Ne Win asked Brig-Gen Sein Lwin – the minister for home and religious affairs at the time[18] – to work with the Sangha and create an administrative system for the increasingly unruly Buddhist Sangha that would both regulate the entire community and punish its unsavoury elements.

From 1979 onwards, Sein Lwin worked hard in cooperation with the *senior* Sangha (emphasis added because younger, less senior sections were not represented at all) who had agreed to create a regulatory framework. A Buddhist congregation was held from 14 to 17 May 1980 involving all nine Buddhist sects[19] in Myanmar: Thudhamma, Shwegyin, Maha-dwara, Mula-dwara, Ah-nauk-chaung-dwara, Veluvana, Nget-twin, Kudo, and Ma-har-yin. In fact, on 1 February of the same year, the Ministry of Home and Religious Affairs had already designated these aforenamed nine sects as the only *legal* ones. This state-Sangha collaboration effectively resulted in unprecedented unity among the various Buddhist sects – especially between Thudhamma and Shwegyin – and their acquiescence to the government's demands that the Sangha be regulated and disciplined. Since then, the government has often claimed that the Sangha in 1980 had among themselves reached a consensus that they needed unity and regulation. However, the minutes of the 1979 and 1980 meetings held among Sein Lwin, his deputies, and the monks representing the different sects as well as the proceedings of the First Congregation say otherwise. Although not explicitly stated, the minutes and proceedings clearly show that the state was indeed in charge and the Sangha, for their own reasons, simply just gave in to the demands of the government officials, as was stated in detail

17 Ibid.

18 Sein Lwin later became president for slightly more than two weeks in 1988 amidst popular protests.

19 In the previous three ecclesiastical court and tribunal Acts and their rules, only Thudhamma, Shwegyin, and Dwara were mentioned as the three major sects. However, this number increased to nine when the first congregation was held in 1980. In comparison to Thudhamma and Shwegyin, the other seven sects had significantly fewer members. For a detailed background to the emergence and development of those sects, see U Maung Maung (Dhamma Gothaka), *Let-shi A-thi-a-hmat-pyu Sangha-gaing 9-gaing A-kyaung* [About Nine Sects that Are Currently Recognized] (Sein Pan Myaing, 1989 [1981]) and Mendelson (n. 10), 84–111.

in the official chronicle of *Ma Ha Na* and another historical account written by a famous monk author, Ashin Kelasa.[20]

Sein Lwin already had a road map for the Sangha, which he and his deputies presented at several meetings before and during the 1980 congregation.[21] However, it was not the case that the Sangha were forced to agree with the government; rather, what transpired was that the government was in charge and the Sangha cooperated. Senior monks told Sein Lwin and his team that their moral authority alone would not suffice to control the huge Sangha membership, and that they needed the power of the state to regulate and discipline themselves. Sein Lwin promised them that the state would help. In this way, the state and the Sangha built rapport and together created the rules for Sangha regulation. In other words, the rules of the religious order were set and enforced with the help of the secular state order.

The Vinaya rules taught by Buddha include 227 rules for male monastics (Bhikkhus) and 311 rules for female monastics (Bhikkhunis). Most of them are concerned with individual conduct, though a few rules provide for communal problem-solving and decision-making. Most importantly, the Vinaya do not dictate any form of punitive measures for male and female monastics who violate the rules. The most severe punishment for the four most serious offences or *Pārājika*s – sexual intercourse, murder, major theft, or falsely claiming supernatural abilities – is excommunication, after which the respective monk(s) may never be allowed to reenter the monkhood. Less severe punishments, such as confessions and corrective training, are meted out for lesser offences such as lying or drinking alcohol.[22] This lack of legal enforceability and punishments appeared to be the impetus for legal cooperation between the state (which effectively owns sanctioning powers as the setter and enforcer of *secular* rules or laws) and the Sangha (as the setter of the *moral* and behavioural standards according to the Tipitaka). Whereas the Sangha lack powers of the state in a secular regulatory, disciplinary, and punitive sense, the state needs the approval of the Sangha to directly and/or indirectly control its members. Both parties need each other so that the legal-criminal apparatus of the state helps to regulate, discipline, and punish the Sangha (as needed). This symbiotic relationship is exactly what emerged in 1980.

It has been almost four decades since the state–Sangha agreement created a legal order for the monkhood. This unity between the state and the Sangha has effectively

[20] State Sangha Maha Nayaka Committee, *Pa-ta-ma A-kyein Gaing-paung-sôn Sangha A-si-a-we-pwe-kyi Hmat-tan* [Proceedings of First All-Sect Congregation] (Department of Religious Affairs Press, 1980), 10–12; Ashin Kelasa, *Pa-ta-ma A-kyein Gaing-paung-sôn Sangha A-si-a-we-pwe-kyi Hmat-tan* [Proceedings of First All-Sect Congregation] (Department of Religious Affairs Press, 1980), 13–17, 21, 23, 28.

[21] Ibid.

[22] For details of the Vinaya, see I. B. Horner, trans., *The Book of the Discipline*. 6 vols. (Pali Text Society, 1949–66). For a critical analysis of the Vinaya as law, see Petra Kieffer-Pülz, 'What the Vinayas Can Tell Us about Law', in Rebecca Redwood French and Mark A. Nathan (eds.), *Buddhism and Law: An Introduction* (Cambridge University Press, 2014), 46–62.

outlawed ideologies, interpretations, beliefs, teachings, and practices of certain monks, lay preachers, and their followers that are deemed unorthodox by *Ma Ha Na*. Several questions thus arise. Why are *certain* ideologies, interpretations, beliefs, teachings, and practices deemed deviant or evil? Who judge(s) them and how are they judged to be so? What are the results of being judged and declared to be deviant? I will address below these questions and their implications on the regulation of religion, which has resulted in the violation of religious freedom rights of deviant groups.

DEVIANCE OR A-DHAMMA-CUM-A-VINAYA AS PART OF THE PURIFICATION OF SASANA

There is no definition of deviance in Myanmar's existing legal documents. However, from the point of view of *Ma Ha Na* and its senior monks, deviance is said to occur when an ideology, teaching, or practice deviates from the teachings contained in the Tripitaka, which alone is deemed to be the authentic canon of Theravāda Buddhism. Hence, the yardstick by which deviance is to be judged and measured is the Tipitaka itself. It is common knowledge among Buddhists in Myanmar that *Ma Ha Na*, as the supreme Sangha council, is obliged to check whether the conduct of a particular monk or group of monks is in line with the Vinaya rules for individual and/or group monastic behaviour. However, the legal and religious issues that have been considered and decided by *Ma Ha Na* are much more extensive because the council has apparently interfered and declared sects and groups (with participants consisting of both monks and lay Buddhists) as illegal.

Although there is no definition of deviance, a general principle may be gleaned from statements made by successive *Ma Ha Na* presiding monks. For example, in his message during a *Ma Ha Na* meeting in 2014, the current Chair Bamaw Sayadaw Kumarabhivamsa stated that there are both a-Dhamma and a-Vinaya that should be dealt with for the effective purification, perpetuation, and propagation of Sasana.[23] By 'a-Dhamma' and 'a-Vinaya', he meant false teachings or doctrines and misconduct respectively.[24] This claim is very important because it elevates the role of senior learned monks to the level of master-interpreters of Buddhism, which contains two other facets of Buddha and Dhamma. Buddha refers to Gautama Buddha, Dhamma refers to his teachings, while Sangha refers to the congregation

[23] 'Thathana-to Than-shin Ti-tan Pyan-pwa-ye Lôk-ngan-kyi-ko Ko-si-ko-nga A-thi-thi Saung-ywet-to-mu-kya-ya-twin Kyi-lin-than-shin-tho Seik-dat-pyin Saung-ywet [In Efforts to Purify, Perpetuate, and Propagate Sasana, We Must All Try to Do So with Pure, Sincere Minds]', *The Mirror* (Yangon, 13 May 2014), 9.

[24] Although Bamaw Sayadaw distinguished between doctrine-related a-Dhamma and conduct-related a-Vinaya, the meaning of a-Dhamma appears to cover both aspects in a broad sense. A-Dhamma is defined as misconduct and false doctrine in A. P. Buddhadatta, *Concise Pali-English Dictionary*, 2nd edn (Colombo Apothecaries' Co., 1968), 12. This definition was most probably provided because Dhamma in theory contains *Vinaya* when it refers to the Tipitaka.

of monastic members who claim to trace their unbroken lineage to the time when Buddha was alive. Buddhists take refuge in these 'Three Jewels' which constitute the central tenets of their faith. In other words, to be or become a Buddhist, devoting oneself to the Jewels is a basic requirement. Gautama Buddha, who would explain his teachings or Dhamma, entrusted the latter to the Sangha. The Sangha thus naturally became the guardian of the Dhamma who then have the final say in deciding whether a doctrine or monastic conduct is Buddhist. Bamaw Sayadaw was therefore apparently emphasizing the role of the senior Sangha or *Ma Ha Na* in the case of Myanmar.

What allowed *Ma Ha Na* to occupy this space? The protagonist was the state. State patronage – or more accurately, state guidance – of the Sangha did not stop at the first congregation in 1980. After the congregation was successfully held, the socialist state once again showed the Sangha the way to further develop Buddhism. At a ceremony on 28 May 1980, where religious honorific titles were being offered to senior and learned monks, Sein Lwin stated that *Ma Ha Na* and its respective bodies should strive towards the 'three P's': the purification; perpetuation; and propagation of Sasana or Buddhism. He also stated that the three activities should be prioritized in this order, since the purification of the Sangha was an urgent task at hand.[25] *Ma Ha Na*'s senior advisor monk, Patthana Sayadaw U Visuddhabhivamsa, responded to this suggestion by proposing that the Sangha be purified in two ways: first, through removing bogus monks from within the Sangha; and second, through removing bogus teachings from the Sasana.[26] This exchange was amongst the first official policies suggested by the state, in cooperation with the Sangha, to purify the Sangha. To remove bogus monks from the order, the first congregation created a religious identification card to be held by the Sangha (which includes monks, nuns, and male and female novices).[27] The 'Buddhist Lent', which falls in the rainy season where temporary monks, nuns, and novices do not enter the order, was chosen to be the period when statistics of the Sangha and their members holding identification cards would be recorded.[28]

The statistics provided in the official chronicle of the Second All-Sect Buddhist Congregation held from 29 to 31 May 1985 shows that there were 253,322 monks and novices, and 20,363 nuns in 1983–4; out of which 218,624 monks and novices and 17,998 nuns had been issued religious identification cards.[29] Interestingly, the project to issue the cards seemed more efficient in the 1980s than in the present day. For example, the documents provided to the attendees[30] at the Fifth All-Sect

25 State Sangha Maha Nayaka Committee (n. 20), 231.
26 Ibid., 233.
27 Ibid., 217.
28 Ibid., 200–01.
29 State Sangha Maha Nayaka Committee, *Du-ti-ya A-kyein Gaing-paung-sôn Sangha A-si-a-we-pwe-kyi Hmat-tan* [Proceedings of Second All-Sect Congregation] (Department of Religious Affairs Press, 1985), 456–7.
30 On file with the author.

Buddhist Congregation held from 11 to 13 May 2014 recorded 560,024 monks and novices and 50,439 nuns in Myanmar according to the Lent tally in 2013–14. However, the 2014 census only recorded 247,765 religious card holders (216,887 monks and novices, and 30,878 nuns). This suggests that about half of the members of the Sangha in 2013–14 did not have identification cards. However, the religious identification cards have arguably helped both the state and *Ma Ha Na* to differentiate registered, legitimate monks from unregistered, bogus ones, and to deal with the problem of bogus monks.

As stated earlier, the other larger project of *Ma Ha Na* was to purify the doctrine itself. The doctrine was thought to be tainted by unsavory, unorthodox, and false teachings, ideas, interpretations and practices (referred to as '*Vāda*' in Pali). Vāda, which basically means 'saying, theory or discussion', implies both abstract notions of teachings, ideas, and interpretations, as well as empirical practices. Hence, in theory, a Vāda is deemed deviant, a-Dhamma, or a-Vinaya if it is not in accordance with or deviates from the teachings and practices of Theravāda Buddhism (as contained in the Tipitaka). While Vāda is usually translated to 'sect' in English, the word actually contains different meanings. Sect may suggest a religious outlier group that neither believes in the mainstream faith nor practises it; in contrast, Vāda does not denote anything about grouping. Broadly speaking, however, the two terms may appear to be interrelated because as long as a Vāda is being propagated, there will be a group of monks and people that believe in, teach, and practice it. This chapter will therefore use both terms interchangeably because they denote the same concept in the case of Myanmar's deviant 'sects'.

III. JUDGEMENTS AGAINST DEVIANT SECTS

What has *Ma Ha Na* done to accomplish its mission of purifying Buddhism? Since its establishment in 1980, *Ma Ha Na* has faced the daunting task of detecting cases in which a-Dhamma and a-Vinaya might have occurred for at least some thirty years since independence in 1948 or fifteen years since the repeal of the Year 1311 (ME) Vinasaya Hta-na and Tribunal Act in 1965. *Ma Ha Na* was apparently very active in declaring several sects or teachings to be deviant in the first few years of its operation. Such a task had never been carried out by the state or the Sangha. Once the Sangha organization was set up in 1980, special Vinaya tribunals – effectively the monastic judiciary – were formed by *Ma Ha Na* to look into certain teachings, ideas, and practices that had been popular within Myanmar in the previous decades. As of 2011, 17 special Vinaya tribunals have been formed to decide on cases allegedly involving a-Dhamma and a-Vinaya. The existence of these tribunals spans the periods of military-dominated socialist rule (1962–88), military dictatorship (1988–2011), and pseudo-civilian regime (2011–16).

Each of the tribunals established thus far follow the same format. Both sides – the defendant, or monks and people who are alleged to believe in and practice a-Dhamma and a-Vinaya, and the plaintiff monks who file charges against the defendant – are allowed to be present in the tribunal proceedings. The tribunals themselves comprise learned monks who are thought to be knowledgeable about the matters in dispute. Both sides are summoned and allowed to explain their versions of the truth, before the tribunal decides which side is correct according to the Tipitaka. Most interestingly, *every one* of the 17 special or dedicated tribunals has decided against the teachings, ideas, or practices of the sects alleged to be deviant. This strongly suggests that the decisions against these deviant sects might already have been made before the tribunals were even formed. More importantly, history tells us that once charges are levelled against a sect, the chances of being acquitted of the allegations are effectively non-existent. Table 8.1 shows the names of the sects and the respective dates of the tribunals' judgements. Most of the Vādas declared to be deviant are related to a-Dhamma, meaning that the teachings, ideas, and interpretations were found to be a-Dhamma or against Theravāda orthodoxy. Also, while most of the Vādas received *total* rejection by the respective tribunals, Tribunals 12 and 14 decided against only a limited list of teachings by Mogok Sayadaw U Vimala (1899–1962) and teachings in the Ten-Day Special Course conducted by U Kittisara at Aung San Tawya Tatoo Monastery in Yangon. Tribunal 12 did not state that all of the teachings by Mogok Sayadaw were deviant; instead, it picked a few teachings and held that their interpretations by the famous monk and meditation master were deviant. It should be noted that this judgement was made posthumously because of Mogok Sayadaw's passing in 1962. Likewise, the judgement by Tribunal 2 was handed down three years after U Okkatha died in 1979. Shin Okkatha[31] was the materialist ideologue monk who was the father of Luthe Luphyit U Okkatha Vāda, Sama dithi Sutesana Vāda, and Shwe Abhidhamma Vāda. Similarly, Tribunal 14 identified only two mistakes in the special course of U Kittisara and held that these were deviant, without requiring the monk to do anything except disown the respective mistakes.

Only three of the sects judged by the tribunals were related to a-Vinaya (being counter to established Theravāda Buddhist rituals and conduct). The consecration rituals for monastic ordination halls that were taught and practised by Twante U Punnyasara's Vāda and Mawlamyine Shwe War Myaing Kyaung Vāda were found to be against Vinaya. Also found to be against Vinaya was the Bhikkhuni (female monastic) Vāda originated by a Myanmar Buddhist nun named Daw Saccavādi who was ordained as a Bhikkhuni in Colombo, Sri Lanka[32] in February 2003 before entering Myanmar in December 2004. In Theravāda orthodoxy, the order of

[31] For details of the case of Shin Okkatha, see Janaka Ashin and Kate Crosby, 'All too Human: The Impact of International Buddhist Networks on the Life and Posthumous Conviction of the Burmese Nationalist Monk, Shin Ukkaṭṭha (1897–1978)', *Journal for the Irish Society for the Academic Study of Religions (JISASR)*, 3 (2016), 219–35.

[32] The Bhikkhuni order was revived in Sri Lanka and Thailand in recent years though it has faced staunch opposition from the mainstream orthodox Sangha in both countries. In Myanmar, it has not emerged since the case of Daw Saccavādi.

TABLE 8.1 *List of Deviant Sects*[33]

No.	Deviant Sect Name	Vinaya Tribunal	Date of Judgement
1	Kyaukthinbaw Vāda	Tribunal 1	23.2.1981
2	Luthe Luphyit U Okkatha Vāda, Sama dithi Sutesana Vāda, Shwe Abhidhamma Vāda	Tribunal 2	29.10.1981
3	Kyaungpan Tawya Vāda	Tribunal 3	26.4.1982
4	Kyaukpon Tawya Vāda	Tribunal 4	7.11.1982
5	U Marlarvara (Yaytashay) Vāda	Tribunal 5	1.4.1983
6	Dhammaniti Vāda	Tribunal 6	15.7.1983
7	Moenyo (North Okkalapa) Vāda	Tribunal 7	4.7.1983
8	Htuntone Lakkyan U Htin's Vāda	Tribunal 8	31.12.1985
9	Twante U Punnyasara's Vāda	Tribunal 9	25.2.1988
10	Mawlamyine Shwe War Myaing Kyaung Vāda	Tribunal 10	7.6.1989
11	Sankalay Vāda	Tribunal 11	16.3.1998
12	Moegok Vinissaya	Tribunal 12	28.3.2005
13	Bhikkhuni Vāda	Tribunal 13	27.5.2005
14	Two Mistakes in Ten-Day Special Course	Tribunal 14	22.6.2006
15	Moenyin U Khemeinda and U Vicittasarabivamsa's Vāda	Tribunal 15	16.10.2006
16	Myitkyina U Vicittasarabivamsa's Vāda	Tribunal 16	17.2.2009
17	Moepyar Sect Vāda	Tribunal 17	15.11.2011

Bhikkhunis is believed to be extinct. Therefore, the order may not be revived without an already existing community of Bhikkhunis, notwithstanding the willingness of male monastics or Bhikkhus to preside over the ordination. Hence, Daw Saccavādi's ordination was held to be against Vinaya.

While the *Ma Ha Na* monks who formed the tribunals in the first place and the monks who subsequently sat on them do not have secular powers of enforcement, their decisions are empowered by law. Monk discussants and attendees at the first congregation of 1980 made – apparently at the suggestion and behest of the state as argued earlier – detailed rules and regulations relating to matters involving sects and other monastic conflicts. However, those rules do not carry secular powers as state laws do. Thus, the SSMNC and its special tribunals need to and have been able to draw upon the power of the state to enforce the orthodoxy that they deem sacred. Once the work of a tribunal is completed and a decision has been made, the tribunal

[33] Details of the tribunal proceedings are available in Ashin and Crosby (n. 5).

sends its decision to the *Ma Ha Na* which then issues an order to inform all hierarchical Sangha organizations at the lower levels about the decision and direct them to take the necessary actions on the ground.

To give legal backing to the work of the tribunals and *Ma Ha Na*, the socialist state promulgated two laws – namely, the Law on Solution of Cases and Conflicts in Accordance with the Rules of the Order (1980), and the Law to Protect Solution of Cases and Conflicts in Accordance with the Rules of the Order (1983).[34] The 1980 law states that all conflicts involving monks must be resolved by monastic Vinaya teams and special tribunals.[35] The 1983 law further reinforces the decisions made by *Ma Ha Na* and its tribunals. The law states that the orders issued by the Ministry of Religious Affairs, following the decisions of the tribunals against the sects, must be obeyed.[36] It criminalizes disobedience by imposing a prison sentence of five years.[37] The decisions of the tribunals thus carry strong legal power and punitive impact. In this way, the state has assisted *Ma Ha Na* to regulate and punish dissidents and opponents from within or outside their own monastic order, when these dissidents preach and practise teachings that are deemed unorthodox or un-Theravāda and judged as such.

That being said, there has only been two cases where actual punishment was meted out by *Ma Ha Na* (with the help of the state), or the state (at *Ma Ha Na*'s request). The first case is that of the Myanmar nun or *thila-shin*,[38] Daw Saccavādi, who had been fully ordained as a bhikkuni or female monastic in Sri Lanka on 28 February 2003. Her ordination was decided as deviant by Tribunal 13 in 2005. At the ceremony on 27 May 2005 where Daw Saccavādi was supposed to sign a pledge that her actions had been deviant, kowtow to the (male) Sangha in attendance, take off her bhikkuni robe, put on the *thila-shin* robe, and read out her pledge. She reportedly failed to read out the pledge. She was then 'remanded in custody and

34 Apart from these two laws that were apparently made by the state to support the work of the senior Sangha, there is another law which has often been used against monks. This is the Law Relating to the Sangha Organization, which was enacted in 1990 by the coup regime's State Law and Order Restoration Council to deal with growing political dissent against the state within the monkhood. This law reiterates that there are *only* nine Buddhist sects in Myanmar and criminalizes the formation of any new sects and Sangha organizations that are not directly under the SSMNC. A detailed discussion of the law and how it has been used is beyond the scope of this chapter.

35 Law on Solution of Cases and Conflicts in Accordance with the Rules of the Order 1980, Section 3.

36 Law to Protect Solution of Cases and Conflicts in Accordance with the Rules of the Order 1983, Section 6.

37 Law to Protect Solution of Cases and Conflicts in Accordance with the Rules of the Order 1983, Section 10.

38 In Burmese, nuns are called *thila-shin* which means possessors of (Buddhist moral or ethical) precepts. But in strict legal terms, they are not part of the monastic order; they are still considered part of the secular world. They are even entitled to ownership of property and inheritance unlike monks or male monastics who have to renounce all secular assets and attachments to enter the order. However, nuns are included in statistics on the monastic population. For details, see Hiroko Kawanami, 'The Religious Standing of Burmese Buddhist Nuns (*thilá-shin*): The Ten Precepts and Religious Respect Words', *The Journal of the International Association of Buddhist Studies* 13.1 (1990), 17–39.

sent to prison where she stayed for 76 days'.[39] She was forced to fulfil the requirement a second time on her release.[40] The second case of the Moepyar Sect will be discussed separately in detail in the text that follows.

At this juncture, it should be noted that the claimed intention of *Ma Ha Na* and the tribunals, as clearly stated by the monks sitting on the council and tribunals on several occasions,[41] is only to stop the spread of the ideas, teachings, interpretations, and practices. Hence, the orders issued by *Ma Ha Na* and the Ministry of Home and Religious Affairs (later known as the Ministry of Religious Affairs) to follow the tribunal's decisions only ask that the leaders and followers of the respective sects disown their teachings, practices, and all missionary material. As long as the sects do not defy the orders and continue to propagate their ideas and practices, the cases are closed and no further action is taken. The tribunals and the orders do not aim at punishing the sects for having deviated from orthodoxy, though this is on the condition that the sects comply with the judgements. *Ma Ha Na* and the tribunals use both their moral power and Buddhist scholarship, as well as the secular power of the state, to make sure that the sects give up their teachings and practices. As the sects are generally unable to counter the combined power of the Sangha and the state, all of the sects – with only one exception – have acquiesced and signed the pledge prepared by *Ma Ha Na* that they will never propagate their Vādas again. The monks from the sects were subsequently even allowed back into the monkhood since, according to the Vinaya, deviance does not result in being permanently ostracized from the monkhood.

IV. THE CASE OF MOEPYAR U NYANA

One case stands out in the trend of peaceful settlement between *Ma Ha Na* and the sects (where the latter obey the decisions of the tribunals and *Ma Ha Na* to discontinue proselytization and disown their beliefs and practices). The case received attention from the international human rights advocacy community in the 2010s owing to the excessive and chronic punishments that were imposed on the leader of the sect. While Tribunal 17 formed by *Ma Ha Na* handed down their 15 November 2011 judgement that the teachings of the Moepyar Sect[42] were deviant, U Nyana (the Moepyar leader) had had a long-running feud with *Ma Ha Na* since at

39 Ashin and Crosby (n. 5), 240.

40 Ibid., 239.

41 State Sangha Maha Nayaka Committee, *Kyaukthinbaw Vāda Vinicchaya* [Vinaya Judgement on Kyaukthinbaw Ideology] (Department of Religious Affairs Press, 1981), 517–18; State Sangha Maha Nayaka Committee, *Moenyo (North Okkalapa) Vāda Vinicchaya* [Vinaya Judgement on Moenyo (North Okkalapa) Ideology] (Department of Religious Affairs Press, 1984) l, m, n, o; State Sangha Maha Nayaka Committee, *Sankalay Vāda Vinicchaya* [Vinaya Judgement on Sankalay Ideology] (Department of Religious Affairs Press, 2009), 395.

42 Moepyar in Burmese means 'sky blue' or 'blue'. The name of the sect seems to be derived from the blue colour of the robe U Nyana dons. A few other authors use 'Moe Pyar' but it makes better sense to use 'Moepyar' because the two words used together refer to the name of a colour.

least 1981. U Nyana studied Theravāda Buddhism as a monk for years at several prominent teaching monasteries across Myanmar. In the early 1980s, he started claiming that he had reached the stage of *ariya* or holiness by seeing the truth. He even informed one-year-old *Ma Ha Na* in 1981 of his *ariya*-hood which they found unconvincing. This interaction led to a decision by *Ma Ha Na* that U Nyana had violated one of the four *Pārājikas* by falsely claiming that he had supernatural abilities. According to the rules, a Buddhist monk must never disclose abilities such as seeing the truth even if the monk has seen the truth. Therefore, in the eyes of *Ma Ha Na*, U Nyana had violated a cardinal Buddhist rule. As mentioned earlier, however, Buddha did not dictate any punishments against such acts. It was probably for this reason that *Ma Ha Na* did not do anything against him.

Unable to accept *Ma Ha Na*'s decision to reject his claim, U Nyana disowned both Buddhism and monkhood and informed the state and *Ma Ha Na* of these renunciations, adding that he had released himself from being part of the Buddhist monastic community in Myanmar. He then stopped wearing the saffron robe and started donning blue clothing. On 10 February 1983, he established a new Vāda, the *Piccuppan Kamma Vāda Buddha Batha*,[43] and started preaching his Vāda. Many of his followers still treated him as a monk. An opportunity later arose for *Ma Ha Na* to take legal action against U Nyana with the help of the state. Sections 5 and 9 of the newly enacted Law to Protect Solution of Cases and Conflicts in Accordance with the Rules of the Order states that a person must never impersonate a monk or novice, and that those in breach of the prohibition may be imprisoned for three years. U Nyana was imprisoned under those sections in 1984 and released in 1986. He was arrested again and imprisoned for 10 years in 1991 under Section 5(e) of the Emergency Provisions Act (1950),[44] which criminalizes the spread of false news while knowing that it is not true. He was released from prison for the second time in 1998.

U Nyana would not give up. He continued to preach his Vāda and accumulated a group of followers that reportedly numbered a thousand or so. In 2010, he was imprisoned again, this time for twenty years in total for breaching Sections 295 and 295(a) of the Penal Code (two years each), Section 6 of the Law Relating to Forming of Organizations (1988) (five years), Section 10 of the Law to Protect Solution of Cases and Conflicts in Accordance with the Rules of the Order (five years), and Sections 12 and 13 of the Law Relating to the Sangha Organization (1990) (three years each). His several attempts at appeal, seeking a presidential pardon, and obtaining a writ of certiorari from the Supreme Court – because he was handed

[43] Despite this official name, the sect is commonly known as the Moepyar.

[44] This notorious law was frequently used by the military regime in the 1990s and 2000s to uproot and punish dissent. One of the first legal moves taken by the NLD government was to repeal the Act by enacting the Law Repealing the Emergency Provisions Act (2016). Many former political prisoners who were arrested and imprisoned under the Act became Members of Parliament after the November 2015 general elections.

down sentences by invoking different laws for the same offences – all failed.[45] He was eventually released from prison in January 2016, by which time he was already seventy-seven years old. U Nyana and his followers found their sect in a new political and social context in Myanmar, which was at that time administered by the democratically elected government led by State Counselor Daw Aung San Suu Kyi. The sect did not discontinue its activities in this new environment, which brought *Ma Ha Na*'s wrath down upon it once again. *Ma Ha Na* again sought to take legal action against U Nyana and his followers, and asked the Ministry of Religious Affairs and Culture (new name of the former Ministry of Religious Affairs after it was merged with the Ministry of Culture since 2016) to act on its decision. The President's Office accordingly issued an order to the local governments of states and regions to help the Ministry with the task, because the sect is largely based in Mandalay with followers across the country. The case was still pending as of March 2017.[46]

The case of the Moepyar Sect tells us two main things. First, *Ma Ha Na* demands complete obedience from the sects. Second, despite its peaceful actions against other sects that willingly or unwillingly obeyed its decisions, *Ma Ha Na* can be vengeful and punitive if it is defied. Whether state organs will impose another prison sentence on U Nyana and his followers in the new political climate remains uncertain. However, the fact that *Ma Ha Na* did not let U Nyana and his sect do as they wished, and the fact that the state acceded to its demands to penalize the sect on behalf of the council, strongly suggest that firstly, deviance as interpreted by *Ma Ha Na* and its tribunals is still a religious crime in Myanmar; and second, the state will continue to cooperate with the council to punish such crimes.

V. CONCLUSION

The argument in this chapter is that there has been extensive regulation and punishment of deviant Buddhist sects in Myanmar over the years since the establishment of *Ma Ha Na* in 1980. Theravāda Buddhist orthodoxy that is accepted as genuine by *Ma Ha Na* and backed by the state has led to legally binding judgements that have declared at least seventeen Buddhist sects and their teachings, ideas, interpretations, and practices to be deviant. Consequently, leaders and followers of the sects have had to give up their beliefs and practices permanently. The only exception thus far is the case of the Moepyar sect and its leader U Nyana, the latter having been imprisoned three times for a total period of thirty-three years since 1984 for his defiance against *Ma Ha Na*'s judgement that his teachings are deviant.

45 Melissa Crouch, 'The Common Law and the Constitutional Writs: Prospects for Accountability in Myanmar', in Melissa Crouch and Tim Lindsey (eds.), *Law, Society and Transition in Myanmar* (Hart, 2014), 141–58.

46 Aung Kyaw Min, '"Moe Pyar" case proceedings delayed', *The Myanmar Times* (Yangon, 16 March 2017).

The regulation and punishment of the sects have been carried out through the combined power of the state and the senior Sangha. In other words, both entities have cooperated on the shared mission to regulate and punish the sects – the Sangha provides the moral sanction for the state to take legal action against the sects, while the state puts the desire of the Sangha into practice. Between the two entities, it is difficult to determine which has greater agency. However, as discussed earlier, it was the socialist state which laid down the rules and regulations for the Sangha to regulate and punish itself using the power of the state. Therefore, it can be argued that the state has been the more important agent in this regard. Furthermore, the most recent case of the Moepyar sect and the current sluggishness of state organs in taking additional action against seventy-seven-year-old U Nyana suggest that the Sangha alone cannot do much without the state's power. Still, the synergistic relationship between the two entities in the past has unfortunately resulted in violations of the *minority* Buddhist sects' right to freedom of religion.

9

The Bureaucratization of Religious Education in the Islamic Republic of Iran

Mirjam Künkler[*]

I. INTRODUCTION: THE REGULATION OF RELIGION AS A UNIVERSAL PHENOMENON

The regulation of religion by the state is a nearly universal phenomenon. No state, as Jonathan Fox's comparative data and corresponding analyses show, can entirely evade affecting religion in some way – be it through the adoption of religious schooling, the state incorporation of religious law, or the official recognition of religion, whether 'merely' for tax purposes or grander institutional or financial support.[1] The United States features the strictest interpretation of a constitutional separation between religion and state, but even the US judiciary has repeatedly been compelled to delineate what it will and will not consider a religious entity.[2]

The regulation of religion by the state always affects religious actors (organizations, individual believers, religious elites/religious authorities) in some way – it is never neutral.[3] Adherents of the religious market paradigm regard the state's role

* An earlier version of this chapter was presented at the Workshop 'Bureaucratizing Islam', organized by Aaron Glasserman at the Center for Interdisciplinary Research Bielefeld, 23–24 October 2014. I thank the participants for comments and questions, especially Dale Eickelman, Aaron Glasserman, Mara Leichtman, and James Piscatori. I also thank Heydar Shadi for a most valuable exchange.

1 Jonathan Fox, 'World Separation of Religion and State into the 21st Century', *Comparative Political Studies* 39.5 (2006), 537–69. Fox shows, for example, that the constitutions of more than fifty states contain a non-establishment clause similar to that of the US Constitution, but that most nevertheless regulate religion in one way or another, or indirectly subsidize religious institutions, despite official commitments to a 'wall of separation' between religion and state. See Jonathan Fox and D. Flores, 'Religions, Constitutions, and the State: A Cross-National Study', *Journal of Politics* 71.4 (2009), 1499–513.

2 Kent Greenawalt, *Religion and the Constitution: Establishment and Fairness*, Vol. 2 (Princeton University Press, 2008); Marci Hamilton, *God vs. the Gavel: Religion and the Rule of Law* (Cambridge University Press, 2005); Christopher L. Eisgruber and Lawrence G. Sager, *Religious Freedom and the Constitution* (Harvard University Press, 2007). For a concise review of US Supreme Court jurisprudence on establishment and free exercise, see Derek H. Davis, 'Law, the U.S. Supreme Court, and Religion', *Oxford Research Encyclopedia of Religion* (2016).

3 Mirjam Künkler and John Madeley, 'Conclusions: The Continued Prevalence of the "Marker State",' in M. Künkler, J. Madeley, and S. Shankar (eds.), *A Secular Age Beyond the West. Religion, Law and the State in Asia, the Middle East and North Africa* (Cambridge University Press, 2018), 342–84.

primarily as distorting the competition, by privileging certain actors over others.[4] Those defending the thesis of 'secure secularization' view the state as a primary explanans for secularization if it provides fundamental welfare functions which renders material reliance on religious organizations largely superfluous.[5]

Anthropologists of religion have drawn attention to how state interference revises and transforms religious practices and identities.[6] On a more macro-comparative level, sociologists of religion have examined how state interference has interacted with societal processes of secularization and sacralization, while political scientists of religion have queried what the regulation of religion tells us about political elites' interests and competition between different government agencies.[7] Recent work in global history has highlighted the potentially transnational character of state interference in matters of religion.[8] No matter what perspective and methodological approach one takes, it will be difficult to look past the profound consequences that state regulation of religion has on the ways religion is conceived and practiced within a given environment: whether and how it unfolds, where, ie in which public and private arenas, and in which forms.

The Islamic Republic of Iran presents a particularly interesting case to study from the vantage point of the regulation of religion, for it features state interference into religious affairs in a multifaceted manner, and often in ways that defy common assumptions about the nature of an 'Islamic state'. Having been established thanks to the triumph of religious authorities in the factional struggles that followed the ousting of the Shah in early 1979, it showcases one of the strongest examples of the state regulation of religious authority, religious law, and religious education. Even though individual religious authorities (Shiʿite clerics) gained unprecedented access to power and resources in the aftermath of the revolution, the same soon began to establish clerical hierarchies in rivalry to existing, mostly bottom-up

4 Paradigmatically, Roger Finke and Rodney Stark, 'Religious Economies and Sacred Canopies: Religious Mobilization in American Cities, 1906', *American Sociological Review* 53.1 (1988), 41–9; Laurence R Iannaccone, 'Introduction to the Economics of Religion', *Journal of Economic Literature* 36.3 (1998), 1465–96.

5 Paradigmatically, Ronald Inglehart and Pippa Norris, *Sacred and Secular: Religion and Politics Worldwide* (Cambridge University Press, 2004).

6 Dale Eickelman, 'Mass Higher Education and the Religious Imagination in Contemporary Arab Societies', *American Ethnologist* 194(1992), 643–55; Richard T. Antoun, 'Fundamentalism, Bureaucratization, and the State's Co-Optation of Religion: A Jordanian Case Study', *International Journal of Middle East Studies* 38.3 (2006), 369–93; Dominik Müller, 'The Bureaucratization of Islam in Southeast Asia', *Journal of Law and Religion* 33(2018), 212–47.

7 A. Kadir Yildirim, *Muslim Democratic Parties in the Middle East: Economy and Politics of Islamist Moderation* (Indiana University Press, 2016); Yüksel Sezgin and Mirjam Künkler, 'Regulation of Religion and the Religious: The Politics of Judicialization and Bureaucratization in India and Indonesia', *Comparative Studies of Society and History* 56.2 (2014), 448–78; Mirjam Künkler, 'The Special Court of the Clergy (Dādgāh-e Vīzheh-ʾye Rūḥānīyat) and the Repression of Dissident Clergy in Iran', in S. Arjomand and N. Brown (eds.), *The Rule of Law, Islam, and Constitutional Politics in Egypt and Iran* (SUNY Press, 2012), 57–100.

8 Clemens Six, *Secularism, Decolonisation, and the Cold War in South and Southeast Asia* (Routledge, 2018).

processes of authority certification, and began to police religious authority in ways hitherto unknown to Shiʿite Islam. Similarly path-breaking changes were undertaken in the realm of law, in so far as the Islamic Republic prided itself for being the first Muslim country (contra Pakistan and Saudi Arabia) to establish a comprehensive civil law system entirely based on Islamic law.[9] A third area in which the state regulation of religion effected dramatic transformations is religious education. Here the long-standing and legendary independence of the religious seminaries (*howzehs*) was gradually undermined through a variety of policies, ranging from the centralization of the admissions and examination processes to the standardization of curricula.[10] It is this third area on which the chapter will focus. Four developments characterize the evolution of religious education since the Revolution of 1979: first, the dramatic expansion of the religious educational sector, with exponential increases in student numbers and the rising significance for state employment of degrees from the religious seminaries. Second, the gradual incorporation into the state administration of the religious seminaries which had enjoyed a centuries-long history of administrative and financial autonomy. This process has resulted in the state takeover of various aspects relating to the religious seminaries, ranging from curriculum design to admissions, finance, examination, and the hiring and firing of teaching personnel. Third, the extension of state-run religious higher education to girls and women, which was close to non-existent prior to the revolution of 1979. Fourth, the narrowing of the women's curriculum since the late 1990s to lower levels of qualification, with the result that women can hardly attain any longer the level of expertise necessary to engage in *ejtehad*, widely considered the highest form of religious authority, required to interpret religious law. It will be argued that these developments have affected men's and women's religious education in different ways. While they have overall strengthened state control over what is taught in the religious seminaries and positioned religious education as the main path towards public (and thus safe and stable) employment, they have resulted in the exclusive purview of the state over women's religious education. As a consequence, women have the choice only to either take advantage of the state-run religious education program on offer, which, however, will not allow them to attain the highest levels of expertise in Shiʿite jurisprudence, or to not opt for religious education in the first place. As such, the state has achieved what I will call the 'exclusive bureaucratization' of women's religious education with the result that private religious education

[9] Said Amir Arjomand, 'Constitution of the Islamic Republic', *Encyclopædia Iranica* VI/2 (1993), 150–8; an updated version is available at www.iranicaonline.org/articles/constitution-of-the-islamic-republic (accessed 10 August 2018); M. Hashemi, *Hoquq-e asasi-ye jomhuri-ye eslami-ye Iran*, Vols. 1–2 (Mojtamiʿ-e Amuzesh-e ʿAli, 1375/1996); Asghar Schirazi, *The Constitution of Iran: Politics and the State in the Islamic Republic* (I. B. Tauris, 1997).

[10] In the following Persian transliterations will be used without diacritics to adhere to the style of the volume. Persian and Arabic plurals are simply indicated with an English plural s; thus *howzehs*, rather than *howzeh-hā*, and *madrasas* rather than *madāris*.

permitting women to attain the highest levels of religious authority is hardly available any longer.

The chapter draws on previously untapped sources in Persian to document the gradual process of state regulation of the religious education sector. Thus far, the extent to which reforms instituted under Khomeini's successor, Khamenei, have led to the state regulation of the Shi'ite seminaries and their attempted state incorporation has received scant attention with the consequence that the independence of the seminaries still tends to be overestimated. Not least because religious education has become the crucial stepping stone towards a career in many of the countries' leading clerical councils and political positions, including that of the next Supreme Leader, the question of the seminaries' independence is of paramount importance. The chapter also covers novel ground in including in the discussion the sector of women's religious education, drawing here on fieldwork conducted among Iranian seminary students in Qom.

II. RELIGIOUS EDUCATION AND THE STATE IN IRAN

A. *Before Bureaucratization: The Seminaries as* nazmi dar bi-nazmi

The locus of religious education in Iranian Shi'ism has traditionally been the religious seminaries (*madrasas*). Even though informal study groups as well as Sufi orders may function as important spaces for religious formation, formal religious authority in Shi'ite Islam has since about the mid-thirteenth century relied on training in the *madrasas*.[11] As elsewhere in the world, with the rise of the modern state, the twentieth-century state bureaucracies of the Pahlavi dynasty (1925–79) attempted to not only stem and push back the societal influence of religious authority but to moreover regulate the affairs previously under their purview, including education and law. Inspired by Mustafa Kemal's radical secularization program in neighboring Turkey, Iran's Reza Shah (1925–41) embarked on his own program of policies aimed at disempowering the Shi'ite clergy and pushing religion out of the public sphere. Religious law and courts were gradually replaced by state courts,[12] and with the spread of state schools and the opening of the country's first university in 1934, secular education gradually crowded out religious schools and a

[11] *Madrasas* had been established at this time in Qom, Ray, Kashan, Abadan, Saveh, Sabzevar and Varamin, as well as in Hilla, Kufa, Najaf, and Karbala in Iraq. See Zaryab, who cautions, 'the overwhelming majority of what were called *madrasas* in the sources were simply dormitories; only a relatively small number offered religious education'. Data for the fourteenth to eighteenth centuries are highly unreliable but by the 1860s various sources indicate the existence of more than 35 *madrasas* in Iran with more than 400 students. By 1922, these had declined to 30 *madrasas* with 210 students. 'Abbās Zaryāb, 'The Madrasa in Shi'ite Persia' (*Encyclopædia Iranica*, III/2 (1989), 184–7; an updated version is available at www.iranicaonline.org/articles/education-v-the-madrasa-in-shiite-persia (accessed 28 March 2018).

[12] Soudabeh Marin, 'La Réception Mitigée des Codifications Napoléoniennes en Iran (1911–1935)', *Droit et Cultures* (*Jus* et le Code Civil) 48.2 (2004), 107–31.

secular higher education became the preferred career path for the more affluent. By the 1960s, the roles of the Shiʿite clergy, which until the early twentieth century had included adjudicating over legal disputes and managing the grammar schools in most towns and villages of the country, had been reduced to running the mosques and keeping the scholarly tradition alive.[13] In contrast to his father's generation, by the 1960s an Iranian could well go through life without interacting much with the *ʿulama* at all: no longer would he need to rely on a cleric for marriage, for solving a dispute, and for attaining an elementary education.

Even though Reza Shah and his son Mohammadreza (r. 1941–79) aimed to gradually obliterate the significance of religious schools and seminaries for the educational sector, they did not interfere with the seminaries' internal affairs. How the seminaries were run, how they recruited teachers and students, how they generated and managed their finances, the level of salaries and stipends they paid, what they taught, and how they taught it – all of these matters were largely left to the clergy's devices,[14] in sharp contrast to Mustafa Kemal's Turkey for example, where in 1924 religious education was eradicated entirely and reintroduced much later only under the state's aegis. Even though in the early 1970s Mohammadreza Shah instituted a Religious Corps (*Sepah-e Din*) of officers who were trained in the public universities' Islamic Studies programs and dispatched to the countryside to propagate a type of Islam that was friendly to the Shah's policies, he did not force this regime-friendly version of Islam onto the seminaries.[15] Part of the reason that the *howzehs* became one of the strongest hotbeds of anti-Shah sentiments and mobilization in the late 1970s was precisely that the Shah's governments had not integrated the seminaries into the state bureaucracy but largely respected their autonomy.[16] Accordingly, the relationship of the seminaries and their patrons towards one another in the pre-revolutionary era has been characterized as one of *nazmi dar bi-nazmi* (order within disorder), where schools and scholars competed with one another for students and societal support without any formal hierarchy between them.

[13] On why Shiʿite religious authorities can be referred to as a 'clergy' (for which a Persian terminological equivalent exists, *ruhaniyat*), see Rainer Brunner, 'Shiʿite Doctrine: Hierarchy in the Imamiyya' (*Encyclopædia Iranica*, 1 October 2010), www.iranicaonline.org/articles/shiite-doctrine-ii-hierarchy-emamiya (accessed 28 March 2018).

[14] Michael M. J. Fischer, *Iran: From Religious Dispute to Revolution* (University of Wisconsin Press, 1980).

[15] Richard Yann, 'Le Rôle du clergé: tendances contradictoires du chi'isme iranien contemporain', *Archives de Sciences Sociales des Religions* 55.1 (1983), 5.

[16] The Arabic word *hawza* (plural *hawzat*) literally means 'property, district, territory', not unlike the concept of 'campus' in the Western university system. In the Persian context the *hawza* (Persian *howzeh*) is increasingly used to denote not the entire complex of religious seminaries but an individual seminary.

B. The Seminaries under Ayatollah Khomeini

Shortly after the 1979 revolution and the return of Ayatollah Khomeini to Iran after sixteen years in exile, the new elites embarked on a full-fledged cultural revolution (*enghelab-e farhangi*) in the course of which universities and cultural institutions were closed and reorganized to take account of the changing political climate. Ayatollah Khomeini was soon referred to in official outlets and revised school curricula as 'the Imam',[17] an honorific title reserved previously to the twelve Shiʿite imams. In other words, he was rhetorically elevated to the twelve outstanding authorities who had led the Twelver Shiʿite community since its founding. Professed belief in '*velayat-e faqih*', the principle of the 'guardianship of the jurist' upon which the new polity was based, became a requirement for public employment.[18] As could be expected, the religious seminaries became a major recruitment ground for new elites in the state's bureaucracies and affiliated agencies, and the *howzeh*s experienced a general revival under the new regime: the number of students doubled between the mid-1970s and the early 1980s.[19]

For the most part, the religious seminaries flourished under Supreme Leader Ayatollah Khomeini (1979–89). The *howzeh*s are traditionally based on religious endowments which are financed by (voluntary) religious taxes, *khoms* (chiefly, 20 per cent on profits) that believers pay to the source of emulation (*marja*ʿ) of their choice. (Every Shiʿite believer should follow one source of emulation.) There are at any given time only a dozen or fewer such sources of emulation in the world, and believers must choose a living *marja*ʿ. Different sources of emulation (*maraje*ʿ) therefore run and care for the upkeep of different seminaries in the Shiʿite centres of learning, that is Qom in Iran and Najaf in Iraq, as well as cities of secondary importance, such as Mashhad, Shiraz, Tabriz, and Esfahan in Iran; Kerbela and Hilla in Iraq; and Damascus in Syria. Under Ayatollah Khomeini's tenure, the financial independence of the *howzeh* remained largely untouched. Sources of emulation, both Iranian and non-Iranian, continued running their *howzehs* in the cities of Iran, recruiting students at their own discretion from Iran and other countries of the Shiʿite world (and indeed beyond).

Exceptions to this were religious seminaries run by grand ayatollahs challenging Khomeini's newly acquired power as political Leader. Grand Ayatollah Shariat-Madari was the most prominent adversary to Khomeini, whose followers went so far as to form a political party in 1978 fighting the Khomeiniists in pursuit of a different kind of Islamic Republic. After having been subjected to ghastly scenes during a short stay in

[17] Jalal Matini, 'Bahti dar baraye sabiqeh-ye tarikhi-ye alqab wa ʿanawin-e ʿolama dar madhab-e shiʿa', *Iran Nameh* 1 (1362/1983), 560.

[18] Said A. Arjomand, *The Turban for the Crown: The Islamic Revolution in Iran* (Oxford University Press, 1998), 101.

[19] ʿAqiqi Bakhshayeshi, *Yeksad sal-e mobarezah-ye rohaniyat-e motaraqqi*, Vol. 4 (Daftar-e Nashr-e Navid-e Eslam, 1361/1982), 159.

prison during the revolution,[20] Shariat-Madari was put under house arrest where he died in 1986. His educational center in Qom, the *Dar al-tabligh*, a beacon of modernist scholarship in the Shiʿite world, was closed down.[21] The seminary of another grand ayatollah, Seyyed Hasan Tabatabaei-Qomi from Mashhad, was torn down under the pretense of necessary restructuring plans of the local Imam Reza shrine, after the grand ayatollah had expressed his opposition to the revolutionary forces.[22]

While Khomeini by and large did not interfere with seminary life apart from the said exceptions, it was under his leadership that the state gradually began to regulate aspects of religious education – the beginning of a bureaucratization (and state incorporation) process that fully unfolded under his successor Khamenei (1989–). A Council for the Management of the *Qom Howzeh (shora-ye modiriyat-e howzeh-ye ʿelmiyeh Qom)*[23] was founded in 1980, which attempted to progressively bring seminaries under its control by offering financial grants.[24] A first step in this process was to institute new modes of certification for religious authorities. Previously, the most successful seminary students would complete three cycles of a *howzeh* education, each lasting for about four to eight years,[25] and eventually graduate by receiving an *ejazeh* of *ejtehad*, a permission to engage in independent legal reasoning on the basis of the sources, from their main teacher, a grand ayatollah.[26] With this *ejazeh* (permission), they would be a *mojtahed* (a person qualified to engage in *ejtehad*). A

20 See Minister of Intelligence Reyshahri's memoirs on how he took pleasure in abusing the grand ayatollah. See M. Mohammadi Reyshahri, *Khaterat-e siyasi: 1365–1366* (Muʾassasah-ʾi Mutalaʿat va Pizhuhishʹha-ye Siyasi, 1369/1990).

21 It was ultimately integrated into a new regime-controlled institution, the *daftar-e tablighat-e eslami howzeh-ye ʿelmiyeh Qom.*

22 Künkler, 'The Special Court of the Clergy (Dādgāh-e Vīzheh-ʾye Rūḥānīyat) and the Repression of Dissident Clergy in Iran' (n. 7), 57–100.

23 http://howzeh-qom.ir. The center's activities are funded by the Supreme Leader's office.

24 Ali Shirkhani and Abbas Zari, *Tahavvulat-e howzeh-ye ʿelmiyeh Qom: Pas az piruzi-ye enqelab-e eslami* (Entesharat-e Markaz-e Asnad-e Enqelab-e Eslami, 2005).

25 The first level, *muqaddamat* (introductions), usually lasts up to six years depending on the qualifications of the student upon entering the program. It includes training in Arabic language, logic, rhetoric, theology, philosophy, history of Islam, Qur'an, *feqh* (jurisprudence) and *osul-e feqh* (principles of jurisprudence). The second level, *sotuh*, takes about four years and deepens the study of *feqh* and *osul-e feqh*. Beside these two, theology, philosophy, *rijal* (science of narration) and *diraya* (hadith studies) are also taught. The third cycle consists of the *dars-e kharej* (external studies), which is not based on one particular text but discussion-focused learning between a grand ayatollah and his students, spanning a variety of subjects in *feqh* and *osul-e feqh*.

26 Roy Mottahedeh, 'Traditional Shiʿite Education in Qom', in A. O. Rorty (ed.), *Philosophers on Education: Historical Perspectives* (Routledge, 1998), 451–7; Devin J. Stewart, 'Ejāza', *Encyclopædia Iranica*, VIII/3 (1998), 273–5 (an updated version is available at: www.iranicaonline.org/articles/ejaza [accessed 8 August 2018]); Aron Zysow, 'Ejtehād in Shiʿism', *Encyclopædia Iranica*, VIII/3 (1998), 281–6 (an updated version is available at: www.iranicaonline.org/articles/ejtehad (accessed 8 August 2018)). To become a village preacher, or a functionary in a state department with responsibility for religious affairs, one would usually have completed the second cycle (*sotuh*). To teach a seminary or university course or to reach higher administrative positions in the state bureaucracy would require completion of the third cycle (*dars-e kharej*), or at least study in this cycle for some years.

student would aim to collect as many *ejazeh*s from as many high-ranking authorities as possible. Most *mojtahed*s remain at the level of being a *hojjatoleslam* (an honorific title, literally meaning 'a proof of God'), while a few may rise higher in the hierarchy through recognition of their scholarly distinction by their peers, at which point they would be referred to as an *ayatollah* ('sign of God'). The most distinguished ayatollahs would rise to the status of grand ayatollah, *ayatollah al-ozma* ('great sign of God'), when a sufficient number of followers (*moqallid*s) will refer to the juristic works of the ayatollah, published in his treatise (*resale-ye amali-ye*), and seek guidance from him.[27] With more and more followers who pay their religious tax to him, he will emerge as a *marja*, a source of emulation, and be able to establish his own *howzeh* as well as invest the collected funds into other institutions, such as libraries, mosques, hospitals, and other institutions serving the community. The production of religious authority remained essentially the same throughout the Pahlavi dynasty: it was a combination of bottom-up certification driven by those who would follow an emerging authority, and peer recognition.[28]

The Islamic Republic changed this system when in 1982 it endowed an existing body with the task of officially recognizing individual religious authorities with a corresponding rank. The Society of Teachers of the Qom Seminaries (*jame'eh-ye modarressin-e howzeh-ye 'elmiyeh-ye Qom*) had been founded in 1961 to coordinate and promote throughout the country the religious teachings of the seminaries and to serve as a guard against the encroachment of the Pahlavi state. In 1982, it was elevated from an interest group to a para-statal organization whose head is appointed by the Supreme Leader and which keeps a registry of religious authorities and their ranks in the country. When one reads that a cleric has been 'demoted', such as has happened to a number of clerics supporting the green movement in 2009 (including grand ayatollah Yusuf Sane'i), it means the Society of Teachers of the Qom Seminaries has changed his rank. De facto, endowing the Society with the task of officially recognizing religious authorities as such has altered the production of religious authority in nothing short of a revolutionary manner. Of course one needs to be cognizant of the fact that official recognition is only a small part of what constitutes religious authority and many believers may be unaffected by it in their choice of a *marja'*. Nevertheless, it can result in severe financial and status repercussions, as those not or no longer officially recognized may lose access to teaching positions, the possibility to give student salaries, and thereby to attract a student body to begin with.

With the consolidation of the Islamic Republic, new employment opportunities were created for the graduates of the *hozwzeh*s. As law was Islamized, judges in courts were replaced by graduates of the religious seminaries, and a number of state institutions, from the ministries to state-funded religious endowments (*bonyads*)

27 Brunner (n. 12).
28 Ibid.

became institutions led by members of the clergy.[29] The social class of the clergy, pushed out of society into the academic towers of the seminary under the Shah, now became the major recruitment ground for public service. Studying in the *howzeh*s opened up a lucrative career path, with assured employment and public benefits in store at the end.

Facing challenges from within the clergy early in the revolution, Khomeini as Supreme Leader began to appoint the Friday prayer leaders in the major cities. Henceforth it was from the registry of the Society of Teachers of the Qom Seminaries that individuals would be selected as Friday prayer leaders and for public service positions. Those not included in the registry at a rank required for the position would not be considered. Being included in the registry at a particular rank is not, however, necessarily a reflection of either having acquired that rank through learning and scholarly distinction, or entirely a result of the evaluation of the members of the Society. When needed for a particular position, the state-run media may also 'manipulate' a given cleric's status, by repeatedly referring to him as an *ayatollah* rather than a *hojjatoleslam*, for example. This happens frequently; the current head of the judiciary, Sadeq Ardeshir Larijani, is an example of this strategy. Conversely, the media may also refer to a given cleric with a rank lower than he is known for, with the result that the Society of Teachers of the Qom Seminaries may eventually demote him. Thus even though the members of the Society and the leaders of the state-run media are appointed by the Supreme Leader, there are factional struggles between his appointees that make for contention and contestation within the system.

When 'Ali Khamenei, president of the Islamic Republic (1981–9) and a *hojjatoleslam* at the time, was chosen by the Assembly of Experts as Khomeini's successor in 1989, the Society of Teachers of the Qom Seminaries repeatedly attempted to include him among the list of *maraje'*, sources of emulation.[30] Even regime insiders and hardliners, however, protested against this dramatic promotion and twice the Society had to ultimately remove his name from the list again. The manoeuvre did help, however, in cementing his status as an ayatollah among the public. Over time he has succeeded in centralizing his influence over the clergy and in using state resources to buttress his claims to the *marja'iyat* (office of being a source of emulation) both inside

[29] Graduates of the Shi'ite seminaries are employed in all branches of government, in para-statal organizations, state-owned companies, and the military.

[30] After Khomeini's death, grand ayatollah Golpayegani (d. 1993) and then grand ayatollah Mohammad 'Ali Araki (d. 1994) were among the few candidates recognized as *maraje'* by the Society of Teachers of the Qom Seminaries, and followers of Khomeini had been recommended to choose Golpayegani and then Araki as their new *marja'*. When Araki passed away in 1994, however, the Society published a new list of candidates for the *marja'iyat* which included Khamenei's name. Grand ayatollahs from within and without Iran objected resolutely to Khamenei's inclusion in the list, insisting that he lacked the required jurisprudential credentials to be considered for the *marja'iyat*. After some back and forth between regime-sponsored advocacy of Khamenei on the one hand and vociferous protest against his nomination, Khamenei asked the Society to withdraw his name.

and outside Iran to such a degree that today he is indeed considered a *marja'*, although his distinction as a juristic thinker has hardly improved since the 1990s.

C. *The Seminaries in Post-Khomeini Iran*

While Khomeini largely left the seminaries to their own device, and used his power as Supreme Leader primarily to neutralize individual rivals, his successor has taken a more comprehensive approach to the *hozwzehs*. Post-Khomeini Iran has witnessed a considerable transformation in the institutions of religious learning: not only has the number of students significantly increased during Khamenei's tenure (1989–), from 20,000 in the mid-1980s to more than 60,000 by 1996, to about 150,000 in 2018, the relationship between the *howzeh* and the state has also changed dramatically.[31] While a few *howzehs* have successfully evaded state intervention and retained their pre-revolutionary independence from the state, since the late-1990s most have been subjected to various institutional reforms that have increased state oversight of their personnel, their curricula, and their finances.[32]

The most important state instrument in these institutional reform projects has been the Supreme Council of the Seminary (*shora-ye ali-ye howzeh-ye 'elmiyeh*), a clerical body newly founded in 1991, whose members are directly appointed by the Supreme Leader, 'Ali Khamenei.[33] With the founding of this council, the locus for drawing up state policies towards the Shi'ite seminaries was taken out of the Ministry of Higher Education and placed exclusively in its hands. The Council has undertaken various educational reforms aimed at the standardization of curricula, and control over the leading personnel in the seminaries. It now oversees nearly all but a handful of the important seminaries across the country. The previously mentioned Council for the Management of the *Qom Howzeh*, an administrative body staffed by technocrats, was placed under the new clerical council, which consists to a large part of political appointees. Since 2010, these two institutions have branches in each Iranian province, and each provincial branch oversees all of the seminaries in that particular province.[34]

One of the most important reforms Khamenei has championed has been the modernization of the *howzeh* education, thus primarily concerning the style rather

[31] On the number of *howzeh* students in the 1970s, see Zaryāb (n. 10). For more recent numbers, Haddad Adel and others (eds.), 'Howzeh-ye 'Elmiyeh, Shi'i Teaching Institution', in *Encyclopaedia of the World of Islam* (EWI Press, 2012); Kari Vogt and Frida Austvoll Nome, 'Islamic Education in Qom: Contemporary Developments', *Acta Orientalia* 6935 (2008), 38; and http://howzeh-qom.ir. To put these numbers into perspective, it needs to be born in mind however that the number of students in the secular education sector has risen in much greater proportion: from 170, 000 in 1976 to about 5,000,000 in 2015.

[32] A Firuzi, Seyr-e tarikhi-ye tashkil-e shura-ye 'ali va modiriyat-e hawza (*Payām-e Ḥowzeh*, Vol. 1, 1373/1994), 7–23; Vogt and Nome (n. 29).

[33] For the site of the Supreme Council of the Seminary, see www.shorayeaali.com/

[34] Saeid Golkar, 'Cultural Engineering under Authoritarian Regimes: Islamization of Universities in Post-revolutionary Iran', *Digest of Middle East Studies* 21.1 (2012), 1–23.

than the content of learning. The three traditional cycles of the seminary education have been replaced by BA and MA degrees, thus streamlining religious education with that of the universities. While the duration of the three cycles of the seminary education used to be in principle unlimited, the new degree programs involve term limits and the organization of study programs with clearly defined modules that lead to the attainment of said degrees. Thanks to the new degree structure, students can now move more easily between secular and religious institutions, and combine degrees from both spheres.

Under the initiative of the Supreme Council of the Seminary, teaching materials have been reorganized to the effect that it is no longer one teacher teaching one book, but instead textbooks that contain a comprehensive curriculum of several subjects (e.g., *manteq* [logic], *hekmat* [theosophy], *feqh* [jurisprudence], etc.) at a given level. The duration of study has been formalized (with sequences set for modules that build on one another), and end of program-examinations have been set out and standardized across seminaries. In terms of pedagogy, memorization (*tikrar*) has been replaced by the encouragement of interaction between teacher and student also at the lower levels (at the higher levels this was a principle of religious learning all along).[35] Classrooms have been redesigned with chairs, tables, boards, often also computers, and as such hardly resemble any more the traditional teaching style where students sat on the floor around a charismatic teacher. With the redesigned classrooms, modern teaching methods and textbooks, the *howzeh*s of Qom in the 1990s moved years ahead in terms of style compared to centres of learning in neighbouring Iraq and in Lebanon. (Since the revival of the seminaries in Iraq after the fall of Saddam Hussein in 2003, the *howzeh*s of Iraq have experienced similar modernization processes but no comparable process of state incorporation and standardization.)

The same institutions that have driven the modernization of religious learning in Iran have, however, also been the chief engines of bringing the religious seminaries under the aegis of the state. Most importantly, the cited principle of 'order within disorder', describing the internal diversity of the seminary landscape, has been replaced by centralization and standardization. This begins at the level of personnel. Whereas admission to the universities of the country has always been organized by way of a *concours* (a countrywide admissions exam akin to the French model), entrance to a religious seminary was always subject to the final approval of the grand ayatollah running a given seminary, and his representatives (*vakil*s). Since the mid-2000s, an admissions process to the *howzeh*s through a centrally organized *concours* has been instituted, a process which only very few seminaries have managed to resist. Students who have passed the *concours* are allocated to a specific *howzeh* depending on their achieved grade and their indicated preferences.

35 Discussion and critique (*mobahetha, enteqat*) are an integral part of the higher levels of a madrasa education.

The monthly stipends for the students, hitherto set by the individual *mojtahed*, are now fixed by the Council for the Management of the *Qom Howzeh*.[36] Moreover, they are no longer paid by the individual seminary, but instead centrally through the Management Council, with the result that stipends of politically active or non-conformist students can easily be withheld without involving and informing the students' teachers and mentors.

The Supreme Council of the Seminary determines the disciplines to be taught in each *howzeh* and the educational levels and degrees on offer. Independent state-run graduate schools (*marakaz takhassosi*) have been set up where non-juridical subjects of the Islamic sciences are now taught (previously exclusively in the seminaries), including *tafsir* (Qur'anic commentary) and Qur'anic sciences, theology, history of Islam, *hadith* (sayings of the prophet), and Islamic philosophy.[37] Applicants need to have completed the second traditional cycle or a BA degree in order to take the admissions exam. The upshot of this has been a compartmentalization of the Islamic sciences that shields the juridical fields (considered paramount for the attainment of religious authority) from 'dilution' of the more mundane fields of study. It also allows the state to better control admissions to the most advanced degrees in the juridical sciences, especially training in *ejtehad*, and to thereby closely monitor who will and who should not become part of the future generation of *mojtaheds*. This is important not least because in theory the Supreme Leader of Iran is elected and 'supervised' by a clerical Assembly of Experts (*Majles-e Khobregan*), popularly elected every eight years by the people, for which only those may run as candidates who have attained the *mojtahed* rank. The Assembly meets twice a year and asks the Supreme Leader for a report. It could theoretically replace him during these meetings through the vote for an alternative candidate, but it has never come to such a vote of no confidence in the Assembly's history.

The examinations for all levels of study are now centrally conducted and the degrees officially recognized by the Ministry of Higher Education. The examination for the highest degree of study, the attainment of an *ejazeh* of *ejtehad* (previously granted by the individual ayatollahs who ran particular seminaries) has been moved to the administration of the Society of Teachers of the Qom Seminary.[38]

Once students have graduated, the Supreme Council of the Seminary has the task of deciding who will be dispatched when to which parts of the country to engage in *tabligh* (Islamic propagation). It assigns the village and city preachers and the prayer leaders in the *hoseiniyehs* (study centres for Shiʿite laymen and -women).

[36] This excludes a handful of distinguished *howzehs*, such as the Feiziyeh in Qom, which has managed to remain financially and managerially autonomous.

[37] Official website of Qom Howzeh: http://howzeh-qom.ir.

[38] In addition, the Assembly of Experts conducts its own *ejazeh* examinations for those seeking candidacy in this clerical council. This is perceived by many high-ranking clerics as an act of disrespect, as it creates a parallel system of certification, bypassing their own authority.

Apart from introducing BA, MA, and PhD degrees in the seminaries, under Khamenei's aegis the administration has strengthened the nexus between the religious and secular institutions of higher learning through three other reforms. In 1996 Khamenei called on the Minister of Higher Education to further Islamize the secular universities of the country. To that end, a committee was formed with representatives of the Shiʿite seminaries to review the study programs and texts used in the humanities and social sciences.[39] Second, since 2010, state-run theological seminaries have been set up inside 67 of the country's 110 university campuses, so that academic study at the universities can now be complemented by religious seminary courses. This further erodes the autonomy and attractiveness of the once independent *howzehs*, in so far as students may now turn to the state-run theological seminaries inside the universities for reasons of convenience. Third, under Khamenei an introductory Islamic Studies course has been made mandatory for students of secular education programs, thus creating a new presence of *ʿulama* on secular campuses.[40]

Beside the reforms in the domestic realm, the Islamic Republic has opened religious study centres (book clubs) around the world from Daressalam in Tanzania to Kargil in India, and Makassar in Indonesia,[41] where books by Iran's leading clerics are disseminated for free and from where local students are recruited for travel to and study in Iran.[42] These are funded by the cultural offices in Iranian embassies, offices that are not under the supervision of the Foreign Ministry, but under supervision of and funded by the Supreme Leader's office.

Overall, with the accession of Khamenei to the Supreme Leader's office the sphere of religious education has experienced its most profound transformation since the constitutional revolution of 1906. The role of the state in interfering with the recruitment of students and teachers, the levels of stipends and salaries, and most importantly the curricula and teaching methods is unprecedented. Although a few *howzehs* have been able to resist the incorporation into the state bureaucracy, the level of state involvement today far surpasses the Shah's attempts to interfere with the internal affairs of the religious seminaries.

39 S. Golkar, 'Cultural Engineering under Authoritarian Regimes: Islamization of Universities in Post-revolutionary Iran', *Digest of Middle East Studies* 21.1 (2012), 1–23.

40 Importantly, as Golkar (2012) notes, some of the reforms have only partially been implemented because from 1997 to 2005 the Ministry of Higher Education and later the universities were staffed by reform-minded officials who pursued other goals. During the reformist parliament (2000–2004), the universities gained the right to hold elections for their top administrators (chancellors and deans), to develop their curricula and syllabi, and to select their faculty members (previously the right of the Supreme Council of Cultural Revolution [SCCR]). These processes significantly increased the reformist presence among university administrators. Under the presidency of Ahmadinejad (2005–2013) the university reforms were reversed and deans once again appointed through the SCCR. Candidates must now apply through a centralized website and the SCCR screens applications, and then proposes two candidates per post to the universities, of whom the latter must choose one.

41 I conducted fieldwork here in 2011 to study the role of religion in Iran's cultural foreign policy.

42 Recently, these have been brought under one central administration under Al-Mustafa International University. See http://fa.alkawthartv.com/news/99348 and http://www.hawzaengland.com.

III. WOMEN'S RELIGIOUS EDUCATION AS AN EXAMPLE OF EXCLUSIVE BUREAUCRATIZATION

Apart from creating a tighter nexus between the *howzeh*s and the state, the 1979 revolution has affected the institutions of religious learning in another significant way. While only very few women had access to a *howzeh* education before 1979, the Islamic Republic has made women's religious education a pillar of its education policy and built not just a handful but dozens of women's seminaries, particularly since the 1990s, throughout Iran and beyond its borders.[43] Most of these are under the directorship of the Centre for Management of Women's [Sisters'] Seminaries (*markaz-e modiriyat-e howzeha-ye ʿelmiyeh khwaharan*), which today oversees more than 320 centers countrywide.[44] In addition to these, a number of informal *maktab*s exist: neighbourhood institutions where women study the Qur'an with a local religious authority and sometimes even *hadith* and *feqh*.

Similar to the realm of the secular universities, where the 1979 revolution created unprecedented opportunities for women's learning,[45] in the religious realm, too, it has dramatically improved women's access to education. In nearly every town today girls and women can seek instruction in one of the state-supported institutions of women's religious learning and seek accredited degrees of higher Shiʿite education. As I develop further below, however, the scope of the religious education on offer is limited. While most men's *howzeh*s allow their students to study up to the highest level, the third cycle (*dars-e kharej*), hardly any *maktab*s and *howzeh*s provide similar opportunities for women. Women are either compelled to join the general *dars-e kharej* courses that high-ranking regime officials (such as Khamenei and Sadeq Larijani) offer, which are highly politicized or, if they seek intensive study in the *howzeh*s, their specialization is limited to family law (*feqh-e khanevadeh*).[46] Such a focus is not sufficiently broad to enable one to seek the eventual rank of *mojtaheda*. Accordingly, no high-ranking female religious scholar has emerged from the

[43] Keiko Sakurai, 'Women's Empowerment and Iranian-style Seminaries in Iran and Pakistan', in K. Sakurai and F. Adelkhah (eds.), *The Moral Economy of the Madrasa: Islam and Education Today* (Routledge, 2011), 32–59; Keiko Sakurai, 'Shiʿite Women's Seminaries (howzehye 'elmiyyeh-ye khahran) in Iran: Possibilities and Limitations', *Iranian Studies* 45.6 (2012), 727–44; Keiko Sakurai, 'Making Qom A Center of Shiʿi Scholarship: Al Mustafa International University', in M. Bano and K. Sakurai (eds.), *Shaping Global Islamic Discourses: The Role of Al-Azhar, Al-Madinah and Al-Mustafa* (Edinburgh University Press, 2015), 41–72.

[44] Geographically, the only exceptions to this are the province of Khorasan, where the 'Centre for Management of Women's Seminaries of Khorasan' is in charge, and the city of Qom, where most *maktabs* for women were merged after the revolution into one seminary, Jameʿat al-Zahra', which is autonomously governed.

[45] With a female literacy rate of more than 80% in the 1990s, the percentage of female students in the universities surpassed 50% in the early 2000s.

[46] See http://paziresh.jz.ac.ir/uploads/pazirest/97/20%420%.pdf.

post-revolutionary seminaries.[47] This, I suggest, is chiefly because by and large, women are in the *howzehs* not to become *mojtaheds* or religious scholars with expertise to (re)interpret Islamic law, but *moballeghs* (propagators). What is more, because the state has the near monopoly over women's religious education, is has achieved the *exclusive bureaucratization* of their training in the Islamic sciences, with the result that alternative channels enabling women to attain the highest levels of religious authority needed to effect legal change (the *ejazeh* of *ejtehad*) are hardly available any longer.[48]

A. *Women's Religious Education at the Turn of the Revolution*

Although accounts exist of individual women's presence in the *madrasas* in Safavid and Qajar Iran,[49] such occurrences were very rare and limited to individual clerical families.[50] During most of the Pahlavi dynasty, hardly any references to women in the religious seminaries are known, as secular girls' schools were set up from the 1910s onwards and henceforth provided an attractive alternative for the daughters of urban elites. The 1960s, however, present a turning point. From the early 1960s onward, women's seminaries were being set up in a handful of towns,[51] and Ayatollah Shariatmadari in Qom went so far as to open a women's wing in his renowned *Dar al-tabligh*.[52] Other institutions soon followed, when the *madrasa Dar al-shifa* established the Centre for Women Studies (*markaz-e motala'at-e zanan*) and Qom's Haqqani School opened a girls' madrasa associated with it, the *maktab-e tawhid*, in 1973/74.[53]

47 During the 2015 ejtehad exam by the Assembly of Experts there were also some female participants: www.radiozamaneh.com/254304. But so far no highly trained female Shiite scholar would consider herself fit to be a high-ranking religious leader. On why Zohreh Sefati does not do so, see Mirjam Künkler and Roja Fazaeli, "The life of two mujtahidahs: Female Religious Authority in 20th century Iran" in *Women, Leadership and Mosques: Contemporary Islamic Authority*, edited by Masooda Bano and Hilary Kalmbach, Brill Publishers, 2011, pp. 127–160.

48 While family law is important and some of the most consequential battles about the interpretation of religious law are fought in the realm of family law (is unilateral divorce by the husband legitimate? Is the first wife's consent required for polygyny? Does the wife require the husband's permission to work? In the case of divorce until what age may the mother retain custody of the children?), expertise in family law is not sufficient to rise in the clerical ranks. It would be unthinkable for a *mojtahed* to have no training in criminal and other public law, and exhibiting expertise in family law only.

49 Maria Szuppe, 'The "Jewels of Wonder": Learned Ladies and Princess Politicians in the Provinces of Early Safavid Iran', in Gavin R. Hambly (ed.), *Women in the Medieval Islamic World* (St. Martin's Press, 1998), 325–47.

50 Roswitha Badry, 'Zum Profil weiblicher "Ulama" in Iran: Neue Rollenmodelle für "islamische Feministinnen"?', *Die Welt des Islams* 40.1 (2000), 7–40.

51 Examples of this trend include *maktab-e fatemeh*, established in 1961 in Fasa, Fars Province; *maktab-e zahra'*, set up in Shiraz in 1964, *Zahra'-ye Athar*, founded in Tehran in 1966, and *madrese-ye 'elmiyeh narges* in Mashhad in the same year, *maktab-e fatemeh* in Isfahan in 1967. Mahtab Rezapoor, 'Enghelab-e Eslami, Bastar Royesh Sabz Howzeh-ye 'Elmiyeh Khwaharan', in *Payam-e Zan*, no. 158 (Ordibehesht, 1384/2005); Künkler and Fazaeli (n. 47).

52 Called *Dar al-Zahra* in 1973, which by 1975 already counted 150 female students.

53 Official website of Howzeh-ye 'Elmiyeh Khwaharan:
www.jz.ac.ir/index.php?option=com_content&view=article&id=160&Itemid=149.

Ayatollah Khomeini was known for his support of women's education, their religious education in particular. When a handful of women who had been educated in the Qom seminaries and who emerged as influential leaders during the revolution shared their disappointment with him over a lack of state support for women's religious education, he agreed to establish a woman's seminary, offering the full *howzeh* education at all three levels.[54] In the order (*hokm*) establishing the first seminary (*Jame'at al-Zahra*) in August 1984, Khomeini declared:

> … the respected ladies of Iran have proven during the revolution that they can stand shoulder to shoulder with men, provide valuable services to Islam and the Muslims in social and political activities, and that they can be leaders in education and the formation of society. Now -thanks be to God- there is an institution being built in the holy city of Qom, the city of knowledge and struggle [*'elm va jehad*], for their training. We hope that with the efforts of the *'ulama* and the leaders of the Qom seminaries, this Islamic goal [of training women in the Islamic sciences] will be realised and be an effective step towards the intellectual growth and flourishing of women's Islamic knowledge.[55]

From early on, a dualism existed in the rationale for women's religious education, between those who genuinely believed in the ability (and right) of women to attain religious authority and those who saw religious education for women as an instrument to further inculcate the values of the 1979 revolution. As Hoodfar and Sadr comment, the interest of the first group 'lay purely in theological education with the radical goal of becoming a female *mojtahed* […]. Although their demands fell outside conventional politics, one can consider them pioneers in breaking down one of the strongest walls of exclusion for women. Their goal remains the training of female *'ulama*'.[56]

The second characterized those women who, although having joined the school for theological training, chiefly considered themselves as proselytizers for political Islam; they participated in women's religious gatherings, popularizing the idea of revolution and a religious world order. Among them were Monireh Gorji, the only female member of the Constitutional Assembly in 1979; and Maryam Behrozi, who has been a member of several parliaments since the revolution, and the founding member of the Islamist women's party, the Association of Zeinab. It is unclear where

54 Ṭabaṭaba'i, 'Gerdeham-e Modiran va Masolan ḥawza-ha-ye 'Elmiyeh Khwaharan Sarasar Keshvar' (trans.: 'The Gathering of Managers and Officials of the Women's Seminaries Throughout the Country'), *Payam-e Ḥawza* no. 14 (1376/1997).

55 Cited online at http://www.imam-khomeini.ir/fa/c207_51324/%D8%B5%D8%AD%DB%8C%D9%81%D9%87_%D8%A7%D9%85%D8%A7%D9%85/%D8%AC%D9%84%D8%AF_19/%D8%B5%D8%AD%DB%8C%D9%81%D9%87_%D8%A7%D9%85%D8%A7%D9%85_-_%D8%AC%D9%84%D8%AF_19 (accessed 2 May 2018).

56 Homa Hoodfar and Shadi Sadr, 'Religious Idioms and Rights-Based Demands: Can Women Act as Agents of a Democratization of Theocracy in Iran' (Kevorkian Center Research Workshop, New York University, 30 March 2009), 51.

exactly Khomeini stood between these poles. The fact that he agreed to institute the full *howzeh* education with its three-tiered level that far surpasses the needs of the formation for mere propagators would render credence to the interpretation that he did believe women should be able to become *mojtahedas*, should they wish to.

B. Post-Khomeini Administrative Changes

When Khamenei succeeded Khomeini as the Supreme Leader, the changes he undertook to the men's *howzeh* system were also applied to the newly created women's centers. Mirroring similar institutions that would manage the men's seminaries, the Centre for the Management of Women's Seminaries (*markaz-e modiriyat-e howzeha-ye 'elmiyeh-ye Khwaharan*) was founded, which would henceforth oversee all women's seminaries.[57] While only a handful had existed under Khomeini, Khamenei expanded the women's *howzeh* system across the country. Today, more than 300 such seminaries exist[58] which train about 60,000 young women, two fifths of the overall *howzeh* student body.[59]

Together with the expansion of the women's religious education system a radical curriculum reform was undertaken in 1991.[60] Similar to the modernization process in the men's seminaries, BA and MA programs were introduced, but differently from the men's *howzeh*, the curriculum was also simplified and genderized: a new emphasis was introduced on philosophy and morals as opposed to law and jurisprudence, as well as domestic applications of religious knowledge. According to *hojjatoleslam* Tabataba'i, the director of *Jame'at al-Zahra*, the largest women's seminary, in the new curriculum students study sufficient Arabic to understand the Qur'an, the *hadith* and other key texts. They also study 'socio-political subjects' such as 'fundamentals of the Islamic Revolution', the Iranian Constitution, and Ayatollah Khomeini's will. And finally, they are trained in public speaking as well as practical skills, including *ayin-e zendegi* (rituals of life), *hamsardari* (keeping a married life) and *khanedari* (housekeeping).[61] The classical *howzeh* subjects are also offered, but in a simplified form compared to the way they are taught in the men's seminaries: *manteq* (logic), *osul* (principles of jurisprudence) and *falsafa* (philosophy), as well as *akhlaq* (ethics), *tarikh-e eslami* (Islamic history) and the life of the Shi'ite imams. Most women specialize in Qur'anic exegesis (*tafsir*), theology (*kalam*), ethics (*akhlaq*), or Arabic grammar and syntax. Most consequentially, the *feqh* curriculum in the highest cycle has been narrowed to family law and thus limits

57 Except in Mashhad and Qom, which have their own administrative systems.

58 See http://whc.ir and http://womenhc.com/index.php?panel=bloglist.

59 Although only a part of these completes a full degree. Many use a year in the seminaries as a bridge year, while waiting for admission to their preferred university study course.

60 'Gozaresh az Jame'at al-Zahra' (S)- Tadabir-e Imam -Ghods Sareh'; see https://web.archive.org/web/20101022061553/http://www.jz.ac.ir/fetr/index.php?option=com_content&view=article&id=177&Itemid=143&limitstart=8 (accessed 5 May 2018).

61 Ṭabaṭaba'i (n. 39).

women to seeking only partial expertise in *feqh*. Women graduates can thus acquire the ability of *ejtehad-e mutajazzi* (partial *ejtehad*) but not *ejtehad-e motlaq* (absolute *ejtehad*) in all fields of law. While few scholars would indeed prove their undisputed mastery of all fields of law, expertise in family law is, as noted, of relatively low standing and not sufficient to become recognized as an outstanding *mojtahed* or *mojtaheda*.

Upon embarking on the curriculum reform in 1991, Supreme Leader Khamenei openly conceded his opposition to the previous curriculum which had been identical with the men's curriculum and thus enabled women to seek expertise in any area of *feqh* and to aspire to a career in scholarship:

> From the start I was against the curriculum and always wondered why our thoughtful friends wanted to implement those programmes [as were offered in *Jame'at al-Zahra* in the 1980s]. When you asked them 'why do these young ladies come to the *howzeh*?', they would say, 'they come as we do.' This is while men can use their *howzeh* qualifications in many different ways … but what about our sisters? Shortly before the revolution, I asked the late Mr. [sic] Qoddusi to set up a four-year degree program for these women who came to study in the *howzeh* so at the end of their studies you can give them a degree with which they can lead propagation (*tabligh*) gatherings and so on and they can serve [their community] …[62]

Thus a new emphasis was introduced on *tabligh* rather than *feqh*. Importantly, higher level studies of *dars-e kharej-e feqh* and *osul*, which are required if one aspires to become a *mojtaheda*, were no longer systematically offered, though individual teachers would offer them privately at the request of students.[63]

Overall, the emphasis shifted from jurisprudence to ethics and to courses that combine behavioural and moral formation. The students' career paths attest to this redirection. Despite the spectacular institutional apparatus that the Islamic Republic has erected to promote women's training in religious studies (the largest of its kind in the world), the scholarly fruit is surprisingly difficult to identify. For example, the careers that female graduates of Iran's largest women's seminary, *Jame'at al-Zahra'*, typically choose include teaching religion and Arabic in secondary schools, as well as in cultural centres and bases of the *Basij* (voluntary army). While some graduates become lecturers in the women's seminaries inside and outside of Iran, most engage in *tabligh*, or propagation activities, on completion of

62 'Gozaresh az Jame'at al-Zahra' (n. 4).

63 'Gozaresh az Jame'at al-Zahra', Barnamehaye Amoozeshi', http://jz.ac.ir/post/26-%D9%81%D8%B9%D8%A7%D9%84%DB%8C%D8%AA-%D9%87%D8%A7-%D9%88-%D8%B8%D8%B1%D9%81%DB%8C%D8%AA-%D9%87%D8%A7%DB%8C-%D8%AC%D8%A7%D9%85%D8%B9%D9%87-%D8%A7%D9%84%D8%B2%D9%87%D8%B1%D8%A7-%D8%B3%D9%84%D8%A7%D9%85-%D8%A7%D9%84%D9%84%D9%87-%D8%B9%D9%84%DB%8C%D9%87%D8%A7 (accessed 2 May 2018). News websites make much of the fact that women are allowed to attend the Supreme Leader's *kharej* course: https://www.tasnimnews.com/fa/news/1393/03/17/392936/———. But being permitted to listen to his lectures is hardly equivalent to being enrolled in a full-fledged *dars-e kharej* course at the *howzeh* which covers a diversity of topics in *feqh* and *osul-e feqh*.

their studies.[64] In 2008, of about 450 graduates, 160 sought employment in the ministry of education, the state-run broadcasting corporation or the para-statal religious endowments. A further 140 were sent individually to engage in *tabligh* among the pilgrims in Qom, and 96 to other cities.[65] By contrast, very few *mojtahedahs* (not more than a dozen out of an alleged 12,000 graduates so far) are known to have emerged from the women's religious seminaries since their inception in 1984. The leading female *'ulama* of Iran today, as few as they are, are products of the pre-revolutionary decentralized seminary culture rather than the extensive post-revolutionary apparatus put in place by the state.[66]

IV. CONCLUSIONS

Few states invest as much in religious education today as Iran does. Remarkably, the Islamic Republic reserves these investments not to men, but from the beginning has included women's institutions in the religious education sector. In fact, Iran today has the largest network of religious seminaries for women in the entire Muslim world, a fact that increasingly attracts also foreign students from other parts of the Shi'ite world and beyond. Since the 1979 revolution, and in particular since Ayatollah Khamenei became Supreme Leader in 1989, the state has exerted great efforts at regulating the Shi'ite seminaries and at gradually incorporating them into a growing sector of state-administered religious education.

What lies at the basis of the state's efforts to bureaucratize the Shi'ite seminaries? While Khomeini had used state resources to silence critics and sideline competitors, he in principle supported the independence of the men's religious seminary system. Under his successor Khamenei, the policies towards the religious seminaries have radically shifted. What was limited initially to a modernization campaign of teaching methods and materials in order to render the *howzeh*s a more attractive alternative to a secular education, has resulted in an unprecedented level of state encroachment upon the men's seminaries, motivated mostly by Khamenei's pursuit of the centralization of power and management, but in particular nourished by his (realistic) concern that his strongest rivals inhabit the *hozwzeh*s.

As far as women's religious education is concerned, Khomeini, to the initial surprise of many observers, fully supported it. He made state resources available for the first women's *howzeh* to open its doors in 1984 and to give women access to a full *howzeh* education similar to that offered in the men's seminaries. In that system,

64 Mahdi Jami and Mahdi Kalji, *Az Shahr-e Khoda ta Shahr-e Donya, Sad Sal Tahavol dar Houzey-e Qom* (trans.: From the City of God to the Earthly City [!], A Hundred Years of Transition in the Ḥawza in Qom) (n.d.), 4.

65 Farhangi, 'Tabligh-e Jame'at al-Zahra'', Nameh-ye Jame'a,.

66 Künkler and Fazaeli (n. 47).

women could strive to attain the same qualifications as their male colleagues. His successor Khamenei, by contrast, has exhibited a rather instrumental view on women's religious education. In full awareness of the fact that women can become authoritative interlocutors in debates around legal reform only if fully trained in *ejtehad*, he has cut the qualifying cycle from the women's curriculum and replaced it with a specialization in family law (*feqh-e khanevadeh*). Overall, the focus of the women's curriculum has shifted from jurisprudence to ethics and practical applications. Most significantly, because only the state offers women's religious education, women cannot seek to acquire the needed expertise elsewhere in the country. (For men, a variety of alternatives still exist to supplement a state-controlled *howzeh* education with private lessons in less monitored spaces.) What women gained in this particular field under Khomeini, they lost under his successor.

The result of Khamenei's reforms in the women's religious education sector has been an exponential increase in quantity with a decrease in quality. While every small town today features a religious *madrasa* in which women can learn about their religion, the highest levels of learning, which would qualify one to partake in discourses around legal reasoning and the interpretation of religious law, are not offered. Without that expertise, women can become neither experts in most realms of law – a requirement for most advanced jobs in the public sector that are reserved for the clergy – nor can they emerge as authoritative Shiʿite scholars.

What makes this development even more dramatic for those women truly interested in becoming experts or scholars of Islamic law and jurisprudence is that the Islamic Republic has bureaucratized women' religious education *exclusively*. Before the revolution, women could usually attend the lectures of the Qom teachers and thus learn *dars-e kharej* (the highest level of learning) from a variety of grand ayatollahs and in all fields. Since the expansion of the sector of women's *madrasas* under Khamenei and the limit of *dars-e kharej* to family law, the path to be trained in *ejtehad-e motlaq* (absolute *ejtehad*) as opposed to *ejtehad-e mutajazzi* (fragmented, partial *ejtehad*) has been closed off.

Can the bureaucratization of religious education in Iran be viewed as a form of depoliticization, a motif that often lies at the basis of processes of the regulation of religion? The standardization of curricula, the narrowing of pedagogical content to regime-approved subjects and methods and the centralization of admissions and examination procedures, is not so much geared at depoliticization as it is to ensure that debate and contestation on the basis of religion remain within officially defined discursive spaces.

10

Managing Religious Competition in China

Regulating Provisions of Charitable Activities by Religious Organizations

Jianlin Chen and Loveday J. Liu

I. INTRODUCTION

The contemporary movement to apply the concept of regulation beyond the traditional confines of economic market activities and to encompass a variety of activities such as family, charity, education, and of course, religion is certainly welcome.[1] With regard to the realm of religion in particular, scholarly inquiry into the wide array of regulatory techniques and the profound impacts these state actions exert on complex dynamics among religious institutions, adherents, and the broader society adds important nuances beyond the conventional dichotomous assessment as to whether religious liberty is infringed.[2] Yet whereas this expansion to ostensibly noneconomically motivated activities rightly shines the spotlight on noneconomic values that underpin regulatory choices,[3] it also implicitly treats regulation of such activities as distinct from conventional regulation of the economic/financial market.

[1] Robert Baldwin, Martin Cave, and Martin Lodge, "Introduction: Regulation – the Filed and the Developing Agenda," in Robert Baldwin, Martin Cave, and Martin Lodge (eds.), *Oxford Handbook of Regulation* (Oxford University Press, 2010), 5–6. For a good discussion as to how the approach to labor law in Australia was reconceived into labor market regulation, and the consequential expansion of inquiry beyond employer-employee relationships and formal legal institution, see generally Andrew Frazer, "Reconceiving Labour Law: The Labour Market Regulation Project," *Macquarie Law Journal* 8(2008), 21.

[2] For example, Ofrit Liviatan, "Faith in the Law: The Role of Legal Arrangements in Religion-Based Conflicts Involving Minorities," *Boston College International and Comparative Law Review* 34(2011), 53, 58–9; Robin C. A. White and Clare Overy, *The European Convention on Human Rights*, 5th edn (Oxford University Press, 2010), 315–32, 409–18; Nicholas Gibson, "Faith in the Courts: Religious Dress and Human Rights," *Cambridge Law Journal* 66.3 (2007), 662–79.

[3] Mike Feintuck, "Regulatory Rationales Beyond the Economic: In Search of Public Interest," in Robert Baldwin, Martin Cave, and Martin Lodge (eds.), *Oxford Handbook of Regulation* (Oxford University Press, 2010), 51–6. Cf. Michael Hantke-Domas, "The Public Interest Theory of Regulation: Non-Existence or Misinterpretation?" *European Journal of Law and Economics* 15 (2003), 165, 186–8 (tracing the intellectual history of the "public interest" as a justification for regulation in the United Kingdom and United States and observes that the concept has been used as a vehicle to realize political and moral values).

Drawing on the Law and Religious Market theory,[4] this chapter utilizes the case study of China to first, explain how regulation of ostensibly noneconomically motivated activities (e.g., religion and charity) can be properly conceived as a form of market regulation and, second, how such a conception can add a valuable dimension to the discourse. In particular, this chapter situates China's regulation of charitable activities by religious organizations in the context of recent major legal reform on charity law and highlights the contradictory treatment where, on one hand, the law recognizes the self-interested motivation of participants and donors of charitable activities and accommodates their co-opting of charitable activities to promote or advance commercial interests but, on the other hand, specifically prohibits religious organizations from any religious propagation during provisions of charitable services. This chapter argues that from the perspective of market regulation, such denial of religious "self-interest" hampers the purported policy objectives of promoting greater religious participation in charitable activities but may be justified on the grounds that it promotes religious competition that is normatively desirable.

This chapter is organized into six parts. Part II introduces the religious-economic model that posits the process in which individual religious choices are akin to decisions-making processes in other realms of human activities. Part II further explains how law may be properly conceived as regulation on religious competition (i.e., the methods by which religions may retain and compete for adherents) and the corresponding normative implications on the regulation of religious activities.

The next two parts lay out the case study. Part III outlines the religious demographics and the underlying constitutional and general legal framework of law and religion in China, observing in particular the heavy-handed state control on religious affairs. Part IV examines the Opinions on Encouraging and Regulating Religious Participation of Charity Activities[5] in the the broader context of the newly enacted landmark Charity Law.[6]

Part V applies the insights of Part II to the case study and argues that whereas the Charity Law has embraced the notions that regulation of charitable activities can and should be approached as a form of market regulation, religion should continue to be treated as sui generis to the detriment of policy objectives. Nonetheless, analysis of how the prohibition of religious propagation in provisions of charitable services would impact religious competition reveals that such prohibition may be normatively justified either because such prohibition can steer religions to compete more in the spiritual and theological dimension by limiting the avenues (here being

[4] Jianlin Chen, *The Law and Religious Market Theory: China, Taiwan and Hong Kong* (Cambridge University Press, 2017).

[5] 关于鼓励和规范宗教界从事公益慈善活动的意见 [Opinions on Encouraging and Regulating Religious Participation of Charity Activities] (promulgated February 16, 2012, effective February 16, 2012) (P. R. C.).

[6] 慈善法 [Charity Law] (promulgated March 16, 2016, effective September 1, 2016) (P. R. C.).

charitable services) in which religions can readily translate economic advantages into religious competitiveness or because such prohibition neutralize wealth disparity among religious organizations that are caused by extrinsic factors (e.g., macroeconomic policies). Part VI concludes.

II. LAW AS (RELIGIOUS) MARKET REGULATION

This part draws on the Law and Religious Market theory developed by the first author as a monograph[7] and discusses the legal implications and normative insights that may be garnered from the religious economic model.

A. *Religious Choice under the Religious Economic Model*

The instinctive objection to approaching regulation of religion as market regulation is that it presupposes a religious market (or market for religion), which in turn equates religious choice as ordinary consumer/commercial decisions. This seems implausible, no less given that scholarly research (and perhaps the general public as well) tends to treat religion as a somewhat elusive and mystifying phenomenon.[8] However, the emergence of the religious economic model, an interdisciplinary fusion of sociology and economics, challenges this conventional view and instead treats religious adherents as individual actors *making decisions* concerning religion (e.g., choice of religion and level of participation) in a manner akin to other decisions, namely, to *maximize one's utility*.[9] Thus, a *successful religion* under the model will be one that *for one reason or another*, manages to *more effectively* retain its followers and attract new adherents as compared to its competitors (whether religious or nontheological ideologies).

Some elaboration is inevitably warranted to properly flesh out the numerous complexities and nuances of this economic model, especially for phrases highlighted with underlined italic font that are subjected to common misconceptions.

First and foremost is the assumption of rationality underpinning the "*making decisions . . . to maximize one's utility*" component. This fundamental assumption of economics is controversial, to put it mildly. Yet although there is understandable disquiet at the apparent reduction of the intensely sacred and spiritual matter of religion to mere consumption choices, conventional economic literature has never treated "utility" (and the economic notions of "benefit" and "cost") as simply about

7 Chen (n. 4).

8 James A. Beckford, "The Insulation and Isolation of the Sociology of Religion," *Sociological Analysis* 46.4 (1985), 347, 348, 350; Raymond Firth, "Spiritual Aroma: Religion and Politics," *American Anthropologist* 83.3 (1981), 582, 584.

9 Larry Witham, *Marketplace of the Gods: How Economics Explains Religion* (Oxford University Press, 2010), 12–13; Anthony Gill, *The Political Origins of Religious Liberty* (Cambridge University Press, 2008), 28–31.

monetary and/or pragmatic considerations.[10] "Utility" could well include anything from superficial pleasure, emotional support from a caring network, to profound spiritual fulfillment and sincere divine epiphany.[11] Indeed, research on consumer decisions has revealed consumers may be driven by ethical and other nonmaterialistic concerns[12] in an often complex and elusive cognitive process.[13]

Second, "success" is conceived under the religious economic model as essentially market share – a "*successful religion*" is either dominant in the relevant market (i.e., a solid majority) or is growing faster in relation to other competitors. It is a description of a positive fact without any normative implications per se, whether regarding the merits of the religions or the veracity of its truth claims. More importantly, it does not presume the "success" to be consciously intended. Sociological studies of religions around the globe have frequently reported how religions tend to adopt core characteristics that coincide with the prevailing preferences of the society they operate in, be they theological teachings[14] or methods of worship.[15] Whereas religious leaders are rational actors like the religious adherents they serve and may consciously modify religious doctrines and practices to attract and retain adherents,[16] such modification could well be adopted based on pure theological reasoning without any conscious assessment of its "market impact." Indeed, the same is true for the commercial sphere. Commercial success may be attained in the absence of a conscious profit motive. For example, a restaurant may attain huge popularity and high profitability simply because of its owner's dedicated pursuit of culinary excellence and creativity.[17]

10 Richard A. Posner, *Economic Analysis of Law*, 8th edn (Aspen, 2011), 15–16; Stephen J. Spurr, *Economic Foundations of Law*, 2nd edn (Routledge, 2010), 2–4.

11 Hsing-Kuang Chao, "Conversion to Protestantism among Urban Immigrants in Taiwan," *Sociology of Religion* 67.2 (2006), 193, 196; Joseph B. Tamney, "A Study of Spiritual Involvement," *Sociological Analysis* 27.3 (1966), 146, 150–4.

12 C. B. Bhattacharya and Sankar Sen, "Doing Better at Doing Good: When, Why, and How Consumers Respond to Corporate Social Initiatives," *California Management Review* 47.1 (2004), 9–10; Eleonora Curlo, "Marketing Strategy, Product Safety, and Ethical Factors in Consumer Choice," *Journal of Business Ethics* 21.1 (1999), 37, 40.

13 James R. Bettman, Mary Frances Luce, and John W. Payne, "Constructive Consumer Choice Processes," *Journal of Consumer Research* 25.3 (1998), 187, 207–9.

14 For example, evolving theological teachings and church practices over homosexuality in more liberal parts of the Western world: Allen D. Hertzke, Laura R. Olson, Kevin R. den Dulk, and Robert Booth Fowler, *Religion and Politics in America: Faith, Culture, and Strategic Choices*, 4th edn (Westview Press, 2010), 38–9.

15 For example, the three most successful religions (Pentecostals, Catholic Charismatics, and African diasporan groups) in Latin America share the "common marquee product of pneumacentrism" and the provision of faith healing: R. Andrew Chesnut, *Competitive Spirits: Latin America's New Religious Economy* (Oxford University Press, 2003), 152–4.

16 See also Evelyn Bush, "Explaining Religious Market Failure: A Gendered Critique of the Religious Economies Model," *Sociological Theory* 28.3 (2010), 304, 319–21 (using the case study of the prevalence of patriarchal religions despite the higher religiosity of women to argue for more emphasis to the supply side aspect of the religious economy).

17 Silviya Svejenova, Carmelo Mazza, and Marcel Planellas, "Cooking Up Change in Haute Cuisine: Ferran Adrià as an Institutional Entrepreneur," *Journal of Organizational Behavior* 28.5 (2007), 539, 540–4.

Third, the religious economic model does not reject the existence of divinity and supernatural forces. It is true that sociological research on religious conversions has confirmed the salience of pragmatic and mundane considerations in many religious choices.[18] Such considerations could include economically valuable assistance[19] and a desire to conserve and increase one's social capital[20] or threats of sanctions and violence.[21] Nevertheless, reflecting the "*for one reason or another*" component, "success" in the religious market could well be due to direct divine interventions (e.g., sudden and miraculous "conversion" of an individual)[22] or indirect contributions to religious competitiveness (e.g., through providing financial wealth, electoral success, or military victory).[23]

B. *Law and Religious Market*

Once the concept of religious market is established, it does naturally follow that one function of law will be to regulate the interactive dynamics among the religious leaders and religious adherents or – put more simply – religious competition. This "market regulatory" function of law vis-à-vis the religious market can be perhaps best appreciated through examination of what would occur if there were zero legal restraints on religious competition. Notably, what would emerge is not the idealized portrayal of religious "free competition" where "each [religious group] flourishes according to the zeal of its adherents and the appeal of its dogma."[24] Instead, it is the

18 Barry A. Kosmin and Ariela Keysar, *Religion in a Free Market* (Paramount Market Publishing, 2006), 4; R. Laurence Moore, *Selling God: American Religion in the Marketplace of Culture* (Oxford University Press, 1994), 10.

19 Paul Harvey, "Proselytization," in Philip Goff and Paul Harvey (eds.), *Religion and American Culture* (University of North Carolina Press, 2004), 44; Grace Y. Kao, "*The Logic of Anti-proselytization, Revisited*," in Rosalind I. J. Hackett (ed.), *Proselytization Revisited: Rights Talk, Free Markets and Culture Wars* (Equinox, 2008), 79.

20 Rodney Stark and Roger Finke, *Acts of Faith: Explaining the Human Side of Religion* (University of California Press, 2000), 118–19.

21 See Michael Crowley, "Iraq's Eternal War," *Time* 183.25 (2014), 18, 20–23 (discussing the religious conflicts in Iraq involving the violent and oppressive Islamic State of Iraq and Greater Syria).

22 Fenggang Yang, "Lost in the Market, Saved at McDonald's: Conversion to Christianity in Urban China," *Journal of the Scientific Study of Religion* 44.4 (2005), 423, 433–4.

23 For example, Tamer El-Ghobashy and Maria Abi-Habib, "Shitte 'Soldiers of God' Color Tikrit Battle," *Wall St. Journal* (March 13, 2015), A6 (observing how Shitte fighters attribute their relatively easy military victory against ISIS to their religious faith); Yunfeng Lu, Byron Johnson, and Rodney Stark, "Deregulation and the Religious Market in Taiwan: A Research Note," *The Sociological Quarterly* 49.1 (2008), 139, 143 (discussing the perceived efficacy in granting the wishes of worshippers is an important factor in the success of Chinese folk temples in Taiwan).

24 *Zorach v. Clauson*, 343 U.S. 306, 313 (1952) ("We sponsor an attitude on the part of government that shows no partiality to any one group and that lets each flourish according to the zeal of its adherents and the appeal of its dogma."). This phrase has subsequently become a popular reference phrase by academics: e.g., Jorge O. Elorza, "Secularism and the Constitution: Can Government Be Too Secular?" *University of Pittsburgh Law Review* 72 (2010), 53, 56 n. 4; Mary Ann Glendon and Raul F. Yanes, "Structural Free Exercise," *Michigan Law Review* 90 (1991), 477, 544. See Jianlin Chen, "Deconstructing the Religious Free Market," *Journal of Law, Religion State* 31(2014), 11–22 (discussing

unpleasant history where religious growth is frequently associated with military conquest, imperial expansion, and colonization.[25] This should not be surprising. Sound doctrines and meaningful practices do attract converts but pale in comparison with how coercive faith conversion under threat of death can rapidly swell the ranks of adherents[26] or the brutally efficient eradication of religious competitors through extermination of their adherents, whether directly intended or as an inevitable consequence of conquest.[27]

Fortunately, there is now near universal consensus that military conquest and violence or force should not be a component of religious competition. This in turn drives the enactment of human rights protecting religious liberty and international law denouncing religious violence.[28] Where such legal instruments are effectively enforced,[29] the religious market is affected in two different ways.

First is redistribution. Religions with superior military prowess thrive in the absence of legal prohibition of religious violence. This superior military could be attributed to theological outlooks that are conducive to developing military capabilities[30] but may also reflect extraneous factors such as technologically advanced weaponry.[31] Regardless, legal prohibition will deprive these religions of this potent means of gaining adherents while at the same time benefitting religions

how the different interpretations and combinations of legal components such as definition of religion, Establishment Clause, and Free Exercise, can materially affect the resulting religious market).

25 Ninian Smart, *The World's Religions: Old Traditions and Modern Transformations* (Cambridge University Press, 1989), 490–99, 532–48. See Richard Blake, *Religion in the British Navy, 1815–1879* (Boydell Press, 2014), 156–86 (discussing the range of passive and active manner in which the British navy was involved in the Christian mission and the spread of Christian influence in the British colonies).

26 Gordon A. Christenson,"Liberty of the Exercise of Religion," *Transnational Law and Contemporary Problems* 21 (2013), 721, 728–9; Monica Duffy Toft, "Getting Religion? The Puzzling Case of Islam and Civil War," *International Security* 31.4 (2007), 97, 106–7.

27 For example, the disastrous reduction of native Latin America population by the Spanish Conquistadores through de facto slavery and diseases: Smart (n. 25), 533. See M. D. Litonjua, "Religious Zealotry and Political Violence in Christianity and Islam," *International Review of Modern Sociology* 35.2 (2009), 307, 312–13 (discussing how paganism and heresies in medieval Christendom are wiped out by extermination).

28 H. Victor Condé, "Protection of Religious Freedom under International Humanitarian Law and International Human Rights Law in Times of Armed Conflict," *University of California Davis Journal of International Law and Policy* 5 (1999), 95, 102–7; Leo Gross, "The Peace of Westphalia, 1648–1948," *American Journal of International Law* 42.1(1948), 20, 22–7.

29 Unfortunately, there continued to be many instances where that's the case: Afghanistan: Amalendu Misra, "The Taliban, Radical Islam and Afghanistan," *Third World Quarterly* 23.23 (2002), 577, 580–85; Sudan: Toft (n, 26) 117–24; Iraq: Crowley (n. 21), 20–23.

30 Toft (n. 26), 111. See also El-Ghobashy and Abi-Habib (n. 23) (noting how the Shitte reinforcements in the military success against ISIS are religiously motivated, no less by a fatwa that promised paradise for martyrs in battle).

31 Borzou Daragahi, "Surface Change in Iraq's Politics Allows Deep Wounds to Fester," *Financial Times* (London, September 8, 2014), 2; Peter Marsden, *The Taliban: War and Religion in Afghanistan* (Zed Books, 2002), 46–60.

that are either theologically averse to physical violence or otherwise lacking in military capabilities.

Second, and more important, is pressure or incentive to change. Where military conquest is a permissible form of religious competition, there will be considerable pressure on all religions to respond to this military competition. This may result in reluctant engagement in combat and warfare[32] or even modification of theological doctrines to accommodate participation in military activities.[33] For adherents who unwaveringly uphold their pacifist religious teachings, their responses remain heavily constrained by military competition – either death or flight.[34] Regardless, the final outcome will be a religious market dominated by religions that at least partially orient toward military competition. Walter Russell Mead pertinently observed that "[i]n the modern Middle East, the minorities that have survived, and in some cases thrived, have acquired a military capacity. The Jews, the Kurds, the Armenians, the Maronites and the Druse have not all created states, but they have all built redoubts."[35] Conversely, cultivation of military capabilities is not a common trait for religions operating in regimes where military competition has been legally excluded, as in the case of most modern societies.[36]

C. *Regulating Religious Competition*

This insight of how law (or the absence thereof) has a pervasive influence in shaping the outcome of the religious market introduces a new dimension when examining regulation of religion, namely how law affects religious competition. This new inquiry entails two broad components.

The first component is to identify the impact of the particular piece of regulation on religious competition. This process will encompass the existing examination as to explicit preference and discrimination of specific religions and, more commonly, the overlooked (or at times, insidiously intended)[37] disparate impact of regulation on religions. In addition, and more importantly, this process will investigate how

32 Carolyn Fluehr-Lobban, "Religion, War, and Peacemaking in Sudan: Shari'a, Identity Politics, and Human Rights," in D. S. Timothy (ed.), *Between Terror and Tolerance: Religious Leaders, Conflict, and Peacemaking* (Georgetown University Press, 2011), 109–10.

33 Jennifer Graber, "Mighty Upheaval on the Minnesota Frontier: Violence, War, and Death in Dakota and Missionary Christianity," *Church History* 80.1 (2011), 76, 102–6; John C. Super and Briane K. Turley, *Religions in World History: The Persistence of Imperial Communion* (Routledge, 2006), 103–6.

34 See Harold S. Bender, "The Pacifism of the Sixteenth Century Anabaptists," *Church History* 24.2 (1955), 119, 119–22 (discussing the Anabaptists' insistence of nonviolence in an era of bloody religious conflicts, and the consequent large-scale martyrdom).

35 Walter Russell Mead, "The Plight of the Christians," *Wall St. Journal* (May 16–17, 2015), C1.

36 Andrew Koppelman, "And I Don't Care What It Is," *Pepperdine Law Review* 39 (2013), 1115, 1129 (noting how the criminal law prohibition of violence has rendered religions that "violently crush nonadherents" to be "nearly extinct in the contemporary United States").

37 Gregory C. Sisk, "How Traditional and Minority Religions Fare in the Courts: Empirical Evidence from Religious Liberty Cases," *University of Colorado Law Review* 76 (2005), 1021, 1039; William

regulation affects or alters the precise manner in which religion may compete for adherents. As noted in the previous section, legal prohibition of religious violence removes the military dimension of religious competition. As will be discussed in Part V. B, laws regulating the extent to which religious content may be included in provision of social services is in fact also a regulation on the economic aspect of religious competition. In addition to providing a more nuanced factual account, such identification will facilitate the confronting and discussion of the often overlooked normative question as to whether such a market outcome is actually desired.

The second component is to build on the concern of unintended consequences illuminated in the first component and evaluate the efficacy of such regulations of religious competition. In this regard, the conceptualization of regulation of religion as market regulation facilitates the application of economic analysis to account for considerations such as externality, market failure, initial entitlements, and so on.[38] This process is not necessarily fundamentally different from the normative assessments that are undertaken by more conventional discourse. For example, the issue of externality reflects the conventional analysis as to whether the restraints on religious activities are justified by legitimate and sufficiently compelling public interests.[39] Nonetheless, the economic analysis can provide important refinement and a more holistic assessment. As will be again discussed in Part V.B, the economic inquiry of externality will be triggered even in the absence of any restrictions, given the recognition that regulatory choice includes no state intervention, whereas inquiry as to market failure can identify new circumstances where public interests are implicated.

More fundamentally, appreciating the market regulatory functions of laws related to religions enables a more synchronized and consistent treatment of religious activities with other spheres of activity. As will be elaborated as follows in Part V. A, a major breakthrough of the Chinese charity law reform is the due recognition that the seemingly altruistic endeavors of charitable activities are often motivated by self-interest and that facilitating the realization of such self-interest can help attain the underlying policy objective of developing a more robust charity sector. However, this recognition remains conspicuously absent for religion, where the regulatory push for greater religious involvement in provisions of social services fails to acknowledge, let alone accommodate, the religious "self-interest" of propagating faith and teachings.

R. Hutchison, *Religious Pluralism in America: The Contentious History of a Founding Ideal* (Yale University Press, 2003), 52–4.

38 Cento Veljanovski, "Economic Approaches to Regulation," in Robert Baldwin, Martin Cave, and Martin Lodge (eds.), *Oxford Handbook of Regulation* (Oxford University Press, 2010), 19–27; Joseph E. Stiglitz, "Government Failure vs Market Failure: Principles of Regulation," in Edward J. Balleisen and David A. Moss (eds.), *Government and Markets: Toward a New Theory of Regulation* (Cambridge University Press, 2009), 25–32.

39 Liviatan (n. 2), 58–9; Alastair Mowbray, *Cases and Materials on the European Convention on Human Rights*, 2nd edn (Oxford University Press, 2007), 595–621.

III. SOCIAL AND CONSTITUTIONAL BACKGROUND ON STATE AND RELIGION IN CHINA

A. *Religious Landscape*

There are no precise statistics as to the religious demographic in China given how substantial portions of religious activities are conducted in manners and venues that are not legally authorized.[40] According to the Pew Research Center's 2012 global survey of religious groups, the estimated distribution of the Chinese population as of 2010 was as follows: unaffiliated (52.2%), Chinese folk religions (21.9%), Buddhism (18.2%), Christianity (5.1%), Islam (1.8%), and other religion (1%).[41] By comparison, the Chinese Spiritual Life Survey, a large-scale national survey involving 7,021 respondents and conducted in 2006–2007, found the distribution to be "none" (77.1%), Buddhism (18.1%), Christianity (2.7%), Taoism and Confucianism (0.8%), Islam (0.2%), and other/don't know (1.1%).[42] The divergence may be explained by the potential underreporting of Christians who might participate in technically illegal underground or "house" churches and of Chinese religions adherents who might engage in related Chinese folk religious practices and be considered as religious by Western observers but nevertheless reported no religious affiliations.[43]

An important characteristic of the Chinese religious landscape is the uneven distribution of religious adherents across the country. This is most salient in regions with high concentrations of ethnic minorities, as religious belief is often one of the most important facets of the ethnic minorities' group self-identification. In these regions, the religions closely associated with an ethnicity (e.g., Tibetan Buddhism for Tibetans, Islam for Uighurs and Huis, and Theravāda Buddhism for the Dai ethnicity) may constitute the majority religion in those regions.[44] Other notable regional concentrations of religions include Chinese folk religions in coastal regions in Southeast China[45] and Christianity in the city of Wenzhou.[46] As will be discussed

40 Liu Peng, Brett G. Scharffs, and Carl Hollan, "Constitutional, Legislative and Regulatory Change Regarding Religion in China," in W. Cole Durham, Silvio Ferrari, Cristiana Cianitto, and Donlu Thayer (eds.), *Law, Religion, Constitution* (Ashgate, 2013), 258.

41 Pew Research Center, *The Global Religious Landscape* (2012), 46.

42 Zhao Jianmin, *Religion and Law in China* (Wolters Kluwer, 2014), 18–23; Rodney Stark and Eric Y. Liu, "People's Republic of China: Religions and Churches Statistical Overview 2011," *Review of Religious Research* 52.3 (2011), 282, 286.

43 Katharina Wenzel-Teuber, "People's Republic of China: Religions and Churches – Statistical Overview 2011," *Religions & Christianity in Today's China* II (2012), 29–54; Stark and Liu (n. 42), 284.

44 Zhiebin Xie, *Religious Diversity and Public Religion in China* (Ashgate, 2006), 72–3; Thomas Borchert, "Of Temples and Tourists: The Effects of the Tourist Political Economy on a Minority Buddhist Community in Southwest China," in Fenggang Yang and Joseph B. Tamney (eds.), *State, Market, and Religions in Chinese Societies* (Brill, 2005), 97.

45 Xie (n. 44), 72.

46 Nanlai Chao, *Constructing China's Jerusalem, Christians, Powers and Place in Contemporary Wenzhou* (Stanford University Press, 2011), 1–2.

in Part V.B.2, this uneven distribution coincides with the wealth disparity among different regions in China and implicates how law should regulate the economic dimension of religious competition.

B. Constitutional and Legal Framework

Like most constitutions in the world, including that of the former Soviet Union,[47] the P.R.C. Constitution includes an express provision that proclaims that "[c]itizens of the People's Republic of China enjoy freedom of religious belief."[48] As per the constitutional provision, this right of religious freedom has two components. First, the freedom from compulsion (whether by state or private entities) in terms of religious beliefs (or the lack thereof), and second, no discrimination (whether by state or private entities) on the basis of religious beliefs (or the lack thereof).[49] The same constitutional provision also imposes two qualifiers. First, only "normal religious activities" are protected by the state, and second, there shall be no foreign domination of religious affairs.[50]

Religious activities are heavily regulated under the auspices of the two qualifiers. Only state-prescribed national religious organizations representing the five major religions of Buddhism, Taoism, Catholicism, Protestantism, and Islam are officially allowed.[51] The state is heavily involved in the personal appointment and overall management of these state-sanctioned religious organizations[52] and does cause the religious organizations to adapt their religious teachings in accordance with the prevailing political imperatives.[53] Indeed, religions are exhorted to be compatible with socialism.[54]

47 John N. Hazard, William E. Butler, and Peter B. Maggs, *The Soviet Legal System*, 3rd edn (Oceana Publications, 1977), 90–4, 603.

48 Article 36, 宪法[Constitution] (2004) (P.R.C.).

49 Ibid., Article 36(2) ("No state organ, public organization or individual may compel citizens to believe in, or not to believe in, any religion; nor may they discriminate against citizens who believe in, or do not believe in, any religion.").

50 Ibid., Articles 36(3) and (4) ("The state protects normal religious activities. No one may make use of religion to engage in activities that disrupt public order, impair the health of citizens or interfere with the educational system of the state. // Religious bodies and religious affairs are not subject to any foreign domination.").

51 Ping Xiong, "Freedom of Religion in China under the Current Legal Framework and Foreign Religious Bodies," *Brigham Young University Law Review* (2013), 605, 607; Fenggang Yang, "The Red, Black, and Gray Markets of Religion in China," *Sociological Quarterly* 47.1 (2006), 93, 103–4.

52 Karrie J. Koesel, *Religion and Authoritarianism: Cooperation, Conflict, and the Consequences* (Cambridge University Press, 2014), 45–7; Zhao (n. 42), 18–51.

53 Zeng Chuanhui, "*Coalition and Hegemony: Religions" Role in the Progress of Modernization in Reformed China*," *Brigham Young University Law Review* (2011), 759, 774–5.

54 According to the official explanation, compatibility with socialism consists of a political commitment to "passionately love the country," "support the socialism institution," and "support the leadership of the Communist Party" and does not entail the abandonment of theistic beliefs or religious faith: ¶ 22–7, 宗教工作政策要点 [Key Points on Religious Work Policies] (promulgated March 22, 1996, effective March 22, 1996) (P.R.C.). Sociological fieldwork has also suggested that ostensible but

Building on this narrow scope of recognized religious organization is the ominously vague stipulation that only "normal religious activities" are protected. There is no direct definition of what is normal in the constitution or in other laws. Commentators frequently highlight this undesirable ambiguity that grants broad discretionary power to the administrative agency regulating religious activities,[55] including possibly stipulating that any religious activities not conducted at a legally registered religious site may be deemed as not "normal religious activities."[56] This qualifier has supported various legal sanctions against cults and superstitions.[57]

IV. SOCIAL AND CHARITABLE SERVICE PROVISIONS BY RELIGIOUS ORGANIZATIONS

A. *Background*

Religious organizations have traditionally provided important social welfare functions ranging from health care to education.[58] This is of great importance and generally welcome by the state in the premodern world[59] and remains important amid the growth of the welfare state (i.e., states are increasingly the providers of social services) and the expansion of the regulatory state (i.e., states increasingly regulate the provision of social services)[60] given how some studies have suggested that religious organizations may perform the task better than the government.[61]

superficial acknowledgment of political loyalty and affirmation of political ideology is sufficient for government officials: Jianbo Huang and Fenggang Yang, "The Cross Faces the Loudspeakers: A Village Church Preserves under State Power," in Fenggang Yang and Joseph B. Tamney (eds.), *State, Market, and Religions in Chinese Societies* (Brill, 2005), 50–1.

55 Richard Klein, "An Analysis of China's Human Rights Policies in Tibet: China's Compliance with the Mandates of International Law Regarding Civil and Political Rights," *ILSA Journal of International and Comparative Law* 18 (2011), 115, 133–4; Zhang Qianfan and Zhu Yingping, "Religious Freedom and Its Legal Restrictions in China," *Brigham Young University Law Review* (2011), 783, 791.

56 Lawrence Cox, "Freedom of Religion in China: Religious, Economic and Social Disenfranchisement for China's Internal Migrant Workers," *Asian-Pacific Law and Policy Journal* 8 (2007), 370, 383–4.

57 Article 300, 刑法 [Criminal Law] (promulgated March 14, 1997, effective October 1, 1997, amended February 25, 2011) (P.R.C.). For academic discussion of the criminalization of cult in China, see Guobin Zhu, "Prosecuting 'Evil Cults:' A Critical Examination of Law Regarding Freedom of Religious Belief in Mainland China," *Human Rights Quarterly* 32 (2010), 471, 488–91. See Adam Yuet Chau, "The Politics of Legitimation and the Revival of Popular Religion in Shaanbei, North-Central China," *Modern China* 31.2 (2005), 236, 243–5 (observing the evolving understanding of superstitious activities by the state).

58 Kosmin and Keysar (n. 18), 9; Witham (n. 9), 189–90.

59 Frederick B. Bird, "A Comparative Study of the Work of Charity in Christianity and Judaism," *Journal of Religious Ethics* 10.1 (1982), 144, 163; Frederic Siedenburg, "The Religious Value of Social Work," *American Journal of Sociology* 27.5 (1922), 637, 642–5.

60 Barbra Mann Wall, *American Catholic Hospitals: A Century of Changing Markets and Missions* (Rutgers University Press, 2011), 106; Laurence E. Lynn, Jr., "*Social Service and the State: The Public Appropriation of Private Charity*," *Social Service Review* 76.1 (2002), 58, 65–6.

61 Patrick M. Garry, *Wrestling with God: The Court's Tortuous Treatment of Religion* (Catholic University of America Press, 2006), 153.

In the context of China, the dominance of the state in all aspects of societal life, especially prior to the market reforms in the 1980s, meant that the state is often the primary and sole provider of social services to the population, especially in urban areas.[62] Market reform was successful in stimulating rapid economic growth in the subsequent decades but at the expense of aggravating social and economic inequalities and exposing the deficiencies of the state bureaucracies in meeting the social service needs and demands of population.[63] The fast-aging population – a legacy of the now curtailed one-child policy – further exacerbates the stress on state-managed social service providers. This has contributed to the shift of government policy to permit and encourage greater roles for nonstate entities in the provision of social service providers since the turn of the century.[64]

B. "Encouragement" of Religious Participation in Charity Activities

An integral component of this shift is the Opinions on Encouraging and Regulating Religious Participation of Charity Activities enacted in 2012.[65] This is an important policy document jointly promulgated by six first-tier State Council departments and ministries: Administration for Religious Affairs, United Front Work Department of the CPC Central Commission, National Development and Reform Commission, Ministry of Civil Affairs, Ministry of Finance, and State Administration of Taxation.[66] The Opinions recognize the increasing social tension arising from economic and social transition and how charitable activities by religious organizations are useful components of the development of the Chinese charitable sector, especially given the "deep faith foundation, the long historical tradition, and the higher public credibility" associated with religiously affiliated charitable work.[67]

In terms of specifics, the Opinions set out two categories of measures to encourage greater provision of charitable services by religious organization. First, the Opinions guarantee the enjoyment of state financial support and other preferential policies (e.g., income tax and custom duty exemptions or reductions) for charitable services provisioned by religious organizations.[68] Second, and more significantly, the

62 Weiming Jing and Weiming Tian, 经济转型中的市场社会主义-国外马克思主义的分析与实践检验 [*Market Socialist in the Economic Transition: The Analysis and Practical Examination from Foreign Marxist*] (Economic Management Publishing, 2009), 202–6.

63 Rebecca Lee, "Modernizing Charity Law in China," *Pacific Rim Law and Policy Journal* 18.2 (2009), 347.

64 Jia Xiaoyan and Rong Yichuan, "新中国慈善立法的基调演变：以慈善组织为切入点的分析 [The Evolution of Tone about Charity Legislation of New China: The Analysis of Charitable Organization]," *Hebei Law Science* 32.8 (2014), 69, 71–2.

65 Opinions on Encouraging and Regulating Religious Participation of Charity Activities.

66 For a concise discussion about different types of legislative and regulatory documents, see Albert Chen, *An Introduction to the Legal System of the People's Republic of China*, 4th edn (LexisNexis, 2011), 143–50.

67 Article 1, Opinions on Encouraging and Regulating Religious Participation of Charity Activities.

68 Ibid., Article 6.

Opinions stipulate the permissible avenues in which religious organizations may engage in charitable work. Beyond direct donation (of monies and goods) or setting up a charitable or nonprofit organizations as per existing laws and regulations on such organizations, religious organizations are now expressly allowed to set up charitable projects within the religious organization or premises, henceforth avoiding the need for further registration.[69]

These supports are accompanied by certain restrictions as to the conduct of charitable services. There are the standard exhortations as to the need for accountability and transparency in management to ensure effective delivery of charitable services and avoid abuses and fraud.[70] More relevant to this chapter are the two restrictions specifically tailored to religious organizations, namely the prohibitions against imposition of mandatory levies and fund-raising quotas on adherents in the name of conducting charitable activities[71] and the ban on any religious propagation in the conduct of charitable activities.[72] The normative implications of these measures will be analyzed in the next part. At this juncture, it is simply worth noting this prohibition reflects the general suspicion of the state as to proselytization, both as matter of general principle[73] and in the context of social services provisions. This is particularly salient in the realm of education, an otherwise popular manifestation of social services for religious organizations in other jurisdictions.[74] The Chinese constitutional provision of religious freedom, like the Soviet constitution,[75] explicitly prohibits religious interference with education.[76] Legislation relating to education correspondingly mandates the separation of religion and education,[77] even for private schools.[78] Indeed, all forms of proselytization are prohibited in all schools,

69 Ibid., Article 4.

70 Ibid., Articles 6(3) and 6(4).

71 Ibid., Article 6(2).

72 Ibid., Article 6(1).

73 Francesca Tarocco, "Pluralism and its Discontents: Buddhism and Proselytizing in Modern China," in Juliana Finucane and R. Michael Feener (eds.), *Proselytizing and the Limits of Religious Pluralism in Contemporary Asia* (Springer Science+Business Media, 2014), 245; Ellen S. Reinstein, "Turn the Other Cheek, or Demand an Eye for an Eye? Religious Persecution in China and Western Response," *Connecticut Journal of International Law* 20 (2004), 1, 12.

74 Stephen C. Berkwitz, "Religious Conflict and the Politics of Conversion in Sri Lanka," in Rosalind I. J. Hackett (ed.), *Proselytization Revisited: Rights Talk, Free Markets and Culture Wars* (Equinox, 2008), 204; Robbie B. H. Goh, "Mission Schools in Singapore: Religious Harmony, Social Identities, and the Negotiation of Evangelical Cultures," in Lai Ah Eng (ed.), *Religious Diversity in Singapore* (Institute of Southeast Asian Studies, 2008), 365–6; Wolfgang Gabbert, "Social and Cultural Conditions of Religious Conversion in Colonial Southwest Tanzania 1891–1939," *Ethnology* 40.4 (2001), 291, 299–300.

75 Hazard, Butler, and Maggs (n. 47), 603.

76 Article 36, Constitution.

77 Article 8, 教育法 [Education Law] (promulgated March 18, 1995, effective September 1, 1995, amended December 27, 2015) (P.R.C.).

78 Article 4, 民办教育促进法 [Non-state Education Promotion Law] (promulgated December 28, 2002, effective September 1, 2003, amended November 7, 2016) (P.R.C.).

regardless of whether the proselytization is by staff, students, or other private individuals.[79]

C. New Charity Law: A New Watershed?

The legal reform of the charity sector was furthered by the enactment of the Charity Law in 2016. The legislative purpose of the Charity Law was meant to resolve the existing deficiencies and to facilitate further growth of the charitable sector.[80] In response to such an ambitious scheme, alongside an unmistakably encouraging policy direction, the law provides a regulatory framework that is much more open-minded and comprehensive in comparison with the previous regulations.

First, the law lowers the entry barrier for the charity sector. For the registration of a charitable organization, the law not only gives a clear, exhaustive list of requirements but also sets up the application procedures straightforwardly, leaving little room for the discretionary interventions that commonly plagued Chinese bureaucracy.[81] More importantly, an inclusive, open-ended definition is provided for entities eligible for conducting charitable activities,[82] and at the same time social organizations that are not registered as charitable under the law can still carry out charitable activities "within their capabilities."[83] This overall lowering of the bar addresses the reality that in China, many civil entities devoted to charity purposes are not recognized as legal persons,[84] and in granting them an independent locus for conducting charitable activities, the law will not only give them greater freedom and incentives but on the whole can also attract more resources into the charitable sector. Apart from the more accessible entry previously mentioned, the law also recognizes a wide range of activities that can be engaged in, including the more controversial ones such as the establishment and management

79 ¶16, 关于进一步加强和改进大学生思想政治教育的意见 [Opinions on Further Strengthening and Improving Moral and Political Education for University Students] (promulgated August 26, 2004, effective August 26, 2004) (P.R.C.); chapter 2(2), 关于深化改革加快发展民族教育的决定 [Decisions on Further Reform and Accelerating Development of National Education] (promulgated July 7, 2002, effective July 7, 2002) (P.R.C.).

80 Legal Committee of the Standing Committee of the National People's Congress, 关于《中华人民共和国慈善法（草案）》的说明 [*Explanatory Note on the Charity Law Draft*] (2015).

81 Articles 11–12, Charity Law.

82 Ibid., Articles 3 and 5. According to such a definition, all "natural persons, legal persons *and other organizations*" can now conduct charitable activities.

83 Ibid., Article 111.

84 Typically, many social organizations with religious background in China are not recognized as legal persons, and are thus unable to carry out charitable activities in their own names. See Liu Peng, "宗教法人设立刍议 [On Establishing Religious Legal Person Identity]," in Zhuo Xinping (ed.), 宗教与中国当代社会 [*Religion and Contemporary Chinese Society*] (Social Science Academic Press, 2013), 62–9.

of charitable trusts, and at the same time lowers the bar for certifying charitable activities.[85]

Second, a whole chapter of the law is devoted to outlining the benefits that participants of charitable activities are entitled to, including tax incentives,[86] use of land,[87] financial support in the form of governmental purchase of service,[88] and so forth. Although one cannot turn a blind eye to the many readily observable problems with the provisions, such as the full discretion left to the regulator for the implementation of many benefit-conferring provisions,[89] the chapter still has an important signal effect and the potential to be of more material impact.

Third, as a significant departure from the prior dominant emphasis on state regulatory supervision and administrative control on charitable sector,[90] there is an expansion of the legal rights of both the donors and recipients and enhancement of the obligation of public disclosure and accountability. For example, the donors, when making donations to charitable organizations, may – through a legally enforceable charitable agreement – specify the intended recipients for the donated funds or goods and also enjoy the right to inspect information relating to the management of the donated property.[91] In turn, the charitable organizations and/or recipients may compel the donor through court actions to fulfill the promise of charity donation.[92] Notably, these charitable agreements and other arrangements between the donor and recipient are subjected to the obligation to provide relevant information to the public, such as where there is linkage of charitable donations with commercial activities[93] or where the donor is unable to fulfill the promise of charitable donations because of a change in circumstances,[94] among other general disclosure obligations in relation to finance and operations of charitable organizations.[95] As will be elaborated in Part V.A, these provisions represent a reconceptualization of the charity sector as a charity market and the Charity Law, at least partly, as a form of market regulation.

85 In comparison with the draft, the Law added a requirement of public accessibility to its definition of charitable activities, but concomitantly affirms that urban and rural communal organizations as well as work units (*danwei*) can carry out mutual help activities within the organization. Also, permission from the civil affairs department in charge is not a prerequisite for carrying out charitable activities. For a more specific example, may refer to Article 23 (the article provides that even for public fund raising conducted outside the place of registration of the charitable organization, what is required is mere report filing, instead of seeking administrative permission beforehand).

86 Articles 79–82, Charity Law.

87 Ibid., Article 85.

88 Ibid., Article 87.

89 For example, many of the provisions start with ambiguous terms such as "the state encourages," "the state shall take action," or "the government may."

90 Jia and Rong (n. 64), 74–5.

91 Articles 40 and 42, Charity Law.

92 Ibid., Article 41.

93 Ibid., Article 37.

94 Ibid., Article 41. Interestingly, the donor must report to both the Civil Affairs bureau and the public.

95 Ibid., chapter 8.

V. IMPLICATIONS FROM THE MARKET REGULATION PERSPECTIVES

A. *Disparate Recognition of Rationality*

The significance of the first-ever dedicated legislation on charity in China has naturally attracted much scholarly and public discussion of the matter. Most reflect the general consensus that this is a step in the right direction while separately identifying areas of ambiguity[96] and/or highlighting various areas in need of further reform.[97] Some pieces engage more deeply into the possible paradigm shift, such as the possible transformation of desired public ethics[98] or whether the various facilitating measures should be properly conceived as regulatory in nature instead of industry support policies.[99]

In this regard, there is a strand of discourse that is particularly relevant for this chapter. Chinese scholars have been advocating a more market-based approach toward regulating the Chinese charitable sector and have opined that this shift is reflected in the Charity Law provisions on tax incentives, public accountability, and rights of recipients of charitable donations.[100] These provisions, especially the latter two, are certainly consistent with approaching the Charity Law as a market regulation. Through reducing the information costs associated with monitoring and evaluating charitable organizations and enhancing the incentives (i.e., legal remedies) for such monitoring and evaluation, these provisions sought to co-opt the

96 For example, Su Yanjie, "《慈善法》实施背景下的慈善促进政策落实研究 [Research on Implementing the Charity Promotion Policy under the Charity Law]," *Social Governance Review* 9 (2016), 59, 60–1 (noting the ambiguity and problems of implementing policies of charity promotion that remains ambiguous despite the Charity Law); Xi Ling, "浅议我国新《慈善法》立法评析 [Legislative Analysis of New Chinese Charity Law]," *Legality Vision* 4 (2016), 61, 63–5 (analyzing the legal rights and corresponding enforcement mechanisms newly created by the Charity Law).

97 For example, Wang Siying and Niu Yan, "《慈善法》对中国慈善信托与家族财富传承的作用分析 [Analysis of the Impact of Charity Law on China's Charitable Trust and Family Wealth Legacy]," *Journal of the Lanzhou Institute of Education* 33 (2017), 160–1 (discussing how the new Charity Law has enhanced the ease and effectiveness of charitable trust, and positive impact on use of charitable trust to manage wealth); Xi Ling, 浅议我国新《慈善法》立法评析 [*Legislative Analysis of New Chinese Charity law*], *Legality Vision* 7 (2016), 278 (praising the Charity Law but also noting areas such as transparency of charitable expenditure, privacy rights of beneficiaries which require further situation).

98 Wang Zhengyao and Tian Xiaohong, "慈善法与公共伦理转型 [Charity Law and Transformation of Public Ethics]," *Administration Reform* 7 (2016), 21, 23–4.

99 Hu Minjie, "《慈善法》中的政府促进措施：支持抑或管理 [Promotion Measures in Charity Law: Support or Regulate]," *Jianghuai Tribune* 4 (2016), 16, 18–20.

100 Yu Jianzhong, "构建市场在慈善资源配置中充分发挥作用的法治机制 [Designing a Legal Regime that Facilitate Market Allocation of Charitable Resources]," *China Civil Affairs* 11 (2015), 32–3; Zhang Qilin, "慈善组织间接商业行为之法律规制 [Legal Regulations on Indirect Commercial Acts by Charitable Organizations]," *Jianghuai Tribune* 4 (2016), 10, 14; Xu Huitan, "《慈善法》：不完美的里程碑 [Charity Law: An Imperfect Milestone]," *China Philanthropist* 12 (2015), 34, 38–9.

distinct choices of donors and charitable organizations in enhancing the effectiveness and efficiency of operations in the charitable sector.[101]

However, there is one aspect of the Charity Law that has received little attention but that is an integral component of the charity market approach: namely the recognition and accommodation of the donor's profit motive. Chinese academic commentators have frequently observed that a key breakthrough of the Charity Law is the lowering the costs of charity through crystallization of tax incentives and reduction of regulatory burdens.[102] Yet the Charity Law also includes several provisions that enhance the "benefits" of charitable donation. The most significant is Article 40, which expressly prohibits the use of charitable donations to promote tobacco and any other products of which promotion is prohibited by general law. This exclusionary prohibition clause by necessary implication allows for promotion of products that do not fall into the stipulated categories. Indeed, this legislative appreciation that an enterprise may have a strong incentive to utilize charitable activities as a publicity tool over and beyond general enhancement of the corporate image[103] is echoed in Article 36, which expressly envisaged that a donor may be donating its own enterprise products.[104] Similarly, Article 37 authorizes donors linking their charitable and commercial activities (e.g., performance or sales) to a pledge to partially donate the proceeds for charitable purposes.[105] Notably, whereas such co-opting of charitable activities to achieve publicity and promote commercial purposes has not been explicitly prohibited in the past, such acts by commercial entities do attract significant public controversies amid the ambiguity because of legal lacuna.[106] At a more fundamental level, this represents a departure from the prior approach, which adopted a "pure" conceptualization of public interest that entails the complete exclusion of private benefits.[107]

101 Jia and Rong (n. 64), 74–5.

102 Zhang Biao and Liu JingLing, "民营企业慈善捐赠，市场发展与财务绩效 [Charitable Donations, Market Development and Profitability of Private Enterprises]," *Friends of Accounting* 1 (2017), 70; Hu (n. 99), 16–17.

103 For a discussion as to the possible motives for corporate donations, see Shuo Wang, Yuhui Gao, Gerard P. Hodgkinson, Denise M. Rousseau, and Patrick C. Flood, "Opening the Black Box of CSR Decision Making: A Policy-Capturing Study of Charitable Donation Decisions in China," *Journal of Business Ethics* 128(2015) 665, 666–7; Adrian Sargeant and Kathryn Crissman, "Corporate *Giving in Australia: an Analysis of Motives and Barriers*," *Australian Journal of Social Issues* 41.4 (2006), 477, 479–81.

104 The provision imposed on the donor the obligations as to product liability "in accordance with law." For an analysis, with examples, of how corporate in-kind donations may be used to promote commercial self-interest, see Jacqueline Ferguson, Pamela Hurd-Knief, and Marlene McGuirt, "In-Kind Giving: It's a Good Thing . . . But Don't be Naïve," *Fund Raising Management* 29.6 (1998), 30, 31–2.

105 The provision requires that a donation agreement must been signed with the entities receiving the donation, and to publicly disclose what had actually been donated.

106 Zu Jin, "慈善组织间接商业行为之法律规制 [Legal Regulations on Indirect Commercial Acts by Charitable Organizations]," *Journal of Shandong Police College* 148 (2016), 70, 71; Yu Wan and Huang Qian, "掐"大头"捐零头，一些企业借"慈善"敛财 [Claim Big Donate Little, Some Enterprise Profiting Under Guise of Charity]," *Policy Research and Exploration* 5 (2016), 74.

107 Ma Jinfang, "通过私利的公益保护 [Protecting Public Interest Through Private Interest]," *Tribune of Political Science and Law* 34(3) (2016), 60, 64–6.

This is a welcome move that better reflects the reality of charitable giving. The various disciplines of social sciences have confirmed that philanthropy is far from a simplistic act of altruism or morality and is in fact motivated by a multitude of social, psychological, and of course, economic factors.[108] Indeed, even the understanding of charity as an altruistic behavior does not contradict the core economic assumption of utility maximization rationality, as many people do derive genuine emotional satisfaction (i.e., utility) from assisting others.[109] This recognition not only enables charitable organizations to better design strategies and techniques of soliciting donations[110] but is also instrumental in the development of appropriate regulatory measures and support policies for the charitable sector.[111] At the very least, a calibrated accommodation of the self-interested motives of the participants (be it donor or charitable organizations) will be immensely helpful in achieving the policy objectives of expanding the scope and scale of charitable activities.[112]

This recognition for the general charitable sector can be contrasted with provision of social services by religious organizations in which there is a strict blanket prohibition of the inclusion of any religious propagation. Charity is an integral component in the teachings of many religions.[113] Yet whereas it is typical for such acts of kindness and caring to be regarded in most religious teachings as manifestations of religious morals, some religions, especially those that emphasize evangelism, add a further theological dimension to charitable activities by explicitly conceiving charitable works as a missionary endeavor.[114] Moreover, even

108 For a good discussion as to egoistic, altruistic and mixed motivations behind charitable giving, see Arnold Dashefsky and Bernard Lazerwitz, *Charitable Choices: Philanthropic Decisions of Donors in the American Jewish Community* (Lexington Books, 2009), 11–16; Neeli Bendapudi, Surendra N. Singh, and Venkat Bendapudi, "Enhancing Helping Behavior: An Integrative Framework for Promotion Planning," *Journal of Marketing* 60.3 (1996), 33, 40–43. See also Amihai Glazer and Kai A. Konrad, "A Signaling Explanation for Charity," *American Economic Review* 86.4 (1996), 1019–21 (discussing how – in light of the data indicating the paucity of anonymous donations – charitable donations are often motivated by donor's desire to signal status).

109 Leonard Ray, "Why We Give: Testing Economic and Social Psychological Accounts of Altruism," *Polity* 30 (1998), 383, 393–5; Jerome C. Wakefield, "Is Altruism Part of Human Nature? Toward a Theoretical Foundation for the Helping Professions," *Social Service Review* 67.3 (1993), 406.

110 For example, Gerben Hardeman, Xavier Font, and Jeroen Nawijn, "The Power of Persuasive Communication to Influence Sustainable Holiday Choices: Appealing to Self-benefits and Norms," *Tourism Management* 59(2017), 484, 485–6; Katherine White and John Peloza, "Self-Benefit versus Other-Benefit Marketing Appeals: Their Effectiveness in Generating Charitable Support," *Journal of Marketing* 73.4 (2009), 109, 110–11.

111 Dashefsky and Lazerwitz (n. 108), 125–38.

112 At present, charitable donations constitute about 0.02% of GDP, which pale in comparison with the 2% of those in the United States. Another divergence is the proportion of corporate and individual donation. In China, more than 70% of donation originate from commercial enterprises, in contrast with 75% from individual in the United States: Zhang (n. 100), 12.

113 Bird (n. 59), 164–6.

114 James Leiby, "Charity Organization Reconsidered," *Social Service Review* 58.4 (1984), 523, 530; Martin E. Marty, "Social Service: Godly and Godless," *Social Service Review* 54.4 (1980), 463, 468–9.

nonproselytizing religions are not blind to the effectiveness of charitable works as a means to reach out to and/or retain adherents.[115]

The refusal to allow religious organizations to further their religious "self-interest" of expanding their flock will inevitably dampen the incentives of religious organizations to devote valuable resources and effort to the provision of charitable services, thereby undercutting the purported policy objectives of encouraging greater religious involvement in the provision of charitable and social services. This directly undercuts the policy objectives of the Opinions to co-opt religious organizations to fill the gaps in social services, no less given its recognition that charitable services provided by or affiliated with religious organizations enjoyed "higher public credibility." In any event, there is a glaring inconsistency whereby commercial entities are free to promote their products and businesses in their engagement in charitable activities, but religious organizations cannot spread their religious beliefs in the same process.

B. Beyond Religious Freedom and Toward a "Better" Religious Market

Whereas the failure to apply the same recognition of self-interest to religious organizations' participation in charitable services is arguably a failing in terms of promoting development of the charitable market, it is worth examining the impact of this regulatory restriction on the religious market.

Conventional discourse will prima facie view such measures as undue restriction of religious liberty,[116] especially where the prohibition of religious propagation is applicable even when the religious organizations are not receiving any state subsidies for the provision of charitable services.[117] While not disputing the legitimacy of such critiques, this chapter applies the Law and Religious Market theory and argues that the prohibition may generate potentially beneficial impact on religious competition, namely reducing the salience of economic resources in religious competition and thereby facilitating religious competition that is more spiritually and theologically oriented.

1. Money, Charity, and Conversion

Charitable services can be a potent avenue for religions to spread their faith. Through providing valuable aid and other material assistance, a religious

[115] Susan K. McCarthy, "Serving Society, Repurposing the State: Religious Charity and Resistance in China," *The China Journal* 70 (2013), 48, 55; Moore (n. 18), 273.

[116] Michael D. Waggoner, "Negotiating the New Commons in Religion and Education," in Michael D. Waggoner (ed.), *Religion in the Public Schools* (Rowman & Littlefield Education, 2013), 9–12 (discussing the reaction toward the judicial prohibition of Bible in public schools in the United States).

[117] Helen Rose Ebaugh, Janet Saltzman Chafetz, and Paula F. Pipes, "The Influence of Evangelicalism on Government Funding of Faith-Based Social Service," *Review of Religious Research* 47.4 (2006), 380, 381.

organization can gain access to communities that may otherwise be unreceptive or even hostile to such overtures.[118] The religious organizations may even mandate participation in their religious activities as a prerequisite for receiving the charitable services.[119] The effectiveness of charitable services as a tool of proselytization naturally hinges on the quality of the charitable services provided. Without discounting how religiously inspired dedication and passion may materially improve the delivery of charitable services, financial resources remain a key determinant as to the quality of charitable services, especially in settings such as education and health care, wherein professional (and expensive) expertise is an indispensable component of the services. On a more basic level, religious organizations cannot escape from the realities of the economic sphere where, aside from volunteered services that nonetheless tend to lack stability and expertise,[120] they must procure the desired goods, services, and other resources via the currency of money.

Under such circumstances, a legal regime that freely allows religious propagations and religious content in the provision of charitable services will be highly advantageous for wealthy religious organizations, and the converse is true as well.[121] More importantly, as noted in Part II.B, the selected legal regime will exert corresponding pressure on how religious organizations approach the economic dimension of their activities. Where religious organizations are legally permitted to utilize the provision of charitable services to actively gain new adherents, all religious organizations will have strong incentives to raise sufficient funds to sustain such charitable operations, if only to ensure that there are available alternatives to their adherents so they are not exposed to religiously infused charitable services of rival religions.[122]

2. The Appropriate Regulation for Religious Competition?

From the perspective of regulating religious competition, the question of whether economic superiority should be one of the key factors in a religion's success in the religious market – and thus normatively justifying the corresponding legal regime on

118 Christopher R. Duncan, "Untangling Conversion: Religious Change and Identity among the Forest Tobelo of Indonesia," *Ethnology* 42.4 (2003), 307, 311–13.

119 Sam Wong, "Gendering Religious Capital: A Case Study of Female Mainland Chinese Migrants in Hong Kong," in Niamh Reilly and Stacey Scriver (eds.), *Religion, Gender, and the Public Sphere* (Routledge, 2014), 50; Harvey (n. 19), 44; Kao (n. 19), 79.

120 Priscilla S. Wisner, Anne Stringfellow, William E. Youngdahl, and Lenore Parker, "The Service Volunteer – Loyalty Chain: An Exploratory Study of Charitable Not-for-Profit Service Organizations," *Journal of Operations Management* 23.2 (2005), 143, 144–5; Aubrey Wilson and Gina Pimm, "The Tyranny of Volunteer: The Care and Feeding of Voluntary Workforces," *Management Decision* 34.4 (1996), 24.

121 Jianlin Chen, "Money and Power in Religious Competition: A Critique of the Religious Free Market," *Oxford Journal of Law and Religion* 3.2 (2014), 212, 223–4.

122 Robert P. Weller, "Within and Beyond the Market: Religions, Moralities, and Philanthropies in Chinese Societies," in Jonathan B. Imber (ed.), *Markets, Morals & Religion* (Transaction Publishers, 2008), 241–2.

permissible religious content in charitable services – requires resolution of two key questions.

The first is the fundamental issue of what kind of religion the state hopes, as matter of public policy consideration or otherwise, to emerge as a winner in the religious market. This could be based on theological factors, as per the blood-stained history of religious oppression and policing of doctrinal purity[123] that continues to reflect in the not uncommon practice of state establishment of certain religions.[124] For the specific scenario of regulating religious content in charitable services, the more common and also far-reaching is the dimension of religious competition – should religious competition be based primarily on spiritual and theological reasons? The Law and Religious Market theory highlights the importance of recognizing and confronting this otherwise overlooked question. Nonetheless, the theory does not predicate any particular solution per se, no less because resolution of the question requires engagement with deep philosophical and moral considerations that are beyond the scope of economic analysis. Still, at this juncture, it suffices to point out that where the sacred status of religious liberty is often justified by the perceived moral, emotional, and spiritual benefit of religion both to an individual and society at large,[125] economic competitiveness is at best irrelevant and likely inconsistent with the proffered reasons for advancing religious liberty. Indeed, religious practices that are seemingly outdated and incompatible with the prevailing economic circumstances may facilitate more effective pursuit for spiritual truth – another common justification for religious liberty[126] – precisely because of its renunciation of materialism.[127]

123 For example, Medieval Inquisition; see Carole A. Myscofski, "The Magic of Brazil: Practice and Prohibition in the Early Colonial Period, 1590–1620," *History of Religion* 40.2 (2000), 153; Margaret Mott, "The Rule of Faith over Reason: The Role of the Inquisition in Iberia and New Spain," *Journal of Church and State* 40(1998), 57.

124 David S. Law and Mila Versteeg, "The Declining Influence of the United States Constitution," *NYU Law Review* 87 (2012), 762, 805 (noting that the Establishment Clause is a relatively rarity in the world, with the separation of church and separation appearing in one-third of the current constitutions around the world). The practice is normatively controversial: Julia L. Ernst, "Rethinking the Validity of State Religions: Is Antiestablishmentarianism a Fundamental Prerequisite for the Protection of Religious Rights under International Human Rights Law?" *Northern Illinois University Law Review* 34 (2014), 333, 384–8 (arguing for the abolishment of state religions as a principle of international law while acknowledging that people who hold religious beliefs remained free to influence government policies and/or become members of government). The European Commission on Human Rights has found that establishment of a state religion is not a per se violation of religious freedom: Russell Sandberg, *Law and Religion* (Cambridge University Press, 2011), 67.

125 Andrew Koppelman, "Corruption of Religion and the Establishment Clause," *William & Mary Law Review* 50(2009), 1831, 1907; Steven H. Shiffrin, "The Pluralistic Foundations of the Religion Clauses," *Cornell Law Review* 90(2004), 9, 57.

126 Daniel O. Conkle, "Religious Truth, Pluralism, and Secularization: The Shaking Foundations of American Religious Liberty," *Cardozo Law Review* 32 (2011), 1755, 1757–62; William P. Marshall, "Truth and Religion Clauses," *DePaul Law Review* 43 (1994), 243, 255–60.

127 For example, see David A. Palmer, "Gift and Market in Chinese Religious Economy," *Religion* 41.3 (2011), 1, 15–16 (discussing from a sociological perspective the example of a Taoist's otherworldly

The second is consideration of initial entitlements and extrinsic factors that may distort religious competition. Restrictions on certain avenues that may otherwise translate economic superiority to religious competitiveness may still be normatively desirable even where the state has decided, after robust debate and careful deliberation, that the economic dimension should be a desired part of religious competition.[128] Akin to how reasons why a commercial firm gains dominance in a market implicate the corresponding applications of antitrust law,[129] such restrictions may be justified on the basis that they seeks to neutralize the impact of initial entitlements that are acquired under normatively suspect conditions, such as through colonial imposition.[130] Religions that otherwise have teachings, doctrines, and practices that are conducive to the generating financial wealth[131] may still struggle to economically outcompete religions that possess tremendous resources as part of a colonial legacy. In the specific context of China, there is concern that wealth disparity of religious organizations is driven by the economic policies that dictate uneven economic development between the rural and urban and between the coastal and western-central regions.[132] Such financial advantages are again largely extrinsic to religious practices and doctrines but can nevertheless be influential to the outcome of religious competition.[133] Moreover, given that wealth disparity is particularly salient for religions associated with ethnic minorities who typically inhabit these poorer regions, regulations to dampen the economic dimension of religious competition are arguably helpful to alleviate the emerging social fault lines

religious practices that renders him improvised in terms of material wealth and religious market share).

128 One possible justification is that religious doctrines should be constantly evolving in tandem with the broader social and economic circumstances: Keith N. Hylton, Yulia Rodionova, and Fei Deng, "Church and State: An Economic Analysis," *American Law and Economics Review* 13.2 (2011), 402, 407; Kosmin and Keysar (n. 18), 4.

129 Federico Etro, *Competition, Innovation, and Antitrust: A Theory of Market Leaders and Its Policy Implications* (Springer Science+Business Media, 2007).

130 Tong Chee Kiong, "*Religious Trends and Issues in Singapore*," in Lai Ah Eng (ed.), *Religious Diversity in Singapore* (Institute of Southeast Asian Studies, 2008), 34–5; Prince Sorie Conteh, *Traditionalists, Muslims, and Christians in Africa* (Cambria Press, 2009), 94.

131 For example, some religions may encourage savings, emphasize education, and promote other "economic-friendly" attitudes: Robert D. Woodberry, "Pentecostalism and Economic Development," in Jonathan B. Imber (ed.), *Markets, Morals & Religion* (Transaction Publishers, 2008), 165–7; Luigi Guiso, Paola Sapienza, and Luigi Zingales, "Does Culture Affect Economic Outcomes?," *Journal of Economic Perspectives* 20.2 (2006), 23, 38. Regular tithing is also arguably an efficient and effective way of collecting and consolidating financial resources: Joy Kooi-Chin Tong, "Religious Experience of a Young Megachurch Congregation in Singapore," in Michael Bailey and Guy Redden (eds.), *Mediating Faiths: Religion and Socio-Cultural Change in the Twenty-First Century* (Ashgate, 2009), 168.

132 Jongsung Kim, "Income Inequality in China," *Journal of East Asian Affairs* 24.2 (2010), 29, 33–5; Albert Keidel, "Chinese Regional Inequalities in Income and Well-Being," *Review of Income & Wealth* 55.1 (2009), 538, 542.

133 Nanlai Cao, "In the World but Not of the World: Governing Grassroots Christian Charity in China," in *Charities in the Non-Western World: The Development and Regulation of Indigenous and Islamic Charities* (Routledge, 2013), 187–8 and 192–9.

of class and ethnicity in China,[134] if only as a form of transitional measure before the regional wealth disparity is mitigated by ongoing economic reform.[135]

VI. CONCLUSION

Viewed from the general trend of Chinese legislative reforms since the early 1990s, the new Charity Law is consistent with the ever increasing embrace of market dynamics – and the corresponding conception of laws as market regulation – as a way of understanding and managing social activities. Religion, in contrast, is seemingly the final frontier. Drawing from the Law and Religious Market theory, this chapter's examination of China's regulation of charitable activities by religious organizations highlights how conceiving law affecting the religious activities as market regulation is crucial to appreciate the profound influence of law in the outcome of religious competition and the corresponding normative implications on regulatory design. In addition, this insight is instrumental to ensure broader policy objectives involving the intersection of religion and other sectors not unduly impeded by inconsistent treatment between religion and other forms of human activity.

At the end of the day, that religion – or for that matter, charity – can be analyzed through the same economic assumption of rationality should ultimately not be surprising. After all, they are all undertaken by the same human beings. Same, same but different.[136]

[134] Xiaofei Kang, "Two Temples, Three Religions, and a Tourist Attraction: Contesting Sacred Space on China's Ethnic Frontier," *Modern China* 35.3 (2009), 227, 239 (discussing how Tibetan Buddhists lack funds to construct their own monastery in a bid to increase their religious presence at a religiously sacred site in Sichuan province, in contrast with Han Buddhism, which can draw on donations from wealthy coastal regions).

[135] Kim (n. 134), 46–7.

[136] Jenny Sue Kostecki-Shaw, *Same, Same but Different* (Henry Holt and Co., 2011) (a children's book about the uncanny similarities of the life of two boys despite the ostensibly different environment of America and India where they are respectively from).

PART III

Challenges to State Regulation

11

Regulating Religion through Administrative Law

Religious Conversion in Malaysia beyond Fundamental Rights

Matthew Nelson[*] *and Dian A. H. Shah*

I. INTRODUCTION

As a basic human right, the notion of religious freedom – including the right to choose and change one's religion – is often associated with complex procedural requirements tied to specific forms of state recognition. This administrative link between religious identity and state recognition is particularly important where a change in religion affects one's relationship with related religious laws or institutions (e.g., privileged access to religious education or benefits). The balance between a fundamental right to religious self-identification and the administrative procedures surrounding state recognition raises challenging questions. When do administrative procedures amount to an excessive burden and, thus, a violation of one's fundamental rights? What role should states have when individuals decide to change their religious identification?

Cases of religious conversion are often complex. On the one hand, conversion is tied to religious profession as a fundamental right. On the other, conversion often involves forms of state recognition with all of the administrative requirements this entails: "formal" applications to change one's religion, notarized declarations, detailed paperwork, bureaucratic discretion, and so on. These hurdles move beyond the question of religious profession to include a range of questions about the *manifestation* of one's religious identity within the public realm.

Human rights advocates typically describe the right to profess a specific religion or belief (religious self-identification) as absolute.[1] This is the *forum internum* aspect of one's right to religious freedom (a right to belief in the private realm) as opposed to the *forum externum* aspect – a right to manifest one's belief through public practice

* Both authors thank the participants of the Regulating Religion Workshop held at the National University of Singapore Faculty of Law (December 16–17, 2015) for their comments.

1 Nurjaanah Abdullah, "Legislating Faith in Malaysia," *Singapore Journal of Legal Studies* (2007), 264, 274. See also Manfred Nowak, *U.N. Covenant on Civil and Political Rights: CCPR Commentary* (N. P. Engel, 1993).

and expression.[2] This distinction is evident in numerous international human rights instruments such as the International Covenant on Civil and Political Rights (ICCPR) and the Universal Declaration of Human Rights (UDHR), both of which provide that matters of public manifestation may be subject to constraints established by law. The disagreement, however, relates to what a proper limit to religious manifestation might be. With respect to the *forum internum* aspect, scholars such as Manfred Nowak have argued that the private practice of one's religion (whether individually or with others) cannot be restricted.[3] But even this has not been completely straightforward – even in jurisdictions that guarantee a constitutional right to religious freedom. Constraints are frequently imposed on one's individual right to choose one's religion, including administrative requirements that constitute a regulatory barrier to the state's recognition of one's (ostensibly private) choice. We focus on this latter aspect of state regulation – the introduction of administrative procedures that underpin a state's *recognition* of religious identity.

Administrative procedures are ubiquitous in cases of religious recognition. But what counts as a "reasonable" administrative burden? In this chapter, we argue that administrative and procedural burdens figure as an inevitable feature of state recognition. However, we also argue that, within this realm, questions regarding the "reasonableness" of procedures – in effect, questions that lie at the heart of any effort to understand the *operationalization* of religious freedom – are historically and politically contingent. The operationalization of a fundamental right to religious freedom, in other words, differs from place to place owing to different standards framing the parameters of "reasonable" administrative procedures.

To demonstrate our arguments, we examine the famous religious-conversion case of *Lina Joy* in Malaysia.[4] In this case, historically and politically contingent notions of administrative "reasonableness" emerged as a crucial variable in the state-based operationalization of religious liberty. But our argument is not confined to Malaysia. It extends to Jews in London, Christians in the United States, and many other contexts.[5] In all of these cases, the question is similar: when do the administrative procedures associated with a state's recognition of religious identity amount to an "unreasonable" infringement on that identity and, thus, a violation of fundamental rights? Is there any universal standard to answer such questions?

It is important to stress that registration requirements pertaining to religious identity are not uncommon. Aside from the Malaysian, American, and British cases we discuss, focusing on individual religious identity, a study of 153 states with

[2] See M. Todd Parker, "The Freedom to Manifest Religious Belief: An Analysis of the Necessity Clauses of the ICCPR and the ECHR," *Duke Journal of Comparative and International Law* 17.1 (2006), 91 and Anat Scolnicov, *The Right to Religious Freedom in International Law: Between Group Rights and Individual Rights* (Routledge, 2011).

[3] Parker, ibid. (quoting Nowak [n. 1], 319).

[4] *Lina Joy v. Majlis Agama Islam Wilayah & Anor* [2007] 4, *Malayan Law Journal* 585.

[5] See, e.g., *Burwell v. Hobby Lobby Stores, Inc.* [2014] 573 U.S.; *R v. The Governing Body of JFS* [2009] UKSC 15.

constitutional guarantees pertaining to freedom of worship revealed that 42 percent impose some form of registration requirement with reference to religious groups.[6] Indeed, among those that constitutionalize a "separation" of religion and state, fully 86 percent enforce laws concerning religious registration.[7]

In *Lina Joy*, claims of administrative "unreasonableness" pertaining to religious self-identification were related to the state's insistence that, before it could recognize the identity of a Muslim-to-Christian convert named Lina Joy, Joy would have to complete a series of procedures that did not yet exist. This administrative burden struck many as unreasonable. Yet, for richly contextualized reasons deeply rooted in Malaysia's constitutional and legal history (specifically concerning the bodies that might be charged with defining the relevant policies and administrative procedures underpinning the possibility of state recognition), this procedural burden was judged to be "reasonable."[8] Briefly, Malaysia's Federal Court insisted that specific procedures grounded in deeply contextualized notions of administrative "reasonableness" need not imply a total denial of constitutionally protected religious liberty. In fact, the chief justice who delivered the Federal Court's majority decision did not categorically reject the possibility of a Muslim's renunciation of Islam; he merely suggested that any person seeking to leave the religion must follow the relevant procedures for doing so.[9] In short, the chief justice noted that religious freedom was protected so long as each actor – bureaucratic officials, elected representatives, and private citizens – followed the rules set out in Malaysia to create (and adhere to) relevant procedures. In Joy's case, the chief justice merely suggested that, once Joy had fulfilled the procedures to renounce Islam and the relevant Islamic authorities had "authorized" her apostasy, she could embrace the religion of her choice.[10]

To locate the importance of historically contingent notions of administrative "reasonableness" within the literature regarding religious freedom and human rights, this chapter offers a close reading of one case – the case of *Lina Joy* – in three parts. Part I describes the legal, political, and administrative landscape of Malaysia as this relates to issues of religious conversion away from Islam, drawing special attention to Malaysia's federal structure and its dual court system involving (a) a hierarchy of civil courts (stretching up to the Malaysian Federal Court) as well as (b) a hierarchy of state-level shari'ah courts overseen by state-level sultans who function as the constitutional Heads of Islam in their respective states. Beyond this dual court system, some attention is also paid to the constitutional limits faced by Malaysia's state-level shari'ah courts (in terms of their punitive jurisdiction) and,

6 Jonathan Fox and Deborah Flores, "Religions, Constitutions, and the State: A Cross-National Study," *Journal of Politics* 41.4 (2009), 1499, 1509.

7 Ibid., 1510.

8 *Lina Joy* (n. 4), 607–8.

9 Ibid., 618.

10 Ibid., 612.

since 1988, the jurisdictional limits faced by Malaysia's civil courts vis-à-vis their review of judgments pertaining to shari'ah.

Politically, the role of state-level statutory enactments seeking to highlight the terms of Islamic law in matters of Muslim apostasy will also be discussed, along with the role of Malaysia's Department of Islamic Development, or JAKIM (Jabatan Kemajuan Islam Malaysia), within the Malaysian Prime Minister's Office. With support from JAKIM, several Malaysian states have adopted broadly similar administrative procedures pertaining to Muslim personal law, including marriage, divorce, and conversion *to* Islam. This push in the direction of national standards, however, has not affected conversions *away* from Islam. In fact, different Malaysian states continue to address the issue of Muslim apostasy in different ways, with some – including the Federal Territories in which the case of *Lina Joy* emerged – failing to address it at all. As a constitutional, political, and administrative matter, this is the policy-based procedural lacuna that shaped the fundamental rights of Lina Joy.

Part II provides a detailed reading of *Lina Joy*, highlighting the ways in which Joy's lawyers and the Federal Court opted to set aside the language of fundamental rights in favor of a specific focus on the administrative procedures whereby Joy's religious identity was to be officially recognized. Particular attention will be paid to the policy-based lacuna mentioned earlier and, within this, the legal view that expecting Joy to complete a set of as-yet-non-existent forms could be seen as administratively "reasonable."

Part III examines the literature regarding this lacuna in more detail. Joy herself suggested that, when officials based in Malaysia's National Registration Department (NRD) refused to delete the word "Islam" from her national ID card (a step that was, in many ways, directly shaped by the procedural lacuna we investigate), they were performing a "trick" designed to prevent the state from recognizing her conversion away from Islam.[11] Others, however, tied the presence of this lacuna to specific religious and political factors, including an intrinsic aversion within the Islamic law overseen by Malaysia's state-level shari'ah courts to any recognition for the act of Muslim apostasy itself.[12]

After considering these alternative explanations, we offer another account of the policy-based lacuna that undermined the state's recognition of Lina Joy's conversion, focusing on the relationship between Malaysian legal and political realities (including powerful ideas about the parameters of a "reasonable" administrative procedure for Muslim apostasy within Malaysia's constitutional order). In effect, we draw attention to an historically embedded set of legal and political disagreements regarding the promulgation of relevant administrative standards, noting that these disagreements must be read as a crucial *empirical* variable connecting a fundamental right to religious self-identification with the possibility (or the mode) of state

11 Ibid., 620.

12 See Tamir Moustafa, "The Politics of Religious Freedom in Malaysia," *Maryland Journal of International Law* 29.1 (2014), 481.

recognition in Malaysia. We do not set aside the issue of fundamental rights – already examined at length in the literature regarding *Lina Joy*. Instead, we argue that a deep understanding of local disagreements regarding administrative procedures in Malaysia is essential for those with an interest in grasping the *operationalization* of fundamental rights as they actually unfold on the ground.

Focusing on the operationalization of fundamental rights in a highly politicized context shaped by religious norms, we argue that the operationalization of fundamental rights is politically contingent insofar as it is channeled through official procedures framed by deeply contextualized notions of administrative "reasonableness." Our argument regarding the operationalization of fundamental rights is, thus, an argument focusing on the primacy of politics. Briefly stated: *political* considerations underpin the formal *legal* assessments of administrative "reasonableness" that, in turn, shape the operationalization of each state's recognition of a fundamental right to religious self-identification.

II. CONTEXTUALIZING MUSLIM CONVERSION IN MALAYSIA

To understand the legal context within which Lina Joy's effort to obtain state recognition for her religious conversion unfolded, it is necessary to grasp certain features of Malaysia's Federal Constitution. The British colony of Malaya achieved its independence in 1957 from a set of territories known as the Straits Settlements as well as the Federated and Unfederated Malay States. The Straits Settlements (Malacca, Penang, Singapore, etc.) were directly administered by the British Crown, and in those settlements the terms of Muslim personal law were closely tied to Anglo-Mohammadan law as it had developed in British India. In the Federated and Unfederated Malay states, however, British representatives worked with regional sultans, who retained de jure sovereignty with respect to both Muslim and customary law.[13]

During Malaya's anticolonial nationalist movement, many regional sultans were allied with the United Malays Nationalist Organisation (UMNO), and, after independence, the country arrived at a constitutional settlement that provided for a dual court system separating the country's centralized "civil" courts from its regional (state-level) "Muslim" courts.[14] Malaya was renamed Malaysia in 1963, and in 1976 the country's Muslim courts (overseen by hereditary sultans) were renamed as state-level "shari'ah" courts.

The de jure sovereignty of Malaysia's regional sultans with respect to Islamic law and these state-level shari'ah courts was preserved in Malaysia's Federal Constitution. Article 11(5) protects religious freedom ("subject to public order")

[13] Andrew Harding, *Law, Government, and the Constitution in Malaysia* (Kluwer Law International, 1993), 13.

[14] See generally Hari Singh, "UMNO Leaders and Malay Rulers: The Erosion of a Special Relationship," *Pacific Affairs* 68 (1995), 187.

even as Article 3 stipulates that "Islam is the religion of the Federation". Initially, many of Malaya's regional sultans objected to Article 3, believing it would encroach on their religious authority within their respective states.[15] However, when it was explained that Article 3 was symbolic – indeed, that the state-level religious authority of regional sultans would remain firmly intact – they accepted it.[16] Separate constitutional articles define the ethnic category "Malay" as composed of persons who profess Islam[17] while, at the same time, providing that certain "Islamic" matters will be governed by state-level shari'ah courts overseen by the country's regional or state-level sultans.[18] Together, these articles mean that matters concerning Islam and the personal law of those professing Islam are inextricably tied to the terms of Malaysian federalism and, thus, a delicate balance between Malaysia's central government, its regional sultans, and each state-level legislature.

The jurisdiction of Malaysia's state-level shari'ah courts is limited to matters allocated to them by state-level legislative action.[19] This action, whether in the form of a legislative enactment or a *fatwa* issued by a state-level Mufti, is subject to approval by the relevant sultan before it can be gazetted and transformed into an enforceable law. In Malaysia's Federal Territories (e.g., in the Malaysian capital of Kuala Lumpur), the pattern is similar to that found in regions such as Washington, DC. Local institutions – including state-level shari'ah courts – exist, but it is the federal government that oversees them. In fact it is not a state-level sultan but Malaysia's Yang di-Pertuan Agong (a national "king" elected on a rotating basis from among Malaysia's regional sultans) who oversees the state-level shari'ah courts in Federal Territories such as Kuala Lumpur.[20] This is important because the case of *Lina Joy* originated in Kuala Lumpur.

A. *Muslim Conversion: Legal Debates*

The issue of conversion away from Islam – pertaining both to constitutional issues such as religious freedom[21] and to state-level shari'ah enactments[22] – was initially

15 Dian A. H. Shah, *Constitutionalizing Religion and Religious Freedom: A Comparative Study of Malaysia, Indonesia, and Sri Lanka*. SJD dissertation, Duke University, 2014, 266 (on file with Duke University Library).

16 Joseph M. Fernando, *The Making of the Malayan Constitution* (Malaysia Branch of the Royal Asiatic Society, 2006), 171.

17 Federal Constitution of Malaysia, Article 160(2).

18 Ibid., Article 74. This provision clarifies the legislative powers of Malaysia's federal and state-level governments with reference to the "federal," "state," and "concurrent" legislative lists set out in the constitution's Ninth Schedule.

19 Ibid., Ninth Schedule, List II.

20 For a discussion of the legal, political, and administrative structures surrounding Islamic law in Malaysia, see Farid S. Shuaib, "The Islamic Legal System in Malaysia," *Pacific Rim Law & Policy Journal* 21.1 (2012), 85 and Farid S. Shuaib, "Strengthening Administrative Institutions of Islamic Law in Malaysia: An Overview," *Jurnal Syariah* 16 (2008), 443.

21 Federal Constitution of Malaysia, Article 11.

22 Ibid., Ninth Schedule.

perched in between Malaysia's civil and shari'ah courts, with the civil courts maintaining powers of judicial review. However, since 1988, a constitutional amendment[23] carving out an exclusive sphere of jurisdictional authority for the shari'ah courts – primarily in matters of personal law – has been interpreted to *prevent* this form of judicial review.[24] The amendment, Article 121(1A), was born out of a concern that the two courts were – as evidenced by several cases – issuing conflicting decisions.[25] As a solution, Article 121(1A) was introduced to provide that shari'ah matters specified under List II (Paragraph One) of the constitution's Ninth Schedule (i.e., the state-level legislative list) must be handled *exclusively* by state-level religious courts.[26] It is an important amendment because, in conjunction with existing constitutional and federal statutory limits on the punitive powers of state-level courts – up to three years imprisonment, fines of MYR5000, and six lashes – it means that, although cases of Muslim apostasy are handled by state-level shari'ah courts, efforts to impose capital punishment (regarded, by some, as a suitable punishment for Muslim apostasy) are prohibited.[27] Before *Lina Joy*, Malaysia's Supreme Court (as Malaysia's highest court was then called) declared that each state legislature was required to define an administrative procedure for its shari'ah courts to govern the

23 Ibid., Article 121(1A).

24 See, e.g., Shamrahayu A. Aziz, "Apostasy and Religious Freedom: A Response to Thio Li-Ann," *Malayan Law Journal* 2 (2007), i, v. Cf. Thio Li-Ann, "Apostasy and Religious Freedom: Constitutional Issues Arising from the Lina Joy Litigation," *Malayan Law Journal* 2 (2006), i, xiv–xvi. Thio argues that it is unclear whether the amendment effectively precludes the civil courts from adjudicating apostasy cases and that the view that shari'ah courts possess exclusive jurisdiction over apostasy cases is still contested.

25 Ahmad Ibrahim, "The Amendment of Article 121 of the Federal Constitution: Its Effect on the Administration of Islamic Law," *Malayan Law Journal* 2 (1989), xvii.

26 The provision states: "Except with respect to the Federal Territories of Kuala Lumpur and Labuan, [the state-level list includes] Islamic law and personal and family law of persons professing the religion of Islam, including the Islamic law relating to succession, testate and intestate, betrothal, marriage, divorce, dower, maintenance, adoption, legitimacy, guardianship, gifts, partitions and non-charitable trusts; … [the] creation and punishment of offences by persons professing the religion of Islam against precepts of that religion, except in regard to matters included in the Federal List; the constitution, organisation and procedure of Syariah courts, which shall have jurisdiction only over person professing the religion of Islam and in respect only of any of the matters included in this paragraph, but shall not have jurisdiction in respect of offences except in so far as conferred by federal law, the control of propagating doctrines and beliefs among persons professing the religion of Islam; the determination of matters of Islamic law and doctrine and Malay custom."

27 Within Islamic law, the punishment for apostasy is debated. This issue is not addressed in the Qu'ran; it emerges in various hadith (sayings of the Prophet Mohammad) and, historically, different "schools" of Muslim jurisprudence have stressed different punishments. See generally, Frank Griffel, "Toleration and al-Shāfi'ī and al-Ghazālī on the treatment of apostates," *Bulletin of SOAS* 64.3 (2001), 339, and Yohannan Friedmann, *Tolerance and Coercion in Islam: Interfaith Relations in the Muslim Tradition* (Cambridge University Press, 2003), 121–59. In 1990 Kelantan's Chief Minister (PAS) pressed for the imposition of capital punishment. UMNO suggested a constitutional amendment to enhance the jurisdiction of state-level courts (thereby avoiding accusations of standing in the way of shari'ah); but this idea was later withdrawn. See Andrew Harding, "The Keris, the Crescent and the Blind Goddess: The State, Islam and the Constitution in Malaysia," *Singapore Journal of International & Comparative Law* 6 (2002), 154, 176–7.

process of Muslim apostasy – up to and including discretionary efforts to deter apostasy within existing state-level punitive limits.[28] The Court held that, if states failed to specify any procedure, this did not actually prohibit Muslim apostasy. Instead, the Court simply noted that recalcitrant states (or, in the case of Malaysia's Federal Territories, parliament itself) would have to frame statutory rules for their sultans (or the king) to endorse. This ruling stemmed from the fact that, according to the constitution's Ninth Schedule, explicit legislation was required to endow state-level shari'ah courts with jurisdiction over issues mentioned on the state-level legislative list. And, even then, state legislatures did not have the authority to enact just any law pertaining to Islam; they were limited to the promulgation of laws on a schedule of "Islamic" matters spelled out in Paragraph One of List II.[29] Without specific enabling legislation, in other words, the 1988 constitutional amendment articulated in Article 121(1A) was not sufficient – on its own – to guide or empower Malaysia's state-level shari'ah courts.

Since 1988, however, several court cases have sought to clarify the relationship between Malaysia's federal constitution, including its state-level shari'ah courts, and the question of fundamental rights (with particular reference to the procedures underpinning Muslim apostasy). These cases framed the legal environment within which *Lina Joy* emerged. In 1991, the High Court was asked to decide whether a person from Selangor who had allegedly converted *to* Islam had died as a Muslim.[30] The Court concluded that, because neither the Selangor Administration of Muslim Law Enactment (1952) nor the Islamic Family Law (Federal Territories) Act (1984) specifically mentioned the issue of conversion – in other words, because jurisdiction over this issue had not been transferred to Selangor's state-level shari'ah court by way of explicit legislative action – the matter should be heard by a (civil) High Court instead.[31] But, in 1992, this view was modified in a case known as *Dalip Kaur*[32] concerning the status of a man from Kedah who was said to have converted *away* from Islam before he passed away. In this case, the Supreme Court declared that the civil courts could *not* assume jurisdiction, because matters of Muslim apostasy required expert assessment by a qualified religious authority.[33] Because the Kedah Administration of Muslim Law Enactment (1952) did not clarify the procedural mechanism whereby Muslims might leave Islam (indeed, because there was no explicit legislation clarifying the jurisdiction of Kedah's shari'ah courts in cases of

[28] See generally *Dalip Kaur v. Pegawai Polis Daerah, Balai Polis Daerah, Bukit Mertajam & Another* [1992] 1, *Malayan Law Journal* 1.

[29] Shad Saleem Faruqi, *Document of Destiny: The Constitution of the Federation of Malaysia* (The Star Publications, 2008), 134.

[30] *Ng Wan Chan v. Majlis Ugama Islam Wilayah Persekutuan & Another (No. 2)* [1991] 1, *Malayan Law Journal* 487.

[31] Ibid., 490.

[32] *Dalip Kaur* (n. 28).

[33] Ibid., 9 (concurring opinion by Justice Mohamed Yusoff).

Muslim apostasy at all), however, the Court found that Kedah's civil courts were still empowered, by default, to render a binding decision.[34]

In 1998, however, the High Court adopted an entirely different approach, holding in the case of *Md Hakim Lee*[35] that, even where explicit state-level legislation conferring jurisdiction on state-level shari'ah courts in matters of Muslim apostasy was not in place, there was no justification for granting "default" jurisdiction to the civil courts.[36] On the contrary, according to Idrus Bin Harun (a parliamentary draftsman in the office of the Malaysian Attorney General), *Md Hakim Lee* held that jurisdiction in matters of Muslim apostasy lay with the shari'ah court given its jurisdiction over Muslim religious affairs, "even if no express provisions were provided in [a state-level statute]."[37] Muslim apostasy was left to state-level shari'ah courts, in other words, on the *expectation* that legislative guidance regarding appropriate procedures would be forthcoming: "The fact that the plaintiff might not [yet] have his remedy in the syariah courts," noted Harun, "would not make the jurisdiction exercisable by [a civil] High Court."[38]

The view in *Md Hakim Lee* was later reinforced in a landmark case known as *Soon Singh*,[39] where it was found that although each state (including the Federal Territories) had explicit laws covering conversion *to* Islam, only some had provided their shari'ah courts with explicit jurisdiction over conversions *away* from Islam.[40] In *Soon Singh*, however, the Federal Court concluded that, in cases of Muslim apostasy, the jurisdiction of state-level shari'ah courts could be *implied* given the special religious expertise required to judge such cases.[41] This approach was taken to a different level in a subsequent case known as *Shaik Zolkaffily*,[42] wherein the Federal Court held that where jurisdiction over a specific issue had been conferred to the shari'ah courts – either explicitly or implicitly – but no legal remedy had been specified (by statute) within those courts, it was still the state legislature that was expected to determine the legal remedy within the shari'ah courts.[43] In other words, "the fact that [a litigant] did not [yet] have his remedy in the syariah court would not make the jurisdiction exercisable by the civil court."[44] This is the jurisprudential background that set the stage for *Lina Joy*.

34 Ibid., 7.

35 *Md Hakim Lee v. Majlis Agama Islam Wilayah Persekutuan, Kuala Lumpur*[1998] 1, *Malayan Law Journal* 681.

36 Ibid., 689.

37 Dato Idrus bin Harun, "Interaction between Syariah Law and Civil Law," Inaugural Annual Events (IAE) of the AGCs, Singapore, March 23–25, 2006.

38 Ibid.

39 *Soon Singh v. Pertubuhan Kebajikan Islam Malaysia (PERKIM) Kedah* [1999] 1, *Malayan Law Journal* 489.

40 Ibid., 501.

41 Ibid., 502.

42 *Majlis Ugama Islam Pulau Pinang dan Seberang Perai v. Shaik Zolkaffily bin Shaik Natar & Others* [2003] 3, *Malayan Law Journal* 705.

43 Ibid., 719.

44 Ibid.

During the 1980s and 1990s, several states passed laws specifying a procedure concerning Muslim apostasy to be overseen by their state-level shari'ah courts. In Pahang, Perak, Malacca, and Sabah, these enactments identified Muslim apostasy as an offense – for example, an "offense by persons professing … Islam against the precepts of that religion" (*Constitution of Malaysia*, Ninth Schedule, List II, Paragraph One) – to be punished with fines and/or imprisonment.[45] But, in Negeri Sembilan, steps were put in place allowing state-level shari'ah courts to oversee the process of Muslim apostasy (including three months of counseling and a further one-year cooling-off period) before an official certification of Muslim apostasy could be issued.[46] And, in Johor, the unreported case of *Ismail bin Suppiah*[47] decided by the Kuala Lumpur High Court noted that, as per the (now-repealed) Johor Administration of Islamic Law Enactment (1978), the chief kadi was simply expected to play a mechanical role in registering the non-Muslim name of any Johor-based Muslim who declared himself an apostate.[48] In the Administration of Islamic Law (Federal Territories) Act (1993) and at least four other states, however, the issue of Muslim apostasy was not addressed. The question underpinning the case of *Lina Joy* was therefore as follows: why did this statutory (and, thus, procedural) lacuna persist in Malaysia's Federal Territories even *after* the Federal Court clearly urged it to be filled? This is the procedural question that underpinned specific concerns about the administrative operationalization of religious freedom in Malaysia.

B. *Muslim Conversion: Political Debates*

Apart from this jurisprudential and legislative context, it is important to appreciate the larger *political* context within which Malaysian cases of Muslim apostasy were addressed. Throughout the latter half of the twentieth century, much depended on a pattern of electoral competition between two leading political parties: the right-of-center United Malays National Organization (UMNO) – the dominant collaborator in a ruling coalition known as the Barisan Nasional (BN) or National Front – and the religiously conservative (Islamist) Parti Islam Se-Malaysia (PAS). Since its inception in the early 1950s, PAS projected itself as the only truly "Islamic" party in Malaysia, vowing to form an Islamic state in which only Muslims would hold political power.[49] In fact, for much of the country's history, and especially since the late 1970s when social and political movements took on a more overtly religious

45 See, e.g., Crimes (Syariah) Enactment 1992 (Enactment No. 3 of 1992), Sections 12 and 13, and the Administration of the Religion of Islam and the Malay Custom of Pahang Enactment 1982, Sections 103 and 185.

46 Administration of the Religion of Islam (Negeri Sembilan) Enactment 2003, Section 119.

47 *Ismail bin Suppiah v. Ketua Pengarah Pendaftaran Negara* (R-1-24-31-95) (unreported case).

48 See the Johor Faith Protection Bill 2000, which resembled a bill passed that year in Perlis.

49 Andrew Harding, "Sharia and National Law in Malaysia," in Jan Michiel Otto (ed.), *Sharia Incorporated: A Comparative Overview of the Legal Systems of Twelve Muslim Countries in Past and Present* (University of Chicago Press, 2010), 502–3.

character, UMNO and PAS competed for Malay-Muslim votes – especially in the north and east of the country (a.k.a. Malaysia's Malay-Muslim "heartland").[50]

Central to this ongoing electoral competition has been a push to construct a cohesive Malay-Muslim constituency by "defending" the boundaries of Islam or, at least, appearing to defend Muslim interests. UMNO and PAS, in other words, have frequently sought to "out-Islamize" one another by highlighting issues that touch on Malay-Muslim religious and political sensitivities.[51] This competitive posture stretches all the way from policing various forms of religious orthodoxy to discouraging Muslim apostasy. The government's emphasis on Islam, for instance, was officially expressed during UMNO's 1982 General Assembly, when Prime Minister Mahathir Mohamad stressed that UMNO would ensure Malay-Muslim adherence to various Islamic teachings.[52] In fact, certain reform initiatives took place even before Mahathir assumed office. At the federal level, for instance, the government established a National Council for Islamic Affairs (*Pusat Islam*) under the Department of Religion, which was later reorganized in the office of Prime Minister Mahathir as Malaysia's Department of Islamic Development (JAKIM).[53] Within Malaysia, each state maintains its own Islamic affairs department. However, JAKIM has become increasingly influential over time in coordinating interstate Muslim affairs (particularly insofar as states have become more and more reliant on funds derived from the center).[54] Today, JAKIM's wide-ranging role extends from the vetting of Friday sermons across Malaysia to the issuance of national procedures for determining the end of Ramadan. In the past, the end of Ramadan was determined by states using visual sightings of the moon and/or astronomical calculations.[55] But, when Prime Minister Mahathir stepped in to centralize this moon-sighting process, he reinforced deep-seated federal–state tensions as well as the terms of an enduring rivalry between Malaysia's national executive and its various regional sultans.[56]

JAKIM also recommends draft laws for state-level enactment.[57] In fact, given its persistent political dominance across Malaysia during the 1980s and 1990s (except in

50 Shah (n. 15), 344.

51 Ibid., 386.

52 Gordon P. Means, *Political Islam in Southeast Asia* (Lynne Rienner, 2009), 126.

53 Ibid.

54 See Maznah Mohamad, "The Ascendance of Bureaucratic Islam and the Secularization of the Sharia in Malaysia," *Pacific Affairs* 83.3 (2010), 505.

55 Means (n. 52), 128.

56 Means suggests that Mahathir overstepped the boundaries of his executive authority because Malay rulers possess "constitutionally defined powers … over matters related to Islam." Means (n. 52), 128. However, Shad Faruqi notes that not everything concerning Islam is reserved to the states. Shad Saleem Faruqi, "Jurisdiction of State Authorities to Punish Offences against the Precepts of Islam: A Constitutional Perspective," *The Malaysian Bar* (September 24, 2005), www.malaysianbar.org.my/constitutional_law/jurisdiction_of_state_authorities_to_punish_offences_against_the_precepts_of_islam_a_constitutional_perspective.html (accessed September 2, 2015).

57 Means (n. 52), 126.

Kelantan, where PAS won state-level elections in 1990), the ruling BN found it relatively easy to standardize state-level laws concerning various aspects of Islam. Indeed, even *within* Malaysia's federalized approach to Islam, the link between federal and state-level party politics has generally ensured that shari'ah-based policies governing marriage, the administration of Islam, and certain civil and criminal procedures (albeit not Muslim apostasy) were gradually harmonized over time. But, with reference to the focus of this article (Muslim apostasy), the question is: why did this steady march of standardization fail? Moreover, turning to *Lina Joy*, why was the procedural lacuna left by this failure seen as legally (and administratively) "reasonable"?

III. UNDERSTANDING *LINA JOY*: FROM FUNDAMENTAL RIGHTS TO ADMINISTRATIVE LAW

By the time *Lina Joy* reached Malaysia's Court of Appeal and, then, Malaysia's Federal Court, Joy's quest to obtain state recognition for her religious conversion – by deleting the word "Islam" from her national ID card – was explicitly framed as a case of administrative law rather than fundamental rights. The facts were simple. Initially, Azalina binti Jailani (a.k.a. "Lina Joy") applied to change the name on her ID card (which did not mention her religion), stating that the reason for this change was a "change of religion" from Islam to Christianity. Her application, however, was denied, and Joy was advised to apply again, stating that the reason for her change of name was her "choice" of religion. This time her request was granted, and she received a new ID card with her new name.

Unfortunately, this new card also included her old name on the back. And, owing to a legislative amendment that had come into effect while Joy's application for a new ID card was being processed, her new card also included a description of her religion as "Islam." (The intervening piece of legislation required that every national ID card must specify a Muslim's religion as Islam; and, along the way, the National Registration Department [NRD] claimed that, while it recognized Lina Joy's new name, it had no authoritative documentary evidence stating that Joy had renounced Islam.[58]) When Joy applied to delete the word "Islam" from her ID card, she was ordered to follow the procedures spelled out in Malaysia's National Registration Regulations 1990 (hereinafter, the "1990 Regulations"), which provided her with a set of forms requiring any Muslim applying for a change of name to specify their religion and, then, to provide "[a]ny further documentary evidence as the registration officer may consider necessary to support the accuracy of any particulars submitted."[59]

[58] The same piece of legislation specified that, among the "reasons" given by those seeking to change their name, "change of religion" was no longer permitted.

[59] National Registration Regulations 1990, clause 4(c)(x).

When Joy submitted her forms specifying her religion as "Kristian" (along with a copy of her baptismal certificate), the presiding NRD officer made a notation saying that the religion of the applicant should be retained as Islam because, scanning the NRD records, there was no authoritative documentary evidence stating that, before Joy became a Christian, she had officially abandoned Islam.[60] A mere assertion of religious identity by a private citizen (or a recognized religious authority – in this case, the church that issued Joy's baptismal certificate) was not enough. Instead, the state required a three-way combination of (a) individual self-assertion (i.e., individual profession), (b) an acknowledgement by relevant religious authorities (insofar as each religious community in Malaysia was constitutionally entitled to "manage its own … affairs" [Article 11(3)(a)]), and above all, (c) some type of formal process officially recognized by the state itself. In Malaysia, following the "implied" jurisdiction spelled out in *Soon Singh*, it was the formal administrative procedure associated with this last element that required Joy, as one seeking to leave Islam, to approach a state-level shari'ah court.

Joy insisted that, as per the form she was asked to complete, her baptismal certificate was sufficient to support "[t]he accuracy of any particulars submitted,"[61] since the particulars actually submitted concerned her status as a Christian. However, the NRD contended that, insofar as Joy was seeking to delete the word Islam from her ID card (and, thus, to change her status from what was in the NRD records), the only satisfactory evidence was a certificate of apostasy from a relevant shari'ah court.[62] From Joy's perspective, as a person no longer professing Islam, she was not subject to the jurisdiction of Malaysia's shari'ah courts. However, the NRD argued that it was not her professed status as a "Kristian" but her earlier effort to abandon Islam that was at issue (in deleting the word "Islam"). And, as such, the NRD argued that the procedure for adjudicating this act of renunciation – by implication, because the Administration of Islamic Law (Federal Territories) Act (1993) did not mention Muslim apostasy – involved the shari'ah court.

In effect, the question before the Court was regarded as a routine matter of *administrative* law, albeit one that underpinned the *operationalization* of a fundamental constitutional right: did the NRD act "reasonably" (i.e., within a defensible understanding of administrative discretion) when it required Joy to obtain a certificate of apostasy from a shari'ah court before deleting the word Islam from her ID card? The case was explicitly framed as a case of "Wednesbury" (un)reasonableness, asking whether the administrative decision taken by the NRD was wrong, capricious, perverse, or absurd – indeed, in the language of the Court of Appeal of England and

60 *Lina Joy v. Majlis Agama Islam Wilayah Persekutuan and Others* [2005] 6, *Malayan Law Journal* 193, 202.

61 *Lina Joy* (n. 4), 629.

62 Ibid., 627.

Wales in *Wednesbury Corp*[63] "[s]o unreasonable that no reasonable authority could have ever come to it."[64]

Malaysia's Federal Court, by a 2:1 majority, concurred with Malaysia's Court of Appeal and concluded that, in an *administrative* sense, the NRD *had* acted "reasonably" for at least three reasons. First, the Court argued that the NRD's insistence on authoritative evidence from the shari'ah court confirming that Joy was no longer a Muslim was "reasonable."[65] In particular, the chief justice argued that a mere statutory declaration issued by a person leaving the religion was not enough.[66] Because renouncing Islam was thought to implicate the terms of Islamic law, it was perfectly reasonable for the NRD to require confirmation from the relevant Islamic authorities who were thought to possess the expertise required to adjudicate such matters. In fact, the Court added that if the NRD had accepted a person's "self-declaration" on its own, the NRD might be at risk of "wrongly" designating someone's affiliation with a particular religious group.[67]

Second, agreeing with Malaysia's Court of Appeal, the Federal Court conceded that the relevant Administration of Islamic Law (Federal Territories) Act (1993) granting jurisdiction to the shari'ah courts in various matters did *not* provide any guidance regarding the procedures governing Muslim apostasy. Yet, following *Soon Singh*, the Court declared that the jurisdiction of the shari'ah courts was "implied."[68] In fact, as per *Md Hakim Lee*, the Court accepted the conservative view that the judiciary must avoid filling legislative lacunae on its own; the courts were simply obliged to encourage each state-level legislature to satisfy its own legal role in specifying the relevant procedures.[69] In effect, the Court argued that it was legally "reasonable" to expect each actor within Malaysia's constitutionally defined legal-cum-administrative order to play its required part. The alternative – arrogating legislative powers to the Court on the premise that a radical commitment to institutional centralization was required to ensure a defense of fundamental rights – was rejected. This was because such a move was seen as undermining the underpinnings of Malaysia's constitutional order (including its approach to federalism and a constitutional separation of powers).[70]

Third, it is important to stress that the 1990 Regulations did not offer any clear guidance as to what must be provided to correct erroneous particulars on an ID card. Instead, the Court declared that it was within the administrative *discretion* of each NRD officer to determine which documentary evidence was required "[t]o support the accuracy of any particulars submitted"[71] and that, in cases of Muslim apostasy, it

63 *Associated Provincial Picture Houses Ltd. v. Wednesbury Corporation* (1948) 1 K.B. 223.
64 Ibid., 234.
65 *Lina Joy* (n. 4), 604.
66 Ibid.
67 Ibid., 603.
68 Ibid., 616–18.
69 Ibid.
70 Ibid., 618.
71 Ibid., 603.

was administratively "reasonable" in light of prevailing jurisprudence to expect some type of certification from Malaysia's state-level shari'ah courts.[72] The Court stressed that determining the question of whether a person had renounced Islam was not within the jurisdiction of the NRD and that it was not something "[t]he NRD is … equipped or qualified to decide."[73] In fact the Court in *Lina Joy* held that, even when a certificate of apostasy *was* furnished before the NRD, each NRD officer still possessed the discretion to retain or remove the word "Islam" from an ID card.[74] In *Lina Joy*, the relationship between fundamental rights and administrative discretion (and judicial deference to such discretion) was made abundantly clear.

For comparative purposes, it is interesting to note that at no point did the Court explicitly state that Lina Joy could not change her religion (in keeping with the fundamental rights outlined in Article 11 of the Malaysian constitution). On the contrary, the Court simply came to the conclusion that Joy's exercise of this freedom *in Malaysia* was subject to the relevant state regulations.[75] For the Court, exercising one's rights under Article 11 (as a Muslim) simply required compliance with Malaysia's laws and procedures associated with the renunciation of Islam.[76] In short, the exercise of Joy's religious freedom could not be *recognized* by the state unless specific procedures were followed – procedures closely tied to Malaysia's federal constitutional order and the legal authority of its state-level shari'ah courts.

IV. *LINA JOY*: RIGHTS VS. REASONABLENESS?

Lina Joy argued that the NRD's actions amounted to a form of trickery preventing the state from officially recognizing her conversion. In her submissions at trial (in the High Court), Joy documented an unfruitful back-and-forth with the NRD. The NRD rejected – without articulating any reason – her first application for a change of name (in which she stated that her reason for this change was her renunciation of Islam).[77] She put in a second application almost two years later (again citing conversion as the reason for her name change), but this time the NRD did not respond.[78] She subsequently enquired about the status of her application, whereupon she was told not to disclose her conversion to avoid any difficulties with her application.[79] In fact it was this advice that led Joy to submit a third application, which was subsequently approved (albeit with a new ID card that specified her religion as "Islam").[80] The dissenting judgment prepared by Justice Richard

72 Ibid., 604.
73 Ibid., 602.
74 Ibid., 604.
75 Ibid., 612.
76 Ibid.
77 Ibid., 620.
78 Ibid.
79 Ibid.
80 Ibid., 621.

Malanjum, focusing heavily on the constitutionality of the 1990 Regulations and the matter of official discretion, stressed this protracted series of interactions.[81] In fact, taking up the question of administrative "reasonableness," Malanjum noted that, within Malaysia's existing policy framework, Joy had been faced with an extremely difficult administrative process followed by an almost impossible additional requirement.[82] This requirement required Joy to follow a set of procedures concerning the work of a relevant state-level shari'ah court – a *statutory* set of procedures that, within Malaysia's Federal Territories, did not (yet) exist.

A. *Proceduralizing Apostasy*

Malanjum began his dissenting judgment by accepting that the NRD official who handled Joy's case was entitled to request any documentary evidence "[n]ecessary to support the accuracy of any particulars submitted."[83] He simply reiterated that the particulars actually submitted concerned Joy's identity as a Christian – hence her baptismal certificate – rather than her status as an ex-Muslim. There was an "abuse of power," he noted, when the NRD "[f]ailed to take into consideration a legally relevant factor, namely … the documents submitted by the appellant, … preferring [instead] its policy of requiring a certificate of apostasy from the Federal Territory Syariah Court."[84] This policy – according to Malanjum – was not a step that had been stipulated in the 1990 Regulations. Indeed, turning specifically to the question of "Wednesbury" (un)reasonableness, he drew attention to the matter of completing a set of forms that did not exist.[85] For Malanjum, the NRD's insistence on a certificate of apostasy from the Federal Territory shari'ah court was not only illegal but also administratively unreasonable, "[b]ecause under the applicable [state-level] law, the Syariah Court in the Federal Territory has no statutory power to adjudicate on the issue of apostasy."[86] In short, he noted that the NRD "[r]equired the performance of an act that was almost impossible to perform."[87]

81 Ibid., 625–30. Justice Malanjum added: "[T]he conclusion in the majority judgment that the impugned policy adopted by NRD was reasonable within the test of *Wednesbury Corporation v. Ministry of Housing* (1966) 2 Q.B. 275 has unfortunately missed one cardinal principle. The implementation of the policy has a bearing on the appellant's fundamental constitutional right to freedom of religion under Article 11 of the Constitution. Being a constitutional issue it must be given priority independent of any determination of the *Wednesbury* reasonableness; … before it can be said that a policy is reasonable within the test of *Wednesbury* its constitutionality must be first considered." Ibid., 631.

82 Ibid., 632.

83 *Lina Joy* (n. 4), 626.

84 Ibid., 630.

85 In Malaysia, different rules for different groups are constitutionally permitted in the context of religious personal law. However, Malanjum focused on a rule pertaining only to "Muslims" (whose ID cards had to "state their religion"); he described this as a case of discrimination beyond the realm of Muslim personal law. See ibid., 639.

86 Ibid., 632.

87 Ibid., 644.

This statutory lacuna pertaining to the jurisdiction of the Federal Territory's shari'ah courts thus became the central issue in *Lina Joy*. Did the NRD exercise its administrative discretion in a "reasonable" manner when it sought to chart a course between (a) the statutory *silence* of the Federal Territories regarding the work of its shari'ah courts in cases of Muslim apostasy and (b) the guiding jurisprudence of *Soon Singh* regarding the *implied* jurisdiction of those very shari'ah courts? Crucially, Malanjum did not seek to erase the silence of the Federal Territories by legislating from the bench; instead, he adhered to the work of his predecessors in continuing to press for the promulgation of clearly defined laws in each state. In particular, he stressed that, in cases regarding Muslim apostasy (and, thus, fundamental rights), jurisdiction should never be "implied." Following *Dalip Kaur* (1997), he returned to questions of policymaking and noted that clearly defined procedural guidance *should be* incorporated "[i]n all state enactments to avoid [any] difficulties of interpretation."[88]

B. Regulating Apostasy: State-Level Variation

Outside of Malaysia's courts, however, this case raised one of the most important questions in Malaysia's constitutional and political order: to what extent should various states, including the Federal Territories, be *compelled* to confront the issue of Muslim apostasy via explicit state-level enactments and, even beyond this, to what extent should state-level policies reflect a particular "national" standard? Indeed, if such policies were to reflect a national standard, which standard could be said to reflect an (administratively) "reasonable" standard for regulating – and recognizing – Muslim apostasy?

Focusing on the punitive procedures in Pahang (where would-be apostates were seen as committing a crime and punished with the maximum state-level punishment of six lashes, a MYR5000 fine, and three years' imprisonment), some perceived a basic aversion to any legalization of Muslim apostasy. Former Australian High Court Judge Michael Kirby and Malaysian scholars such as Nurjaanah Abdullah, for instance, read *Lina Joy*'s emphasis on the power of state-level shari'ah courts as, prima facie, a denial of fundamental rights. To protect fundamental rights, they noted, such cases regarding apostasy should be removed from the shari'ah courts and returned to the civil courts forthwith.[89] For Abdullah, the problem lay in the fact that it was virtually impossible to get the required validation from a shari'ah court in most states, as references to such courts were "not merely an administrative or procedural requirement … [but a] control mechanism over individuals who wish to renounce [Islam]."[90] Abdullah added that the very existence of cumbersome shari'ah-court

88 Ibid., 650.

89 Michael Kirby, "Fundamental Human Rights and Religious Apostasy: The Malaysian Case of Lina Joy," *Griffith Law Review* 17.1 (2008), 151, 156; Abdullah (n. 1), 281.

90 Abdullah (n. 1), 283.

procedures was inappropriate in religious freedom cases, as such procedures patently and often willfully "ignore … the reality that whether or not a person has renounced Islam is … a question of fact [and] not of law."[91]

This notion – that state recognition should resemble a frictionless conduit through which religious self-identification could be validated strictly on the basis of an individual's autonomous "choice" of religion – was, however, considered administratively problematic. In fact the judicial majority in *Lina Joy* directly addressed the problems with this view, arguing that such an approach might have the effect of allowing Muslims to renounce Islam merely to avoid certain constraints associated with Muslim personal law (e.g., constraints on the production of a will excluding certain heirs). Similarly, the trial judge in *Lina Joy* suggested in the High Court that a complete absence of administrative regulation – that is, an ability to renounce Islam without going through any religious body – would be problematic insofar as Malaysia's constitution explicitly allowed each religious group to "manage its own … affairs" (Article 11(3)(a)).[92]

A more nuanced view, however, pressing for a sharply limited set of constraints on Muslim apostasy within Malaysia's shari'ah courts, was articulated by Justice Malanjum, who referred to the (now defunct) procedure previously adopted in the state of Johor according to which the powers of a state-level shari'ah court were limited to "registering" individual declarations of conversion.[93] In a similar vein, states like Negeri Sembilan recommended a rather limited set of procedures within which, after attending three months of rehabilitative counseling followed by a one-year cooling-off period (to consider repentance), apostates could expect to receive an official certificate of apostasy issued by the shari'ah court.

These divergent approaches to the proceduralization of Muslim apostasy – stretching all the way from "punitive" Pahang (where existing procedures seemed to overlap with outright prohibition) to "permissive" Negeri Sembilan (where this was not the case) – are important.[94] They are particularly important when it comes to considering what sort of explicit state-level enactments might be introduced in the context of future efforts to move beyond the "implied" jurisdiction in *Soon Singh*. However, as comparative examples, they still ignore the core *political* question that

91 Ibid.

92 *Lina Joy v. Majlis Agama Islam Wilayah & Another* [2004] 2, *Malayan Law Journal* 119, 126.

93 "A clear provision," Malanjum noted, could "[i]mpose an obligation on the relevant authority to … maintain a register of converts who … executed a deed poll renouncing Islam", *Lina Joy*, n. 4, 654. In the end, Malanjum stressed the inevitable overlap between fundamental rights and questions about the "reasonableness" of the administrative procedures operationalizing those rights. He argued that the latter should never stifle the former.

94 Two cases are instructive in this respect. *Daud bin Mamat* and *Kamariah bte Ali* emerged in Kelantan, which (unlike the Federal Territories that framed *Lina Joy*) has an enactment specifying the procedures for apostasy. In *Daud bin Mamat*, the civil court decided that the appellant had to complete a set of required shari'ah-court procedures that he had not yet done. See *Daud bin Mamat & Others v. Majlis Agama Islam & Another* [2001] 2, *Malayan Law Journal* 390 and *Kamariah bte Ali v. Kerajaan Negeri Kelantan & Another* [2002] 3, *Malayan Law Journal* 657.

confronted Lina Joy, namely, why did Malaysia's Federal Territories fail to specify any procedure pertaining to Muslim apostasy at all? As a matter concerning both law and "national" politics, this is the policy-oriented administrative question that framed the experience of Lina Joy.

C. *Politicizing Apostasy: Federal–State Relations*

To explain why the introduction of specific procedures governing Muslim apostasy in Malaysia's Federal Territories was so difficult and, indeed, why the resulting administrative gap (stemming from a persistent statutory lacuna) was seen as "reasonable" by Malaysia's Federal Court, we argue that the problem of religious freedom in Malaysia must be understood in light of (a) historical and political factors pertaining to the country's constitutional architecture and (b) a set of rather delicate (and, to some extent, unresolved) *political* issues involving the distribution of federal and state-level powers in matters concerning religion.

Malaysia's scheme of federalism is center-heavy. Even a cursory assessment of the legislative distribution of powers in the constitution is enough to highlight this fact: List I of the Ninth Schedule lists twenty-seven matters in which the federal parliament possesses exclusive competence; List II provides only thirteen matters falling exclusively to the states. One of these thirteen matters is Islamic law, but as explained earlier, there is a very limited area of Islamic law within which individual states can legislate.[95] Despite the common assumption that all matters having to do with Islam are within the exclusive purview of Malaysian states, and despite the fact that state-level sultans remain the Heads of Islam in their respective states (owing to a carefully engineered compromise during the constitution-making process[96]), the power of the federal legislature and, thus, the power of the federal government in matters concerning Islam is, as noted earlier, substantial.[97] The other point worth reiterating is that the punitive jurisdiction of Malaysia's shari'ah courts is capped by the Syariah Courts (Criminal Jurisdiction) Act 1965. Limiting the kinds of punishment that state-level shari'ah courts can impose, this law emerged from the federal legislature.[98]

When it comes to the issue of Muslim apostasy, however, federal–state relations remain extremely complex. List II reserves to state-level legislatures and the federal parliament (in the case of the Federal Territories) the power to define and punish offences by persons professing Islam against the precepts of that religion (including apostasy). Yet, if Malaysia's federal parliament were to exercise this power – creating

95 See Federal Constitution of Malaysia, Section I.A.

96 See generally Fernando (n. 16) and Shah (n. 15), chapter 2.

97 Laws on Islamic banking, finance, and insurance, for instance, would fall within the purview of the federal parliament.

98 See Jaclyn L. Neo and Dian A. H. Shah, "Hudud and the Struggle for Malaysia's Constitutional Soul," *Constitutionnet* (June 25, 2015), www.constitutionnet.org/news/hudud-and-struggle-malaysias-constitutional-soul (accessed May 5, 2016).

a federal law for the Federal Territories that differed from existing state-level laws on this issue (either in a more "punitive" or a more "permissive" direction) – questions would inevitably arise. Article 75 of the constitution clearly states that federal laws will prevail over any (inconsistent) state-level laws. But, with so many different state-level laws concerning Muslim apostasy, any exercise of the federal legislative power needed to address the procedural lacuna facing Lina Joy could be seen as challenging the legislative remit of the states and, specifically, the power of the sultans to assert their constitutionally defined role as "Heads of Islam" in their respective states. Indeed, federal legislation in this sensitive area might be seen as an effort to pressure Malaysia's state-level sultans to conform to federal standards.

This pressure would not be overlooked by Malaysia's states, particularly since the federal government, through JAKIM, has already stepped up its efforts to standardize "state-level" Islamic laws, including those pertaining to Muslim personal matters like marriage, divorce, and inheritance. It is notable, however, that this push for harmonization has *not* touched the domain of Muslim apostasy (even though the imposition of capital punishment for unrepentant apostates – a measure that has been proposed, at various times, in states like Kelantan and Terengganu – is blocked by Malaysia's federal Syariah Courts [Criminal Jurisdiction] Act 1965). From an historical perspective, efforts to encourage centralization in matters pertaining to Islam remain highly controversial, particularly in light of long-standing frictions regarding the balance of federal and state-level powers.

Malaysia's sultans explicitly raised strong reservations during Malaysia's pre-independence constitution-making process regarding the inclusion of a constitutional provision cementing Islam as the religion of the Malayan federation, fearing that such a provision would shift the locus of authority in Islamic matters to the central government. Indeed, it is only after these sultans received clear assurances that their regional authority in matters regarding Islam would *not* be lost that they agreed to the inclusion of this provision. In fact Malaysia's sultans were assured that, even *if* a federal-level government department were established for religious matters, that department would *not* exist under the purview of an elected federal government – as it does (in the form of JAKIM) today. They were assured that such a department would only serve to "coordinate" the federation and the states under the purview of Malaysia's rotating king (i.e., the Yang di-Pertuan Agong).[99]

Since the earliest days of the constitution-making process, Malaysia's regional sultans have registered persistent concerns about the effect of non-Muslim proselytism on Muslims, suggesting that questions of Muslim apostasy were already a sensitive issue.[100] This is not surprising insofar as Malaysia's sultans derive both their religious authority and political legitimacy from "[M]uslim notions of ...

99 Shah (n. 15), 92.

100 Ibid., 112. It was for this reason that the sultans objected to the inclusion the right to propagate one's religion in the constitution.

rule."[101] Indeed, while the federal legislature may well pass laws to regulate the process of Muslim apostasy in Malaysia's Federal Territories, doing so would almost certainly push the federal government into an enormous political clash. It would, quite simply, stir up a host of questions about the shape of Malaysia's constitutional federalism, with specific reference to religious policymaking and the religious prerogatives of Malaysia's state-level sultans. The statutory gap facing Lina Joy was awkward; but, for historical, constitutional, and political reasons, it is not difficult to understand why the deferential behavior of the NRD, vis-à-vis state-level procedures, was considered administratively "reasonable."

To guarantee harmony between the versions of Islamic law applied in different units of the Malaysian federation, including the Federal Territories, some have suggested that Malaysia should have a Grand Mufti "whose opinions would bind all Muslims."[102] However, Farid Shuaib reports that, so far, this suggestion has received a negative response: "The federal government could not establish such an office," he explains, "unless the states voluntarily agree to subordinate their Muftis to a federal Mufti," and this "the states have resisted."[103] Turning specifically to the pattern of statutory inaction that frustrated Lina Joy, Shuaib notes that the creation of a Grand Mufti able to make fatwas for the whole of Malaysia would require a constitutional amendment. But this is unlikely. Malaysia's regional sultans, he explains, "have shown their readiness to be firm in situation[s] related to their position."[104]

The constitutional amendment that, according to Shuaib, would be needed before Malaysia's parliament could specify a "national" punishment for the so-called "crime" of Muslim apostasy was not introduced during the fifty years that UMNO and its BN coalition held the requisite two-thirds majority in parliament (1957–2008). With the demise of that supermajority in 2008, the policymaking context regulating Muslim apostasy and, therein, the operationalization of religious freedom, has shifted. In short, the possibility of introducing such a constitutional amendment and, then, a "national" law governing Muslim apostasy has declined.

V. CONCLUSION

The right to freely choose one's religion (i.e., religious self-identification) and the formal procedures underpinning a state's recognition of one's faith are closely linked. They are tied together by administrative procedures, but those procedures

101 See M. B. Hooker, "Muhammadan Law and Islamic Law," in M. B. Hooker (ed.), *Islam in South-East Asia* (Brill, 1997), 171, and Donald L., *Horowitz, Ethnic Groups in Conflict* (University of California Press, 2000), 226.

102 Shuaib, "The Islamic Legal System in Malaysia" (n. 20), 111.

103 Ibid. As Shuaib points out, "[t]here is a National Fatwa Committee, which was set up in 1970 and is currently placed within the Department of Islam of Malaysia in the Prime Minister's Office. This Committee may deliberate on issues relating to Islam but its recommendation … is not binding on the states."

104 Shuaib, "Strengthening Administrative Institutions of Islamic Law" (n. 20), 451.

vary from place to place in ways that directly shape the operationalization of religious freedom as a fundamental constitutional right. In Malaysia, the operationalization of religious freedom is shaped by specific administrative procedures, but historical, constitutional, and political contingencies have shaped the way in which those procedures are designed from state to state within the country, including their absence in Malaysia's Federal Territories and certain other states. These contingencies also explain Malaysia's failure to close the procedural gap that prevented Lina Joy from transforming her religious self-identification into a case of state recognition.

Conventionally, religious freedom is understood as an inherently negative right, meaning that states must not encroach on an individual's freedom to choose or change her religion. However, insofar as this right is guaranteed by national constitutions and international human rights instruments, this particular formulation targeting the *forum internum* fails to appreciate the relationship between religious self-identification and the administrative procedures underpinning state recognition. The central issue is this: at what point do the bureaucratic procedures underpinning the state's *recognition* of one's religious self-identification become administratively "unreasonable" in ways that constitute an abuse of one's fundamental rights?

Given the intricacies of Malaysia's legal system, one might appreciate the need to formalize the procedures governing conversion into or out of Islam. For specific historical reasons, the Malaysian constitution carves out a realm of specific (and exclusive) jurisdiction for state-level shari'ah courts in matters pertaining to Islam, suggesting that, at the very least, an official record of one's religious identity is necessary to ensure that the application of shari'ah-based laws is strictly limited to those professing the religion of Islam. Yet, building on this limitation, there have been several cases – particularly in divorce and custody battles – where a spouse converts *into* Islam and then claims that, insofar as he or she is now governed by shari'ah, prior obligations under civil law (e.g., obligations related to spousal maintenance) are no longer deemed to apply.[105] *Lina Joy* reminds us that, legally speaking, forms of religious *identification* are closely tied to formal administrative procedures underpinning state *recognition*.

To obtain state recognition, asking Lina Joy to follow a set of procedures that did not yet exist may seem (normatively) unreasonable – in many ways, an overzealous restriction on Joy's fundamental right to religious freedom. However, the case of *Lina Joy* reminds us that there is much to be gained (analytically) from a detailed empirical understanding of the relationship between religious self-identification and historically contingent questions of procedure – historically contingent questions of administrative procedure that underpin each state's recognition of religious identity and, therein, its manifestations within the public realm. It is this *empirical*

105 See, e.g., *Subashini a/p Rajasingam v. Saravanan Thangathoray & Other Appeals* [2008] 2, *Malayan Law Journal* 147.

understanding of historically and politically embedded debates about administrative procedure (and administrative "reasonableness") that, we argue, deserves more attention among those with an interest in the operationalization of religious freedom worldwide.

The absence of explicit statutory provisions governing Muslim apostasy in Malaysia's Federal Territories was not enough to persuade Malaysia's Federal Court that the regulatory requirements set by Malaysia's National Registration Department (requiring a certificate of apostasy from the relevant shari'ah court) were "unreasonable." On the contrary, the Court held that it was administratively reasonable for the NRD to require this certificate because apostasy was a matter to be addressed according to (state-level) Islamic principles. Requiring such a certificate, in other words, was (a) within the ambit of the administrative discretion afforded to the National Registration Department and (b) not so illogical (in Malaysia) as to fail a "Wednesbury" reasonableness test.

The question of administrative reasonableness in *Lina Joy* also implicated a rather sensitive feature of interbranch constitutional politics. Indeed, for specific historical, political, and constitutional reasons, the Federal Court refused to encroach on Malaysia's state-level shari'ah courts in matters pertaining to Islam. Moreover, it was conscious not to disrupt Malaysia's approach to center–state relations in legislative and judicial matters specifically pertaining to shari'ah. The Court believed that there was a clear constitutional mandate under the Ninth Schedule for Malaysia's state-level shari'ah courts to address these matters, even in the absence of any statutory provisions granting jurisdiction to those courts. Indeed, this exercise of judicial restraint in the face of complex political considerations is not unusual; Malaysia's Federal Court simply concluded that the NRD had acted "reasonably" in the sense of arriving at a course of administrative action that made sense within the context of Malaysian history and politics, the Malaysian constitution, and Malaysian administrative law.

In the end, the Federal Court's approach in *Lina Joy* had the effect of prohibiting – whether intentionally or not – the formalization of Lina Joy's choice of religion, i.e., her religious self-identification. Even if Joy had approached the shari'ah courts of Malaysia's Federal Territories, however, it is unclear which "procedures" she would have been expected to complete to obtain a certificate of apostasy. Without further legislative action, as demanded by the courts, her fundamental rights could not be operationalized and, as a result, her right to religious freedom was denied.

12

Legal Pluralism, Patronage Secularism, and the Challenge of Prophetic Christianity in Singapore

Daniel P. S. Goh

I. INTRODUCTION

Pluralism in its legal, ethnic, and religious varieties is an incontrovertible social fact for postcolonial states, at least in Southeast Asia. In Singapore, a strong state developed to regulate a pluralistic society, thus resulting in a trans-religious state that has used its secular powers to provide patronage support and protection of religions in the service of nation building. Patronage secularism, I argue, is a particular species of republican *laïcité*, in which the separation of state and church does not exist constitutionally, normatively, or practically. Instead, the state seeks to become the patron of religious institutions and in so doing accumulates the social power to become the trans-religious broker in matters of the good and the moral.

Patronage secularism, however, means that the state has to allow for a degree of legal pluralism, where religious institutions could continue to enjoy some social-legal autonomy in governing their own affairs. In recent decades, the rise of prophetic Christianity, particularly nondenominational megachurches practicing Pentecostalism, seeking the transformation of society through evangelism has led to unwitting challenges to the patronage secularism of the Singapore state. I show that this is due to the revelatory practices of Pentecostalism, which has produced new legal cultures in the megachurches that hybridize divine, corporate, and constitutional legalism in ways that seek to engage secularism. I discuss two cases in which megachurches had their brushes with the state and the law, and lost, attesting to the endurance of patronage secularism in Singapore.

My aim in this chapter is to combine the sociology of religion and the sociology of law to turn the mirror back on the debates on the secularization thesis in the West. The state's negotiations of the relationship between secularism and the religious are reminiscent of the process in Western societies, except that this is not a case of a liberal democracy faced by resurgent religion. Neither liberal nor democratic, but bequeathed with the legal traditions, principles, and institutions of the former Western imperial powers, the formation of the secular takes its own path in postcolonial societies such as Singapore. It is also difficult to meaningfully describe the involvement of religion in the public sphere in postcolonial societies as deprivatization or resurgence, as many of these religions take on new modern forms despite their traditionalist identities and narratives. In the case of prophetic Christianity in Singapore, it is the transfiguration of revivalist Christianity indigenous to Asia taking on novel forms of social engagement relevant to the modernization of state and society.[1] The conclusion that I draw from this study is that the main features of the radical redefinition of secularism in the West argued for by Charles Taylor[2] are already evident in the patronage secularism of Singapore, and this problematizes attempts to square this redefined secularism with political liberalism.

II. LEGAL PLURALISM AND PATRONAGE SECULARISM IN SINGAPORE

Secularism derives its political legitimacy not in its liberal and rational departure from its religious opposite, but in its capacity to mediate religious differences and arbitrate religious conflict from a transcultural vantage point. This describes the Singapore state, which, ironically, is often deemed illiberal by political sociologists. Founded in 1819 as a British port settlement, Singapore was a key colonial base in Southeast Asia for more than a century. The migrant population of the thriving commercial town was characterized by tremendous diversity. The European center of the city was anchored by the Anglican and Roman Catholic cathedrals and ringed by local churches of various denominations attended by the native population. The ethnic quarters of the city had dynamic and porous boundaries, such that one could find mosques, churches, Hindu temples, Buddhist temples, and Chinese clan temples sited close to each other. The plural society was carefully managed by the colonial government, which sought to incorporate the myriad religious groups into an overarching framework of imperial loyalty and accommodation through civic rituals and institutions. Rather than the divide-and-rule strategy that scholars often accuse colonial regimes of using to exercise political rule, the colonial government aimed to regulate religion for social harmony through corporatist accommodation. Far from being benevolent, the intention and outcome was a degree of state control of independent religious entities that the colonials feared could abet nationalist movements.

The corporatist accommodation meant that while the state gradually extended and centralized the rule of law over the diverse spheres of life of the native

[1] Terence Chong and Daniel P. S. Goh, "Asian Pentecostalism: Revivals, Mega-Churches, and Social Engagement," in Bryan Turner and Oscar Salemink (eds.), *Routledge Handbook on Religions in Asia* (Routledge, 2014), 402–17.

[2] Charles Taylor, "Why We Need a Radical Redefinition of Secularism," in Eduardo Mendieta and Jonathan Vanantwerpen (eds.), *The Power of Religion in the Public Sphere* (Columbia University Press, 2011), 34–59.

population, it fostered a legal pluralism unique to the colony. This legal pluralism was enhanced in the postcolonial period after Singapore became an independent republic in 1965. For example, the separate legal jurisdiction for Muslims over matrimonial matters established in 1880 was consolidated in the Administration of Muslim Law Act in 1966. The deployment of the Muslim Advisory Board, which started in 1915, to represent matters related to Islam and Malay custom was replaced and enhanced by the constitution of the Majlis Ugama Islam Singapura (Islamic Religious Council of Singapore) as a statutory board with executive powers to regulate Muslim affairs.

For the colonial government, the distinct regulation of Muslim affairs reflected the recognition of the special privileges and rights of the Malays as indigenous peoples of the region in the 1870s, as Singapore became part of the imperial expansion that ultimately formed British Malaya. For the postcolonial state, the special position of the Malays was explicitly recognized in Article 152 of the Constitution of the Republic of Singapore. Article 153 calls for the legislature to "make provision for regulating Muslim religious affairs." This is a seeming paradox when Article 15 of the Constitution on the "Freedom of religion" delineates that

(1) Every person has the right to profess and practise his religion and to propagate it.
(2) No person shall be compelled to pay any tax the proceeds of which are specially allocated in whole or in part for the purposes of a religion other than his own.
(3) Every religious group has the right –
    (a) to manage its own religious affairs;
    (b) to establish and maintain institutions for religious or charitable purposes; and
    (c) to acquire and own property and hold and administer it in accordance with law.
(4) This Article does not authorise any act contrary to any general law relating to public order, public health or morality.

However, it would be a mistake to view this as either a historical peculiarity pertaining to Islam or as an ambivalent state of affairs due to a reactive illiberal state. First, the postcolonial enhancements produced a spectrum of legal pluralism that ranged from strong centralized state regulation, as in the case of the regulation of Muslim religious affairs, to informal control through the regulation of associational life. The regulation of Hinduism takes place through the Hindu Endowments Board, also a statutory board established in law in 1968 and successor to the colonial Mohammedan and Hindu Endowments Board established in 1907 to manage the religious affairs of Indian communities. However, the postcolonial Board only directly manages the four major Hindu temples and seeks to extend its influence to the other temples through the organization of major festivals as well as being the mediator between the state and the temples. Thus, Vineeta Sinha notes the continuities from colony to nation and the informal nature of state regulation – more like "encounters" as she puts it – of Hinduism.[3] In another model, the canon law of the Roman Catholic Church is given explicit legal status by the state and administered as a separate domain parallel to civil law.[4]

Further down the spectrum, the regulation of Chinese religious affairs takes place more loosely through a series of laws. An important law in this respect is the Societies Act, which mandates the registration of almost all types of civic associations, including those pertaining to any religion, ethnic group, clan, nationality, or martial arts. This harks back to the old colonial ordinances regulating Chinese Triad secret societies that dominated the social life of the Chinese migrant communities in Malaya. The Charities Act and the Companies Act also perform the function of regulating many Chinese religious groups, as these often take the legal form of charities, institutions of public character, and nonprofit companies.

A key mechanism is the state's urban planning and allocation of land for religious purposes. Almost all land is owned by the state and leaseholds are tendered out to specified religions to meet the religious needs of the population. Only groups that are registered societies, charities, or nonprofit companies are eligible. Sometimes, as with many proactive Christian groups, religious entities would actively seek to convert underutilized facilities such as old cinema theaters in decaying town centers into religious places of worship. After establishment, the tenure of the places of worship is not secured in perpetuity but dependent on leasehold durations and other powers the state has in repossessing land for developmental purposes. Therefore, religious groups that seek to have a viable social presence in their communities have to treat the state as a patron and not just a neutral arbiter of property and economic transactions.

Second, it would be wrong to see these regulative mechanisms as a Hobbesean response to the specters of religious conflicts by an illiberal regime conditioned by racial and religious strife during decolonization, as Michael Hill has argued.[5] This view plays into the common portrayal of the Singapore state as an enigmatic capitalist autocracy, almost as the opposite number to the Lockean liberal state. Not only that. This interpretation misses out on the formation of the secular regime in Singapore through the state's articulation of religious domains and their regulation vis-à-vis *society* – society as a secular space for the enactment of moral transformation to produce national identity and public goods.[6] This has taken place, as I have argued, through a systematic legal pluralism adapted to each religion and its adherents and developed from the onset of colonial state formation into the postcolonial era.

3 Vineeta Sinha, *Religion-State Encounters in Hindu Domains: From the Straits Settlements to Singapore* (Springer Science+Business Media, 2011), 125–83.

4 Gary F. Bell, "Religious Legal Pluralism Revisited – The Status of the Roman Catholic Church and Her Canon Law in Singapore," *Asian Journal of Comparative Law* 7.1 (2012), 49.

5 Michael Hill, "The Rehabilitation and Regulation of Religion in Singapore," in James T. Richardson (ed.), *Regulating Religion: Case Studies from Around the Globe* (Kluwer Academic, 2004), 343–58.

6 Talal Asad, *Formations of the Secular: Christianity, Islam, Modernity* (Stanford University Press, 2003).

In fact, there is no reason to not interpret the development of secularism in Singapore as attuned to the four goals proposed by Taylor for his diversity-adapted secularism. The Constitution and its institutional enactments secure the freedom of religious affiliation as well as guarantee religious equality. The corporatist accommodation building on colonial legal pluralism aimed to facilitate the public participation of religions while preserving religious harmony. This publicity was an inexorable reality in the colony. Instead of pursuing the privatization of religions, which the colonial state saw as untenable, it sought to manage the plurality and publicity through the rule of law, so as to define and secure the secular domain for government.

Taylor's redefinition exists as a philosophical injunction, but the Singapore case is an actual *historical* reality that shows the articulation of the four aims does not produce a liberal democratic outcome. What we see in Singapore is the emergence of patronage secularism, where the secular is not pitted against the sacred. Instead, both are conjoined domains regulated by the state, whose legitimacy is derived from regulating institutionalized religions, as well as from governing the secular in the productive spheres of the national economy and the making of citizens, harnessing the sacred to produce social goods to drive these spheres. In the incorporation of religious groups into the framework of governance, reinforced by the dispensation of resources and land, the state has emerged as the secular patron of religions.

III. THE CHALLENGE OF PROPHETIC CHRISTIANITY

Singapore has been both the target as well as the base for Christian missionaries since early colonial times. Western missionaries made inroads into the Chinese population in the late nineteenth and early twentieth centuries. By the 1930s, many local churches using Chinese languages had been established and a new generation of local pastors rose to the fore. During the tumultuous decolonization period after the Second World War, Christians played a significant role as an anticommunist bulwark. After independence, during the 1970s and 1980s, Christians adapted to the rapid industrialization and modernizing social changes. In this period, the liberals who championed the social gospel were increasingly hemmed in by state regulation and crackdowns. These culminated in the 1987 administrative detentions of Catholic social workers and activists accused of engaging in a "Marxist conspiracy" to subvert the state. This took place in the wave of democratization and liberalization sweeping through East and Southeast Asia at the time, and the extrajudicial actions of the government came under heavy international and domestic criticism.

After several years of political maneuvers, the single-party political regime survived the democratic challenge and strengthened its position vis-à-vis organized religion, especially Christianity. The Maintenance of Religious Harmony Act was enacted in this period, giving powers to the state to stop religious figures from crossing the line between the religious and the political and to keep the peace between religions, especially if the peace is disturbed by active proselytization. Vineeta Sinha has shown that the Act, the powers of which have not been used, acts more powerfully to enshrine the position of the secular state as the protector of religious harmony, as well as the trans-religious agent to secure the inevitable religious diversity in Singapore.[7] However, in so doing, I argue, the state also entrenches itself as the patron of religious institutions, guiding and working with religious groups to engage society along approved routes.

While the Act was primarily motivated by the perceived need to discipline political religion, it was also motivated by the rise of evangelical Christianity in Asia. At the time of enactment, the latter concern was with evangelical Christians disturbing the peace through aggressive proselytization. Into the gap vacated by the liberals, independent Pentecostal churches founded by charismatic local pastors who left mainstream churches grew rapidly among the Chinese in the 1990s.[8] They accounted for the bulk of the increase of percentage of the resident population who professed themselves as Christians, from just below 10% in the 1980 Census to nearly 15% in the 2000 Census to more than 18% in the 2010 Census. On the other hand, the percentage of those professing to be Taoists or following traditional Chinese religions fell from 30% to 11% from 1980 to 2010. Those now professing to be Buddhists (33% in 2010) or stating they are not religious (17% in 2010) account for the drop not accounted for by conversion to Christianity. Several of the fast-growing independent Pentecostal churches have become megachurches with attendance at services or membership crossing the 10,000 mark. The first to do so was Faith Community Baptist Church led by Lawrence Khong, who had aspired to lead the entire evangelical Christian community in Singapore. Membership had remained at 10,000 for more than a decade because of his controversial leadership. Three other churches have surpassed Faith Community Baptist in numbers, drawing mainly young people from the new middle classes.[9]

The social influence of the megachurches greatly extends beyond the numbers, aided by strong financial capital accumulated by mandatory tithing and relentless donation drives. Many of the churches participate in the social sector with charity outreach arms. Faith Community Baptist has one of the most established outfits, TOUCH Community Services, with a strong presence in aging and poorer public housing estates. Some also have considerable presence in the commercial and property sectors. In collaboration with state-owned and private capital, both New Creation and City Harvest owned shopping and commercial complexes with large exposition and concert halls, partly to address the lack of mass worship spaces.

7 Vineeta Sinha, "Theorising 'Talk' about 'Religious Pluralism' and 'Religious Harmony' in Singapore," *Journal of Contemporary Religion* 20.1 (2005), 25.

8 Daniel P. S. Goh, "State and Social Christianity in Postcolonial Singapore," *Sojourn: Journal of Social Issues in Southeast Asia* 25.1 (2010), 54.

9 Terence Chong, "Megachurches in Singapore: The Faith of an Emergent Middle Class," *Pacific Affairs* 88.2 (2015), 215–35.

The megachurches have also ventured into the entertainment business, seeking to bring their Christian values and message into the mass media and popular culture sphere. As I have argued, these forays into the secular public sphere are displacements of the more traditional bible-toting proselytization, which hit its limit in the 2000s owing to pushback by the other religions as well as informal interventions by the government that led to several pastors issuing public apologies for hurting religious harmony.[10] Faith Community Baptist's foray into the secular social sector and City Harvest's entanglements in the popular entertainment business, and their challenges to the legal pluralism and patronage secularism in Singapore, are the two cases I discuss in this chapter and in the next two sections.

Compared to the other religious adherents, Christians have historically been left largely to their own devices by the state. The National Council of Churches of Singapore was formed in 1974, after the Council of Churches of Malaysia and Singapore split. The latter could be traced to its founding as an anticommunist bulwark in 1948, supporting the British regime during the emergency war against communist insurgents. The National Council, led by the Anglicans, Methodists, Lutherans, and Presbyterians, represents mainstream Christian interests vis-à-vis the state in an ad hoc manner. As emerging influential congregations, the megachurches engage the patronage secularism of the state in a different way. The resultant relationship is more transactional than the relationship of peerage between the mainstream denominational churches and the state. This is due to the need for the megachurches to carve out a space for themselves in Singapore, both physically and socially.

When I first conducted field research at City Harvest in 1998, the church was renting the disused Hollywood Theater just on the eastern outskirts of the city center to hold its services, but was aggressively raising money for a permanent building. It was also searching intensely for its identity as a church in Singapore, and began to build a reputation for itself as a church for youthful pop concert–like worship with a cosmopolitan urbane attitude and open-door "Church Without Walls" approach led by the dynamic couple, founding pastors Kong Hee and Ho Yeow Sun. The church was allocated land out in Jurong West, far away from the city center, in a public housing estate in the western industrial heartland and moved to its new premises in 2001.[11] In the schema of patronage secularism, City Harvest would be allocated land to build a church to serve the spiritual needs of the population, more than four-fifths of which were homed in public housing.

10 Daniel P. S. Goh, "Pluralist Secularism and the Displacements of Christian Proselytizing in Singapore," in Michael Feener and Juliana Finucane (eds.), *Proselytizing and the Limits of Religious Pluralism in Contemporary Asia* (Springer Science+Business Media, 2014).

11 Melody Zaccheus, "City Harvest Church Returns to Suntec Premises after Revamp," *The Straits Times* (Singapore, July 8, 2013), www.straitstimes.com/singapore/city-harvest-church-returns-to-suntec-premises-after-revamp (accessed June 2, 2017).

The church also gained recognition through its social work arm, the City Harvest Community Services Association, which had a distinctive focus on youth empowerment services. In 2002, the church started City College, a self-styled social enterprise to tutor underachieving students for high school examinations, while imparting life skills and values for excellence and service. O School was started soon after to become the largest street dance school in Southeast Asia, helping to sanitize youth street culture and provide employment to underprivileged youths. At the peak of its engagement with patronage secularism, City Harvest participated in the state's Chingay Parade in 2008, the annual street processional celebration of the multiculturalism of the nation and the global city.[12] The church contributed a float item called Solid Rock, featuring a secular story with religious undertones. The float was styled as a medieval castle, with young church members clad in armor and weapons acting out the defense of the castle against dark forces on the streets of downtown Singapore.

The hint of spiritual warfare in City Harvest's Chingay 2008 float was uncharacteristic of the church. However, for Faith Community Baptist, spiritual warfare was a central plank of the church's teaching and identity. The church was among the wave of aspiring megachurches that moved into disused movie theaters in the late 1980s and early 1990s. In that period, standalone theaters with large auditoriums were losing out to multiplexes located in new shopping malls and quickly became relics in maturing public housing estates. Many new churches led by entrepreneurial and independent-minded pastors saw these old auditoriums as a better alternative to state-allocated land for religious purposes, the lease of which was halved from sixty to thirty years in 1990. In 1992, Faith Community Baptist moved into the former Liberty Theater in Marine Parade Town. At the end of the decade, the church bought the Dalit Theater in Bukit Merah Town and the ninety-nine-year lease for the land zoned for commercial use, converting it into the TOUCH Community Theater for the church to expand into the arts sector and for its charity arm, TOUCH Community Services, to use as its primary base. In 2014, the church rebuilt the theatre – now renamed Gateway Theatre – into a nine-storey building with a 950-seater theatre and a 300-seater black box theatre space.[13] Nevertheless, the use of commercial land for religious purposes required the tacit approval of the state, which allowed it as long as the church was meeting the religious and social needs of the residents. In fact, TOUCH Community Services worked very closely with the state to provide a wide range of social services to strengthen the nuclear heterosexual family as the social buffer and basic building unit of social life, in line with the familial ideology of the state.

[12] Daniel P. S. Goh, "State Carnivals and the Subvention of Multiculturalism in Singapore," *British Journal of Sociology* 62.1 (2011), 111.

[13] Melody Zaccheus, "Church Builds $50m Arts Hub in Bukit Merah," *The Straits Times* (Singapore, October 28, 2015), www.straitstimes.com/singapore/church-builds-50m-arts-hub-in-bukit-merah (accessed June 2, 2017).

The dual location of Faith Community Baptist in the suburban public housing heartlands, one in the East of Singapore and the other in the West, with continued secondary presence in the city center at Suntec City Convention Centre, was not only strategic, but also fitted into the territorial imagination of spiritual warfare. Through the 1990s and into the 2000s, founding pastor Lawrence Khong led the LoveSingapore Movement to unite the Protestant churches and mobilize them for intensive proselytization to win the city over for Christ.[14] The discourse of spiritual warfare dominated the Movement, which saw itself in battle over the city with the demonic forces of secular culture, and for which practices such as territorial prayer-walking and high-ground praying over strategic locations were organized. Khong was the first among the megachurch pastors to lead his church into the breach of secular culture, establishing Gateway Entertainment in 2000[15] to bring Christian values into the arts and entertainment. In parallel with his pastoral work, Khong transformed his hobby for performing magic into a profession and began to perform magic shows to reach out to the unconverted and transmit wholesome family values.[16] This foray to sanctify the secular reached a personal climax for Khong in 2009, when he performed the finale for the Chingay Parade.[17] The megachurch pastor as illusionist was an ironic spectacle that fitted well with the state's multi-culturalism, as it showed the liberal embrace of the state's patronage of religion.

However, the fundamental prophetic character of the megachurches' evangelical Pentecostal faith could not be easily tamed. Given the autonomous space to anchor and grow its institutions for engaging secularism and the public sphere, the mega-churches produced their own hybrid legal cultures. City Harvest's "Church Without Walls" and Faith Community Baptist's emphasis on spiritual warfare each produced their own interpretations and practices of the law befitting the church's prophetic mission. As the megachurches pushed out into the public square to transform its secularism, they posed unwitting challenges to the patronage secularism of the state.

IV. ADULTERY AND THE RELIGIOUS EXCEPTION TO WORK

Faith Community Baptist's championing of the nuclear heterosexual family took place amidst profound changes to the social landscape. While most individuals still adhere to the familial ideology promoted by the state, blended families were becoming more common and accepted as well, causing the state to accommodate blended families by tweaking welfare and public housing policies. At the same time, the lesbian, gay, bisexual, and transgender (LGBT) movement gained tremendous ground through its annual Pink Dot rallies to promote acceptance of homosexual

[14] Lee Siew Hua, "The ST Interview: Singapore Churches' Mr Unity," *The Straits Times* (Singapore, April 20, 2011).
[15] "Minister, Magician and Polo Player," *The Straits Times* (Singapore, April 20, 2011).
[16] Lee, "The ST Interview: Singapore Churches' Mr Unity" (n. 19).
[17] Tay Suan Chiang, "Chingay Set to Sizzle," *The Straits Times* (Singapore, January 24, 2009).

relationships as loving and stable dyadic relationships. After years of government-sanctioned approbation and persecution, the movement achieved considerable success by staying away from advocating marital rights and focusing on gaining social acceptance.[18] The rallies have attracted more than 20,000 supporters each year, while the government has suspended the enforcement of anti-homosexuality laws. From their vantage point of spiritual warfare, Khong and his supporters thought they were losing ground in a slippery slope from tolerance of private homosexual relationships to the acceptance of the "homosexual lifestyle."[19]

In August 2013, the government's manpower ministry ordered Faith Community Baptist to compensate a former employee for dismissing her "without sufficient cause" during her pregnancy.[20] The compensation amount was very small – $7,000 in salary and maternity benefits. But the church objected. According to media reports, the woman, an administrative staff at the church, was dismissed in September 2012 after she was found to be pregnant with the child of a male co-worker.[21] The woman was married at the time, while the co-worker was a divorcee. The co-worker had been dismissed earlier in a separate case of misconduct involving a breach of confidentiality and the pregnant worker was put through counseling to end the adultery.[22] After eight sessions of counseling,[23] the woman continued to refuse to end the relationship and the church dismissed her when she was seven months pregnant.[24] The woman then complained to the Ministry of Manpower, which came down on her side after around ten months of investigation, mediation, and negotiation with the church.[25] In a long explanation to church members on his Facebook page, Khong wrote,

> At the end, we were left with no other option but to terminate her with just cause on the grounds of her continued involvement in this illicit relationship, as this illicit relationship is against the teachings and doctrines of the Bible, and our belief in leading an exemplary Christian life. As much as we wanted to avoid this recourse, it was simply not possible for her to continue working for the church while leading such a lifestyle. However, we did not want to leave her in a lurch and continued to extend our care and compassion for her. While we could not offer her severance pay

[18] Lynette J. Chua, *Mobilizing Gay Singapore: Rights and Resistance in an Authoritarian State* (Temple University Press, 2015).

[19] Elgin Toh, "Lawrence Khong: I Told the Minister to Send Me to Jail," *The Straits Times* (September 7, 2013).

[20] Toh Yong Chuan, "Compensate Woman Fired for Adultery, Church Told," *The Straits Times* (Singapore, August 20, 2013).

[21] Ibid.

[22] Lawrence Khong, "Lawrence Khong (FCBC)" (*Facebook*, August 23, 2013), www.facebook.com/lawrence.khong.fcbc (accessed June 29, 2016).

[23] Ibid.

[24] Toh, "Compensate woman fired for adultery, church told" (n. 19).

[25] Jeanette Tan, "Church Pays $7,000 Compensation for Dismissed Pregnant Staff Who Had Affair" (*Yahoo!* Singapore, August 28, 2013), https://sg.news.yahoo.com/church-pays–7-000-compensation-for-dismissed-pregnant-staff-who-had-affair-162329331.html (accessed June 2, 2017).

> as she was being terminated on just grounds, we encouraged her to apply for the LoveSingapore fund, knowing she would need financial assistance and emotional support.[26]

The remarkable thing about Khong's explanation was the *legal* thinking behind not offering the dismissed employee severance pay, which would allow the church to avoid the tussle with the government. Under orders from the ministry, the church agreed to pay but refused to concede the dismissal was "without sufficient cause." The Employment Act protects expectant women from unfair dismissals from the fourth month of pregnancy onward.[27] The government usually interprets sufficient cause as related to work performance or misconduct that would bring serious disrepute to the organization. Because family life is deemed to be a private realm and regulated and provided for as such, and employment is regulated as a public matter, the government could not admit adultery and engagement in illicit relationships as sufficient cause. On the other hand, Khong's counterargument was that the church was fundamentally an organization ministering to the spiritual needs of the people and secular law must permit moral reasons derived from religious beliefs as just causes for dismissal of employees. On intense public criticisms for failing in Christian compassion, Khong further explained,

> There is a gross misunderstanding between compassion and forgiveness versus action taken to ensure purity in the church leadership. . . . We spend time praying for and with the person concerned. This is called discipleship. We are not called just to have to accommodate everyone in the church. We are called to make disciples. Paul tells us to do the following: 2Tim. 3:16 All Scripture is God-breathed and is useful for teaching, REBUKING, correcting and training in righteousness, 2Tim. 4:2 Preach the Word; be prepared in season and out of season; correct, REBUKE and encourage – with great patience and careful instruction. Titus 1:13 This testimony is true. Therefore, REBUKE them sharply, so that they will be sound in the faith Titus 2:15 These, then, are the things you should teach. Encourage and REBUKE with all authority. Do not let anyone despise you.
>
> . . . This has always been the church's position. I expect the Christians and even MOM [The Ministry of Manpower] to respect that. It has nothing to do with lack of compassion. It has to do with maintaining a high moral standard for those who are in Christian ministry and leadership. This is for the protection of the members. This is part of compassion and love for the sheep.
>
> When this person was terminated in spite of us allowing her to resign quietly and therefore would be given her due compensation, we have no choice but to

[26] Khong (n. 21).

[27] Section 84(1)(a)(i), for notices of dismissal given before May 1, 2013. The Employment Act has since been amended to protect female employees at any time of her pregnancy where the female employee has served the employer for a period of three months or more immediately preceding the day the notice is given (Section 84(1)(b), for notices of dismissal given on or after May 1, 2013).

> terminate her. Involuntary termination does not allow us to give compensation. . . . I TOTALLY DISAGREE with MOM that there is insufficient ground for her termination and I am prepared to sacrifice my life and everything I have to maintain this position.[28]

I quote Khong at length to show how the church's legal argument was grounded in the church's demand for strong discipleship and strict discipline for its leaders underpinned by Biblical injunctions and the spiritual warfare worldview – they were no mere employees, but key officers in God's spiritual army. What the state considers to be the private affairs of individuals, and thus not to be admitted into the public square for deliberation, was a wholly legitimate consideration for the church precisely because it was to be considered a private organization with its own religious rules under the legal pluralism that has prevailed in Singapore. The church was willing to compensate if the offending staff member would resign and keep the issue private, but could not compromise without undermining the internal authority of the church when she claimed her employment rights, refused to resign, and thus made the issue a public and secular one. Just over a month later, Faith Community Baptist made an unprecedented appeal to the High Court to clarify the government's decision.[29] In its statement, the church, while invoking the patronage relationship with the state, called on the Constitution and the legal pluralism that has secured secular democracy as well as religious harmony,

> FCBC has always been respectful of the governmental authorities. We are constantly praying for and interacting with them as they lead the nation. . . .
>
> Having said that, whilst we respect the authorities and believe that they have been established by God over us, in light of Minister's decision, we are concerned about any far-reaching repercussions this decision has on FCBC as a church or for that matter all religious organisations, in our continuous attempts to uphold the values of our faith as we lead and watch over our flock.
>
> Specifically, we sincerely hope that the Courts can give guidance on where we stand with reference to the constitutional rights of religious bodies in the management of their religious affairs, which we believe include the hiring and dismissal of staff, the moral standards expected of staff at a level that reflects the ethos and values of the organisation. . . .
>
> We are mindful of the gravity of this application, and we recognise any outcome may have a bearing beyond our own organisation and affect the religious community at large – Christian or otherwise. We therefore trust and pray that the Courts will be able to help us move forward as an organisation that seeks to uphold the

[28] Lawrence Khong, "Lawrence Khong (FCBC)" (*Facebook*, August 24, 2013), www.facebook.com/lawrence.khong.fcbc (accessed June 29, 2016).

[29] Toh Yong Chuan, "Church Wants Review of Minister's Order to Compensate Axed Employee," *The Straits Times* (Singapore, October 2, 2013).

values of God – yet coexisting with all in our secular society that thrives on democracy and religious freedom.[30]

The Ministry responded, asserting its position as the secular patron of religious harmony and the multireligious constitution of the nation,

> Many different religions co-exist and thrive in Singapore; it is part of our make-up as a nation. Individuals and religious organisations are free to practise their respective faiths. However, our system of governance is a secular one and everyone has to abide by the laws of the land regardless of race, language or religion. The laws regarding employment constitute one such area. Employment laws have to be applied equally to all regardless of their religion.[31]

This set the stage for a deadlock for the High Court to adjudicate. The National Council of Churches Singapore quickly interjected, stating that the issue should not framed as a state–church matter and sided with the government's position that the case concerned the employer–employee relationship as regulated by the Employment Act and common law.[32] In May 2014, the judicial review was granted leave by the Court.[33]

A year later, Faith Community Baptist unexpectedly dropped the review. The church said that it had come to understand the rationale for the minister's decision and accepted that "every decision of the Minister would depend on the unique facts of each case." Therefore, as "a responsible religious body/corporate citizen of this nation," the church accepted the decision. Still, the church insisted "that moral conduct can in appropriate circumstances be governed by the terms of employment, where such conduct would affect the moral authority required in the performance of a job." However, the church affirmed that it remained "committed to the well-being of our nation, more so as she celebrates the year of Jubilee."[34] By interpreting the minister's decision as an exception made for each unique case and then asserting the exception that should be given to a religious group, the church called a truce that preserved both the sovereignty of the state and the church, even if only precariously and temporarily. There were two other exceptions implied in the statement that related to patronage secularism in particular. The first is the

30 Lawrence Khong, "Statement by Reverend Lawrence Khong" (Faith Community Baptist Church, October 2, 2013), www.fcbc.org.sg/spstatement/ (accessed June 2, 2017).

31 "Church's Dismissal of Pregnant Worker: The Manpower Ministry Responds," *TODAYonline* (Singapore, October 3, 2013), www.todayonline.com/singapore/manpower-ministrys-response (accessed June 29, 2016).

32 "FCBC Case Not a Matter of 'Church vs State', Says NCSS," *TODAYonline* (Singapore, October 10, 2013), www.todayonline.com/singapore/judicial-review-not-matter-church-vs-state-says-nccs?page=1 (accessed June 2, 2017).

33 Selina Lum, "Church Gets Green Light to Challenge Minister's Decision," *The Straits Times* (Singapore, May 30, 2014).

34 Faith Community Baptist Church, "Official Statement on MOM Judicial Review" (*Faith Community Baptist Church [FCBC] Singapore*, May 18, 2015), www.fcbc.org.sg/about/news/official-statement-mom-judicial-review (accessed June 29, 2016).

implication that it is because the church was a responsible religious body *and* corporate citizen of the nation, working with the state for the national good, the church accepted the government's decision on this specific case (though not its position). The second is the implication that the church's commitment to the nation and that 2015 was the special golden jubilee year were both factors in the church's decision to drop the review. The jubilee year was important because the government invested numerous resources and sought to work with all local organizations to mobilize the population for a grand celebration.

The political context had also changed dramatically since 2013. In June 2014, Khong and the LoveSingapore movement he led upped the ante against the LGBT movement, attempting to hold a counter-rally against Pink Dot to affirm the nuclear heterosexual family at the Padang, a national field that was a stone's throw away from where Pink Dot was held. FamFest was canceled after the government rejected the application because the location was unsuitable.[35] Subsequently, Faith Community Baptist and other churches joined Muslims to wear white in a show to defend traditional family values.[36] Founding Prime Minister Lee Kuan Yew died in March 2015 and a massive public outpouring of emotions crystallized the national sentiment and bolstered support for the ruling party, which had been on the defensive vis-à-vis a democratizing and liberalizing society. The general election was looming when Faith Community Baptist dropped the review and the church later implicitly endorsed the ruling party in the general election in September, by calling for his church to pray for "a strong government that has a clear mandate" to make decisions favoring the long-term good of the nation instead of pandering to the short-term demands of the people, and "empowered to take moral leadership in the nation."[37]

All things considered thus, the political calculus favored a renewal of patronage secularism. The state was carefully negotiating the balance between the liberalizing demands led by diverse groups making secular political pitches and the conservative reactions led by religious groups, trying to remain above the culture war while facilitating the groups to debate in the public square in search for a compromise. As the liberalizing forces had been increasing their leverage with the state, mobilizing social support and corporate sponsorship, it was perhaps seen as necessary for religious groups to remain on the good side of their patron and assert their counter-influence on the state. However, as the series of exceptions made by Faith Community Baptist to preserve the legal pluralism in their dropping of the judicial

35 Janice Tai and Melody Zaccheus, "Red Dot Family Day Planned for Padang Cancelled," *The Straits Times* (Singapore, May 7, 2014).

36 "Church Groups' Followers Wear White to Make a Stand," *The Straits Times* (Singapore, June 30, 2014).

37 Lawrence Khong, "Pray for a Strong Government" (*Faith Community Baptist Church [FCBC] Singapore*, September 1, 2015), www.fcbc.org.sg/celebration/our-thoughts-this-week/pray-strong-government (accessed June 29, 2016).

review shows, the challenge to the patronage secularism has not diminished, only suspended.

V. THE CHURCH AS SECULAR CORPORATION

In the case of City Harvest, the tussle with the state went to the courts. Though both are Pentecostal megachurches, City Harvest is very different from Faith Community Baptist. The latter emphasized discipleship and discipline for spiritual warfare and had been contented to allow its church membership to hover at around 10,000 to cultivate dedicated troopers. City Harvest was growth-oriented and preached healing for success and prosperity.

While Faith Community Baptist deepened the church's roots in the public housing heartland, investing $50 million to build a community and arts center in place of the old theater it had been using in Bukit Merah,[38] City Harvest sought to move back close to the city center after its relocation to its allocated place in Jurong West. Barely a few years after the church moved into its Jurong West premises, a titanium-clad $48 million building packed with the latest technologies,[39] and looking out of place in the public housing estate, City Harvest began looking for a sizable plot of land for a large building with good transport accessibility in the city center. In 2010, the church invested $310 million to become co-owner of Suntec City,[40] a premier shopping, convention and office complex anchoring one bank of Marina Bay, the new center of the global city. City Harvest's main objective was to secure the use of the 12,000-seat auditorium to cater to its self-reported 33,000 members then.[41] The longer-term vision was further church growth and closer integration into the secular global economy, so that the church could Christianize the flows of global capitalism.

This was yet another key difference between Faith Community Baptist and City Harvest. Pastor Khong's magic shows and the Gateway Entertainment projects were aimed at transforming families and community life in an intimate manner, one stage show at a time. Through its Crossover project, City Harvest's Pastors Kong and Ho sought to latch on to global culture flows to Christianize it. Crossover was started in 2002 as a project inspired by the "Church Without Walls" approach. The vision was for "members to be in the marketplace, for the marketplace, and to serve the marketplace" with "the Cultural Mandate," which is to engage "contemporary culture with relevance, and creatively serving our society with authenticity as successful, model citizens for the glory of God."[42]

38 Zaccheus, "Church Builds $50m Arts Hub in Bukit Merah" (n. 12).

39 "Singapore's Super Church-Builders: Kong Hee," *The Straits Times* (Singapore, July 17, 2010), Saturday Special Report.

40 Esther Teo, "City Harvest Paying $310m to Become Suntec Co-owner," *The Straits Times* (Singapore, March 7, 2010).

41 Ibid.

42 City Harvest Church, "The Origins of the Crossover" (*The Crossover Project*), www.chc.org.sg/crossover/english (accessed June 30, 2016).

The last part invokes patronage secularism and signals to the state that the Crossover project is intended to serve social needs. This was important because the church attracted controversies as early as 2003, when the press reported on unhappiness among church members for City Harvest's close support for Ho's pop music career. Known as Sun Ho in the pop music field, Ho was getting traction in East Asia, and was one of the five nominees for the Favorite Music Artist from Singapore award at the MTV Asia Awards that year. One member publicly alleged the church was pushing sales of Ho's pop music albums to members and screening her music videos in church, thus unethically mixing the secular with religion, and that church funds were improperly used for promoting the albums.[43]

While the member later apologized and retracted his allegations under the threat of libel suits,[44] the controversy showed that the Crossover project contained inherent contradictions. To achieve success in the pop music field, the church would have to invest huge amounts of capital, time, and energy to promote the project as a *secular* project with the religious messages toned down. Members contributing their donations to the church become stakeholders who demanded some accountability, but the church treated the membership as constituting a captive market to help promote the project. It certainly did not help that Ho was the founding pastor's wife and had to suspend her worship-leader ministry to cross over to the secular realm. It could be interpreted that the church was a platform for Ho's personal aspirations to become a pop star, the concert-like worship sessions being the training ground for her performances as well as the launching pad for marketing her success. Things got worse when Crossover tried to break into the US pop music market in 2007 with the music video, *China Wine*, which showed a scantily-clad Ho dancing suggestively with rappers.[45]

It was during the same time the nonprofit sector in Singapore was being hit by a series of scandals involving celebrity leaders mishandling donated monies, including that of a Buddhist monk who used pop star endorsements and worked closely with the state to establish the Ren Ci Hospital.[46] The disgraced monk was sentenced to jail in October 2009 for misappropriating hospital funds for loans made to companies and persons linked to the monk, who accumulated real estate properties around the world.[47] City Harvest cleared the governance review of large charities by the Commissioner of Charities in 2008 in the wake of the Ren Ci scandal.[48]

43 Samuel Lee, "I Have Done Nothing Wrong," *The Straits Times* (Singapore, January 20, 2003).

44 Bryna Sim, "He Dared to Ask about Use of Church Funds," *The Straits Times* (Singapore, June 28, 2012).

45 Ng Huiwen, "Idea Was to Spread Gospel via Pop Music," *The Straits Times* (Singapore, October 25, 2015).

46 Salma Khalik, "Ren Ci Under Probe for Financial Discrepancies," *The Straits Times* (Singapore, November 8, 2007).

47 *Public Prosecutor v. Goh Kah Heng alias Shi Ming Yi and Another* (2009) SGDC 500.

48 Hoe Yeen Nie, "Clean Bill of Health for Big 7; but Some Areas of Governance Need Cleaning Up," *Today* (Singapore, September 11, 2008).

However, in May 2010, just a couple of months after City Harvest announced the purchase of Suntec City for its ambitious growth plans, the police began investigation into the church accounts because of complaints of misuse of church funds made to the Commissioner.[49] In June 2012, Kong Hee and four other church leaders were arrested on charges of misappropriating funds to finance Ho's music career.[50] The government charged the leaders with conspiring to wrongly channel $24 million to Ho's artist management firm and a company owned by a church member, and more than $26 million later on to cover up the initial misappropriation after the church's auditor flagged the transactions as questionable.[51]

During the course of the trial, which attracted considerable publicity, it was revealed that the 2003 incident involving the unhappy member led to the setting up of the artist management company dedicated to managing Ho's crossover forays into secular pop music.[52] Before the attempt to break into the US pop music market, the company provided lighting and audiovisual services to City Harvest for the church's worship services, employing the same staff who used to be employed by City Harvest to provide those services.[53] The increased financial needs due to the US foray led to the church leaders to propose dipping into the church building fund, made up of donations from members and supporters earmarked for the search for larger and more central premises than the Jurong West building, to purportedly invest in the artist management company to finance Ho's campaign.[54]

The defendants argued against the charges of criminal breach of trust by way of intention. They argued that they love the church and did not intend to cause harm or loss to the church.[55] They claimed that their sole motivation was the cultural mandate of the Crossover vision and there was neither dishonesty nor conspiracy. Lawyers, auditors, and the church's Management Board were purportedly consulted on the plans. Moreover, the cultural mandate meant that it was morally permissible to temporarily use church funds for the Crossover project and the funds would be made good when the project was successful, which had to be because it was a mandate given to the church from God. During the trial, Kong Hee's twelve-page "confession letter," written as the authorities began the probe in 2010, was presented to the court as evidence of his pure motives. In the letter, the summary of which was published by City Harvest, Kong admitted to negligence and mistakes and prayed that the authorities would help City Harvest, Singapore Christianity and local charities "navigate through this very unfortunate and damning situation" that he had caused. Kong ended the letter pleading for leniency and "a chance to make

49 Melissa Sim, "Police Probe 17 Linked to City Harvest Church," *The Straits Times* (Singapore, June 1, 2010).

50 Ignatius Low, "5 City Harvest Leaders Arrested," *The Straits Times* (Singapore, June 27, 2012).

51 Leonard Lim, "City Harvest Case: $50m Misused," *The Straits Times* (Singapore, June 28, 2012).

52 *Public Prosecutor v. Lam Leng Hung and other appeals* (2017) SGHC 71 ("*Lam [HC]*") [23].

53 Ibid. [24].

54 Ibid. [27]–[28].

55 *Public Prosecutor v. Lam Leng Hung and others* (2015) SGDC 326 ("*Lam (DC)*") [187].

amends to become a better person and Christian minister," saying that he realized his mistakes only after reviewing them with lawyers from a top law firm, that "in all honesty" he "did not make any of those decisions with the intention of personal gain."[56]

The plea to the authorities to guide the church and Singaporean Christians points to the patronage secularism. But more importantly, the admission to honest *legal* mistakes on hindsight and repeated claims to moral purity, when taken together with the refusal to plead guilty to criminal breaches of trust, show that the church leaders interpreted the law governing corporate bodies through the prism of their religious mission. As Justice See Kee Oon stated in his decision at first instance, "Thus they convinced themselves that it was both morally and legally permissible to temporarily use the money from [City Harvest Church]'s funds when they knew it was not."[57] The judge found the accused guilty, saying, "no matter how pure the motive or how ingrained the trust in one's leaders, regardless of the context in which the trust operates, these do not exonerate an accused person from criminal liability if all the elements of an offence are made out."[58] The religious motives did play a part in the sentencing by the judge, who balanced the prosecution's call for a deterrent sentence with moderate sentences of eight years for Kong and between twenty-one months and six years for the others.[59] After the sentencing, Kong and the other defendants filed appeals against both the verdicts and sentences, while the prosecution also filed appeals against the sentences it thought were too light. The majority of a three-judge bench allowed the defendants' appeal and reduced the criminal breaches of trust charges and sentences for all defendants. The current sentences stand at three years and six months for Kong, and between seven months and three years and four months for the others.[60]

Accustomed to the legal pluralism, Kong and his leaders were acting out their prophetic Christianity in a way that fused their legal understanding with the moral purpose of the divine cultural mandate. The result was an inevitable challenge to the state at a time when rogue charity leaders were undermining patronage secularism by abusing the patronage for their own benefit. Kong did not see the Crossover project as ultimately benefiting his wife, who even when living the lavish material lifestyle of a pop star in Hollywood and in Singapore, was seen as merely acting out the divine mandate to evangelize pop music consumers as authentically as one should. Hence, Kong could not see his actions as criminal. After each verdict was handed down, Kong apologized to his congregation for the suffering members had to endure because of their faithfulness to the church and him, not for what he had

56 City Harvest Church, "City Harvest Trial: Contents of Kong's 'Confession Letter' Revealed," *City News* (September 11, 2014), www.citynews.sg/2014/09/city-harvest-trial-contents-of-kongs-confession-letter-revealed (accessed June 30, 2016).

57 *Lam (DC)* (n. 61) [495].

58 *Lam (DC)* (n. 61) [501].

59 *Public Prosecutor v. Lam Leng Hung and others* (2015) SGDC 327.

60 *Lam (HC)* (n. 58) [419]–[434].

done.[61] In 2015, promises were made to improve governance, so that the church would rise about the tribulations and achieve a new "CHC 2.0" vision of renewed growth.[62] In 2017, Kong said he had confidence in CHC's new leadership, which he said had put in place good corporate governance, and pledged that "whatever happened in the past will never repeat itself in the future."[63] The prosecution has filed a criminal reference referring questions of law arising from the split High Court decision to the Court of Appeal and has indicated that it intends to ask the apex court to reinstate the original convictions.[64] The appeal is pending at the time of writing, but the challenge of prophetic Christianity to patronage secularism was sealed.

VI. CONCLUSION

In his revision of Western secularism, Taylor argues that a democracy "demands a 'people' with a strong collective identity" and therefore "obliges us to show much more solidarity and much more commitment to one another in our joint political project than was demanded by the hierarchical and authoritarian societies of yesteryear."[65] Postcolonial Singapore experienced this demand to forge a people with strong collective identity urgently when it became independent half a century ago. Under a dominant ruling party, the country built upon the Westminster model of democratic representation and carved out a unique political trajectory that scholars have tagged as something like authoritarianism. A large part of this trajectory involved the state's deliberate and conscious production of the secular domain, which was formed upon the colonial patronage of religions. The secular is not defined against religion or by it, but in relation to diverse religions as the domain of the trans-religious state that secures religious harmony and facilitates religious participation in the public sphere and in the production of social goods. The secular state works closely with *religions* to produce the solidarity and commitment between citizens needed for the young nation. There was no secularization in the last fifty years, but the formation of the secular that also led, quite deliberately and with design, to the rise of religions in the public sphere.

Legal pluralism is a necessary consequence of the patronage secularism. This pluralism is distributed across the different religions, with Christianity enjoying the greatest degree of autonomy. This autonomy did not mean separation from

[61] Ng Huiwen, "Kong Hee Tells Church Members: Pastor Is Sorry," *The Straits Times* (Singapore, October 25, 2015); Ng Huiwen, "CHC Founder Kong Hee Tells Church He Is 'Deeply Sorry'," *The Straits Times* (Singapore, April 8, 2017).

[62] Ng Huiwen, "Kong Hee Tells Church Members: Pastor Is Sorry," *The Straits Times* (Singapore, October 25, 2015).

[63] Ng Huiwen, "CHC Founder Kong Hee Tells Church He Is 'Deeply Sorry'," *The Straits Times* (Singapore, April 8, 2017).

[64] Attorney-General's Chambers, "The City Harvest Church Case: *Lam Leng Hung & Ors v. PP*; Prosecution Files Criminal Reference" (*Attorney-General's Chambers*, April 10, 2017), www.agc.gov.sg/DATA/0/Docs/NewsFiles/CHC%20Press%20Release_web.pdf (accessed June 4, 2017).

[65] Charles Taylor (n. 2), 44.

patronage secularism. The churches depended on the state's control of land and regulation of the property market as well as the social sector to maintain and deepen their relevance to the population. Indeed, once the more liberal branches of Christianity championing social justice were crushed by state repression in the early decades of independence, the fastest-growing Christian churches were the ones who worked closely with the state. Faith Community Baptist and City Harvest were the two largest Pentecostal megachurches in Singapore at one point, and the financial capital the two churches had built up through donations and tithes would have been useless if they could not translate into charity outreach and property development, both of which necessitated state patronage in different degrees.

Yet, because of the prophetic nature of their Pentecostal founding, the two megachurches were not contented with their allotted place in the national landscape of diverse religious coexistence. Faith Community Baptist and City Harvest sought to create "gateways" or "crossover" into secular culture to Christianize it. The former became extremely focused on the defending the nuclear heterogeneous family from promiscuity, dysfunctionality, and homosexuality. The latter became obsessed with the global flows of pop culture and sought some form of Christian success and achievement in the international cross-Pacific field of pop music. In the process, both churches unwittingly challenged the secularism of the law, bringing their hybrid interpretations of the law afforded by legal pluralism to bear in the face-off with the state in the courts.

13

Equality in Secularism

Contemporary Debates on Social Stratification and the Indian Constitution

M. Mohsin Alam Bhat

I. INTRODUCTION

The transnational legal literature has often approached secularism as a normative doctrine that organizes institutions regulating religion in public life. Scholarship on India is not an exception. Considerable ink has been spent on a normative and historical assessment of the content of secularism under the Indian constitution. The very prospect of separating religion and state in a deeply diverse and religious society makes this scholarly treatment both exciting and challenging. Add to this the range of recognition that the Indian Constitution grants organized religion: it safeguards individual religious freedom, while at the same time granting protection and autonomy to religious denominations and institutions in their affairs.[1] It mandates state intervention in favour of religious reform, particularly the access of historically excluded groups and castes to places of worship.[2] Constitutional jurisprudence has consistently – but not without occasional apprehension – maintained the 'personal law system' that governs the family laws of different religious communities.[3]

It is little wonder then that some of the most influential accounts of secularism in India stress the uniqueness of the Indian constitutional experiment. Rajeev Bhargava, a prominent scholar who defends the Indian version of secularism, concedes that 'a confusing, somewhat contradictory, picture on secularism emerges from a reading of the constitution'.[4] However, he argues that secularism in India is

[1] The Constitution of India 1950, Articles 25 and 26.

[2] Ibid., Article 25(2) provides that the right to freedom of religion will not obstruct the state's power of 'regulating or restricting any economic, financial, political or other secular activity' associated with religious practice, or measures of 'social welfare and reform or the throwing open of Hindu religious institutions' to all sections of Hindus.

[3] For a discussion of some of the themes in personal laws, see Gerald James Larson, *Religion and Personal Law in Secular India: A Call to Judgment* (Indiana University Press, 2001); Catharine A. MacKinnon, 'Sex Equality under the Constitution of India: Problems, Prospects, and "Personal Laws"', *International Journal of Constitutional Law* 4 (2006), 181.

[4] Rajeev Bhargava, 'India's Secular Constitution: Ideas, Practices, Controversies', in Zoya Hasan, E. Sridharan and R. Sudarshan (eds.), *India's Living Constitution* (Anthem Press, 2005), 105. See also

not a purely procedural principle separating religion from politics; rather, it is a 'multi-value' doctrine where the state's 'principled distance' from religion can still accommodate concerns of diversity, unity, and peace. Another scholar, Gary Jocobsohn, prefers to describe Indian secularism as 'ameliorative': a doctrine that mandates, rather than impedes, the mitigation of historically entrenched religious divisions and recognition of difference.[5] These normative approaches have succeeded in refuting critiques based on straitjacketed accounts of secularism. Instead of locating secularism in the West alone, their contextual depth has helped us to focus on the histories of secularisms.

Nevertheless, this methodology may have its blind spots. The Indian state institutions have often fallen short of the normative promise of secularism. Religion-inspired reasons – directly or through proxies – have come to dominate the legislative agenda.[6] Institutions have not maintained their neutrality, among other things, in dealing with the concerns of security and protection of minority populations.[7] The Indian literature has yet to consistently probe and problematize secularism's ubiquitous inconsistency in the institutional mechanisms of the country. My argument is that explaining these as aberrations is explaining them away.[8]

This chapter is motivated to address, in part, this facet of Indian secularism. I argue that Indian secularism, as a regulatory practice, is far more slippery and disjointed than most contemporary accounts may concede. Indian secularism is marked by patterns of contradictory constructions of what counts as 'religious' as opposed to 'secular'. Thus, the everyday regulation of religious claims through secularism often does not offer a coherent normative content, but is more of a negotiation with religious claims that are seen to be dangerous.

Brenda Cossman and Ratna Kapur, 'Secularism's Last Sigh: The Hindu Right, the Courts, and India's Struggle for Democracy', *Harvard International Law Journal* 38 (1997), 113.

5 Gary J. Jacobsohn, *The Wheel of Law: India's Secularism in Comparative Constitutional Context* (Princeton University Press, 2005).

6 One example of this is the wave of anti-conversion laws that have been enacted across various Indian states. For an account of these laws, see South Asia Human Rights Documentation Centre, 'Anti-Conversion Laws: Challenges to Secularism and Fundamental Rights', *Economic and Political Weekly* 43 (2008), 63; Laura Dudley Jenkins, 'Legal Limits on Religious Conversion in India', *Law and Contemporary Problems* 71 (2008), 109.

7 Sectarian violence, particularly against religious minorities, has been part of everyday life. For the history and politics of sectarian violence, see Steven I. Wilkinson, *Votes and Violence: Electoral Competition and Ethnic Riots in India* (Cambridge University Press, 2006); Ashutosh Varshney, *Ethnic Conflict and Civic Life: Hindus and Muslims in India*, 2nd edn (Yale University Press, 2003).

8 Gyanendra Pandey makes a similar critique in the context of secularism and sectarian violence in India: "Academic discourse … tends to push the moment of [sectarian] violence into the realm of the exceptional and aberrant … It is to suggest that events … do not represent the real flow of Indian history: they are exceptional, the result of unusual conjunctures. It is to pretend that their occurrence on the scale and with the frequency that we have seen in the 1980s still makes no fundamental difference to the essential 'secularism' of the people and to our cherished national traditions: 'secularism', 'non-violence', 'peaceful co-existence'." Gyanendra Pandey, 'In Defence of the Fragment: Writing about Hindu-Muslim Riots in India Today', *Economic and Political Weekly* 26 (1991), 559, 565, 566.

I study some patterns of this negotiation and disjuncture by comparing two 'fragments' – texts that capture divergent and localized episodes – of secularism's institutional life in India.[9] Both fragments reflect the Indian state's response to different minorities' claims of equality and inclusion in the country's affirmative action regime.

My first fragment is the opinion of Raghuram J in *Archana Reddy* – a case dealing with the constitutionality of quotas for Muslims.[10] In *Archana Reddy*, the High Court of the state of Andhra Pradesh was asked whether the state's Muslim affirmative action policy – which had resulted from years of Muslim demands – could sustain the challenge of secularism, specifically the constitution's provisions against discrimination on the ground of religion. Raghuram J's opinion – part of the majority – was a vehement statement of why affirmative action for religious groups violated this secular principle.

I place this statement of secularism next to the second fragment – the 'Note of Dissent' of Asha Das, the member-secretary of the National Commission for Religious and Linguistic Minorities (also known as the Misra Commission after its chairperson).[11] The Misra Commission was constituted by the central government to investigate the need for Muslim affirmative action in light of the growing evidence of the community's socio-economic marginalization. One of the chief issues on its agenda was the long-standing demand by the *Dalit* Muslims for affirmative action. As I will explain in greater detail in the text that follows, the *Dalits*, or the erstwhile untouchable castes, are given a range of affirmative action benefits under the Constitution. However, the *Dalit* converts to Islam and Christianity have been excluded from this regime. The *Dalit* Muslims have thus been demanding the removal of this religious bar. The Misra Commission was the first government-instituted panel to assess the legal grounds of the exclusion in order to make recommendations to the state. While the majority of members agreed with the *Dalit* Muslim demand, Das filed a dissent that presented the first articulate defence of the exclusion. She insisted that the religious exclusion was not discriminatory and thus not a violation of the principle of secularism.

My purpose in comparing these two fragments is not to derive a normative rationale underlying Indian secularism. Rather, this approach aims to do the opposite – to explore its slippages and ambiguities, diversities and contradictions.

9 I use the term 'fragments' in a similar manner as how some historians have used it – as an eclectic set of texts that push us to reconsider entrenched understandings of historical narratives. See Gyanendra Pandey, *Routine Violence: Nations, Fragments, Histories* (Permanent Black, 2006), 47. Pandey uses fragments 'to indicate certain kinds of historical sources: I include among these fragments often neglected by orthodox historians, a weaver's diary, a book of poems on riots written by a little known local poet, women's writings … '.

10 *B. Archana Reddy v. State of Andhra Pradesh* [2005] MANU/AP/0682/2005.

11 Ministry of Minority Affairs, *Report of the National Commission for Religious and Linguistic Minorities* (Government of India, 2007) (Misra Commission Report), 156.

This methodology aligns itself with what Kim Lane Scheppelle calls 'constitutional ethnography'. According to her:

> The goal of constitutional ethnography is to better understand how constitutional systems operate by identifying the *mechanisms* through which governance is accomplished and the *strategies* through which governance is attempted, experienced, resisted and revised, taken in historical depth and cultural context. While any one specific constitutional setting has distinctive and ungeneralizable features, each constitutional context also has *logics* that link various specific features found in the particular case into patterns whose traces may also be visible elsewhere with different specific manifestations.[12]

My fragmentary approach is well suited to explore, in Scheppelle's words, 'a set of repertoires that can be found in real cases and that provide insight into how constitutional regimes operate'.[13] As a scholar of constitutional ethnography of secularism writes, this methodology of studying constitutionalism highlights 'the multivalenced and often conflicting meanings, understandings, and implications of constitutional discussions for diverse and fractured polities'.[14]

In line with the spirit of this methodology, I will attempt to bring out the tensions underlying Indian secularism. What is significant in my choice of fragments is that they give a constitutional frame to the political positions that are widely endorsed in India. In fact, at least for the time being, both positions reflect the dominant political and institutional understanding of religious minority claims of inclusion. Interestingly, though, my exploration should reveal that they are based on deeply conflicting understandings of religious identity and social stratification. In deploying secularism, institutional actors conceptualize the minority religious Muslim community in incompatible ways. In Raghuram J's opinion in *Archana Reddy*, affirmative action for Muslims as a group was unsustainable because of the internal heterogeneity of the community; whereas in Das's note, the inclusion of *Dalit* Muslims was unsustainable because they were *only* Muslims, without other intersecting identities. While the former interpreted religious identity as illusory, the latter treated religious identity as exhaustive. This patent contradiction has done little to undercut the power of secularism, as a discourse, in responding to both Muslim claims of inclusion.

To study secularism from the perspective of the debates on affirmative action is potentially illuminating. In much of the literature, the central cases of secularism concern questions of cultural accommodation (for example, multiculturalism) or the identity of a constitutional polity (for example, the imposition of religious law in

12 Kim Lane Scheppele, 'Constitutional Ethnography: An Introduction', *Law & Society Review* 38 (2004), 389, 390–91.

13 Ibid., 391.

14 Jeffrey A. Redding, 'Secularism, The Rule Of Law, and "Shari'a Courts": An Ethnographic Examination of a Constitutional Controversy', *Saint Louis University Law Journal* 57(2013), 339, 340–41.

theocratic or quasi-theocratic states). Social stratification and group subordination are not the usual routes to theorize about secularism. My hope is that this approach will shed light on some counter-intuitive aspects of secularism as regulation, particularly how certain citizenship claims in India are understood or interpreted as 'religious' claims, and thus deemed to be anti-secular. In the two fragments I discuss, institutional actors construct the Muslim claims – which are against group subordination and marginalization – as 'religious' instead of 'secular'. Curiously, these institutional actors do not interpret analogous claims emerging from caste groups on the similar register of 'religion'. This contrast invites us to investigate the background of these institutional presuppositions that draw the boundaries of Indian secularism.

In the rest of this chapter, I will juxtapose my chosen fragments and evaluate the consequent implications. In Section II, I describe the historical and constitutional antecedents of the Indian affirmative action regime. I focus on the constitutional regime of affirmative action for the erstwhile untouchable castes or the 'Scheduled Castes'. I also give an account of how the interpretation of equality under the Indian constitution came to accommodate affirmative action, particularly quotas, for the marginalized low-caste groups. In doing so, I also introduce the grounds of the Muslim demands for affirmative action. In Section III, I give an account of secularism as an institutional tactic in addressing these demands. My aim here is not only to elaborate on the *form* of constitutional arguments that Raghuram J and Das proffer, but also to explore the complex understanding of religious identity and social stratification that facilitates their positions. My focus will be on showing how their respective arguments are in fact based on contrasting views of Muslim social stratification, and the construction of the 'religious' that secularism is meant to curtail.

It is these contradictory constructions of social stratification and religious identity that I attempt to make sense of in Section IV. My aim is not to give an exhaustive historical account of this tension, which I have tried to do elsewhere.[15] I will only address how a significant articulation of secularism under the Indian Constitution is contingent on constructing religious identity as being separate from social stratification. I will argue that during the Indian constitutional framing, secularism emerged as a formula to neutralize claims of both religious and caste minorities. Constitutional framers accomplished this by adopting different strategies that worked in tandem: minority caste claims were treated as a problem of social stratification, and thus of social and political power; in contrast, religious minority claims were rejected. It was precisely this contrast between caste and religious identity that sustained the constitutional formula of secularism. This has left a

[15] See M. Mohsin Alam Bhat, *Conflict, Integration and Constitutional Culture: Affirmative Action and Muslims in India*. J.S.D. dissertation, Yale Law School, 2017.

seemingly deep impulse within Indian secularism to *not* interpret claims of religious minorities as claims against subordination.

II. EQUALITY AND THE INDIAN AFFIRMATIVE ACTION REGIME

A. 'Caste' and the *Dalit* Reservation Regime

Politics in India has a habit of subjecting the country's affirmative action regime – famous for accommodating historically marginalized caste communities – to regular bouts of tension. Caste groups have led the most prominent mobilizations for inclusion in the affirmative action regime.[16] Consequently, they have also had the biggest impact on shaping the contours of the regime. By the early 2000s, various iterations of Muslim mobilizations started arguing that affirmative action had left the minority unattended. Their visible social and political marginalization, they argued, mandated their inclusion in the existing regime.[17]

Before I come to the structure of affirmative action in India, it is pertinent to first define 'caste'. Caste is a social and economic institution that is based on a status gradation of endogamous occupational groups. In some accounts, this caste hierarchy spans four caste clusters or *Varnas*: the *Brahmins*, or priestly classes; *Kshatriya*, or warrior classes; *Vaishya*, or mercantile classes; and *Sudra*, or low classes. Outside the pale altogether are the outcastes and pariahs – the *Dalits*. Each of these classes further comprises thousands of caste groups.[18]

The *Dalits* at the bottom of the hierarchy have traditionally faced, and continue to face, extreme forms of untouchability and violence.[19] They have also been forced to engage in menial labour, including sanitation, cleaning, and handling dead animals (for example, for leather). The *Dalits* have also historically been prohibited from owning land or getting educated. All this has been enforced through systems of violence, both physical and religious. The caste system gets endorsement from some fundamental Hindu scriptures, particularly the *Manusmriti*, which laid down rules to maintain caste 'purity' in areas such as social interaction and marriage.

16 For more information on the history of caste mobilization for reservations, see Christophe Jaffrelot, *India's Silent Revolution: The Rise of the Lower Castes in North India* (Orient Blackswan, 2003).

17 For accounts of Muslim reservation demands, see Theodore P. Wright, 'A New Demand for Muslim Reservations in India', *Asian Survey* 37 (1997), 852; Mohammad Sajjad, *Muslim Politics in Bihar: Changing Contours* (Routledge India, 2014).

18 For a short sociological introduction to the topic, see M. N. Srinivas, 'Some Reflections on the Nature of Caste Hierarchy', *Contributions to Indian Sociology* 18 (1984), 151.

19 See Oliver Mendelsohn and Marika Vicziany, *The Untouchables: Subordination, Poverty and the State in Modern India* (Cambridge University Press, 1998); 'Hidden Apartheid: Caste Discrimination against India's "Untouchables"'. *Human Rights Watch* (12 February 2007), www.hrw.org/report/2007/02/12/hidden-apartheid/caste-discrimination-against-indias-untouchables (accessed 29 April 2017).

Since its inception, the Indian Constitution has provided an eclectic model of affirmative action, popularly known as 'reservations'. Two of these are relevant to my argument. The first is reservations for the *Dalits*. The constitutional category of the 'Scheduled Castes' (SCs) is meant to capture this group. Backed by a long and inspiring political mobilization on the part of the untouchables,[20] the constitution prohibited the practice of untouchability in 1950.[21] It also instituted proportional representation for the SCs in the political branches. At the same time, the Constitution enabled the state to provide affirmative action, including quotas, in government employment and educational institutions.[22]

The constitutional text did not specify the social groups that would qualify as SCs. Neither did it lay down any explicit test for their identification. It only provided a procedure: Article 341 left the first enumeration of the SCs to the president, with subsequent changes to be affirmed by parliamentary legislation.[23] The first enumeration was done in a presidential order issued in 1950 ('1950 Order'), with periodic additions every few years.

While the constitution did not provide a criterion for the selection of SCs, the institutional practice has been to rely on 'extreme social, educational and economic backwardness arising out of the traditional custom of untouchability'. As Galanter and Dushkin have noted,[24] this process of identification, far from being clear, has remained a combination of political and bureaucratic exercises. One reason for this lack of clarity is the historical and territorial diversity of caste practices, including those of untouchability.

In the 1950 Order, the president restricted the SC category to only those who professed to be Hindu. Subsequent alterations not only expanded the enumeration, but also came to include Sikhs (1956) and Buddhists (1990) in the category. However, both Muslims and Christians have been left out. This means that a *Dalit* who converts to either religion would lose her SC status. This also means that Muslim and Christian groups that historically engaged in occupations analogous to those of the SCs, and that went through the same or comparable socio-economic conditions, would not be covered. This is a particularly stark anomaly: many *Dalit* Muslim and Christian communities are known by the same names and live alongside their Hindu, Sikh, or Buddhist compatriots. The only difference is their religious conviction.

20 For a compelling account of *Dalit* politics in India, particularly before Independence, see Anupama Rao, *The Caste Question: Dalits and the Politics of Modern India* (University of California Press, 2009).

21 The Constitution of India 1950, Article 17.

22 Ibid., Articles 15(4) and 16(4).

23 Ibid., Article 341 ('The President may … by public notification, specify the castes, races or tribes or parts of or groups within castes, races or tribes which shall for the purposes of this Constitution be deemed to be Scheduled Castes.').

24 See Marc Galanter, 'Untouchability and the Law', *Economic and Political Weekly* 4 (1969), 131; Lelah Dushkin, 'Scheduled Castes Policy in India: History, Problems, Prospects', *Asian Survey* 7 (1967), 626.

The *Dalit* Muslim mobilization arose to politicize precisely this anomaly. While demands for inclusion were already being made by the *Dalit* Christians,[25] it was only in the mid-1990s that a number of platforms – with concrete agendas of *Dalit* Muslim inclusion – started to form. One of the earliest specimens was the *Dalit* Muslim Morcha, in the Indian province of Bihar. While it started as a coalition of a number of low-caste Muslim occupational groups voicing various shared demands of the state, by 1996, the Morcha started mobilizing around the specific demand of inclusion in the SC category.[26]

Organizations such as Morcha have argued that the religious test in the 1950 Order is discriminatory on the ground of religion, and thus a violation of equality and secularism. This has not been a straightforward claim. In order to be persuasive, *Dalit* Muslim organizations have argued that the institution of caste is trans-religious; caste is a 'socio-professional' category that is shared by all religions in India. Consequently, the whole gamut of disabilities that flow from the *Dalit* identity – untouchability, social stigma, and social and economic marginalization – are shared by all the *Dalits* irrespective of their religious faith. Evidence from the social sciences increasingly supports this view. Sociologists such as Imtiaz Ahmad have argued that the Indian Muslim community reflects caste-like features in part because the converts to Islam had carried their ascriptive identities and occupations to the new faith.[27] In 2006, a government-instituted report studied the socio-economic conditions of *Dalit* Muslims and *Dalit* Christians.[28] It not only noted the existence of caste-like stratification among Muslims, but also found data that the marginalization of *Dalit* Muslims was comparable to that of their 'Hindu' counterparts.

All these developments have brought the *Dalit* Muslim and Christian demand to the forefront of political discourse. In 2008, a *Dalit* Christian organization approached the Supreme Court to challenge the constitutionality of their exclusion. Soon, *Dalit* Muslim organizations impleaded as parties. These petitions await their final hearing.[29]

[25] For a discussion of *Dalit* Christians, see A. K. J. Wyatt, 'Dalit Christians and Identity Politics in India', *Bulletin of Concerned Asian Scholars* 30 (1998), 16; Lancy Lobo, 'Visions, Illusions and Dilemmas of Dalit Christians in India', in Ghanshyam Shah (ed.), *Dalit Identity and Politics: Cultural Subordination and the Dalit Challenge* (SAGE, 2001), 242.

[26] See M. Mohsin Alam Bhat (n. 15), 168–225; Yoginder Sikand, 'A New Indian Muslim Agenda: The Dalit Muslims and the All-India Backward Muslim Morcha', *Journal of Muslim Minority Affairs* 21(2001), 287.

[27] See Imtiaz Ahmad, *Caste and Social Stratification among Muslims in India* (Manohar, 1978).

[28] Satish Deshpande, *Dalits in the Muslim and Christian Communities: A Status Report on Current Social Scientific Knowledge* (Government of India, 2006), http://ncm.nic.in/pdf/report%20dalit%20%20reservation.pdf (accessed 2 September 2017).

[29] *Mohd. Sadiq v. Union of India* [2006] Writ Petition (C) No. 46 of 2006; *Akhil Maharastra Khatik Samaj v. Union of India* [2008] Writ Petition (C) No. 13 of 2008; *Centre for Public Interest Litigation v. Union of India* [2004] Writ Petition (C) No. 180 of 2004.

B. *'Backward Classes' and Muslims*

A very different set of affirmative action claims arose from a separate genre of political and social formations. By the early 2000s, numerous Muslim organizations started demanding that Muslims, as a group, must be recognized as the beneficiaries of affirmative action. The Muslim organizations were addressing a different set of constitutional norms: the power of the state to provide affirmative action, including quotas, for the category of the 'other socially and educationally backward classes' or 'other backward classes' (OBCs) – 'backward' being the constitutional euphemism for the marginalized.

The OBC category, which was introduced in the constitution through an amendment in 1951, has a long and checkered history. Its antecedents lie in the pre-Independence practice of providing reservations and representation to 'backward' castes and communities.[30] After its introduction in the constitutional text, the controversy has been about the role of caste in the determination of beneficiaries. The only textual standard for the identification of OBCs is the test of 'social and educational' backwardness and lack of state representation. But the fact that the category is called the backward *classes* led to a prolonged legal battle over the role that caste identity should play in the identification of beneficiaries of the OBC category. The specifics of this debate are not relevant here. The only thing I will highlight is the conclusion of this debate by the early 1990s: The Supreme Court in *Indra Sawhney* held that caste groups could be the beneficiaries of affirmative action *provided* there is evidence of their socio-economic and educational backwardness, and inadequate representation in public employment.[31] To assess the 'social backwardness' of a caste, the Supreme Court – endorsing the views of the Backward Classes Commission – held that, inter alia, caste status, occupation, and participation of women in the workforce would be the relevant tests.[32]

The OBC regime endorsed by *Indra Sawhney* included a few Muslim subgroups. Over the years, a discrete demand emerged for the recognition of Muslims as a separate beneficiary of affirmative action. Muslim organizations argued that not only had a number of Muslim groups been left out of the policies, but also those who had been included did not obtain any benefits from the quotas. Muslims, they argued, could not compete with the better off backward classes.[33] These organizations insisted that the abysmally low Muslim representation in public employment and education reflected this precise failure of affirmative action to ensure equal participation.

30 See Marc Galanter, *Competing Equalities: Law and the Backward Classes in India* (University of California Press, 1984), 17–39.

31 *Indra Sawhney v. Union of India* [1992] Supp (3) SCC 217.

32 *Report of the Backward Classes Commission – First Part* 52 (Government of India, 1980).

33 See Syed Shahabuddin, 'Association for Promoting Education and Employment of Muslims, National Convention on Reservation: Working Paper', *Muslim India* 143 (1994), 498; Iqbal Ansari, 'On Reservation for Muslims: Rationale and Modalities', *Muslim India* 143 (1994), 501.

By the mid-2000s, the data collected by government-instituted reports started to support some of these arguments. Most prominently, the Sachar Committee Report – an inquiry committee set up by the central government to collect empirical evidence on the matter – found that based on most socio-economic indicators, Muslims were among the most deprived socio-cultural groups in the country.[34] The Committee recommended a range of affirmative action benefits for the community that fell short of quotas. The Misra Commission, which was constituted almost simultaneously, addressed the issue more directly. The Commission, under its terms of reference, had been asked to assess the legality and desirability of affirmative action among religious and linguistic minorities. It recommended reservations for Muslims *as a group*. It also looked at the *Dalit* Muslim demand for inclusion, and by a majority, recommended the removal of the religious bar. Asha Das, the only member from the state bureaucracy, came to a different conclusion. She filed a 'Note of Dissent', arguing that the exclusion of Muslims and Christians from the SC category was desirable – and constitutional.

While these debates were evolving, some state governments – most prominently the government of Andhra Pradesh – introduced a quota policy for Muslims. This provoked a number of constitutional challenges in the state's High Court. In each of these cases, the High Court has struck down Muslim quotas. One such case was *Archana Reddy*. And one such opinion was Raghuram J's.

III. CONFRONTING MINORITY CLAIMS OF INCLUSION

From a legal perspective, the two Muslim demands are oriented differently. The *Dalit* Muslim claim, in contesting the religiously circumscribed boundaries of the SC category, is making an argument of parity. The argument is that the right to equality is implicated because the *Dalits* – irrespective of their religious identity – share a common social experience of historical marginalization. It is this commonality across religions that makes their exclusion, as Muslims, discriminatory. The Muslim reservation demand, on the other hand, is based on a conception of difference. The argument is that religious identity – particularly minority Muslim identity – reflects empirically verifiable socio-political and economic marginalization. The non-recognition of the specificities of minority experience constitutes political injustice and perpetuates inequality.

These differences notwithstanding, secularism is implicated in the state responses to both these claims. Courts and other state institutions have been asked to evaluate whether affirmative action for the religious group stands up to scrutiny under the principle of secularism, and whether the exclusion of citizens from constitutionally mandated affirmative action on the sole basis of their religious identity violates

[34] Prime Minister's High Level Committee, *Social, Economic and Educational Status of the Muslim Community in India: A Report*. Sachar Committee Report (Government of India, 2006), www.minorityaffairs.gov.in/sites/default/files/sachar_comm.pdf (accessed 2 September 2017).

secularism. Addressing these questions, Raghuram J's opinion and Das's note of dissent, once juxtaposed against each other, reveal the tensions and continuities in secularism as a regulatory practice. In this section, I will show how the model of secularism deployed in these fragments asserts contradictory accounts of the Muslim community.

A. *The Illusory Muslim Community*

Archana Reddy was the second case in a series of constitutional challenges against Muslim quota policies in the state of Andhra Pradesh. In 2004, the state government introduced the first version of the policy, which provided for a separate quota of 5% in public employment and education for Muslims. The Andhra Pradesh High Court struck down the order on the ground that the government had not proceeded to gather relevant evidence of socio-economic marginalization of Muslims in the state, as was required by the Supreme Court in *Indra Sawhney*.[35] The decision compelled the state government to refer the issue to a commission, which eventually came to the conclusion that Muslims in the state were socio-economically backward as a matter of evidence. The state government accepted the commission's report and reinstituted the quota. This policy was challenged in *Archana Reddy*.

The High Court's opinions in *Archana Reddy* went in divergent directions. All the judges agreed that the quota policy was unconstitutional, but all gave different grounds. Nazki J held that Muslims as a community could be the recipients of affirmative action provided that their backwardness is manifest in evidence. In his view, however, the commission's report had not collected adequate data along relevant criteria that spoke to the peculiarities of Muslim marginalization. Raghuram J and Rao J, in their separate judgments, agreed that the policy was unconstitutional. However, unlike Nazki J, they held that quota policies could *never* target religious groups like Muslims. Raghuram J's opinion, in particular, was a sharp rejection of religion-specific affirmative action policies. According to him, such 'religion-explicit' policies threatened the 'carefully organized constitutional system of secular democracy'.[36]

To be sure, Raghuram J and Rao J were in the minority on the question of whether Muslims could be treated as a class of beneficiaries for affirmative action.[37] My interest in Raghuram J's opinion is not because it laid down a binding precedent on the issue. Rather, it is of great relevance because it represents the dominant institutional position on Muslim affirmative action.

35 *T. Muralidhar Rao v. State of Andhra Pradesh* [2004] (6) ALD 1 (L.B.).

36 *Archana Reddy* (n. 10), [18] (Raghram J).

37 Nazki J (writing for himself and Reddy J) and Ramana J disagreed with Raghuram J and Rao J, and held that while the Muslim quota policy in front of them was unconstitutional, this did not preclude treating Muslims as a beneficiary class.

Raghuram J derived the content of secularism from the Constitution's equality provisions: Articles 14 and 15 of the Constitution prohibit discrimination on the grounds of sex, religion, caste, and race. According to the judge, these anti-discrimination provisions reflect the 'basic and transcendental value' of the prohibition against religion specific action. As he said in his judgment, 'religion specific conferral of benefits or imposition of burdens, offend the Constitution'.[38]

But in and of itself, this position is paradoxical: if the Constitution had prohibited both religious *and* caste discrimination, why was 'religion specific' affirmative action more objectionable than caste-based ones? Raghuram J's answer lay in his assessment of the Muslim community itself. According to him, it was impermissible to treat the Muslim community (and presumably any religious community) as a node of constitutional recognition because it was not a truly coherent community. The Muslim community, in his view, was a 'heterogeneous social class' consisting of 'identifiable and distinct insularities'.[39] Raghuram J argued that the evidentiary basis for Muslim affirmative action was 'irredeemably flawed' because it proceeded on the assumption that Muslims were an 'integrated, homogeneous social class'.[40] It did not separately recognize the 'distinct constitutional classes' which may just happen to be Muslim. This was a crucial argument. The existence of intra-Muslim diversity made Muslims, as a group, an illegitimate node of constitutional recognition for the purpose of affirmative action. The state government had misrecognized the legitimate constitutional classes. These could not be religious groups but only caste groups – Muslim or otherwise.

Raghuram J. argued that the caste system pervaded Hindu and non-Hindu religions in India. This had less to do with the fact that religions such as Islam and Christianity were egalitarian. Rather, caste – as a form of status and stigma – existed among Muslims as well:

> On conversion to other religions, having regard to the negative socio-cultural influence that the Hindu caste system has had on other religious collectivities as well, those converted to the other religions from the lower castes of the Hindus, suffer a lower level of esteem even amongst the members of the religious community to which they had converted. It is in these circumstances that the several judgments pointed out, a measure of casteism, factually though not formally, exists in other religions as well.[41]

This was in line with the sociological literature I alluded to earlier. It also resonated with parts of *Indra Sawhney*. In response to the concerns of the minority judges that the adoption of caste as a criterion for OBC identification would leave out religious minorities for the category's ambit, the majority judges in *Indra Sawhney* had

38 *Archana Reddy* (n. 10) [33] (Raghuram J).
39 Ibid. [68] (Raghuram J).
40 Ibid. [78] (Raghuram J).
41 Ibid. [111] (Raghuram J).

insisted that caste or caste-like stratification was shared among all religious groups.[42] But in his majority opinion in *Indra Sawhney*, Jeevan Reddy J also noted that the choice of caste did not preclude the possibility of choosing religion as a basis of identification. In *Archana Reddy*, the state relied on these passages to argue that religion, like caste, could be the basis of identifying affirmative action beneficiaries. But Raghuram J insisted that these passages in *Indra Sawhney* were 'theoretical' at best. After all, it was caste quotas – rather than religion-based affirmative action – that was in front of the *Indra Sawhney* court.

Raghuram J's reasoning reflected his inability to perceive minority religious identity as a relevant form of social stratification. While there may be social diversity among Muslims – much like any social conglomerate – the central question is: what is the relevant barometer for 'homogeneity' that constitutional recognition for affirmative action demands? Evidence shows that Muslims are substantially socio-economically disadvantaged compared to other social groups, and suffer from ghettoization and insecurity. These elements of marginalization appear to be shared across the diversity within Muslims.[43] Consequently, Raghuram J's assertion about the diversity of the Muslim community begs the question: why should the *common* experience of subordination – as a religious minority – not lend adequate homogeneity to Muslims for affirmative action?

The very fact that this alternative did not register a presence in Raghuram J's opinion suggests that his articulation of secularism was not based solely on a sociological account of Indian Muslims. It was also based on an implied construction of religious identity – as normatively irrelevant, unwieldy, and illusory. In Raghuram J's opinion, socio-economic marginalization is shared across religious groups, and the marginalized are 'unfortunate and disadvantaged, simpliciter'. The 'misfortunes are religion … neutral'.[44]

The implied assertion that religious identity is illusory was accompanied by the danger that was posed by its recognition. According to Raghuram J, religion specific quotas 'divide the society, accentuate prejudices, and retard a civil society'.[45] Instituting such policies provides perverse incentives for people to convert to Islam.[46] While he did not state this explicitly, Raghuram J was alluding to the perennial anxiety of 'demographic aggression' by religious minorities – the fear

[42] *Indra Sawhney* (n. 31) [399] (Sawant J); [83] and [94] (Reddy J).

[43] See Sachar Committee Report (n. 34), 237 ('Our analysis shows that while there is considerable variation in the conditions of Muslims across states … the Community exhibits deficits and deprivation in practically all dimensions of development. In fact, by and large, Muslims rank somewhat above SCs/STs but below Hindu-OBCs, Other Minorities and Hindu-General (mostly upper castes) in almost all indicators considered …. In addition to the "development deficit", the perception among Muslims that they are discriminated against and excluded is widespread, which exacerbates the problem.').

[44] *Archana Reddy* (n. 10) [112] (Raghuram J).

[45] Ibid. [35] (Raghuram J).

[46] Ibid. [124] (Raghuram J).

that Muslims and Christians will overrun the Hindu numerical majority through religious conversion. The distribution of constitutional benefits to religious minorities qua religious minorities would thus be driven 'by nothing more substantial than competitive political compulsions' at the expense of constitutional principles.[47] These elements in Raghuram J's articulation of secularism are not only widely held, but also reflect the contemporary institutional position.[48]

In Raghuram J's articulation of secularism, the Muslim community was constructed as politically inauthentic – fragmented, heterogeneous, and socially diverse. More interestingly, it constructed 'religious' claims of social groups as opposed to 'secular' claims: claims of caste minorities were to be interpreted as secular; but similar claims of religious minorities were to be interpreted as pertaining to religion and thus contrary to secular constitutional values. Note that this difference has less to do with the substance of the claims – both types of claims were based on subordination and marginalization. Rather, this had to do with *who* was making the claims. I shall come back to this point in Section III.

B. *The Exhaustive Muslim Identity*

If religious identity is sociologically and constitutionally inauthentic, what are the possibilities of legitimate modes of inclusion? The next fragment reveals that routes to other political and constitutional possibilities may not be easily available.

In 2004, the central government constituted the Misra Commission and set it the task of recommending welfare measures, including reservations, for the socio-economically backward sections among the religious minorities. This was the first time such a commission had been explicitly asked to look into the entire array of Muslim demands. In its 2007 report, the Commission endorsed the *Dalit* Muslim claim. According to it, caste is 'a social phenomenon shared by almost all Indian communities irrespective of their religious persuasions'.[49] It noted that since 'no special benefits can be given to any community or group on the basis of religion', religious exclusion from the SC category violated the constitution. It went on to recommend that the SC status should be completely de-linked from religious identity: ' … a willful change of religion on his part should not affect adversely his or her Scheduled Caste status – as that would in our opinion conflict with the basic constitutional provisions relating to equality, justice and non-discrimination on

47 Ibid. [33] (Raghuram J).

48 A recent example is the ruling party's objections to Muslim quota policies in the state of Telangana. See 'Telangana: Muslim Quota Move Will Be Fought Politically, Legally, Says BJP', *The Indian Express* (Mumbai, 28 March 2017) (where the state BJP leader is reported to have said that 'the BJP would fight against this religious reservation, dividing people on religious lines and for vote bank politics, politically on one hand and legally on the other'), http://indianexpress.com/article/india/telangana-muslim-quota-move-will-be-fought-politically-legally-says-bjp-4589581/ (accessed 2 September 2017).

49 Misra Commission Report (n. 11), 143.

religious grounds'.[50] Note that at least to the extent of conceptualizing the relationship between caste and religious identity, the Commission's recommendation was in line with *Archana Reddy*.[51]

This conclusion, however, was not unanimous. Asha Das, the member-secretary of the Commission, disagreed with the other members on the *Dalit* Muslim question. According to Das, religious exclusion from the SC category was not discriminatory – and thus did not violate the secular principle – because Islam and Christianity 'originated outside India'[52] and did not recognize the caste system.

Das is not alone in taking this line of defense. A wide range of political actors, particularly from the Hindu right wing, have argued that since the Hindu religious dogma recognizes the caste system, the boundaries of the SC category must be limited to 'Hindu' *Dalits*. In response to the fact that the category has been extended to Sikhs and Buddhists – neither of which recognize the caste system – they have argued that both are 'Indic religions' and thus part of the 'Hindu fold'. In other words, the SC category must remain limited to the 'Hindu family of religions' and not non-Indic religions.[53] This argument conceptualizes caste as a matter of religious doctrine. Moreover, it divides religions between the Indic and non-Indic, while including the former in the larger rubric of Hinduism. This, of course, leaves out the *Dalit* converts to Islam and Christianity from the SC category altogether.

It is clear that Das's view of caste diverged from *Archana Reddy* and the litany of sources that it relied on. In *Archana Reddy*, caste was understood as an authentic form of social stratification – or a 'constitutional class' as Raghuram J called it – to the exclusion of religious identity. Das treated caste as a religious phenomenon – related to religious doctrine rather than a wider social phenomenon of exclusion.

Moreover, in *Archana Reddy*, religious community was illusory. In Das's note, however, religion was an overarching – even an exhaustive – identity. The idea of the social that Das implicitly endorses in her understanding of caste discrimination is noteworthy. The only reason why the existence of caste within one's religious faith is relevant is if the religious faith circumscribes the social possibility of discrimination. *Dalit* Muslims and Christians argued that in spite of their religions not recognizing the caste system, in practice, they continued to face social exclusion and segregation – the marks of caste-related status discrimination. They also argued that regardless of whether other Muslims engaged in caste discrimination, *Dalit* Muslims continued to face discrimination by other citizens. After all, most of the *Dalit* Muslims had continued in their traditional occupations, and they 'continue to be part and parcel

50 Ibid., 154.

51 For a critique arguing that the Commission's position, including the dissent, reinforced the Hindu national character, see Rupa Viswanath, 'Commissioning Representation: The Misra Report, Deliberation and the Government of the People in Modern India', *South Asia: Journal of South Asian Studies* 38 (2015), 495.

52 Misra Commission Report (n. 11), 163.

53 See M. Mohsin Alam Bhat (n. 15) 182–6; Tanweer Fazal, 'Scheduled Castes, Reservations and Religion: Revisiting a Juridical Debate', *Contributions to Indian Sociology* 5 (2017), 11.

of the Indian society which is still largely caste based'.[54] By circumscribing the *Dalit* identity within religious identity, Das was implicitly suggesting that cross-community experiences of exclusion were not the concerns of the Constitution.

Das's silencing of the intersectional experiences of *Dalit* Muslims can also be found in other arguments for religious exclusion. Take the case of another bureaucratic fragment. In 1996, in the face of growing demand for Christian inclusion in the SC regime, a cabinet note was circulated among the central government ministers.[55] The note categorically opposed the removal of the religious bar. Its primary ground was the pragmatic maintenance of the status quo: adding Christian converts would open a can of worms, encourage Muslims to make similar demands, and potentially generate a political backlash from the Hindu right wing. But beyond these concerns, there was a specific construction of religious identity as essentially *bounded and separate* from caste disabilities. The note argued that the 'Scheduled Caste converts to Christianity … do not constitute a caste but a religious group'.

Das's dissenting note resonated with the construction of social identity visible in the cabinet note. Caste as social stratification was affixed to religious dogma and theology, and *not* the everyday experiences of caste-based exclusion. In doing so, the experiences of *Dalit* Muslims are rendered specious on the register of caste. Moreover, the Muslim community is rendered bounded and immutable.

Such reasoning implicated the legitimate boundaries of a secular state. Das insisted that the very recognition of the *Dalit* Muslim claim would amount to a 'formal introduction of caste system in Islam/Christianity and changing the basic tenets of the religion, *which will be outside the jurisdiction of both the Parliament and the Judiciary*'.[56] If caste discrimination existed in minority religious institutions, then it was not the responsibility of the state to recognize this as constitutionally relevant social stratification: These are 'issues to be addressed primarily by the religious leaders through reform within their system'.[57] While she did not elaborate on the grounds of her objection, the animating idea was that secularism mandated that the state *not* interfere in the internal religious matters of religious groups: ' … *the very competence of the State* – executive, Parliament or even judiciary – to introduce "caste" into religions that profess egalitarian regime is questionable.'[58]

IV. DEPOLITICIZING RELIGION, DOMESTICATING CASTE

In the two fragments I have discussed, secularism is sustained by diametrically opposite views of Muslim identity and Muslim social stratification. In *Archana*

54 This was the argument explicitly made by *Dalit* Muslim groups before the Commission. See Misra Commission Report (n. 11), 164.

55 Ministry of Welfare, Government of India, 'Note for the Cabinet (Secret) regarding Recognition of Scheduled Caste Converts to Christianity as Scheduled Castes', No. 12016/30/90-SCD (R. Cell).

56 Misra Commission Report (n. 11), 163 (emphasis added).

57 Ibid., 164.

58 Ibid., 165 (emphasis added).

Reddy, Raghuram J rejected Muslim affirmative action on the ground that the Muslim community was fragmented and illusory. Das defended religious exclusion from the SC category by asserting that secularism demanded non-interference in the Muslim community – as a bounded and exhaustive religious identity. Beyond these contradictory conceptions of the Muslim community, these institutional fragments expose a more intimate dimension of Indian secularism. Raghuram J and Das were comparing the various claims that aimed to assuage group subordination and marginalization. In doing so, they constructed certain claims as 'religious' and others as 'secular'. Only the former invited secularism to limit group recognition and state intervention.

This is most palpable in Das's note. The *Dalit* Muslim claims have mobilized socio-economic evidence to establish their historical and contemporary marginalization. They have contended that caste as social stratification must be interpreted beyond religious doctrine – and through the sociological analysis of stigma and discrimination. But in response to the *de-sacralization* of social stratification, Das invoked secularism to discipline *Dalit* Muslim claims. At the same time, she interpreted the *Dalit* caste as being essentially religious – and located in the Hindu religious scriptures. Ostensibly, this interpretation of caste as religion did not pose an affront to her articulation of secularism.

Similarly, in *Archana Reddy*, Raghuram J distinguished between two sets of claims. The first mobilized the evidence of caste-based marginalization and subordination, while the second focused on the socio-economic and political subordination faced by religious minorities. Again, it was only the latter that invited disciplining. Raghuram J bracketed the latter set of claims as 'religious' and contrary to secularism.

How, then, did *certain* questions of marginalization get constructed as 'religious' and others as 'secular'? This question draws on the constructivist approach to secularism, particularly the approach taken by Talal Asad. As Asad has famously argued, secularism is not a straightforward separation of religion and state. It reflects complex forms and mechanisms through which the 'religious' domain is constructed. While law aims to separate religion and state, according to Asad:

> … formal constitutions never give the whole story … [T]he nation-state requires clearly demarcated spaces that it can classify and regulate: religion, education, health, leisure, work, income, justice, and war. The space that religion may properly occupy in society has to be continually redefined by the law because the reproduction of secular life within and beyond the nation-state continually affects the discursive clarity of that space.[59]

I argue that the construction of 'religion' in both fragments is a product of India's constitutional history. This historical pedigree of Indian secularism lends itself to

[59] Talal Asad, *Formations of the Secular: Christianity, Islam, Modernity* (Stanford University Press, 2003), 201.

acting as a regulatory practice that counters the sting of religious minority claims that are considered dangerous.

I am being careful in making this argument. I am not suggesting that this is the only way in which the interpretive work on Indian secularism has proceeded or can proceed. After all, both Muslim claims that I discuss assert adversarial interpretations of equality and secularism. Therefore, I do not intend to propose an essential meaning of Indian secularism. Rather, I wish to highlight the historical contingencies that have shaped the tensions surrounding the interpretation of Indian secularism. Moreover, my aim is not to provide a comprehensive historical account of the construction of 'religion'.[60] Rather, I wish to highlight how Indian secularism was constituted through contrasting treatments of 'religion' and 'caste' – within the logic of nation-state formation – during the constitution-making process. It is this contrast that continues to dominate many institutional iterations of secularism in India: constructing religious minority claims as 'religious' and anti-secular.

Secularism under the Indian constitution emerged as a constellation of norms in the context of addressing minority claims.[61] What was often described as the 'minority problem' included the political demands of both religious minorities and the low-caste 'untouchable' minority. Much to the consternation of the Congress Party–dominated Constituent Assembly that was given the task of framing the Constitution, the minorities demanded separate political representation in the new republic. At the start of the deliberations in 1948, the Assembly conceded on the issue of proportional political representation for all minorities. However, by 1949, it adopted a contrasting attitude towards religious and caste minorities. It maintained political representation for the latter in the form of the SC category, but religious minorities were left bereft of any special rights beyond cultural and religious rights.[62]

Scholars have offered numerous explanations for the distinctive treatment of religious and caste claims. The most prominent explanation is the dramatic role of religious violence that accompanied the partition of the country in 1947 and the birth of Pakistan. The partition also weakened the bargaining power of the religious

[60] For more detailed accounts that I draw my argument from, see M. Mohsin Alam Bhat (n. 15), 176–88; Cassie S Adcock, 'Debating Conversion, Silencing Caste: The Limited Scope of Religious Freedom', *Journal of Law and Religion* 29 (2014), 363; Shabnum Tejani, *Indian Secularism: A Social and Intellectual History, 1890–1950* (Indiana University Press, 2008); Ravinder Kumar, 'Gandhi, Ambedkar and the Poona Pact, 1932', *South Asia: Journal of South Asian Studies* 8 (1985), 87; Rochana Bajpai, *Debating Difference: Minority Rights and Liberal Democracy in India* (Oxford University Press, 2011).

[61] See Rochana Bajpai, *Debating Difference: Minority Rights and Liberal Democracy in India* (Oxford University Press, 2011), 95: 'Secularism in the nationalist scheme was the answer to problem of the creation of an integrated nation-state and a common national identity out of competing allegiances not only of religion, but also of race, caste, tribe, and language'; Niraja Gopal Jayal, *Representing India: Ethnic Diversity and the Governance of Public Institutions*, 1st edn (Palgrave Macmillan, 2006), 2.

[62] Constitution of India 1950, Articles 25 and 30.

minorities – particularly the Muslims – in the Assembly.[63] The anxiety of sectarian or 'communal' division formed the political backdrop to addressing the Minority Problem. It also constituted the substance of the secular formula that aimed to facilitate 'integration' and national unity.[64] Consequently, the orientation of secularism during the deliberations had less to do with the legitimacy of religious discourse in public life, and more to do with the scope and extent of group recognition.[65]

Secularism was based on a framing that separated the issue of religious minorities from that of caste. As Rochana Bajpai has noted, for the members of the Assembly, the recognition of religious identity reflected group affiliations that were divisive and unwarranted.[66] Consequently, the Assembly rejected any recognition of religious identity beyond religious and cultural autonomy. In contrast, as the deliberations of the Assembly proceeded, the *Dalits* were removed from the label of 'minorities' and accommodated within the discourse of 'backwardness' – as a form of social stratification deserving constitutional redress.[67] Members argued that recognizing the SCs for affirmative action would alleviate their social, educational, and economic 'backwardness' by integrating them into the social mainstream and promoting national development. Thus, religious groups were the subject of the multicultural concerns of the Constitution, while low-caste groups were the subject of its socio-economic ameliorative agenda.

It may be tempting to approach this contrasting treatment of religious and caste identities, as many scholars have done, simply as a normative shift towards social stratification as the basis of affirmative action.[68] This is true to a significant extent: socio-economic marginalization did become the legitimate standard for the recognition of social groups. However, my argument is that the process of this framing also

63 See Ralph Retzlaff, 'The Problem of Communal Minorities in the Drafting of the Indian Constitution', in R. N. Spann (ed.), *Constitutionalism in Asia* (Asia Publishing House, 1963), 55; Granville Austin, *The Indian Constitution: Cornerstone of a Nation*, 2nd edn (Oxford University Press, 1999), 151–4. There is some evidence that some religious minority leaders traded political safeguards in exchange for religious, educational and cultural rights. See Bajpai (n. 60).

64 See Bajpai (n. 61), 78–84; James Chiriyankandath, '"Creating a Secular State in a Religious Country": The Debate in the Indian Constituent Assembly', *Journal of Commonwealth & Comparative Politics* 38 (2000), 1.

65 See Chiriyankandath (n. 64), 8.

66 See Bajpai (n. 61), 88–96, 122.

67 Ibid., 110–12, 125–6, 134.

68 For example, Rochana Bajpai appears to suggest this when she argues that in recognizing the claims of caste minorities, the '… nationalists were not conceding here what they had rejected in the case of religious minorities: the relevance of the social identity of representatives for representation …. Legislative quotas for Scheduled Castes were intended as one among several provisions for the amelioration of their social and economic disadvantage. The mechanisms whereby legislative quotas would contribute to this end were not detailed, but these pertained to representation only tangentially, to the extent of ensuring the inclusion of members of hitherto excluded groups.' Ibid., 126. See also Gurpreet Mahajan, 'Indian Exceptionalism or Indian Model: Negotiating Cultural Diversity and Minority Rights in a Democratic Nation-State', in Will Kymlicka and He Baogang (eds.), *Multiculturalism in Asia* (Oxford University Press, 2005), 288.

tells us how the constitution makers conceptualized caste and religious identities. During the deliberations, social stratification came to be conceptualized precisely in the juxtaposition between caste and religious identities. While the members were sensitive to inequality in caste, they predominantly interpreted religious identity as merely religious and cultural difference. The members' reluctance to recognize religious identity as a basis for affirmative action not only reflected their view that religious difference was irrelevant for political representation; it also reflected that they perceived religious difference as *only* 'religious' – distinct from social stratification as in the case of caste.[69]

Here, I am extending the argument that Shubnum Tejani makes in the context of India's constitution making. Tejani argues that it was the 'language of liberalism' in 1947 that impeded the attempts of Muslim representatives in the Assembly to articulate their case on the grounds of inequality.[70] In her view, caste-based affirmative action could be – and was – defended as a measure to eradicate caste division and inequality, but religious minorities could not lay claim to these grounds because 'the premise of state secularism was precisely *non*-intervention'.[71] According to her: '[T]he challenge of difference that religion posed to the secular state lay in its *identity, not its inequality*. The transition from nationalism to a secular democracy required religious minorities to forgo any claim to inequality.'[72]

While the limitations of the liberal repertoire may be a contributory factor,[73] the framers did not treat all potentially religious divides as being incontrovertibly against secularism. In fact, a significant section of the Assembly interpreted 'untouchability' and caste differences specifically in religious terms. Affirmative action for caste minorities was understood to be a form of penance for upper caste Hindu religious discrimination.[74] In other words, there was nothing obvious in treating the question of religious minorities as a solely 'religious' – as opposed to a 'secular' – question.

Thus, while my reading aligns with Tejani's argument, there is something more at play: the contrast between identity and inequality was itself a product of secularism that emerged during the deliberation process. The dominant section of the constitution makers only saw certain kinds of inequalities as constitutionally relevant social stratification. Inequalities that pertained to the erstwhile minority problem came to be constructed as 'religious', thereby inviting secularism's imperative of non-interference and separation.

69 The religious minority members of the Assembly did come to argue – admittedly through vague formulations – in favour of the idea that religious identity should also be seen as a form of social stratification. See Bajpai (n. 61), 164.

70 Shabnum Tejani, *Indian Secularism: A Social and Intellectual History, 1890–1950* (Indiana University Press, 2008), 263.

71 Ibid., 264.

72 Ibid. (emphasis added).

73 I depart from Tejani's somewhat implicit claim that liberalism had enough motivating power during the Constituent Assembly debates to determine the rights of caste and religious minorities in the postcolonial state.

74 See Bajpai (n. 61), 136–7.

The two institutional fragments must be seen in this light. The antecedents of Raghuram J's opinion in *Archana Reddy* – where he was reluctant to *see* the inequality of minority religious identity – lie in the circumscribed construction of constitutionally relevant social stratification. While Raghuram J could appreciate the religious-ness of Muslim identity, he interpreted it as inauthentic for the purposes of the state's ameliorative role. This background also explains the tension in Das's note. The questionable severing of caste and religion allowed Das to approach the *Dalit* Muslim demand as a 'religious' issue, restricting the possibility of state redress. The purely religious formulation of the *Dalit* caste did not appear paradoxical to her: caste was social stratification, and religious difference just 'religious'.

V. CONCLUSION

My aim in this chapter was to move away from approaching Indian secularism as a stable normative matrix that determines the relevance and scope of religion in public life. The focus on fragments that invoke and apply secularism opens up the possibility of studying the everyday interpretive dynamics of secularism as a regulatory practice. This inquiry exposes the tensions and slippages in secularism's institutional life, which are often flattened in theoretical discussions about the relationship between religion and law.

Specifically, I argued that Indian secularism regulates minority claims through contradictory conceptions of community identity. If Raghuram J in *Archana Reddy* interpreted the Muslim community as heterogeneous and illusory, Das interpreted it as eliminating any intersectional claims. My point is not that these views are well founded or that they cannot be made compatible. In fact, I desisted from making any normative claim in this regard. Rather, my point is that elite institutional expressions of secularism, such as in *Archana Reddy* and in the Misra Commission Report, have remained in a state of tension. And this, in itself, has not undercut the power of such expressions of secularism to regulate political claims.

Approaching Indian secularism as a regulatory practice in this manner also points us toward its constructivist dimension. The category of 'religion' does not precede the 'secular'. My account shows that historical contingencies and institutional regulatory practices constantly shape the boundaries of what counts as 'religious'. The presence of religious discourse in defining a practice or category does not automatically pose an affront to Indian secularism. In Das's note, caste defined in purely religious doctrinal terms was a secular creature. But it was the *Dalit* Muslim claim – asserting the de-sacralization of social stratification – that could not find a home in Das's interpretation of secularism.

Interestingly, these conflicting conceptualizations and constructions also reflect the possibility of negotiation. Indian secularism's meaning is elastic precisely because its everyday institutional life is contradictory. In their ongoing struggles,

Dalit Muslims have relied on these institutional positions – that assert their religious community's heterogeneity – to argue for inclusion in the SC category. The supporters of Muslim quotas continue to make their case by analogizing the historical recognition of caste to social stratification: They argue that the institutional appreciation of caste inequality must lead to a similar appreciation of other forms of sociopolitical inequalities. Both arguments await a hearing in the Indian Supreme Court. My account shows that these Muslim political actors are not merely participating in an enterprise of generating a more coherent model of Indian secularism. Their burden is not only to push the state institutions to agree on a view of Muslim social stratification. The stakes are higher. Their burden is also to recalibrate the entrenched construction of 'religion' that obscures inequality and subordination.

14

Beyond the State and the Hawza

Legal Pluralism and the Ironies of Shi'i Law

Haider Ala Hamoudi[*]

I. PRESUMPTIONS OF CONFLICT

Perhaps the easiest way in which to demonstrate the rather obvious manner in which Twelver[1] Shi'i juristic rules can, and frequently do, clash with state law in a rather fundamental fashion is by way of an example. The following rule, taken from the juristic compendium of the current *primus inter pares* of Najaf's high clerics, Grand Ayatollah Ali Sistani, offers a useful illustration:

> It is not permissible to have sexual intercourse with a wife who has not reached nine years of age, whether it be a permanent marriage or a temporary one.[2] However, there is no problem with all of the other enjoyments, such as grasping with appetite, kissing, hugging, and "thighing."[3] If he does have sex with her before she reaches nine, and he does not tear her, then the stronger opinion is that there is no consequence to him other than the sin itself [i.e. there are no legal consequences].

[*] The author would like to thank Michael Helfand, Mirjam Künkler, and Clark Lombardi for their generous comments and support. Special thanks to Daniel Goh, Arif A. Jamal, and Jaclyn Neo as well as the Centre for Asian Studies at the National University of Singapore for the opportunity to present this chapter at the conference "Regulating Religion: Normativity and Change at the Intersection of Law and Religion."

[1] This chapter deals exclusively with that branch of Islam known as Twelver Shi'ism, as opposed to the many schools of Sunnism, or even other schools of Shi'ism, which differ from Twelver Shi'ism in important ways. As the eminent Robert Gleave describes it: "Twelver Shi'i belief is characterized by a conviction that during the Prophet's lifetime, Ali (his cousin and son in law) was designated as leader of the Muslim community, and Twelver Shi'ites, unlike other Shi'i groups, consider there to have been twelve such leaders (Imams) descended from (and including) Ali who were the rightful heirs of the Muslims." Robert Gleave, *Inevitable Doubt: Two Theories of Shi'i Jurisprudence* (Brill Academic Publishers, 2000), 1.

[2] Respecting the peculiarly Shi'i institution of "temporary marriage," see Ali Al-Sistani, *Minhaj Al-Saliheen* (Dar al-Muwazza' al-Arabi, 2008), Vol. 3, paras 229–61 [hereinafter Sistani]. It is also further discussed in the main text.

[3] The term "thighing" is no more a word in Arabic than it is in English, and is derived merely by taking the noun "thigh," *fakidh* in Arabic, and putting it into a verb form. Notwithstanding its absence from most modern Arabic language dictionaries, the meaning of the term in the context of this particular ruling is rather obvious.

Tearing is the ripping of the urinal and menstrual pathways, or the menstrual and anal pathways, or all three, such that they are combined.

If he does tear her, then there is no exit from the legal effects of the marital relationship, and flowing therefrom are all of its rules from inheritance to the prohibition of a fifth[4] [wife] to the prohibition of her sister with her,[5] and other [rules]. It is said, "he is prohibited from having sex with her again," but the stronger opinion is the opposite, especially if the injury heals through treatment or otherwise. It is true that he must pay blood money for the tearing, which is the blood money of a soul[6] if he divorces her, and the more common opinion is [he must still pay blood money] even if he does not [divorce her], though this is not free of doubt. And he is obligated to support her so long as she is torn even if she is disobedient or he divorces her, and as precaution[7] even if she marries after the divorce.

If he penetrates his wife after she reaches nine and tears her, she is not prohibited from him, nor is the blood money due. But as precaution, the obligation of supporting her [exists] as if the tearing was before reaching nine. . . .[8]

These rules, which are not of Grand Ayatollah Sistani's making but indeed widely repeated among jurists operating within the Shi'i tradition,[9] create obvious conflicts with modern international norms respecting gender equality and human rights that need not be recounted here. For our purposes, it suffices to note that they also stand in stark contrast with prevailing Iraqi law in a number of significant ways.

4 Shi'ism, much like Sunnism, does not permit a man to marry more than four permanent wives at one time. Judith E. Tucker, *Women, Family, and Gender in Islamic Law*, 1st edn (Cambridge University Press, 2008), 56. Thus, as explained more fully later in the main text, Sistani is effectively saying that if a man "tears" his wife by engaging in sexual intercourse with her before she reaches the age of 9, then for purposes of the four-wife limit, she remains his wife even if he divorces her.

5 This refers to the prohibition against a man marrying a wife and her sister polygamously at the same time, though he can marry them sequentially, following the death or divorce of one. See Sistani (n. 3), paras 174, 177. Essentially, therefore, based on the foregoing passage, a man cannot marry the sister of his wife if he "tore" his wife before the age of 9, whether or not he divorces her.

6 As with Islamic law generally, Shi'ism imposes upon those who are the victims of intentional injury (or their kin, if the injured party dies) the right to exact retaliation or the receipt of what is known in Islamic law as *diyya*, or blood money, for the injury. See Abdul Majid Al-Khu'i, *Minhaj Al-Saliheen*, Vol. 3 (1992), 83 [hereinafter Khu'i]. However, injury caused by mistake is generally compensable only through payment of blood money. See Khu'i (n. 7), 95. While making no mention of retaliation, Sistani indicates here that a child wife who suffers severe injury from a husband's penetration of her is entitled to the same blood money as would be available if he had killed her – the "blood money for a soul."

7 The Shi'i principle of "precaution" is complex and difficult to summarize. It suffices to note that Shi'i jurists often ascribe significant levels of doubt to their rulings, and therefore often obligate believers to undertake certain actions that *might* be obligatory, or avoid certain actions that *might* be prohibited, out of precaution. Haider Ala Hamoudi, "Sex and the Shari'a: Defining Gender Norms and Sexual Deviancy in Shi'i Islam," *Fordham International Law Journal* 39 (2015), 25, 37. The ruling cited here is an example of the former phenomenon – it is not *certain* that a husband who has caused tearing to his wife must support her financially even if she marries another husband after he divorces her. However, it is likely enough to be rendered an obligation, out of precaution.

8 Sistani (n. 3), para 8.

9 See Hamoudi (n. 8), 93–4 (discussing the issue in greater detail).

First, Iraqi law specifically prohibits the marriage of individuals who have not reached the age of 18, though the age may be lowered to 15 under certain circumstances.[10] Certainly the idea of a child of the age of 9 marrying is not at all contemplated, let alone a child *under* 9. Indeed, Iraqi law renders it a crime for a family member to compel any individual into marriage without his or her specific consent.[11] This renders the marriage of a child under 9, who plainly lacks such capacity to consent, per se criminal.[12]

Second, a wife who is severely harmed by her husband has immediate grounds under Iraqi law to seek a judicial dissolution of her marriage.[13] By contrast, the specific consequences, according to Grand Ayatollah Sistani, of severe physical harm that accompany vaginal or anal penetration of a child too young to accommodate it are instead *the obligatory continuation of the legal effects of the marriage.* Thus, based on the preceding passage, Grand Ayatollah Sistani permits the husband to divorce the wife. However, in such a case, the husband gains no advantage, in that he must continue his legal obligations of support even if she marries another and she remains one of his wives for the purposes of the four-wife limit, among other things. No mention is made at all of the injured wife's right to dissolve the marriage.[14] Moreover, so long as the marriage remains in place, her obligation of "obedience," which effectively translates to her obligation to be available to her husband for his sexual satisfaction,[15] remains in place. Her refusal to fulfill this obligation entitles the

[10] Personal Status Code of Iraq, No. 188 of 1959, as amended [hereinafter "Personal Status Code"] Articles 7–8.

[11] Ibid., Article 9(1).

[12] The conclusion that a child under 9 is not an adult and therefore not capable of consenting to marriage is not one with which Shi'i jurists would disagree. The jurists in such cases vest capacity to marry in the father or paternal grandfather of the child. Sistani (n. 3), para 57. ("The father and paternal grandfather of the male or female child exercise guardianship [in matters of marriage].") As noted in the main text, the Personal Status Code specifically renders it criminal for a father or paternal grandfather to exercise such authority in a manner that compels the marriage of a minor.

[13] Article 40(1) of the Iraqi Personal Status Code reads as follows:
"Each of the spouses may seek a judicial dissolution if one of the following causes is satisfied: If one of the spouses causes harm to the other, or their children, in a manner that renders the continuation of married life impossible." It is difficult to imagine a more paradigmatic case of harm rendering marital life impossible than a husband whose penetration causes a combining of menstrual and urinal pathways into one.

[14] Elsewhere in his compendium, Sistani indicates that a wife may seek a judicial dissolution of her marriage if her husband "hurts her, or is cruel to her, other than in a religiously legitimate manner." Sistani (n. 3), para 360. However, under the juristic rules, the husband's primary right in marriage is to the sexual enjoyment of his wife, and he is permitted to penetrate his wife after the age of 9. Thus, it is difficult to see how any harm arising from the penetration after the age of 9 could be described as anything but "religiously legitimate." The same result would not necessarily hold for a child under 9, as any penetration there would seem to be devoid of religious legitimacy.

[15] See Sistani (n. 3), para 350 ("the disobedience of a wife is established by her refusal to obey her husband in the manner that she is obligated, and this is in not enabling him in his rights in his enjoyment of her, and included within this is her refusal to remove repellents which oppose his enjoyment and pleasure of her . . . ").

husband to take a series of incremental measures in retaliation, culminating in moderate physical discipline.[16]

Third, injuries to the person are adjudicated in Iraqi law on the basis of the principles of the Iraqi Civil Code, which are familiar to any modern civilian lawyer. A person is entitled to be fully compensated for all injuries that are caused by the wrongful act of another.[17] These include "moral" injury, which would encompass emotional harm as well as harm to reputation.[18] The juristic rules pronounced by Sistani provide no compensation for emotional harm, nor indeed for physical harm, unless they result in the severe injury of "tearing."

Fourth, a husband who causes severe physical harm to his wife is almost surely criminally liable under Iraqi law. Even if it is true that Iraqi courts provide some dispensation to husbands to engage in physical disciplining of their wives (a separate problem of its own), it is also true that Iraqi criminal courts routinely prosecute husbands for physical injuries to wives that are less severe than "tearing."[19]

Fifth, and finally, Sistani references the possibility of a "temporary" marriage with a child wife, effectively an arrangement wherein a man pays a dower to the wife in order to engage in sexual enjoyments with her for a period of time that could be anywhere from an hour or less to a year or more.[20] This type of sex for dower arrangement, discussed extensively in Sistani's compendium,[21] is not recognized in the Iraqi law as a permissible form of marriage.

Admittedly, I have deliberately selected this provocative illustration in order to highlight discrepancies between juristic and state law. There are countless other areas where such tensions do not arise, and where religious rules are broadly consonant both with Iraqi law as well as with broader understandings of contemporary human rights. Nevertheless, the example I have selected is hardly the only one where a rule in Sistani's compendium lies in some tension with state law. References to the stoning of adulteress lesbians[22] and the freeing of slaves to expiate for the sin of a killing by mistake[23] are other obvious examples. (Under Iraqi law, adultery is a misdemeanor[24] and slavery has been prohibited since the state was

16 Ibid., para 353.
17 Civil Code of Iraq, No. 40 of 1951 [hereinafter "Civil Code"], Articles 202–7.
18 Ibid., Article 205(1).
19 For a series of recent Iraqi cases that address the twin issues of legal physical discipline directed against a wife on the one hand and illegal battery of a wife on the other, see Haider Ala Hamoudi and Mark Cammack, *Islamic Law in Modern Courts* (Aspen, 2018), 454–61.
20 Sistani (n. 3), 3.
21 Ibid., paras 229–61.
22 Ibid., para 380.
23 Ibid., para 746.
24 See Penal Code of Iraq, No. 111 of 1969 (as amended), para 377 (imposing a penalty of "jail" for adultery). See also Penal Code (n. 46), para 89 (indicating that any term for "jail" cannot exceed one year).

created.[25]) If the exercise is expanded to include other, earlier leading scholars of Najaf, among them Sistani's immediate predecessor as Najaf's *primus inter pares* jurist, Grand Ayatollah Khu'i, then the discrepancies become even starker.[26]

The tensions are thus quite clear. A Grand Ayatollah cannot reasonably believe both in the legitimacy of a father's contracting his child into marriage, and in the legitimacy of a state law that criminalizes precisely this conduct. It cannot be that sex with a 10-year-old wife that causes severe harm is a criminal battery that deserves compensation for all material and moral harm done and that the primary consequence of such sex is the continuation of the legal effects of marriage. Finally, and most obviously, it cannot be both that a child wife so injured has a right to dissolve the marriage, and that she has a continued obligation of sexual obedience to the husband who injured her.

The presumed manner in which Shi'i jurists are understood to manage these obvious contradictions is through one of two approaches. The more long-standing approach is commonly referred to as Quietism.[27] The Quietist jurist is aware of the existence of state law and does not resist it. Instead, he regards state law as some sort of epiphenomenon from which the believer ideally isolates herself until it is removed and replaced with some form of ideal Islamic law. Within Quietist political theory, such perfect justice can be established only upon the eventual reappearance of an infallible Hidden Imam, the Mahdi, whose name is invoked several times a day by the faithful, and who is called upon by them at those times to emerge from his hiding.[28] To the Quietist, the best approach to state law is to endure it as one endures all ordeals, follow God's Law as closely as might be feasible, and await the Mahdi's return.[29] It is no ideal state of affairs to be sure, but a divinely ordained one, which

25 Cindy J. Smith and Kristiina Kangaspunta, "Defining Human Trafficking and Its Nuances in a Cultural Context," in John Winterdyk, Benjamin Perrin, and Philip Reichel (eds.), *Human Trafficking: Exploring the International Nature, Concerns, and Complexities* (CRC Press, 2012).

26 Grand Ayatollah Khu'i, for example, includes a recommendation in favor of female genital mutilation in his compendium, referring to it through the historic Shi'i juristic phrasing of "the curtailment of the maidens." Khu'i (n. 7), para 1382. More broadly, as discussed in greater detail in the main text that follows, the section on lawful sexual relations in Khu'i's compendium includes references not only to marriage, but also to the right of male masters to have sex with female slaves. Khu'i (n. 7), paras 1320–40 (laying out a section entitled "on the permission of the enjoyment of female slaves and lawful sex with them").

27 Sarvenaz Bahar, "Khomeinism, the Islamic Republic of Iran, and International Law: The Relevance of Islamic Political Ideology," *Harvard International Law Journal* 33 (1992), 145, 162 (". . . the denial of legitimacy to existing forms of government during the period of ghaiba lends itself to at least two possible interpretations – one leading to quietism in the absence of the Twelfth Imam and the other to activism.").

28 See ibid., 162 (noting that Quietism is a means to deny legitimacy to the existing government in the absence of the Hidden Imam).

29 See, e.g., Hamid Algar, *The Roots of the Islamic Revolution* (Open Press, 1983), 25 (noting, with respect to Iranian clerics at the start of the twentieth century that "[i]t was held . . . that a totally legitimate authority was, in the nature of things, impossible, given the continuing occultation, or absence, of the Imam from the world. It was held that all that could be done in his absence was to limit the inevitable illegitimacy to existing rule.").

God will choose one day to end by ordering the Hidden Imam to reappear to establish perfect justice.

The other, more contemporary approach, developed in the latter half of the last century by the Najaf-trained jurists Muhammad Baqir al-Sadr and Ruhollah Khomeini, is for the juristic class to seize the reins of power directly and enact positive state law themselves on the basis of the rules derived by the jurists over the centuries.[30] Such a legal system might not be ideal in the absence of the Infallible Imam, given the very real possibility of juristic errors and omissions in interpretation.[31] However, it is argued, this is not a reason to fail to try to establish as close a legal system to ideal Islamic law as might be possible during the Mahdi's absence.

The distinctions between the two approaches, and the presumed political contestation between advocates of the two, has been the subject of much worthy academic commentary.[32] However, it also might be noted that the two approaches share important similarities. In particular, they both manage to retain some sense of purity and logic as concerns the relationship of state law to Islamic law, and they do this by delegitimizing state law and indeed the state itself, to the extent that the state departs from Islamic law norms. In no case is the existence of a law prohibiting marriage before the age of 18, or criminalizing the forced marriage of a minor by her father, deemed in any way an ideal state of affairs. Plainly, in both cases, ideal justice is provided only by the implementation of Islamic law, not a law of the state that is inconsistent with Islamic law. The only difference between the two approaches relates to *who* has the authority to implement religious law, and *what* is to be done when other rules happen to prevail. For the Quietist, only the Mahdi may implement the law because, among other things, only the Mahdi fully knows it. For the juristic revolutionaries, the jurists may implement it as best as they can on behalf of the state in their role as deputies in the Mahdi's absence, pending his return.

30 Chibli Mallat, *The Renewal of Islamic Law: Muhammad Baqir As-Sadr, Najaf, and the Shi'i International* (Cambridge University Press, 1993), 59–62.

31 As noted in n. 8, Shi'i juristic texts are infused with references to doubt respecting the validity of particular rulings, and therefore often indicate that a particular action is obligatory as a matter of "precaution." The acknowledgment of such doubt demonstrates acute juristic awareness that, in the absence of the Mahdi, the full extent of the law cannot really be known and that, therefore, errors and omissions are almost certain to exist. See also Gleave (n. 1), 248 (describing uncertainty in the content of the law as "a permanent feature of the Shi'i legal tradition" after an early, formative period).

32 See generally, e.g., Algar (n. 30); Bahar (n. 28); Mallat (n. 31); Hamid Mavani, "Analysis of Khomeini's Proofs for al-Wilaya al-Mutlaqa (Comprehensive Authority) of the Jurist," in Linda S. Walbridge (ed.), *The Most Learned of the Shi'a: The Institution of the Marja' Taqlid* (Oxford University Press, 2001), 183; Devin J. Stewart, "The Portrayal of an Academic Rivalry: Najaf and Qum in the Writings and Speeches of Khomeini 1964–78," in Linda S. Walbridge (ed.), *The Most Learned of the Shi'a: The Institution of the Marja' Taqlid* (Oxford University Press, 2001), 216.

II. CONTEMPORARY REALITIES

The search for purity and logic in approaching legal order is, however, often a fruitless one. It never seems to exist in actual social spaces. One would be hard pressed to identify a Quietist or a revolutionary who did not depart from their adopted political theory in important ways in order to accommodate secular state laws in some manner or another. For example, Grand Ayatollah Muhsen al-Hakim, who was the leading Najaf jurist during the 1960s, was reported both to have regarded the activist Khomeini frostily because of Khomeini's political activism,[33] and to have pressured his own protégé Sadr into limiting his forays into politics.[34] These are the actions of a classic Quietist. On the other hand, he is also known to have vigorously demanded the repeal of the Iraqi Personal Status Code in 1959, and to have issued a fatwa declaring it a sin – indeed, an act of crimnal apostasy – to join the Communist Party, both of which show significant willingness to interfere in political affairs at times.[35] The consequent implicit *legitimation* of the state and state politics deserves more emphasis than it often receives. After all, if the Grand Ayatollah declares it sinful to join the *Communist* Party because of its affiliations with atheism, then it is difficult to avoid the implication that it is *not a sin* to be politically active, and indeed join other political parties. Similarly, opposition to the Personal Status Code implies that other law that is enacted and unopposed is somehow legitimate.

Conversely, if Khomeini once maintained that Islam had all the laws necessary to govern a state, and there was no need for Western transplants, the messy reality of statehood forced a significant reconsideration of these notions. Iranian contract law, for instance, remains governed by the Civil Code, which adopts a very civilian structure to address the subject. This is in stark contrast to the comparable juristic rules promulgated by Khomeini himself.[36] Thus, faced with a discrepancy between juristic rules and state law, Khomeini not only tolerated but also indeed *embraced state secular law* and did not seek its forceful repeal. Again, the matter deserves more attention than it has received, given its obvious tension with any pure principles of juristic supremacy over conflicting state law.[37]

But it is in the case of post-Ba'ath Najaf generally, and Grand Ayatollah Sistani in particular, where the stark incongruity of a dual embrace of both Quietism and political activism has been most obvious. The fact is, Sistani's interventions into politics go well beyond the mere implicit and indirect endorsement of the state's activities in the manner of his predecessors. One of his earliest, and most widely reported,

33 Stewart (n. 33), 223.

34 T. M. Aziz, "The Role of Muhammad Baqir al-Sadr in Shi'i Political Activism in Iraq from 1958 to 1980," *International Journal of Middle Eastern Studies* 25 (1993), 207, 210.

35 Ibid., 209.

36 Qanun-i Madani [Civil Code] 2007, Article 190 (Iran) (Mostafa Shahabi trans.).

37 For a richer discussion of this subject in the specific context of post- revolutionary Iran, see Haider Ala Hamoudi, "The Death of Islamic Law," *Georgia Journal of International and Comparative Law* 38 (2010), 293, 317.

interventions involved the dissemination of a memorandum wherein he insisted that the only legitimate drafters of Iraq's Constitution were those elected directly by the Iraqi people.[38] When those elections finally came about, the support given by Sistani to the premier Shi'i Islamist party was unmistakable, even if the Grand Ayatollah himself did not offer an express endorsement.[39] Clearly, this is not classical Quietism, and the state is not in Sistani's vision an entity from which the devout believer is alienated. Instead, it is a state where the citizen not only *may* play an important role, but also one in whose affairs the citizen *has a religious duty* to be proactively involved.

Yet, at the same time, Najaf's frequent interventions into state affairs on everything from anticorruption[40] to the content of school curricula[41] clearly is not some sort of surreptitious effort to remake Iraqi law into a replication of juristic rules. In fact, the only highly publicized effort to replace state law with juristic rules lies in the area of personal status, which covers family law and inheritance. Thus, Iraq's existing (and largely Islamic) Personal Status Code has been subject to attack from Najaf, and from Islamist political forces supported by Najaf, since its inception. These objections have only grown in ferocity since the Saddam regime was removed from power.[42] The most recent effort at repeal and replacement took place in 2014. It received the approval of the Iraqi Cabinet, but was never voted on by the legislature, partly because between the Cabinet's endorsement and the legislature's vote, the terrorist insurgency network that refers to itself as the Islamic State managed to take over one of Iraq's largest cities, forcing a reassessment of political priorities.[43] Thus, for now, the existing Personal Status Code remains unamended

38 Ali A. Allawi, *The Occupation of Iraq: Winning the War, Losing the Peace* (Yale University Press, 2007), 203, 210 (quoting the relevant memorandum and describing it as a "bombshell").

39 Ibid., 390 (noting that the Shi'i Islamist electoral list, the United Iraqi Alliance, had among its candidates three of Sistani's top deputies, and that the clerical academies mobilized voters to support the list).

40 Tim Arango, "Senior Cleric Wades in Politics to Offset Iran," *New York Times* (November 1, 2015).

41 Haider Ala Hamoudi, *Negotiating in Civil Conflict: Constitutional Construction and Imperfect Bargaining in Iraq* (University of Chicago Press, 2013), 198.

42 Najaf's jurists had long been opposed to the Iraq Personal Status Code of 1959, with the prominent cleric Muhammad Bahr al-Uloom publishing a lengthy pamphlet against it shortly after it had been enacted. Ibid., 100–101. That opposition did not abate over the years. In fact, during the period in which the United States was still in control of Iraq, Shi'i Islamists on the Iraq Governing Council unsuccessfully sought its immediate repeal. Ibid., 99. That effort resulted in Article 41 of the current Iraq Constitution, which in somewhat murky language appears to contemplate at least the possibility of Iraqis returning to Islamic law rules to govern their affairs. The Article, however, indicates that the matter is supposed to be "organized" by law, and Iraq's Federal Supreme Court has held that until such a law is enacted, the Article is effectively nonjusticiable. See Ibid., 203–4. As noted in the main text, such a law was proposed, and in fact received the endorsement of the Cabinet, but was never voted into law.

43 Haider Ala Hamoudi, "Resurrecting Islam or Cementing Social Hierarchy: Reexamining the Codification of 'Islamic' Personal Status Law," *Arizona Journal of International and Comparative Law* 33 (2016), 329.

despite the obvious Shi'i Islamist displeasure with it. It is difficult to know how long this state of affairs might continue.

Beyond the law of personal status, however, there is very little agitation from religious forces for broad legal change. Without noticeable objection from Najaf, Iraqi law has in fact changed very little since the fall of the Saddam regime. The Iraqi Civil Code – that bedrock of Iraqi private law that hardly reflects the substance of juristic rules – has not been amended at all, nor has there been any effort to try to amend it to conform it to juristic rules.[44] Most of Iraq's core legal architecture likewise remains largely unchanged, including the Penal Code, civil and criminal procedural laws, and the Commercial Code, to name only a few examples.[45]

In fact, instead of the *state* accommodating juristic rules, something of the reverse is happening, where it is the jurists who are implicitly accommodating the modern Iraqi state in its rulemaking capacities. The manner in which jurists do this most often is by simply omitting their own contrary rules. Hence, for example, in a remarkable footnote in the section of his compendium addressing the rules of marriage, Grand Ayatollah Sistani indicates that he will not discuss the rules that concern lawful sex between a master and his female slaves because slavery is not a matter with which modern society is "afflicted."[46] In other words, recognizing the obvious contrast between Shi'i traditional rules and modern state law that has now spanned decades, Sistani effectively concedes to the latter, and permits Shi'i rules on this subject to fall into near absolute obsolescence. This was not the position of Sistani's predecessors, who continued to recite these rules for decades notwithstanding their obvious conflict with longstanding Iraqi law and indeed broad international *jus cogens* norms.[47]

44 Iraq's Civil Code was developed by the premier Arab jurist of the twentieth century, Abdul Razzaq al-Sanhuri. There has long been scholarly debate respecting the extent to which it in fact owes significant fealty to the *shari'a*, as Sanhuri at least at times claimed was the case. Enid Hill, *Al-Sanhuri and Islamic Law* (American University of Cairo Press, 1987), 71–83 (describing the debate at length and taking the position that the Civil Code was in fact more Islamic than is commonly believed); cf. J. N. D. Anderson, "The Shari'a and Civil Law: The Debt Owed by the New Civil Codes of Egypt and Syria to the Shari'a," *Islamic Quarterly* 1 (1954), 29 (describing the Code as more European than Islamic). For the purposes of this chapter, it suffices to note that the Civil Code is not, and does not purport to be, a compilation of Shi'i juristic rules. To the extent it is Islamic at all, this is because it engages in "some of the supposed fundamental principles of . . . medieval *Sunni* rules, informed heavily by Roman law and Continental European law." Hamoudi (n. 38), 310 (emphasis added).

45 See, e.g., Penal Code of Iraq, No. 111 of 1969, as amended from time to time; Criminal Procedure Code, Law No. 23 of 1971, as amended from time to time; Civil Procedure Code, Law No. 83 of 1969, as amended from time to time; Commercial Code, No. 30 of 1984, as amended from time to time. To be sure, some of these laws are modestly amended from time to time in the post Ba'ath era, even as they were amended occasionally before then. See, e.g., Law No. 10 of 2016 (amending the Civil Procedure Code to change slightly the jurisdiction of the trial courts); Law No. 15 of 2009 (adjusting the definition of the felony of false reporting of criminal activity in the Penal Code). However, these modest changes almost never have anything to do with Islamic law.

46 Sistani (n. 3), para 10.

47 See Khu'i (n. 7), paras 1320–40; Muhsen Ibn Mahdi Tabataba'i Al'Hakim, *Mustamsik Al-Urwa Al-Wuthqa* 14 (1983), 179–96.

Of course, this deference is only partial. As the opening passage shows, Sistani continues to recite detailed rules respecting the marriage of children that conflict unambiguously with state law. Moreover, the fact that Sistani implicitly endorsed an electoral list that has repeatedly promised to repeal the Personal Status Code suggests he certainly does not view the state's conflicting law in that particular instance as legitimate.

Thus, the Grand Ayatollahs of Najaf *intervene* in affairs of the state, *legitimize* certain aspects of the state's legal architecture, and yet in other contexts *continue to agitate in favor of* rules that do not accord with the law of the state. The jurists are thus involved in the simultaneous rejection and acceptance of state law.

In other words, far from the pure world of the Quietist, entirely alienated from the law of the state, or of the revolutionary, who seeks to conform the state to the pronounced law of the jurist, Najaf has overtly opted for a third course, a type of legal hybridity, where inconsistent legal orders exist alongside each other in a rather ironic fashion. The product may very well be untidy, and certainly it lacks elegance, but as Justice Holmes indicated more than a century ago, the life of the law is driven not by logic, but by experience.[48] Najaf's methods in that respect are remarkably well adapted to the social fields where they are deployed, as the next section shows.

III. IRAQI LEGAL PLURALISM

As Larry Rosen once remarked with respect to the Moroccan experience, and as is no less true in the Iraqi experience, relevant actors in the applicable social field exhibit "a very diminished sense of contradiction among identifiably distinct legal orders" that coexist alongside each other.[49] That is, in deferring to different legal regimes with different rules to address different areas of their lives, Iraqis generally regard them each as part of the fabric of a general social order, without emphasizing or indeed paying much heed at all to the inconsistencies across the respective regimes. Thus, in promulgating rules that lie in some contradiction to state law, Najaf's jurists do not trouble the masses of Shi'a devout throughout Iraq for the most part. Those masses are perfectly content to defer to those juristic rules when they seem fit, and ignore them when they do not, without sensing any sort of logical contradiction while doing so.

To be more specific, there are three primary legal systems that prevail throughout the Shi'i dominated areas of Iraq. The first is the formal law of the state, the second is Islamic law, as pronounced by the Najaf jurists, and the third, no less important than the first two, is the law of the tribe.[50] Of course, this description is general and these

48 Oliver Wendell Holmes, Jr., *The Common Law* (1883), 1.

49 Lawrence Rosen, "Legal Pluralism and Cultural Unity in Morocco," in Baudouin Dupret, Maurits Berger, and Laila Al-Zwaini (eds.), *Legal Pluralism in the Arab World* (Kluwer Law International, 1999), 92–3.

50 See Haider Ala Hamoudi, "Decolonizing the Centralist Mind: Legal Pluralism and the Rule of Law," in David Marshall (ed.), *The International Rule of Law Movement* (2014), 135, 148–9.

orders may apply with greater or lesser relevance among various classes and in various locations. For a secular Shi'i living in a relatively upscale part of Baghdad, Islamic law may not play a role at all beyond the ceremonial. For a devout one intimately connected to the clerical classes in Najaf, it is quite possible that tribal law is a near irrelevance. Broadly speaking, however, *substantial numbers of* Shi'a living in Iraq regard these three systems as controlling some aspect of their lives.

The first part of this discussion has already shown the manner in which Islamic law and state law stand in some contrast. This is no less true of Iraqi tribal law. Perhaps most prominently, the compensation system for private wrongs appears to be a unique amalgam of Islamic and state law. On the one hand, in particular for the taking of a life, there is some reference to the "blood price," as measured in sheep, which is plainly Islamic in origin and knows no recognition in the state.[51] On the other hand, compensation for moral wrongs and insults to honor are taken extremely seriously by the tribes, somewhat seriously in Iraqi law, and not mentioned at all by the juristic rules. Beyond this, the Iraqi tribes engage in practices condoned neither by Islamic nor state law, among them the trading of women as compensation for injury, a practice that is diminishing in importance, and the killing of youths involved in some sort of unsanctioned romantic affair, a practice that is not diminishing in importance at all.[52]

The three systems are thus inconsistent with each other, and yet Iraq's Shi'a manage to organize their affairs around them in a manner that diminishes the possibility of overt conflict. Thus, for example, with the obvious exception of honor killings, Iraq's Shi'a defer to the state to address criminal matters. Blood feuds between tribes do erupt from time to time, but field research has suggested that the tribes prefer to use mechanisms of state law to punish, rather than rely on their own methods of escalating retaliation, precisely to avoid costly and lengthy feuds that attract the attention of the state.[53]

On the other hand, in attempting to settle private compensation for wrongs, the population is not enthused with the highly imperfect state justice system. There is no particularly strong desire, however, to use Islamic law, which does not regard harm to reputation and honor as compensable. Accordingly, tribal law tends to be

51 Respecting the nature of the blood price and when it falls due, see n. 7. The blood price can be measured on the basis of various items, including gold, silver, camels, and sheep. Muhammad Hasan Al-Najafi, *Jawahir Al-Kalam Fi Sharh Shara'i Al-Islam* (Abbas al-Quchani, ed. 1981) (ca. 1841) 4 [hereinafter Jawahir]. As noted in the main text, Iraqi tribes tend to use sheep, given their value among those tribes relative to animals such as camels or cows, which are quite rare and serve little purpose in Iraq.

52 The means by which Iraqi tribes manage disputes that arise as for wrongs that occur among them is set forth in detail in Haider Ala Hamoudi, Wasfi H. al-Sharaa, and Aqeel al-Dahhan, "The Resolution of State and Private Disputes in the South of Iraq: Toward a Cooperative Model of Pluralism," in Michael Helfand (ed.), *Negotiating State and Non-State Law: Challenge of Global and Local Legal Pluralism* (Cambridge University Press, 2015), 215–60.

53 Ibid., 247–8.

deployed broadly to address such matters.[54] The compensation processes can be informally combined with state law criminal process (if, for example, there is a need for punishment), but beyond that, much of Iraq's population does not involve the state at all to adjudicate these sorts of matters.

Finally, there is the matter of personal status law, where Islamic law prevails. Nearly every Iraqi *eventually* marries in state court, because it is necessary to do so in order to receive important state benefits.[55] However, even a day-long visit to a personal status court in any part of the country will reveal significant numbers of people coming to the court to "marry" who already have young children, and who thus obviously have long been married by a religious cleric, often at a time when it was not legal for them to do so.[56] While in theory the husband is supposed to be jailed for committing a crime in such instances,[57] the state in fact defers to Islamic law and judges seemingly never seek to enforce that crime.[58] Even urban Iraqis, who register their marriages relatively quickly, often have a private religious ceremony at home before the legal marriage takes place.[59]

This context helps to provide a more robust understanding of Najaf's actual *legal* role in the relevant social field, and the manner in which it seeks to regulate it. In some areas, such as criminal law, its role is slight, and accordingly, it often does not even bother to pronounce rules. For example, the jurists do not agitate in favor of state recognition of the limited number of crimes with harsh punishments set forth in revelatory text. These crimes, referred to as the *hudud* (*hadd* sing.), are theoretically quite important, even if evidentiary rules make their actual enforcement in many cases nearly impossible.[60] Yet they remain, within Iraq, entirely unrecognized in the penal law. Part of the reason for this is that there is no expectation or desire within the social fabric to have Najaf rulings govern criminal law. By contrast, there is a strong desire to see Iraq's own existing, secular penal law applied more effectively. Hence, when Grand Ayatollah Sistani calls on the state to protect places of worship from attack, which includes bringing those responsible to justice for the attacks, he makes no mention of traditional Shi'i rulings on these subjects.

A somewhat similar juristic deference to the state applies as to the law of contract, though the juristic legitimation of the state is less robust in that context. Unlike

54 Ibid., 230.
55 See Hamoudi (n. 51), 150.
56 Hamoudi and Cammack (n. 20), 19–21.
57 Personal Status Code, Article, 10(5).
58 Hamoudi and Cammack (n. 20), 19–21.
59 Hamoudi (n. 51), 150.
60 The premier juristic compendium in modernity, the *Jawahir al-Kalam* of Shaykh Mohammad Hasan al-Najafi, provides extensive reports to the effect that, to quote a representative sample, "the carrying out of the scriptural punishment nourishes the earth more than rain lasting forty days and nights." Muhammad Hasan Al-Najafi, *Jawahir Al-Kalam Fi Sharh Shara'i Al-Islam* (Abbas al-Quchani ed., 7th edn, 1981) (ca. 1841), Vol. 41, 256. That said, the same source also points out that to prove the *hadd* of fornication, four male witnesses must testify to the act of penetration. Ibid., 296–7. This renders the prosecution of the fornication a theoretical necessity and a practical near impossibility.

criminal law, where the juristic rules are largely omitted, modern juristic compendia do continue to discuss commercial contracts at some length, together with rules that seem at some tension with the state law, and indeed with modernity.[61] A particularly relevant example is the preference for oral contracts witnessed by two male Muslims over written ones.[62]

Yet Najaf is aware enough of the world not to expect these rules to have any actual relevance across broad sectors of the population, even if it does continue to pronounce them. Thus, the Federal Supreme Court heard a constitutional challenge in 2010 to a provision in the Evidence Law requiring contracts over a certain value to be in writing. The Court found that the provision not only failed to contravene Islam, but indeed was harmonious with its teachings. In so doing, the Court ignored juristic rules entirely, and proceeded with its own exegesis of Qur'anic text. The Court insisted on the basis of this exegesis that in fact there was a strong Islamic preference for contracts in writing, thereby reaching a conclusion that was very nearly the polar opposite of the juristic one.[63] Despite the fact that the Court effectively assumed the role of jurist and usurped Najaf's presumed authority to determine what Islamic law was, Najaf made no public objection to this decision that I have been able to locate. The jurists are thus seemingly unconcerned with the nearly complete obsolescence of Islamic contract law in modern Iraqi law, even as they continue to recite the rules of Islamic contract law in their compendia.

A final area of Islamic law deference relates to tort. Because compensation for private wrongs is also not a matter on which Islamic law is expected to apply, but rather tribal law is, again there is implicit deference to alternative legal orders. Grand Ayatollah Sistani may make oblique reference to the blood price from time to time, as the passage set forth at the start of this chapter shows. However, the detailed rules on the subject – concerning the value of a life and each body part or organ, who is responsible for paying, how these values change across gender and religion, and when retaliation might be claimed instead of a blood price – are not included in his substantial works.

In very stark contrast, the sections on marriage and divorce in Sistani's compendium set forth in extensive detail the rules concerning the entering into marriage, the obligations on each party to the marital contract once the marriage is concluded, the legal consequences of the marriage, and the same respecting divorce.[64] Moreover, unlike contract law, there is, as discussed earlier, both political contestation of the state's Personal Status Code, and broad social practice that favors the religious rules over the state law in this context.

[61] In fact, most of the second volume of Sistani's compendium is dedicated to the subject of contracts and commercial matters, though there is a substantial concluding section on wills and the charitable trusts known as *waqfs*.

[62] Sistani (n. 3), paras 51–5. The same rules respecting special dispensations for the disabled is reflected in Khu'i (n. 7), para 51.

[63] Federal Supreme Court of Iraq, Decision 60 of 2010.

[64] See Sistani (n. 3), paras 1–240.

The foregoing indicates that there is a method in Grand Ayatollah Sistani's determinations respecting what to legitimize and what to contest. Simply stated, he is aware of which Islamic law rules matter in the actual world, and which rules do not. He is seeking to focus most of his attention on the former, while either declining to mention the latter, or discussing them while seeming to implicitly concede their descent into oblivion among all but the most scholastic of followers.

Having laid out this thesis, and my support for it, it is important to note two important limitations with respect to it. First, the determination of which religious rules deserve emphasis and which are deemed fit for obsolescence is a complex matter that extends well beyond the social expectations respecting potential application. Hence, to provide perhaps the most interesting example, Grand Ayatollah Sistani does not lay out rules for the strict punishments associated with the *hadd* of fornication because there is no expectation that the state will or should enforce them. However, he does at least reference the rule requiring stoning of a married woman engaged in an act of lesbianism, which is no more likely to apply in modern contexts than the stoning of any other person engaged in nonmarital sex.[65] The reason seems to relate more to a desire to condemn homosexuality from an ethical perspective, even if the prohibition is not expected to be part of the state's legal system. Such additional considerations are worthy of more attention than I am able to give them here. For now, it suffices to note that my position in this chapter is that the explicit or implicit diminishment of the importance of some rules while demanding the recognition of others through a thorough recounting of them depends in significant part, but certainly not exclusively, on broader social expectations respecting the extent of their applicability.

Second, it is not and has never been my suggestion that Najaf only *intervenes* in state affairs when it pertains to areas of law in which juristic rules play a significant role. This is demonstrably not true, as juristic rules have next to nothing to say about many of Najaf's most prominent interventions into Iraqi political affairs, among them the desirability of open electoral lists,[66] anticorruption measures,[67] a parliamentary system of governance, and democratic constitution making.[68] Clearly Najaf views itself as a vital political actor, with a right and indeed an obligation to insert itself into any number of matters relating to statecraft, some of which have nothing to do with Islamic law at all.

My point, rather, is that in involving itself in state affairs, Najaf both *legitimates* the state in a manner that appears to violate Quietist principles, but at the same time *fails to take it over* in the manner that the revolutionary might demand. Najaf, that is, has found a way to manage its affairs in a manner that accords less with the strictures

65 See Sistani (n. 3), para 380.

66 Haider Ala Hamoudi, "Identitarian Violence and Identitarian Politics: Elections and Governance in Iraq," *Harvard International Law Journal* 51(2010), 82, 87.

67 Arango (n. 41), 1.

68 Andrew Arato, *Constitution Making Under Occupation* (Columbia University Press, 2009), 86–7.

of any pure political theory of governance and more with the conflicting, inconsistent, and self-contradictory realities of the Iraqi social experience.

IV. CONCLUSION

The purpose of this chapter has been to describe the manner in which Najaf jurists have chosen to regulate the Iraqi Shi'i social field, alongside both the state and Iraqi tribes. The result is a regulatory system that is pluralistic and reliant on inconsistent legal orders. However, this means of using state and nonstate authorities to regulate a religious policy does not lead to inevitable tension among the different social orders. To the contrary, the chapter shows that the different authorities tend to work alongside each other in a fashion that minimizes the potential of conflict among them as they operate in their respective regulatory capacities.

Specifically, as concerns the efforts of the clerics to regulate the social field alongside the state, the chapter shows that the jurists eschew the formally elegant and logical, but ultimately unworkable, theories of Quietism on the one hand, where the state is an illegitimate epiphenomenon preceding the return of the Mahdi, and revolutionary Islamism on the other, where the goal is to refashion the law to conform to the rules of the jurists. Instead, Najaf implicitly adopts the lessons of the legal pluralists because it is aware of its competition with alternative legal systems and their regulatory mechanisms, and Najaf prefers to avoid modalities of conflict with those regulatory mechanisms, even as they avoid conflict with it, and with each other. Thus, even as Najaf legitimates the state generally with political interventions, it simultaneously promulgates and seeks enforcement of rules in areas of law where its rulemaking capacity remains relevant, even if those rules are in plain tension with state law. In other areas, where the competing state law, or nonstate tribal law, is preferred, Najaf tends to deemphasize or even omit mention of its own inconsistent rules. The resulting means of regulating a religiously ordered society is not one that is elegant or pure, but is one that is remarkably well adapted to the social milieu in which it is deployed.

Index

accommodation demands, with religious diversity, 3
acculturation mechanisms, in Vietnam, 165–7
complexity in state management of religion, 167
human rights and, 166
internalization of freedom of religion, 166–7
legitimacy through, 166
ADJARI. *See* Agama Djawa Asli Republik Indonesia
Administration of Muslim Law Act (AMLA) (1966) (Singapore), 125, 257–8
administrative law, 244–7
administrative reasonableness, 234–6
administrative state, 28–9
administrative unreasonableness, 234–6
adultery, 264–70
affirmative action, 15
in India, for Muslims, 278, 279–80, 281
as caste group, 281–3, 295
for *Dalits* reservations, 281–3
as other backward classes, 284–5
as SC, 282–3
secularism and, 279–80
Agong, Yang di-Pertuan, 238
Ahmadiyyah community, 111–12
Amarapura Nikāya fraternity, 89–90
AMLA. *See* Administration of Muslim Law Act
anti-colonial national movement, in Malaysia, 237
apostasy laws, 56–7, 120
Islamic law and, 239
Lina Joy case and, 248–53
federal-state relations and, 251–3
politicization of, 251–3
proceduralizing of, 248–9
regulation of, 249–51
under state policy, 249–51
in Malaysia, 241–2
Archana Reddy case, 286–9, 290–2, 296
Asad, Talal, 6, 8
Ashin, Janaka, 170
atheism. *See* Marxist-Leninist atheism
Australia
labor law in, 207
market regulation in, 207
authoritative rules, in regulation of religion, 42
authority, 65–75
civil, 80
conflict between state and religious institutions, 66
cultural, 74
in liberal political theory, 67
religious, 60, 68–71, 80
'hurting feelings' argument, 68
for Religious-Zionists, 73
secular liberalism and, 67–8
state, 71–5
over Gaza disengagement, 73–4
over religious disobedience, 74
Religious-Zionists and, 73
Ultra-Orthodox response to, 71–2
in Ultra-Orthodox Judaism, 66–71
'Da'as Torah' doctrine, 69–71
'gdolei hador', 69–71
state authority and, 71–2
in *Talmud*, 68–9
values and, 65–8
autonomy, 59–60
religious, 123

Baha'i religion, 114–15
Balinese religions, 108
Bangladesh, Islam as state religion in, 3
Berger, Peter, 5, 60–1
Bill on Protecting Religious Groups (Indonesia), 99
Bin Harun, Idrus, 241

Black, Julia, 50, 54
blasphemy laws, 56–7, 120
Brunei, Islam as state religion in, 3
Buddhism, 2–3. *See also* Theravāda Buddhism
  in Cambodia, 3
  constitutionalism and, 80–1, 97
  increased population under, 2–3
  in India, 282
  in Indonesia, 113
  Mahayana, 171
  monastic land, 25
  monasticism, 80–1
  in Myanmar
    sects of, 175–6
    types of, 171
  in Singapore, 135–6
  in Sri Lanka, as state religion, 89–90
  Vajrayana, 171
  in Vietnam, 160
Buddhist Councils, 172
Buddhist Temporalities Ordinance (Sri Lanka), 91
bureaucratic state, 28–9
bureaucratization
  exclusivist, 189–90
  of religion, 46–7
  of women's religious education, 189–90, 200–5, 206
Burma. *See* Myanmar

Cambodia, Buddhism as state religion, 3
Canada
  Ktunaxa Nation aboriginal community in, 31
  religious freedom in, 28
capacious definition of religion, 30–1
capitalist autocracy, Singapore as, 259
Casanova, Jose, 4, 5
caste
  affirmative action regimes for, 281–3
  defined, 281
  domestication of, 291–6
  hierarchy with, 281
  among monks, 89–90
  among Muslims, 287
  other backward classes, 284–5
  scheduled castes, 282–3, 294
  social stratification through, 294–5, 297
caste politics, in India, 282
Catholicism, in Vietnam, 160–1
charitable services, in China
  by corporate and individual donations, 224
  by religious organizations, 217–21, 225–6
  spread of religion through, 225–6
Charities Act (Singapore), 259
charity, religion and, 9
Charity Law (2016) (China), 220–1, 229
  benefits under, 221
  market regulation under, 222–3
  public accessibility under, 221
  state regulatory supervision under, 221
charity law, commercial interest and, 214
China
  charitable services in
    by corporate and individual donations, 224
    by religious organizations, 217–21, 225–6
    spread of religion through, 225–6
  Charity Law, 220–1, 229
    benefits under, 221
    market regulation under, 222–3
    public accessibility under, 221
    state regulatory supervision under, 221
  charity law in, 214
  constitutional framework in, 216–17
    state and religion under, 215–17
  Law and Religious Market Theory in, 208, 209–14
    incentives to change in, 213
    market regulatory functions in, 211–13
    military power as factor in, 212–13
    religious competition in, 213–14
    religious economic model in, 209–11
  legal framework in, 216–17
  market regulation in, 222–9
    under Charity Law, 222–3
    rationality and, recognition of, 222–5
  regulation of religion in, 216–17
  religious competition in
    entitlements and, 228–9
    extrinsic factors for, 228–9
    freedom of religion influenced by, 227
    in Law and Religious Market Theory, 213–14
    regulation of, 226–9
    restrictions on, 228
  religious demographics in, 215–16
  religious markets in, 225–9
  religious organizations in
    background for, 217–18
    charitable service provisions in, 217–21, 225–6
    social service provisions in, 217–21
    state encouragement of, 218–20
  social context in, for state and religion, 215–17
  social organizations in, legal status of, 220
  socialism in, 216–17
Christianity. *See also* Catholicism; prophetic Christianity
  increased populations under, 2–3
  in Indonesia, 106, 108, 114
Church of Scientology, 22–3
civil authority, 80

Civil Code, in Iraq, 306
civil religion, 77
  in Singapore, 126
colonialism
  in Asia, 1
  in Malaysia, 237
  in Myanmar, 173
  as religious pilgrimage, 1
  in Singapore, 257, 258
  in Sri Lanka, historical legacy of, 92–3
  Thirty Years Religious War and, 1
command and control model, 42
commercial interest, charity and, 214
communalism, 295
Communists
  in Indonesia, 114
  in Vietnam, 161
communitarian ethos, 40
compensation for injuries, under Iraqi law, 301
competition. *See* religious competition
complexity. *See* social complexity
confessional states, 38, 40
Confucianism, 2–3
  in Indonesia, 106, 113
constitutional ethnography, 279
constitutional globalization, 277
constitutional jurisprudence, 276
constitutional law
  in China, 216–17
    state and religion under, 215–17
  regulation of religion and, 39–41, 43, 52
  soft, 128, 131
Constitutional Order (Singapore), 123–7
  anti-establishment clause, 125–6
  religious identity under, 124–5
constitutional patriotism, 126
constitutionalism
  Buddhist, 80–1, 97
  relational, 120–1, 127
  secular, 277
constitutions
  in Indonesia, religion in, 100–1
    Provisional Constitution of 1950, 102–3
  religious freedom in, 25
  in Singapore, as Constitutional Order, 123–7
    anti-establishment clause, 125–6
    religious identity under, 124–5
  in Vietnam, regulation of religion under, 150–1
Convention for the Elimination of all Forms of Discrimination against Women, 128
cooperationist model, of state religion, 123
co-regulation processes, 43
corporatist accommodation, in Singapore, 257–8
Country of Particular Concern (CPC), Myanmar as, 169–70
cultural authority, 74
cultural mandates, in Singapore, 270, 272–3
cultural theory, 52
culture wars, in Singapore, 139–43

'Da'as Torah' doctrine, 69–71
Dalits, in India
  affirmative action for, 281–3
  as Christians, 282
  Muslim organizations for, 282–3, 292
Daoism, 2–3
Daw Aung San Suu Kyi, 169, 170, 185
Declaration of Religious Harmony (Singapore), 51
decline of belief, in secular theory, 4
Degar Republic, in Vietnam, 159
democracies. *See also* secular democracies
  pluralism and, 144
depoliticization of religion, 291–6
deprivation phenomenon, 5
deviant sects, in Myanmar, 179–85
  definition of, by State Sangha Maha Nayaka Committee, 177–9
  Moepyar U Nyana, 183–5
  punishment of, 186
  regulation of, 186
  Vinaya tribunals, 179–81
dialectical regulation, 34
discursive process, of regulation, 34
disobedience. *See* religious disobedience
diversity, religious
  in Asia, 2–3. *See also specific countries*
    accommodation demands of, 3
    geopolitical factors for, 3–4
    inter-faith, 25
    intra-faith, 25–6
    as regulatory marker, 21
  principled pluralism and, 123
Diwali, 29
Doctrine of the Elders, 171–2
Durkheim, Émile, 60–1, 77

economic globalization, 277
economic model. *See* religious economic model
education. *See* religious education
egalitarian societies, 40–1
Emergency Provisions Act (1950) (Myanmar), 184
Employment Act (Singapore), 266
epistemic plurality, 34–5
equality, 59–60
  in India, 281
essence-based definitions, of regulation, 39
  for legal regulation, 147–8

essential practices test, 31–3
exclusivist bureaucratization, 189–90

fatwas, 48
fiqh (jurisprudence), 197, 200, 204
Five Principles, in Indonesia, 99, 113
fragmentation in meaning, 30
free conscience, 120, 121–2, 126, 143
freedom of religion, 25
  administrative reasonableness and, 234–6
  administrative unreasonableness and, 234–6
  in Canada, 28, 31
  in China, 227
  human rights and, 25, 233
    international, 119–20
  in India, 276
  legislative state and, 27
  operationalization of, 234
  principled pluralism and, 121–2
  in Singapore, 27–8, 258
  in Vietnam, 155–6
    acculturation mechanisms and, 166–7
freedom of speech, in Singapore, 130–1

'gdolei hador', 69–70
Geertz, Clifford, 11, 100–1
gender practices, by religious minorities, 54
globalization. *See* constitutional globalization; economic globalization
'Great Unity' strategy, 161–3
grid, in cultural theory, 52
groups, in cultural theory, 52

Halakha. *See* Jewish law
Hanifah, Abu, 106
harmony. *See* religious harmony; social harmony
hawza, 191, 192, 196, 203–5
heresy, 120
heterodox beliefs, 24
  in Indonesia, 109–10
Hinduism, 2–3
  essential practices test and, 31–3
  increased populations under, 2–3
homosexuality, in Singapore, 140–2, 264–5
Human Development Index, 7
human rights. *See also* minority rights
  International Covenant on Civil and Political Rights, 234
  in Myanmar, violations of, 169–70
  religious freedom as part of, 25, 233
    forum externum aspect of, 233–4
    forum internum aspect of, 233–4
  statist approach to, 164
  Universal Declaration of Human Rights, 102–3, 234
  in Vietnam, 166
Human Rights Watch, 154–5
'hurting feelings' argument, 68

ICCPR. *See* International Covenant on Civil and Political Rights
independence movement, in Indonesia, 100
India
  affirmative action regime in, 278, 279–80, 281
    for caste groups, 281–3, 295
    for *Dalits* reservations, 281–3
    for Muslims, 284–5
    for other backward classes, 284–5
    for scheduled castes, 282–3
  anti-conversion laws in, 277
  Archana Reddy case, 286–9, 290–2, 296
  Buddhists in, 282
  caste in
    affirmative action regimes for, 281–3
    domestication of, 291–6
    among Muslims, 287
    other backward classes, 284–5
    schduled castes, 282–3, 294
    social stratification of, 294–5, 297
  caste politics in, 282
  communalism in, 295
  Dalits in
    affirmative action for, 281–3
    as Christians, 282
    Muslim organizations for, 282–3, 292
  depoliticization of religion in, 291–6
  equality in, 281
  essential practices test in, 31–3
  freedom of religion in, 276
  Indra Sawhney case, 286–9
  minority inclusion in, claims for, 285–91
  Misra Commission in, 278, 285, 289–90
  Muslims in
    affirmative action regime for, 284–5
    caste among, 287
    Dalits as, 282–3, 292
    development deficits for, 288
    as illusory community, 286–9
    inclusion claims by, 285–91
    quota policy for, 286, 288, 289
    religious identity for, 289–91
  religious conversion in, 282
  religious minorities in, 293–4
  secular constitutionalism in, 277
  secularism in, 293, 295
  Sikhs in, 282
individualist societies, 40–1

Indonesia
  Agama Djawa Asli Republik Indonesia in, 109–11
  Ahmadiyyah community in, 111–12
  Baha'i religion in, 114–15
  Bill on Protecting Religious Groups, 99
  Buddhism in, 113
  Christianity in, 106, 108, 114
  Communists in, 114
  Confucianism in, 106, 113
  fatwas in, 48
  Five Principles in, 99, 113
  independence movement in, 100, 101–2
  Islam in, 100–1
    promotion of, 101
    public acknowledgment of, 106
  legal structures in, 102–3
  Majelis Ulama Indonesia in, 48–9, 116
  Ministry of Religion, 100–1
    recognition of existing religions by, 105–7, 113
    religious holidays under, 106
    social harmony goals of, 103–4
  Ministry of Religious Affairs, 47
  Muslims in, 100–1
  national ideology in, 99, 113
  New Order regime in, 114
  patronage in, 105
  Provisional Constitution of 1950, 102–3
  regulation of religion in, 108–13
    of Balinese religions, 108
    changes to, 113–15
    contemporary challenges to, 115–16
    of fringe religious groups, 110–13
    of heterodox groups, 109–10
    of world religions, 108–9
  religion in
    definitions of, 99–100, 101, 102, 103–5, 115–16
    in Java provinces, 107
    marriage rights and, 105
    in national constitution, 100–1
    social harmony through, 103–4
  Sufi brotherhood in, 111
  Suharto in, 114
  Universal Declaration of Human Rights and, 102–3
Indra Sawhney case, 286–9
intentionality, in religious regulation, 44, 57–8
inter-faith diversity, of religion, 25
International Covenant on Civil and Political Rights (ICCPR), 234
international human rights, religious freedom and, 119–20
Inter-Religious Organization (IRO), 51
intra-faith diversity, 25–6
Iran, 188–90
  Civil Code, 306
  Islamic law in, 194–5
  regulation of religion in, 188–9
  religious education in, 189, 190–9, 205–6. *See also* women
    bureaucratization of, 200–5, 206
    under Khameini, 193–4, 196–9, 205–6
    under Khomeini, 192–6
    in Qom, 190, 192, 194, 195, 197
    through religious seminaries, 190–1, 192–9
    state changes to, 194–5
    Supreme Council of the Seminary, 196–9
  Shi'ism in, 188–9
  Shiite clerics in, 188–9
  Supreme Council of Cultural Revolution in, 199
Iraq. *See also* Shi'ism
  Civil Code in, 306
  law in, 300–3
    compensation for injuries, 301
    for dissolution of marriage, 300–1
    for marriage, 299, 300, 301
    for physical abuse, 301
    tribal, 308–9, 310, 312
  legal pluralism in, 307–12
  Najaf, 192, 304–7, 309, 310, 311–12. *See also* Sistani, Ali
    as center of learning, 192
    jurists in, 305, 312
  Personal Status Code in, 300, 304, 305, 310
  personal status law in, 309
  Shi'i jurists in, 302–3
    in Najaf, 305, 312
    Quietism and, 302–3, 304–6, 312
IRO. *See* Inter-Religious Organization
Islam. *See also* Muslims
  heterodox beliefs, 24
  increased populations under, 2–3
  in Indonesia, 100–1
    promotion of, 101
    public acknowledgment of, 106
  jihadism, 33
  in Malaysia, 3
  orthodox beliefs, 24
  Qur'an and, 204
  radicalization, 33
  as state religion, 3
Islamic Family Law (Federal Territories) Act (1984) (Malaysia), 240, 242
Islamic law, 239. *See also* Shari'a
  apostasy under, 239
  in Iran, 194–5
  women's authority under, 201, 202

Islamic Religious Council (MUIS), 125, 138
Israel
  law and religion in, 61–5. *See also* Jewish law
    Torah, 64
  religion demographics in, 61–2
  Religious-Zionists in, 63–5
    Jewish law and, 64–5
  secular population in, 65
  Supreme Court in, 62, 64
  Ultra-Orthodox in, 63–5
Israel Defense Force (IDF), 64–5

James, William, 60–1
Java, diversity of religion in, 107
Jewish law
  'Da'as Torah' doctrine, 69–71
  Judaism and, 62–3
  Religious-Zionists and, 64–5
jihadism, 33
Judaism. *See also* Israel
  increased populations under, 2–3
  Jewish law and, 62–3
  Ultra-Orthodox, 63–5
judges. *See* jurists
jurisdiction, for shari'ah courts, 239
jurisdictional control, in Sri Lanka, 81, 89–96
  under Buddhist Temporalities Ordinance, 91
  during nineteenth century, 92–4
  over monastic property, 90–2
  over monks, 89
jurisprudence. *See also* fiqh
  constitutional, 276
jurists
  guardianship of, 192
  in Najaf, 305, 312
  Shi'i, 302–3
    Quietism and, 302–3, 304–6, 312

Kemal, Mustafa, 190, 191
Khamenei, 'Ali, 190, 193–4, 195–9, 205–6
  women's religious education under, 203–5, 206
Khomeini, Ruhollah (Ayatollah), 190, 192–6, 303
  religious education for women in, 201–2

labor law, in Australia, 207
Laffan, Michael, 101
Larijani, Sadeq Ardeshir, 195
law. *See also* administrative law; constitutional law; legal regulation
  Islamic, 194–5
  Jewish, 62–3
  religion and, 9–11, 61–5
    Torah, 64
  religious personal, in Malaysia, 248
  socialist, 146–7
  tribal, in Iraq, 307–9, 310, 312. *See also* Iraq
Law and Religious Market Theory, 208, 209–14
  incentives to change in, 213
  market regulatory functions in, 211–13
  military power as factor in, 212–13
  religious competition in, 213–14
  religious economic model in, 209–11
Law on Belief and Religion (2016) (Vietnam), 45, 152–6, 167–8
  legitimacy of, 156
  scope of, 156
Law Relating to the Sangha Organization (1990) (Myanmar), 172, 182, 184–5
Law to Protect Solution of Cases and Conflicts in Accordance with the Rules of the Order (1983) (Myanmar), 182, 184
Lee Hsien Loong, 29, 131
Lee Kuan Yew, 129, 269
legal pluralism, 256, 257–60, 267–8, 273–4
  in Iraq, 307–12
  from patronage secularism, 274–5
legal regulation
  definitions of, 147–8
    essence-based, 147–8
    pattern-based, 147–8
  economic activity through, 148
  macro-political linkages, 148
  in Vietnam, conceptual framework for, 147–50
    as scholarly inquiry, 147–8
    scope of, 147
legitimacy, in Vietnam, for regulation of religion, 168
  through acculturation mechanisms, 166
  under Law on Belief and Religion, 156
Lenin, Vladimir I., 163
liberalism
  authority and, 67–8
  regulation of religion and, 52–3
  religious institutions and, state institutions in conflict with, 59–60
  secular theory and, 5–6
  state institutions and, religious institutions in conflict with, 59–60
liberal-secular states, 52, 53–4
liberty, 59–60
Lina Joy case, 234–7, 244–53
  administrative law and, 244–7
  Muslim apostasy claims and, 248–53
    federal-state relations and, 251–3
    politicization of, 251–3
    proceduralizing of, 248–9
    regulation of, 249–51
    under state policy, 249–51

National Registration Department, 244–9, 255
Wednesbury reasonableness in, 245–6, 247–53, 255
literacy rates, for women, 200
LoveSingapore movement, 269

madrasas. *See* religious seminaries
Mahayana Buddhism, 171
Maintenance of Religious Harmony Act (MRHA) (Singapore), 56, 128–9, 260–1
Majelis Ulama Indonesia (MUI), 48–9, 116
Malaysia. *See also Lina Joy* case
administrative reasonableness in, 234–6
administrative unreasonableness in, 234–6
anti-colonial national movement in, 237
bureaucratization of religion in, 46–7
colonialist history in, 237
Islam as state religion in, 3
Islamic Family Law (Federal Territories) Act, 240, 242
Jabatan Kemajuan Islam Malaysia in, 46–7, 236, 243–4, 252
Johor Administration of Islamic Law Enactment, 242
Kedah Administration of Muslim Law Enactment, 240–1
Muslim apostasy in, 241–2
National Registration Department in, 236
in *Lina Joy* case, 244–9, 255
Parti Islam Se-Malaysia in, 242–3
regulation of religion in, 46
religious conversion in, 125
legal debates over, 238–42
for Muslims, 237–44
political debates over, 242–4
religious freedom in, 254
religious personal law in, 248
Selangor Administration of Muslim Law Enactment, 240
shari'ah courts in, 238, 241–2, 246
United Malay Nationalist Organization, 237, 242–3
Zakat administration in, 46–7
marginalization of religion, 4
markers, regulatory, 12, 30–5
capacious definition of religion, 30–1
dialectical process, 34
discursive process, 34
epistemic plurality, 34–5
essential practices test, 31–3
regulatory dynamism, 33–4
scope of, 19
market regulation
in Australia, 207
in China, 222–9
under Charity Law, 222–3
rationality and, recognition of, 222–5
in Law and Religious Market theory, 211–13
marriage
in Indonesia, 105
under Iraqi law, 299, 300, 301
for dissolution of marriage, 300–1
Shi'ism and, 299
Marxist-Leninist atheism, 159, 162
megachurches, in Singapore, 261–2, 263–4
militant secularism, rejection of, 120
Mill, John Stuart, 68
Ministry of Religion, in Indonesia, 100–1
recognition of existing religions by, 105–7, 113
religious holidays under, 106
social harmony goals of, 103–4
Ministry of Religious Affairs (MORA), 47
minorities. *See also* women
in India, 285–91
religious, 11, 12, 41, 56
gender practices by, 54
in India, 293–4
minority rights, 15
Misra Commission, 278, 285, 289–90
modernity, secular theory and, 8
modes of religious regulation, 44–51
co-regulation, 48–9
through legislative rules, 44–6
public, 46–7
self-regulation, 49–51, 54
Moepyar U Nyana sect, 183–5
monastic land, 25
monasticism, Buddhism and, 80–1
monks
castes among, 89–90
in Myanmar, legal orders for, 176–7
saṅgha, 80–1, 82
saṅgha monks
hierarchical order for, 83
reform movements for, 84
in Sri Lanka, 90–2
in Sri Lanka
fraternities for, 89–90
jurisdictional control over, 89, 96
in political parties, 95–6
property of, 90–2
saṅgha monks, 90–2
multiculturalism, rejection of, 120
Muslims. *See also* India, Muslims in
increased populations of, 2–3
in Indonesia, 100–1
in Myanmar, 169–70
religious personal law for, 248

Muslims (cont.)
  Rohingya, 169–70
  in Singapore, 141
Myanmar
  British colonization of, 173
  Buddhism in
    sects of, 175–6
    types of, 171
  as CPC, 169–70
  deviant sects in, 179–85
    definition of, by State Sangha Maha Nayaka Committee, 177–9
    Moepyar U Nyana, 183–5
    punishment of, 186
    regulation of, 186
    Vinaya tribunals, 179–81
  Emergency Provisions Act, 184
  human rights violations in, 169–70
  Law Relating to the Sangha Organization, 172, 182, 184–5
  Law to Protect Solution of Cases and Conflicts in Accordance with the Rules of the Order, 182, 184
  National League for Democracy in, 169
  nuns in, 182
  regulation of religion in, 46, 173–4
    legal acts for, 173
    under Monastic Code of Conduct, 173–4
  Rohingya Muslims in, 169–70
  Saffron Revolution in, 169
  State Sangha Maha Nayaka Committee, 170, 179–85
    definition of deviance for, 177–9
    purpose of, 179
  Theravāda Buddhism in, 169–70, 171–7, 185
    Buddhist Councils and, 172
    definitions of, 171–2
    Doctrine of the Elders in, 171–2
    legal orders for monkhood, 176–7
    Vinaya rules in, 176
  Vinaya in
    as deviant sect, 179–81
    Theravāda Buddhism and, 176

Najaf, 302, 304–7, 309, 310, 311–12. *See also* Sistani, Ali
  as center of learning, 192
  jurists in, 305, 312
al-Najafi, Mohammad Hasan, 309
National League for Democracy, 169
National Registration Department (NRD), 236
  in *Lina Joy* case, 244–9, 255
nationalism, 77–8
'Neturei Karta', 76–7
New Order regime, in Indonesia, 114
NRD. *See* National Registration Department

OBCs. *See* other backward classes
official control, 81
  in Thailand, 81–9
Ordinance on Belief and Religion (2004) (Vietnam), 45, 151–2
  implementation provisions in, 152
  scope of, 151–2
orthodox beliefs, 24
other backward classes (OBCs), 284–5

Pakistan, Islam as state religion in, 3
Parti Islam Se-Malaysia (PAS), 242–3
patriotism
  constitutional, 126
  in Vietnam, 161
patronage secularism, 256, 257–60, 268–9
  development of, 260
  legal pluralism as consequence of, 274–5
  renewal of, 269–70
pattern-based definitions, of legal regulation, 147–8
Personal Status Code, in Iraq, 300, 304, 305, 310
personal status law, in Iraq, 309
physical abuse, under Iraqi law, 301
pluralism. *See also* principled pluralism
  defined, 120–1
  democracy and, 144
  legal, 256, 257–60, 267–8
    from patronage secularism, 274–5
  religious, 2
  religious regulation influenced by, 39
plurality. *See* epistemic plurality
polycentric regimes, 42, 43–4
post-secularism
  in Asia, 7–9
  definitions of, 7–8
principled pluralism
  core values of, 121–7
    public squares under, 122
    reasonable accommodation principles, 122
    recognition of religion, 122
    religious autonomy, 123
    religious diversity, 123
    religious liberty, 121–2
  defined, 120, 144
  militant secularism and, rejection of, 120
  multiculturalism and, rejection of, 120
  scope and definition of, 121–3
  in Singapore, 123–7, 137–8, 144–5
  Singapore Constitutional Order and, 123–7
    anti-establishment clause, 125–6
    religious identity under, 124–5

theocracy and, rejection of, 120
privatization thesis, 5
prophetic Christianity, in Singapore, 260–74
growth of megachurches for, 261–2, 263–4
homosexuality and, 264–5
National Council of Churches and, 262, 268
treatment of adultery in, 264–70
Provisional Constitution of 1950 (Indonesia), 102–3
public interest
regulation in name of, 207
religious regulation and, 43
in Vietnam, 149
public regulation, 46–7, 49, 50, 58, 148
private self-regulation and, 48, 50
public religions, 6
public spheres, differentiation from private spheres, 4, 6
public square, 122, 136–8

Qom, as center of learning, 190, 192, 197
Society of Teachers of the Qom Seminaries, 194, 195
quasi-autonomous non-government organization (quango), 48–9
Quietism, 302–3, 304–6, 312
Qur'an, 204

radicalization, 33
Rāmañña Nikāya fraternity, 89–90
rationality
market regulation and, recognition of, 222–5
in religious economic model, 209–10
reasonable accommodation principles, 122
regulation. *See also* legal regulation; market regulation; public regulation; self-regulation
contexts for, 20–7
demographic, 20–2
intra-faith challenges, 25–6
polarization, 26–7
religious diversity, 21
definition of, 10
challenges with, 22–5
markers, 12, 30–5
capacious definition of religion, 30–1
dialectical process, 34
discursive process, 34
epistemic plurality, 34–5
essential practices test, 31–3
regulatory dynamism, 33–4
scope of, 19
public interest as justification for, 207
scope of, 10–11, 36–7
states' role in, 27–30
administrative, 28–9
bureaucratic, 28–9
legislative, 27
political statements and, 29
table of cases, 37
regulation of religion, 9–11
in Asia, 9–11. *See also specific countries*
authoritative rules in, 42
bureaucratization in, 46–7
command and control model, 42
communitarian influences on, 40
conceptualization of, 40–1, 42
in confessional states, 38, 40
constitutional law and, 39–41, 43, 52
co-regulation processes, 43
definitions of, 38–9, 42
essence-based, 39
in egalitarian societies, 40–1
expansion of, 41–4
in individualist societies, 40–1
intentionality in, 44, 57–8
through Islamic Religious Council, 48–9
judicialization and, 40
under Law on Belief and Religion, 45
liberalism and, 52–3
in Malaysia, 46
modes of, 44–51
co-regulation, 48–9
through legislative rules, 44–6
public, 46–7
self-regulation, 49–51, 54
non-binding rules in, 42
non-economic goals of, 43
non-state processes, 42
under Ordinance on Belief and Religion, 45
pluralism as influence on, 39
public interest and, 43
purpose of, 39–44, 143
regimes of, 51–7
liberal-secular states, 52, 53–5
in non-liberal regimes, 55–7
polycentric, 42, 43–4
religious market theory and, 187–8
religious uniformity through, 56–7
social, 42
social policies through, 43
under Society Act, 44–5
through state agencies, 46–7
in Thailand, 96–8
unintentional processes, 42
as universal phenomenon, 187–90
relational constitutionalism, 120–1, 127

religion, in Asia. *See also* civil religion; freedom; regulation of religion; religious authority; state religion; *specific countries*
anthropologists of, 188
authority of, 60, 80. *See also* theocracy
women and, 201, 202
bureaucratization of, 46–7
in women's religious education, 189–90
charity and, 9
civil, 77
through colonialism, 1
competition and. *See* religious competition
definitions of, 99, 101, 102
capacious, 30–1
diversity of, 2–3. *See also specific countries*
accommodation demands and, 3
geopolitical factors for, 3–4
inter-faith, 25
intra-faith, 25–6
as regulatory marker, 21
economic model. *See* religious economic model
education and *See* religious education
harmony as result of, 56
law and, 9–11
marginalization of, 4
minorities and, 11, 12, 41, 56
gender practices by, 54
pluralism and, 2
public, 6
separation of state and, in secular theory, 7, 8–9
sociologists of, 188
state, 3
religious authority, 60, 68–71
'hurting feelings' argument, 68
women as, under Islamic law, 201, 202
religious competition, 213–14
in China
entitlements and, 228–9
extrinsic factors for, 228–9
freedom of religion influenced by, 227
in Law and Religious Market Theory, 213–14
regulation of, 226–9
restrictions on, 228
religious conversion, 233. *See also Lina Joy* case
anti-conversion laws, in India, 277
in India, 282
in Malaysia, 125
legal debates over, 238–42
for Muslims, 237–44
political debates over, 242–4
religious disobedience, 74
religious economic model, 209–11
rationality in, 209–10
success in, 210
supernatural forces in, 211
religious education
in Iran, 189, 190–9, 205–6. *See also* women
bureaucratization of, 200–5, 206
under Khameini, 193–4, 196–9, 205–6
under Khomeini, 192–6
in Qom, 190, 192, 194, 195, 197
through religious seminaries, 190–1, 192–9
state changes to, 194–5
Supreme Council of the Seminary, 196–9
in Iraq, 192
religious freedom. *See* freedom of religion
religious harmony
in Indonesia, 103–4
in Singapore, 55–6
Declaration of Religious Harmony, 51
Maintenance of Religious Harmony Act, 56, 128–9
religious institutions, state institutions in conflict with, 59–61
authority and, 66
over values, 59–60
political liberalism and, 59–60
religious organizations, in China
background for, 217–18
charitable service provisions in, 217–21, 225–6
social service provisions in, 217–21
state encouragement of, 218–20
religious personal law, in Malaysia, 248
religious seminaries (*madrasas*), in Iran, 190–1, 195, 196–9
under Khameini, 193–4
under Khomeini, 192–6
religious uniformity, 56–7
religious volunteers, 135
Religious-Zionists, 63–5
Jewish law and, 64–5
state authority and, 73
Rohingya Muslims, 169–70

sacrality, 75–6
construction of, 76
sacred, 60–1
as concept, 75–6
protection of, 75–8
public squares as, 122
Saffron Revolution, 169
Saṅgha Act (1902) (Thailand), 85
Saṅgha Act (1962) (Thailand), 81–5
origins of, 83
saṅgha monks under, 80–1, 82, 83, 84
saṅgha monks
in Sri Lanka, 90–2
in Thailand, 80–1, 82

hierarchical order for, 83
reform movements for, 84
SCCR. *See* Supreme Council of Cultural Revolution
Scheduled Castes (SCs), 282–3, 294
SCs. *See* Scheduled Castes
sects. *See* deviant sects
secular constitutionalism, 277
secular democracies, 267–8
secular liberalism, authority and, 67–8
secular theory, 4–9
Asia and, 4–6
reconceptualization of theory in, 7–9
decline of belief in, 4
deprivation phenomenon and, 5
differentiation of public and private spheres, 4, 6
fragmentation in meaning and, 30
liberalism and, 5–6
marginalization of religion in, 4
modernity and, 8
privatization thesis in, 5
separation of religion and state in, 7, 8–9
in Western contexts, 4, 8–9
secularism. *See also* post-secularism
affirmative action and, 279–80
defined, 5
in India, 293, 295
in Israel, 65
militant, 120
patronage, 256, 257–60, 268–9
development of, 260
legal pluralism as consequence of, 274–5
renewal of, 269–70
secure, 187–8
in Singapore, 126–7
strict, 5–6
secure secularization, 187–8
Sedition Act (Singapore), 130
self-regulation, of religion, 49–51
mandated, 50, 54
shari'ah courts
jurisdictional authority of, 239
in Malaysia, 238, 241–2, 246
Shi'ism
intentional injury victims in, 299
in Iran, 188–9
jurists and, 302–3
in Najaf, 305, 312
Quietism and, 302–3, 304–6, 312
marriage laws in, 299
precaution principle in, 299
Twelver, 298
Shiite seminaries, in Iran, 190–1, 192–6
Shintoism, 2–3
Sikhism, 2–3
in India, 282
Singapore
Administration of Muslim Law Act, 125, 257–8
banking reform proposals in, 138
Buddhism in, 135–6
as capitalist autocracy, 259
Charities Act, 259
churches as secular corporations, 270–4
civil religion in, 126
colonial history of, 257, 258
Companies Act, 259
Constitutional Order, 123–7
anti-establishment clause, 125–6
religious identity under, 124–5
corporatist accommodation in, 257–8
cultural mandates in, 270, 272–3
culture wars in, 139–43
Declaration of Religious Harmony in, 51
Employment Act, 266
freedom of religion in, 27–8, 258
freedom of speech in, 130–1
homosexuality in, 140–2
Inter-Religious Organization in, 51
Islamic Religious Council in, 125, 138
judicial court in, 27–8
legal pluralism in, 256, 257–60, 267–8, 273–4
LoveSingapore movement, 269
Maintenance of Religious Harmony Act, 56, 128–9, 260–1
missionary history in, 260
Muslims in, 141
patronage secularism in, 256, 257–60, 268–9
development of, 260
legal pluralism as consequence of, 274–5
renewal of, 269–70
principled pluralism in, 123–7, 137–8, 144–5
prophetic Christianity in, 260–74
growth of megachurches for, 261–2, 263–4
homosexuality and, 264–5
National Council of Churches and, 262
treatment of adultery in, 264–70
public squares in, 122, 136–8
racial-religious harmony in, 55–6
regulation of religion in, 51, 126, 127–43
through balancing of religious interests, 132–5
through civil orders, 137
consultive leaders and, 136–8
through controllers, 128–32
cooperative partners in, 135–6
through public orders, 132–5
religious diversity in, 2, 121
religious harmony in, 55–6
Declaration of Religious Harmony, 51

Singapore (cont.)
Maintenance of Religious Harmony Act, 56, 128–9
religious volunteers in, 135
rule of law in, 127
as secular democracy, 267–8
secularism in, 126–7
Sedition Act, 130
Societies Act, 44–5, 132, 259
as soft authoritarian state, 128
soft constitutional law in, 128, 131
Taoists in, 131
terrorist threats in, 128
Undesirable Publications Act, 132
urban planning in, for religious purposes, 259
Sistani, Ali (Grand Ayatollah), 298–302, 304–7
Siyam Nikāya fraternity, 89–90
social complexity, in Vietnam, 147
social harmony, in Indonesia, 103–4
social organizations, in China, 220
social policies, through religious regulation, 43
social regulation of religion, 42
social stratification, in India, 294–5, 297
social welfare, 9
socialism, in China, 216–17
socialist institutional space, 158–67
expansion of, 164–7
'Great Unity' strategy, 161–3
for Marxist-Leninist atheism, 159, 162
socialist legality, in Vietnam, 163–4
characteristics of, 163
scope of, 163–4
socialist regimes, Vietnam as, 159–61
Societies Act (Singapore), 44–5, 132, 259
soft constitutional law, 128, 131
Sri Lanka
Buddhism as state religion in, 89–90
colonialism in, historical legacy of, 92–3
jurisdictional control in, 89–96
under Buddhist Temporalities Ordinance, 91
during nineteenth century, 92–4
over monastic property, 90–2
over monks, 89
monks in
fraternities for, 89–90
jurisdictional control over, 89, 96
in political parties, 95–6
property of, 90–2
saṅgha monks, 90–2
regulation of religion in, 96–8
regulatory crises in, 94–6
SSMNC. *See* State Sangha Maha Nayaka Committee
state authority, 71–5
over Gaza disengagement, 73–4
over religious disobedience, 74
Religious-Zionists and, 73
Ultra-Orthodox response to, 71–2
state institutions, religious institutions in conflict between, 59–61
authority and, 66
over values, 59–60
political liberalism and, 59–60
state religions, 3
cooperationist model of, 123
State Sangha Maha Nayaka Committee (SSMNC) (Myanmar), 170, 179–85
definition of deviance for, 177–9
purpose of, 179
stateness, 97
statist human rights, 164
Statman, Daniel, 68
stratification. *See* social stratification
strict secularism, 5–6
Sufi brotherhood, 111
supernatural forces, in religious economic model, 211
suprarationality, 35
Supreme Court, in Israel, 62, 64

Talmud, 68–9
Taoists, 131
Taylor, Charles, 5, 257, 274
Thailand
official control in, 81–9
regulation of religion in, 96–8
regulatory crises in, 85–9
Saṅgha Act (1902), 85
Saṅgha Act (1962), 81–5
origins of, 83
saṅgha monks under, 80–1, 82, 83, 84
Wat Phra Dhammakaya movement in, 86–9
Theravāda Buddhism, in Myanmar, 169–70, 171–7
Buddhist Councils and, 172
definitions of, 171–2
Doctrine of the Elders in, 171–2
legal orders for monkhood, 176–7
Vinaya rules in, 176
Thirty Years Religious War, 1
Tibetan Buddhism. *See* Vajrayana Buddhism
Tin Maung Maung Than, 170
Torah, 64
tribal law, 307–9, 310, 312
Twelver Shi'ism, 298

UBSV. *See* Unified Buddhist Sangha of Vietnam
UDHR. *See* Universal Declaration of Human Rights
Ultra-Orthodox Judaism, 63–5
  authority and, 66–71
    'Da'as Torah' doctrine, 69–71
    by 'gdolei hador', 69–70
    state, 71–2
    in *Talmud*, 68–9
  disengagement from Jewish population and, 76
  'Neturei Karta' and, 76–7
UMNO. *See* United Malay Nationalist Organization
Undesirable Publications Act (Singapore), 132
Unified Buddhist Sangha of Vietnam (UBSV), 160
United Malay Nationalist Organization (UMNO), 237, 242–3
United States (US), separation of church and state in, 33, 187
United States Commission on International Religious Freedom (USCIRF), 169–70
Universal Declaration of Human Rights (UDHR), 102–3, 234
US. *See* United States

Vajrayana Buddhism, 171
VBC. *See* Vietnam Buddhist Church
Vietnam
  acculturation mechanisms in, 165–7
    complexity in state management of religion, 167
    human rights and, 166
    internalization of freedom of religion, 166–7
    legitimacy through, 166
  Buddhism in, 160
  Catholicism in, 160–1
  communist ideology in, 161
  Degar Republic in, 159
  freedom of religion in, 155–6
    acculturation mechanisms and, 166–7
  as highly-regulated state, 146
  Law on Belief and Religion, 45, 152–6, 167–8
    legitimacy of, 156
    scope of, 156
  legal regulation in, conceptual framework for, 147–50
    as scholarly inquiry, 147–8
    scope of, 147
  methodological approach to, 146–7
  officially recognized religions in, demographics for, 146
  Ordinance on Belief and Religion, 45, 151–2
    implementation provisions in, 152
    scope of, 151–2
  patriotism in, 161
  regulation of religion in
    binding standard-setting in, 150–6
    in Constitution, 150–1
    defined, 149
    framework for, 150–8
    institutional theories for, 149
    through laws, 150–6
    legitimacy of, 168
    through monitoring institutions, 156–7
    private interest theories for, 149
    public interest theories for, 149
    revolutionary approach to, 162–3
    through sanctioning, 157–8
    statist rights and, 164
  regulatory space in, 149–50
  social complexity in, 147
  socialist institutional space in, for religion, 158–67
    expansion of, 164–7
    'Great Unity' strategy, 161–3
    for Marxist-Leninist atheism, 159, 162
  socialist legality in, 163–4
    characteristics of, 163
    scope of, 163–4
  as socialist regime, 159–61
  Unified Buddhist Sangha of Vietnam in, 160
Vietnam Buddhist Church (VBC), 160
Vinaya
  as deviant sect, 179–81
  Theravāda Buddhism and, 176

Wat Phra Dhammakaya movement, 86–9
Weber, Max, 60–1
Wednesbury reasonableness, 245–6, 247–53, 255
welfare. *See* social welfare
women
  religious authority of, in Islam, 201, 202
  religious education for, in Iran
    administrative changes for, 203–5
    bureaucratization of, 200–5, 206
    in girls schools, 201
    hawza system for, 203–5
    under Khameini, 203–5, 206
    under Khomeini, 201–2
    literacy rates, 200
    during 1979 Revolution, 201–3
    Qur'an, 204

Zakat administration, 46–7, 239